Philosophy Begins in Wonder

Stephen D. Schwarz

With Kiki Latimer

En Route Books and Media, LLC
Saint Louis, MO

En Route Books and Media, LLC
5705 Rhodes Avenue
St. Louis, MO 63109

Contact us at
contactus@enroutebooksandmedia.com

Cover credit: Katie Latimer
Copyright © 2022 Stephen D. Schwarz and Kiki Latimer

ISBN-13: 978-1-956715-27-9
Library of Congress Control Number: 2022931004

All rights reserved. No part of this book may be reproduced, stored in a retrieval system, or transmitted in any form, or by any means, electronic, mechanical, photocopying, or otherwise, without the prior written permission of the author.

Dedicated in Gratitude
to
Dietrich von Hildebrand

(1889–1977)

My Godfather, Life-long Friend, Mentor, Professor
who awakened and nurtured in me the Spirit of Wonder

In Gratitude

This book is the culmination of a lifetime dedicated to philosophy done in a spirit of wonder. Many people contributed to my life's vocation in pursuit of philosophical truth, especially the following:

To my dear mother Leni Schwarz and my dear father and philosophy professor Balduin Schwarz, I have deepest gratitude.

To Saint Edith Stein who held me in her arms when I was a baby, and who no doubt prayed for me and the safety of my family as we fled Nazi Germany; to her I give gratitude.

To Edmond Michelet who offered us safe haven and passage through France—deepest gratitude for his life saving actions.

To Mother Grace Dammann who offered my father a position at Manhattanville College, which assured our passage to the United States—such heartfelt thankfulness.

To Dietrich von Hildebrand, my professor and friend, and to his wife Alice von Hildebrand, my deepest gratitude. Many wonderful philosophical colleagues graced my life, and I am especially grateful to Ronda Chervin, Fritz Wenisch, and Fr. Ron Tacelli for their deep friendship and encouragement.

To my dearest friend, colleague, and co-author, Kiki Latimer, my heart is ever deeply grateful. Your dedication to our friendship, philosophical discussions, and writing projects has enabled me to make the dream of this book a reality.

Above all, deep gratitude to my wife Sherry, whose steadfast love has blessed my life, and to our children Elizabeth, Stephen, Margaret, and Mary, and to our grandchildren Gretchen, Elise, and Nicholas. My life has been lived out in gratitude, joy, and wonder; for this I ultimately give thanks to God.

In Memoriam

Elise Jackson (2002-2013)
Beloved granddaughter

PHILOSOPHY BEGINS IN WONDER

OVERVIEW AND CONTENTS OF THE BOOK

INTRODUCTION: PLATO WAS RIGHT

Plato was right when he said that philosophy begins in wonder and that wonder is the spirit of a philosopher. The aim of this book is to spell out concretely and specifically how this is so and to show that wonder is really the core of philosophy and the true way to do philosophy. Wonder embraces all that is valid and worthwhile in philosophy, and, in this way, it is our door to reality.

PART ONE: THE HUMAN PERSON

1	THE HUMAN PERSON: What does it mean to be a person?	1
2	PERSONAL IDENTITY AND UNIQUENESS: Are you always the same person?	17
3	PERSON-BODY DISTINCTION: Are you distinct from your body?	27
4	PERSON-BODY UNITY: Are you united to your body to form one being?	51

PART TWO: MUSIC, PERCEPTION, MEMORY and LANGUAGE

5	MUSIC: Where does it exist? In the score? In the playing? In the hearing?	77
6	PERCEPTION: How do you see things? How do you hear things? Touch? Smell?	85
7	MEMORY: The past is gone; how then can you reach it in your memory?	101
8	LANGUAGE: What makes a sound or a symbol a word? What is a meaning?	109

PART THREE: TIME, CAUSALITY, FREEDOM, DETERMINISM & FREE WILL

9	TIME: Does time pass? The past: gone; the future: not yet; the present: how long?	127
10	CAUSALITY: Is there a connection between cause and effect? If so, can we know it?	147
11	FREEDOM: Different kinds. Decision freedom and spontaneous freedom.	165
12	DETERMINISM AND FREE WILL: Is determinism true? Do we have free will?	181

PART FOUR: TRUTH

13	TRUTH: What makes something true? What is that something? Is truth objective?	217
14	KNOWLEDGE AND BELIEF: Different kinds. Belief and doubt. Belief and faith.	241
15	OPINIONS: Different kinds. Can opinions ever be knowledge? Facts and opinions.	257
16	THE LOVE OF TRUTH: How does this relate to evidence? To doubt? Scepticism?	275

PART FIVE: BASIC AND PRACTICAL ETHICS

17	TRUTH AND RELATIVISM: Is there an objective good and evil, right and wrong?	299
18	GOOD AND EVIL: What different kinds of good and evil are there?	329
19	ACTIONS: What should I *do*? Actions as right or wrong. Some theories of actions.	347
20	LOVE: The supreme good. Is it unconditional? Is it from the heart or from the will?	361

Overview and Contents of the Book

PART SIX: VIRTUE ETHICS

21	FORGIVENESS: Different forms of forgiveness. What forgiveness is not.	375
22	GRATITUDE: Different forms of gratitude. The benefits of being grateful.	391
23	LOYALTY: Is loyalty always a virtue? To whom should we be loyal?	407
24	HONESTY and HUMILITY: Two basic virtues. What is true humility?	415

PART SEVEN: ULTIMATE QUESTIONS

25	WHY IS THERE SOMETHING AND NOT JUST NOTHING? Absolutely nothing?	427
26	THE MEANING OF LIFE: Is human life meaningful? Sources of meaning?	441
27	LIFE AFTER DEATH: Is it possible? What is required for it? Is it actual?	471
28	GOD: Is God real? Pointers away from God. Pointers to God. Seeking God.	513

EPILOGUE 539

CHAPTER 1
THE HUMAN PERSON

"Compared to the reality of the human person, this chair doesn't even exist."
    -Dietrich von Hildebrand in a classroom lecture

[1] WHAT IS A PERSON?

I am a person; you are a person. *But what is a person?* Have you ever stopped to think about this, to wonder what it means to be a person? We make an important distinction between persons and things. But why do we do this? A person is not like a thing which is only an "it." A person has dignity and rights while a thing like a rock doesn't. But, after all, aren't both persons and things like rocks physical realities since they occupy space and have weight, size, shape, and color? Sometimes they seem to be interchangeable: both a person and a machine can lift a rock; and certain machines, computers, can calculate, can "remember" and do other mental work.

And yet isn't a person very different from a thing? Why? Why is there a difference between a person opening a window and a thing, an automatic device opening that window? The person *knows* he or she is opening the window. He opens it because he *intends* to open it, not because he is triggered by some mechanism. He is *conscious* of what he is doing. None of these are true of a thing. They are true only of persons. What, then, is a person?

[2] SOME ESSENTIAL CAPACITIES OF A PERSON

What insights into the reality of a person can we get by reflecting in wonder on ourselves, on what we are and what we can do as persons? Here is a list that can get us started:

One, a person is a being capable of saying "I." What a remarkable power! Imagine a squirrel walking towards a pile of nuts and imagine further that this squirrel is saying to himself, "I want those nuts." Wouldn't that be amazing? Wouldn't such a squirrel be a person? Contrast a squirrel that cannot say "I" with the imaginary squirrel above, for in this difference lies part of the essence of what it means to be a person: the being that can say "I"; that can say "I" inwardly, to himself, regardless of whether he or she can say it out loud.

The squirrel's body is unlike ours; but is that decisive? A being that says "I" might have a differently shaped body. Couldn't we humans have differently shaped bodies and still be persons? What, after all, is the role of the body in the capacity to say "I"? Does a being who can say "I" even need a body? And is the squirrel's inability to speak English or any language significant? Wouldn't he be a person if he could say "I" in any language, or just inwardly?

For many people a squirrel is not a being capable of saying "I." For them to imagine a squirrel that could say "I" would be to superimpose an altogether new level of being on the ordinary squirrel. The squirrel, it seems, is somehow aware of the nuts, but not of *himself* as desiring the nuts. Perhaps this view is mistaken; perhaps a squirrel is capable of saying "I." If so, he is a person and as such he is like us. But the same contrast used earlier would remain. The squirrel that can say "I" presents an altogether new reality, a new level of existence over the one that is merely drawn towards the nuts, but cannot say "I" and know himself as being so drawn.

Wonder: can a squirrel say "I"? Isn't animal existence something mysterious? Animals are so close to us in some ways and yet so distant in others. Are pets closer to us than squirrels because of the close interaction pets have with us? Is their nature changed by this interaction and brought closer to being persons? Picture a dog playing with children; isn't it a perfect fit?

How amazing to be able to say "I"! Only a person can do this, and it is one of the deepest marks of the person. Let us delve a little more deeply into this. There seem to be at least two dimensions of this capacity to say "I." The first is the capacity for *perfect self-reflection*. A person, and only a person, has this marvelous and mysterious capacity to turn back perfectly on himself. Matter as it is familiar to us, such as wood or soil or water, is always one part next to the other. Animal consciousness seems to be only outward to objects, and not also inward to a self.

But a person can turn inward to himself, so that the subject of consciousness is also its own object. I can focus, not only on objects outside myself, but also on myself, the one that is doing the focusing. A dog can surely feel pain; but can he think of *himself* as feeling this pain?

The second dimension is *ultimate self-possession*. As a person I *possess* myself, while a non-personal being can only be possessed by another. I exist for myself, as a subject knowing and possessing himself intimately and at all times that I am conscious. A non-personal being can exist only as an object for others, not for itself; possessed by others, not by itself.

Does a baby possess himself? Can he or she say "I"? It seems not. Shall we conclude that he or she is not a person? Don't most of us think of a baby as a real person, just a small person, one not yet fully developed, physically and mentally? We might say that a baby has the *being* of a person, though he or she cannot yet *function* as a person, which includes being able to say "I." (We will examine this distinction in chapter 2, section 8.) For now, we can then simply say that a being who can say "I" is a person and that generally a person has the capacity to say "I." However, the next viewpoint, the person as "you" does apply to a baby.

Two, a person is a being that can be addressed as "you." We can see further what the essence of the person is when we reflect on the simple word *you*. Picture the following. This is a crazy example but also a vivid one that that helps to clarify this point. On a cold winter day a person gets into his car and says, "Come on, please start up!" He is addressing his car as *you*. How amazed he would be if the car replied "OK, I will"! In that case he would have been justified in really meaning to say *you* for then the car would be a person.

Why can't a car say this? Why is it that one cannot talk to car? These may seem to be silly questions but aren't they really wonder questions that help us come to a deeper and more explicit understanding of what it means to be a person? The car owner can't really talk to his car; he merely does as if he could. He can give the car voice commands; but the car cannot understand them, it cannot know it has received them and it cannot intend to carry them out. We have only external events, not the inner reality of a personal being who can understand, know and intend things. Actually, isn't what we call *the car* basically a set of parts put together so that they function as a whole, a machine capable of movement? Compared to a person, the car really has no individual "being" of its own, nor do each of its parts considered separately; it is just there, "asleep." But a person exists in an altogether new way; he is "awakened."

But suppose a person says this, not to his car, but to his computer. Imagine a computer far more advanced than present computers in problem-solving abilities. It's still a machine, not a person. It can be given commands, but it cannot understand them or intend to carry them out. It has only external events, not the inner reality of a personal being. So it still can't be addressed as a person, a "you" despite its complexity. It cannot say "I." It doesn't possess itself as a person; it isn't conscious. In fact, isn't it even further removed from being a person than a squirrel? A squirrel is conscious, and perhaps we can address a squirrel and try to elicit a response.

Some people hold that eventually computers will be persons. Instead of having a living-organism-brain they will have a mechanical-electrical-brain. Both kinds of brains are physical things; why should the kind of physical thing a brain is make any difference in regard to whether or not it is a person? But doesn't this assume that for persons it is the brain that thinks?

Shouldn't we question this assumption? Perhaps it isn't the brain that thinks. It's *you the person* who thinks; and you are not your brain. You have a brain, you use a brain, but you are a reality distinct from your brain. We will return to this topic in chapter 3.

Consider another case. I call out to what I take to be a person at a distance, but I get no reply. Later I realize it was only a cleverly made dummy. I feel a letdown. The reality that I thought was there wasn't there. What I thought was there was another person, a *you.*

I talk to *you.* In doing this, I assume that my words are taken up by you because you are a person, a being capable of understanding my words; that they *reach* into your inner being, your consciousness. Contrast this with the case of the car, and with talking into a tape recorder or a telephone where no one is listening at the other end. In all these cases my talking merely causes physical changes in the surrounding area. It does not reach *you*, a person.

Wonder: how amazing is this link between two persons in speech. How is it possible that by uttering certain sounds I reach you as person?

Three, a person is a being capable of understanding. How familiar understanding is. But what a remarkable power! Reflect on it, and you will discover still another avenue by which to understand (!) the nature of the person.

Take a simple example of understanding. You tell a joke, one that you find really funny. You come to the punch line, but your friend just stares at you with a blank look. After a few seconds he bursts out laughing. "Oh! Yes, I get it!" What happened? What does it mean to "get a joke"? It is one of many forms and levels of this remarkable human capacity: to understand. You understand a joke, a strategy, the rules of a game, why another person did something, a proof in mathematics, why a certain historical event occurred, how a machine works, a point someone makes in a conversation, an ethical truth, what a person is, what understanding itself is, and so much more.

Do you understand what understanding is? Can you describe it? It seems to be one of those things you know well until someone asks you for a description or explanation. Shall we say it is like a spiritual "seeing into" things on the analogy of seeing with the eyes? When we understand we go deeper than merely seeing. Compare one person who sees a machine with his excellent eyesight but has no idea how it functions -- with another person who has poor eyesight but understands it well enough to be able to repair it.

Or shall we compare understanding to touch, and say that to understand a truth means to grasp it spiritually? Our language uses both metaphors: "Oh yes, I see"; and "He finally grasped it." Both metaphors convey the idea of a person going out of himself and participating with reality in a certain way, a remarkable way.

There is also the metaphor of getting: "Ah yes, I get it." Here the picture is a person receiving something and being inwardly changed through understanding. Wonder and reflect on your life to try to understand how profoundly you have been affected over the years by what you have understood. Doesn't understanding give us a profound contact with reality? Wouldn't you be isolated without it, unable to function as a person, in your own being and with others?

How is understanding related to memory? How is it related to imagination? When I understand how a machine works do I accomplish this by imagining its mechanism in my mind? How is understanding related to reasoning? To knowledge? What does it mean to know? Does all knowing involve some understanding?

Try to deny understanding and try to give a good reason why it doesn't exist. Maybe someone will agree with you—after he understands your good reason! Isn't it interesting that certain realities cannot be denied without implicitly reintroducing them? Doesn't this mean that we can know their existence with an absolute certainty?

There is a sense in which the whole essence of a person is contained in this notion of understanding. Pascal seizes on this when he remarks:

> Man is but a reed, the most feeble thing in nature; but he is a thinking reed. The entire universe need not arm itself to crush him. A vapor, a drop of water suffices to kill him. But if the universe were to crush him, man would still be more noble than that which killed him, because he knows that he dies; and the advantage the universe has over him, the universe knows nothing of this. By space the universe encompasses and swallows me up like an atom; by thought I comprehend the world.[1]

Pascal refers to "thinking" and uses the term "knows"; but in this context these can be understood as referring to "understanding" and "understands." That is, man is more noble than the universe because he *understands* the advantage the universe has over him and that he dies.

What a profound thought! The whole physical universe, in all its immense vastness and awesome power is less than a single person! For a person *knows* and *understands* himself and his relation to the universe, while the universe knows and understands nothing.

---

[1] Blaise Pascal, 1623-1662, French philosopher, mathematician, scientist, inventor. *Pensées*, #347 and #348.

Four, a person is a being who has freedom. I'm tempted to steal but then I decide not to. When I freely decide this, I exercise my freedom. Suppose I had decided to steal; I would then be morally responsible for this. After deciding I can act on that decision; I can initiate and control my actions. Freedom can also be exercised in other ways, as when I make a free inner response such as loving and affirming another person. But what is freedom? In what sense are we free? In what ways are we not free? We will turn to these topics in Part Three.

Five, a person is a being who can be morally good or evil. A dog runs into a fire to save a child. Does this mean the dog has done a deed that deserves to be called morally good? Does it mean that he is morally good? By what criterion do we answer these questions? Isn't it by the criterion of *personhood*? If we think the dog is morally good, isn't it because we credit him with being a person? And if we don't think he is morally good (though no doubt in his own way very admirable) isn't it because we don't think he is a person? If the idea of an impersonal being as morally good or evil strikes us as impossible, isn't this because we understand that only persons can be morally good or evil? We will return to moral goodness and evil in Part Five.

Six, a person is a being who can use language. I do not merely utter sounds; I use words to mean something, as in "what did you mean by saying that?" As noted above, when I talk to you, I assume that my words are taken up by you; that they reach into your inner being, your consciousness, you as a person.

Wonder: can some animals use language? If they can, would this show that these animals are persons? Or is what we call animal language something different? How could we ever know? We can never get inside an animal's consciousness.

Seven, only a person can laugh and appreciate humor. Of course, one may be a person without any sense of humor but if there is a capacity to see (to understand) what is funny, must it not be a person who has this capacity? Imagine a dog who could get a joke and laugh. Wouldn't he be a person? Isn't it so that only persons can laugh and appreciate humor?

Eight, only a person can make and receive a promise. Even with all the similarities between dogs and human persons, can we imagine a dog who could make a promise? Or a dog who understands and receives a promise we make to him? Assume the language barrier is somehow overcome; can we make sense of trying to communicate a promise to a dog? If we can't, isn't this because we see that dogs, even with all their many wonderful and person-like features, are not persons? Isn't it so: only persons can make and receive promises?

Nine, only a person can appreciate beauty. Think of beautiful music, beauty in nature, in a painting. What does it take to experience beauty? Isn't it being a person? If a dog or a cow could be moved by the beauty of Bach or Mozart, wouldn't it have to be a person?

Ten, only persons have a history. This feature applies to persons not as individuals but in the totality of all persons. Have you ever realized that animals have no history? Can you imagine an ancient history or a modern history of beavers? Beavers continue to build their dams in the same way, one generation after the next. Humans invent new and better ways. Isn't it true that only persons can make inventions? And that only persons have cultures? Can you imagine a beaver culture? And then another beaver culture different from the first?

Wonder: What do these realities—history, inventions, and cultures—reveal about the nature of being a person?

[3] CONSCIOUSNESS

We have reflected on some of the important things we can do as persons. A fundamental feature common to all these is consciousness; specifically, personal consciousness.

Wonder: what is consciousness? It is so real and yet so hard to describe. It's what you have right now as you're reading this and thinking about; it's what you don't have when you're under total anesthesia while in surgery. It's so real, but it's not

Chapter 1: The Human Person

real the way we often think of reality: as a rock or an electric current in a wire or a magnetic field. All these we can either see or touch or measure by scientific instruments. Consciousness is very different from these; we can't get at it in the ways we can get at physical things. With scientific instruments we can see *that* you are conscious, but we cannot see *your consciousness itself*. It is not the kind of thing we could ever see with our eyes. With scientific instruments we can detect signs of consciousness; but a sign of x is not the same thing as x itself. Breathing is a sign that you are alive as a person, but it is surely not the same thing as being a living person who can say "I" and understand things. So, consciousness is something beyond the physical realities that we can see and touch and measure by our scientific instruments. Yet it is real, even more real and more important and central to our lives as persons than these other things. What kind of reality is it then? And what does that tell us about what it means to be real?

There is consciousness of things: I'm aware of the things around me, a noise, an odor, someone who just came into the room; I'm aware of something that worries me, a pain in my body, memories; and so, so much more. But isn't the core reality just pure consciousness? That is, consciousness itself? Isn't this something more basic than the consciousness of things which we described above as awareness? Can we be conscious of things if we are not first of all and primarily just conscious? The "of" form varies all the time and in countless ways, while the "just being" form, pure consciousness, is there all the time (as long as it's not lost) as a single reality underlying it and presupposed for it.

Is consciousness a physical reality? Certainly, it depends on the brain and proper brain functioning. But what is consciousness in itself? Seeing depends on the eyes and the brain and their proper functioning. But *seeing in itself* is something else, an experience of persons who have consciousness. Once again, what is consciousness itself? Does it have spatial extension, with size and shape and weight, texture, and color? Wouldn't it be hard to claim that it does? Shall we say that it is a non-physical reality? But if so, it is surely not like an abstraction such as humanity. Surely there is a radical difference between personal consciousness and other things:

- Personal consciousness is a *concrete reality*.

- Humanity and other such things are *abstractions*.

A person is a single, individual *concrete* being who can feel pain or joy or sorrow, can know something, can love another person, can make a morally relevant decision, can learn how to play the violin, and so much more. A person can be known and loved as a person. Isn't this, being a *concrete* reality, a level of reality far above the thin reality of a mere abstraction like humanity? And isn't being a *concrete* reality a significant part of what it is to be a person?

What then is the relation between being a person and consciousness? First, can one be a conscious being without being a person? Higher animals and probably other animals as well are surely conscious. But are they persons as described above? Recall promising: you can't make a promise to an animal because it doesn't "get" it; it can't get it. Second, can you be a person without being conscious? Surely you can, for you remain a person when you're not conscious, as when you are under total anesthesia. You retain the *being* of a person even though you are now unable to *function* as a person, where functioning as a person refers to being able to say "I," to understand, to act morally, to understand a joke and all the other things in our list above. We will return to the being-functioning distinction.

So, what is consciousness? If it's not an abstraction, and if it's not physical, then what is it? Is it something of its own, not a reality that can be subsumed under a broader heading like abstract or physical? Shall we say it is spiritual, meaning it is a concrete reality but not physical? And if it is spiritual, how is it related to the body? In some ways I am my body; but I am also not my body, for I am conscious, and consciousness is not a physical reality. I *am* my body, but I am also *not* my body. How can this be? These are big topics, as we will see later on.

[4] PERSONS AND HUMAN PERSONS

We often assume that the two terms, *person* and *human person*, refer to the same thing. But is this really true? Imagine a being that fits the description of *person* given above as the ten essential capacities of a person such as the sense of self in saying "I" for functioning as a person; also, the two essential features of being a person, identity (I am always *me, the same* person) and uniqueness (there is *only one me*), features which we will examine in the next chapter. Why would such a being have to be a member of the human race? Isn't it clear that he or she would not have to be one of us in this sense? Through wonder we can expand our horizons.

If we follow this line of thinking we can conclude: all human persons are persons, but not all persons are necessarily human persons; there could be other kinds of persons as well. In Judeo-Christian and Moslem theology, God is a Person, the Absolute Person and angels are persons, but they are not human persons. The basic capacities for functioning as a person and the two features for being a person (identity and uniqueness) all apply essentially to persons, to all persons, not just human persons. They are aspects of the very nature of a personal being. They were described in human terms because human persons are the only ones we know directly through our experience. But what we grasp here about our nature as persons applies not only to us but to any personal being. Reflecting on ourselves as persons takes us beyond ourselves and gives us insight to the essence of personhood as it applies to any person, not just a human person.

A key to understanding the difference between *persons* and *human persons* is by asking: is having a body essential for being a person? Yes and no: for a human person in his present state, *yes*; for a person as such, *no*. If there are angels, they are persons but not bodily persons.

Another way to see this difference is by considering the question of the possibility of life on other planets. The term *life* can of course simply mean biological life. But what is usually meant is the interesting question whether there are other beings out there who are in significant ways like us; that is, whether they are persons. If so, they would not be *human persons*, members of the species Homo sapiens. But they would surely be *persons*, beings who had the ten essential capacities of functioning as a person and the features essential to being a person.

[5] SOME KEY TERMS IN THE PHILOSOPHY OF THE PERSON

What key terms are important in the philosophy of the person? We have considered two main ones, *person* and *consciousness*; and there is also the term *soul*.

What do these terms mean and how are they related to each other? Here are some of the main points:

1. Person is the most important and basic term and the theme of sections 1-4.
2. Consciousness is a key feature of persons; specifically, an essential feature of functioning as a person (such as saying "I," thinking, listening and talking) but it is not essential to being a person.
3. Consciousness implies being a person, when it is understood as personal consciousness. If you are conscious, you are a person.
4. Being a person does not imply consciousness. You are a still a person while under total anesthesia. You have the being of a person even though you cannot function as a person: saying "I," understanding a philosophical problem, making a moral decision, etc.
5. Soul in its traditional sense refers to the non-physical dimension of the human person. Saying we have souls means we are not entirely material beings; there is more to being a person than the body. This more is the soul. Saying we don't have souls means we are entirely material beings. Could we be persons if we didn't have souls?
6. Soul in this sense is therefore a purely philosophical concept, not a religious one. The question whether we have souls is a philosophical question, to be decided purely by the use of reasoning. There is no appeal to religious faith.
7. Soul is important for the question of immortality: will I continue to exist after my death? Surely my body will not continue to exist as a living thing. If I continue to exist it will be me as a person, my soul; in that sense and in that context the soul is the real me.
8. Soul is also important for the question of personal identity. One theory holds that it is the soul that accounts for this identity.
9. Soul is what makes you a person and all that goes with it: consciousness, all the powers rooted in consciousness such as saying "I" and thinking; plus identity and uniqueness. We are of course intimately united to our bodies, and we even form one being with our bodies. Still, it is not the

body that accounts for consciousness, identity, and uniqueness; it is the soul. We are conscious because we have souls, not because we have bodies. The body is drawn into our consciousness and consciousness relies on the proper functioning of our body; but body and consciousness remain essentially distinct in their basic reality. We will explore these topics later on.

[6] ARE ANIMALS PERSONS?

Many people, animal lovers in particular, would say yes, or go in that direction. There is surely a wealth of evidence in their favor. A dog warns his master of a fire, a dog rescues a child from a fire, a dog protects children, a dog plays with a group of children on the lawn and seems like one of them, a cat rescues a small dog trapped in a ground area below with steep sides, a lion embraces a person in what looks like real love, a tiger embraces a person who has just saved his life in what looks like real gratitude. Many more stories can be added. Don't they all point in the same direction, that animals are a very much like persons? That perhaps they are persons?

But there is also another side. Imagine a dog who tells you in the morning: I slept poorly last night. That would surely be the sign of a person. But isn't the actual dog far removed from an imaginary dog who could say that? In general, while we certainly communicate with dogs and speak words to them, can we actually talk to them? Are they capable of language in the full human sense, even the simple language that a child is capable of? Are they capable of abstract thought, even simple abstract thought? Consider: half a loaf of bread and half a candy bar have the common element *half*; that's easy for you to get; can a dog get it? We can count the number of chairs in the lecture hall; can a dog do this? Would he be a person if he could?

Let us reflect again on promising and animals. Imagine someone saying to a dog "I promise you that I will take you for a walk later today." Doesn't that strike you as odd? More than that, isn't it clear that it is absolutely impossible to make a promise to an animal? Imagine the dog "getting it"; that is, understanding that it is a promise and not just a statement of fact; and then accepting it as a promise and holding the person making the promise as bound to fulfill it. "You promised!" High as dogs stand on the ladder of intelligence, isn't still clear that promising (both accepting promises and making them) is beyond their reach? Or, if it isn't, that they are actually persons after all? All this is meant not only as a wondering about animal intelligence or capability but also as a coming to a deeper grasp of what it means to be a person. A person is a being who can actually make and receive promises; and who can understand what it means to make and receive a promise.

Surely dogs and other higher animals are much more than simply non-persons. But are they persons in the full sense, the way human beings are persons? Are they semi-persons? Maybe we need new categories? Surely there is much here for our wonder; and for our realizing how much we don't know.

[7] THE MYSTERY OF BEING A PERSON: DREAMS

In many ways I know myself; I know who I am, I know what I am. I am a person with all the features noted here, both for being a person and for functioning as a person. In having a thought, I also know that I have a thought and what that thought is. But there are other ways that confront us with deep mystery: I do not know my own being as a person. Consider dreams when we are asleep (as opposed to day-dreams).

In one way my sleep-dream is *very much me*. It is "inside" me, not in the inter-personal world of human relations outside me; only I have a direct awareness of it. When I tell my dream to someone else much of it is lost; all the intimacy and directness are lost.

But in other ways my dream is *not at all me*. In general dreams come at me; often I seem to have little control over them. Generally, I do not invent them, and I do not shape them. And I often wonder: why did I dream that? In most case I have to answer: I don't know. It's as if they came to me from a totally alien and foreign source, something which is not me at all.

And yet in another way they do come from within me. What part of me? Is there a realm of my being as a person that lies outside of what I know as my own being? How can this be?

Dreams are me and not me. How can this be? Isn't the whole world of dreams very mysterious? Surely it is a cause for wonder! There is the wonder at the mystery of dreams, what they are, how they originate; and wonder at the mystery of the human person as one who dreams.

[8] THE MYSTERY OF THE COMING INTO BEING OF A PERSON

The development of a human being in the womb is such an amazing thing! A tiny sperm smaller than a period at the end of a sentence and a not-much-bigger ovum: each by itself is a biological organism that cannot lead to anything further and will soon die. But if they unite a radically new being comes into existence, a zygote; a being that will grow and develop into what we recognize as a human person. Didn't each of us begin our existence as a tiny one-celled zygote? Isn't it strange to say but true: I was once a zygote? And then during the nine months in the womb that tiny being grows into a full-term, highly developed baby. Isn't this amazing?

Just on the biological level this is a source of wonder. But then *consciousness* comes in. How does this happen? Even if we were to fully understand all the amazingly complex details of the biological development of all the organs, tissues, and other body parts, isn't the infusion of consciousness an altogether new and incredible phenomenon? How simple biological structures lead to more developed ones is one thing; but how any level of biological development leads to something so radically different as consciousness is quite another. A cause for wonder!

But there is even more than that. What comes into existence is a *person*! Recall the reality of being a person: a being who can say "I" and understand and make promises. What is developing is the body of a person, with a mouth that will enable the person to speak; with a human face that we will recognize as that of a friend; a loving face or an angry face. In some cases, it means the development of a person with amazing abilities, a Bach or an Einstein.

A final source of wonder: consider that the tiny one-celled being at the beginning of this amazing journey already carries within itself the potential for the *next generation.*

CHAPTER 2
ARE YOU ALWAYS THE SAME PERSON?

THE QUESTION OF PERSONAL IDENTITY

[1] PERSONAL IDENTITY AND THE IDENTITY OF THINGS

Are you the same person now as the day when you born? Of course, you are, else it would not be the case that it was you who were born that day. But haven't you changed? In fact haven't you changed considerably, even radically? Your body then and your body now are radically different. You were an infant then; you are a mature grown-up now. All the things you know now you didn't know then. The same is true for so much else, such as the skills you now have but didn't have then. If you've changed so much, how can you still be the same person? Think of physical objects; when they change radically, don't they lose their identity? You eat a tomato, you chew it and swallow it; it gets digested and is so completely changed that it loses its original identity. Why doesn't the same apply to you and to human persons generally? It seems we don't ever lose our identity as persons the way a tomato loses its identity as a tomato. But why not? What is it that makes us different?

Is the answer perhaps in this direction: persons and things like tomatoes are very different in terms of their identity; they have *different kinds of identity*? In what ways are they different?

First, can the identity of a person ever be lost? What could it mean to lose your identity? Isn't it so that no matter how much you change you are always *you*, the same person? Consider an example. Karl is a guard in a Nazi camp, a very cruel and sadistic guard. But then, much later in his life he has a dramatic, soul-shaking moral and religious conversion. He sees the evil of what he used to do, deeply repents it and now strives to be the exact opposite of what he used to be; he tries very hard to be a very loving person. Isn't he in a very real sense "a new person" in that his character has changed so dramatically? But in another, even deeper sense, isn't he still *the same person*? Didn't the radical change occur in the life of one and the same person? After the conversion can he not truthfully say "I was once a cruel Nazi guard"? And when he says this, doesn't he mean that I now and the former Nazi guard are one and the same person?

If this is so we can say that personal identity means: I am always the same person. When I change, I do not change into another person, I do not become another person. I always remain the same person. The deep metaphysical fact that personal identity can never be lost is captured by the simple phrase: I am always me. As long as I exist at all I am always me, the same person.

What follows from this is the huge difference between these two phrases:

- "I am always the same." This is clearly false: I change.
- "I am always the same person." This is true, this is personal identity.

Second, there seems to be another point, closely related to the first. Isn't the identity of persons absolute as opposed to being a matter of degree? Consider another example, a wooden ship. If you change a few of its planks, can it not still be considered the same ship, with no loss of its identity? Change a few more: isn't it still the same ship? But if you keep changing the planks until you have finally changed all of them, will it not then be the case that you no longer have the same original ship? That the original ship will have lost its identity? But at what point in this set of changes has the original identity been lost? It seems impossible to say. Doesn't this mean that the identity of a ship is not something definite and clear-cut, but merely something that attaches loosely to the ship? Isn't it something that is mainly of practical use, as in identifying it (and not another ship) as the one legally owned by a certain person? Can we say that the ship's identity as "the same ship" over a period of time is merely a matter of degree, perhaps even only a matter of practical convenience? Doesn't the identity of a person, his being "the same person" over a period of time stand in radical contrast to this because it is absolute? A ship can be more or less the same ship as before; but a person: isn't he either absolutely the same person or not at all the same person? Isn't it true that there can be no in-between?

Our experience bears this out. You see someone who looks like your old friend Jim. Is it Jim? You're not sure; you approach him and see if he recognizes you, and if you recognize him. But isn't one thing quite certain: it's either that particular person or it's someone else, there's no in-between? Isn't it clear that there can't be a relative, matter-of-degree identity with a person as there is with a ship? And doesn't it follow from this that identity for persons means something radically different from what it means for ships?

Third, isn't there also this difference? Radical changes not only do not destroy personal identity in that personal identity can never be lost (first point); they are meaningful only because of personal identity. What is striking about the Nazi guard who converts? Isn't it precisely that it is one and the same person who is first extremely evil, and is then very good? Suppose there were two persons, one evil and the other good; wouldn't this point be lost? Here then we have a striking difference between the two kinds of identities: radical changes wipe out the thin identity that mere things have; but radical changes play a significant role in the identity of persons in that radical changes become highly significant only on the basis of personal identity.

A brief summary may be helpful. Personal identity means I am always the same person; I am always me. This holds even through radical changes:

1. Radical changes do not destroy or take away personal identity; it can never be lost.
2. Personal identity is absolute: totally present or totally absent, never in degrees.
3. Radical changes are meaningful only because of personal identity.

Personal identity can never be lost: as long as I exist at all I am always me. But do we not sometimes say that a person acquires a new identity? He changes so much that we say he has a new identity. We might say of Karl, the former Nazi guard, that he is now a different person. Yes, we say this, but what do we mean? Do we mean that he is literally a new, different person, no longer the same "I" or the same "me"? Do we not rather mean that he, the very same person, has changed so dramatically that we now view him very differently? Isn't it simply that the term "identity" as used here is meant to convey two related ideas, his dramatic change in character and our now viewing him very differently? Identity in this second sense then refers to "what a person is known as." That of course often changes. Thus, we have:

- Personal identity primary sense: who you really are, the same person, never changes.
- Personal identity secondary sense: what you are known as, which can change.

[2] PERSONAL IDENTITY AND OUR EXPERIENCE

Isn't personal identity fundamental to our experience? Isn't it foundational for memory? Isn't our memory possible only on the basis of our continuity through our personal identity? I now remember an experience I had in the past, such as (say) a summer in Vermont. Isn't this possible only if the "I now" who remembers the experience is the same person as the "I then" who had the experience that took place in the past and is now remembered?

Doesn't the same structure apply also to intending? I now intend to go to the library later today. Doesn't this mean that the "I now" who intends to go there and the "I later" who will carry out this intention must be the same person? Isn't deliberating similar? "I now" who deliberate and "I later" who do what was decided in the deliberation must be the same person.

Aren't there also cases of dual identities? Think of gratitude. You save my life. I am immensely grateful to you! First there's my identity: I-now am grateful for what was done for me-then; must it not be the same I-me in both cases? Second, isn't there also your identity as the doer of the deed and the receiver of my gratitude? I-now am grateful to you-now for what you-then did for me in the past; must it not be the same you in both cases?

Are there other cases of dual identity? Think of promising, asking for forgiveness and granting forgiveness. In each case there seems to be my identity and your identity:

Chapter 2: Are You Always the Same Person?

My identity: I-later who will keep the promise must be the same person as I-now who makes the promise.

Your identity: you-later to whom I will keep my promise must be the same person as you-now to whom I make the promise.

My identity: I-now who ask for forgiveness must be the same person as I-then who did the wrong for which forgiveness is now sought.

Your identity: you-now of whom I ask forgiveness and you-then who was wronged must be the same person.

My identity: I-now who grant forgiveness: the same person as the one who was wronged.

Your identity: you-now being granted forgiveness: same person who inflicted the wrong.

Here is a little story that brings out dramatically the significance of personal identity and its role in our experience. A woman is robbed as she attends her store. The robber flees. Later she is called to the police station and asked to identify a suspect. "Is he the man who robbed your store?" She says he is. "Are you sure?" "Yes, I'm absolutely sure." "Is there no doubt in your mind?" "No, there is absolutely no doubt; he's the one!" As she walks out of the police station, she sees a second suspect just being brought in. He looks exactly like the first suspect whom she swore is the man who robbed her. She is horrified! In an instance she realizes that the actual robber could just as easily be the second man as the first one. The first one could be innocent! Yet she identified him with absolute confidence. "What if I was mistaken?" What underlies this drama is the question of personal identity: which of the two suspects is the same person as the real robber?

[3] SOME THEORIES ABOUT PERSONAL IDENTITY

What accounts for personal identity? How is it to be explained, especially its being so different from the identity of things like ships? Several theories have been proposed:

The Memory Theory. The classic expression of this theory is John Locke who refers to memory as consciousness. The idea is that my memory of myself in the past is what makes me the same person as that person in the past. He says:

> For, since consciousness always accompanies thinking, and it is that which makes everyone to be what he calls self, and thereby distinguishes himself from all other thinking things: in this alone consists personal identity, i.e., the sameness of a rational being; and as far as this consciousness can be extended backwards to any past action or thought, so far reaches the identity of that person; it is the same self now it was then; and it is by the same self with the present one that now reflects on it, that the action was done.[1]

Memory is certainly a sufficient condition for personal identity. As we have already seen memory is possible only on the basis of the continuity of personal identity. The "I now" who remembers a past experience must be the same person as the "I then" who had the experience. Thus, it is clear that if there is memory there must be personal identity; memory suffices to ensure that there is personal identity.

But is memory a necessary condition for personal identity? Is it true that if there is no memory there cannot be personal identity? Is it true that "If there is personal identity there must be memory"? Isn't it rather false for the following reasons?

---

[1] John Locke, *Essay Concerning Human Understanding*, 2e, 1694, from chapter 27.

(1) Didn't I exist before my earliest memories? I cannot remember being born and the many moments following soon after my birth; but wasn't it was me, the same person I am now, who was born then and had those early moments of existence? And, of course, I cannot remember the time before my birth in my mother's womb; but again, if I existed at all at that time, wasn't it me who existed then? If not, how could it I be that I exist now?

(2) Suppose I suffer amnesia, so that there is a period in my past life of which I have no memories. Was it not I, the same person I am now, who suffered this amnesia? If not, what does it mean to say that I suffered amnesia? My consciousness cannot be extended backwards to this past time in my life; yet doesn't my identity reach that far back and indeed before that time? Doesn't the same hold for being unconscious during total anesthesia? My consciousness does not reach to that time; but wasn't it me, the same person I am now, who existed during that time?

(3) The memory theory cannot account for the future; it is entirely past-looking. But isn't my personal identity important also for the future? We plan to do certain things in the future, we anticipate the future; we deliberate what to do, we hope for good things, we fear evil things; and all these of course refer to the future, to my future as the same person I am now.

(4) Doesn't the memory theory also fail in regard to the meaning of personal identity as it applies to other persons? Recall the story about the store robbery and the two suspects. Which of them is the same person as the actual robber? Isn't this is a matter of correctly identifying another person, his memory or lack thereof having nothing to do with this? If he were to forget his doing the deed of robbing the store, if he in fact did it, isn't he the guilty person?

(5) Isn't the most fundamental criticism of the memory theory that it has it backwards? Isn't the following true? It is not that memory is a necessary condition for personal identity; it is rather that personal identity is a necessary condition for memory. Personal identity is basic; memory comes

later. This point, parallel to the one above that memory is a sufficient condition for personal identity, was made by Joseph Butler:

> And one should really think it self-evident, that consciousness of personal identity presupposes, and therefore cannot constitute, personal identity, any more than knowledge, in any other case, can constitute truth, which it presupposes.[2]

The Whole Body Continuity Theory. This is the idea that you are the same person as long as you exist continuously in the same body. Initially this may seem to work well, as we do remain in our bodies for our whole life. And we identify other persons in this way: you are the same person if I recognize your body, especially your face, as the same. But several problems arise; perhaps the most interesting is the logical possibility of bodily transfer. Locke considers this; he asks us to imagine a prince and a cobbler changing bodies and what it would be like for each to be considered the other. A more recent example of this is the movie, "Freaky Friday"[3] in which a mother and her teen daughter switch bodies. Each has to adapt to the other's usual life for one freaky Friday.

If person A goes into the body of person B (and vice versa), doesn't the identity of person A go along into the new body? And doesn't this mean a separation of personal identity from the previous body, that is, a break in bodily continuity? And doesn't this show that bodily continuity is not the essence of personal identity? It seems to be neither necessary nor sufficient, as bodily transfer shows. Of course, bodily transfer cannot in fact be carried out as in these fanciful cases. But consider their logical possibility: they do not seem to involve any logical contradiction. Isn't this enough to show that personal identity does not mean whole body continuity?

The Brain Continuity Theory. Given this objection to the whole body continuity theory those who want to find the meaning of personal identity in bodily conti-

---

[2] Joseph Butler, *The Analogy of Religion*, 1736, First Appendix.

[3] Based on a novel by Mary Rodgers; screenplay by Heather Hatch; released August 6, 2003.

nuity turn to the brain. The idea is that you are the same person if you have the same brain. But suppose my brain is gradually modified, one part removed and replaced by another that has the same function as the other part but is numerically distinct. Think of the ship being rebuilt plank by plank as in our example above in section 1. During the brain modification procedure my life goes on as before; I hardly notice any difference. But at the end of the procedure don't I have a different brain? Still, if it is I who now have a different brain must this I not be the same person as before?

Our conclusion seems to be this: my identity as a person is not the identity of my body. Perhaps we can go even further. Do I have the same body now that I had as a newborn baby? The cells in my body have replaced one another every seven years, so I no longer have the same body. Doesn't this mean that I do not really have bodily continuity with my body now and as a newborn baby? Hasn't my body therefore lost its identity as a physical reality? But am I not the same person now as the one who existed as a tiny baby and had that baby body? Doesn't this mean that the two are essentially different? I am not the same person because of my body or my bodily continuity; I am the same person despite having had a different body in the past.

The soul as the basis of personal identity. Both the memory theory and the bodily theories seem not to account for the reality of personal identity; that as long as I exist, I always exist as me, the same person. Let us look at one more theory. If my identity is not a capacity I have as a person (my memory), nor my body, then it must lie in me; it must lie in me as a person; it must be part of the essence of what I am as a person. The traditional term for this is the soul.

This theory goes back to Plato, particularly his Phaedo. Plato held a particular version of the soul theory, one that emphasized the radical distinction, even separation, of soul and body. What is being suggested here is a broader theory that reflects later developments emphasizing soul-body unity, holding that a human person is a single being, soul and body as two dimensions of one person. Today the term mind is generally used in place of soul, as in the "the mind-body problem." The term soul should be understood as referring to the non-physical dimension of the person and is meant in a purely philosophic sense, not in a religious one.

In one way we can say that the soul is the real you. In the movie "Freaky Friday" when the mother and her daughter switched bodies it was the soul of each that went into the body of the other. But in another way the real you is the whole person, body-soul, as in "you are now standing up"; not just your body and surely not just your soul, but you, the whole person.

Can we then say that I have personal identity, that I am always the same person because of my soul? Can we then say it is not the body that confers identity on the person but quite the opposite, that it is the person as soul that confers identity on the body? Don't I experience my body over time as always my body, hence in that sense as the same body? Isn't the experienced identity over time that my body has given to it through my soul, through my being as a person?

None of the three theories we considered before the soul theory seems to have room for the possibility of life after death, or human immortality. The reality and supreme importance of life after death is actually the main concern of Plato in his Phaedo. And many of us, maybe all of us, wonder about this; we wonder whether death is the absolute end of our existence. Is it? Or will we continue to exist after the death of our bodies? The significance of this question for us here is that the meaning of immortality is essentially that of personal identity: will I continue to exist in a life after death, the same "I" who exists now? If I do I will of course be changed. I will not have the body I now have. How then will I exist? Perhaps we can adopt a formula:

- I now exist in a bodily way.
- I then will exist in some other way, *I the same person.*

CHAPTER 3
PERSON-BODY DISTINCTION

[1] INTRODUCTION

What is a person? What does it mean to be a person? This was our topic in the last two chapters, but it calls for further reflection, for more wonder. Specifically, is a person his or her body? Doesn't our immediate experience give us a two-fold contradictory answer? That is:

Yes, I am my body: I feel it to be me. When my body is cold, I am cold; when you see my body you see me; when you touch my body you touch me; when I swim it is my body that makes the swimming movements; when I carry a suitcase it is with my body, my arm and my hand.

No, I am not my body: I think but my body doesn't think; I am conscious but my body like any other physical thing (such as a tree) is not conscious; I am a loving person but my body is not a loving being; I feel happy or sad or worried, but my body doesn't feel such things.

One of the wonders of the human person is that these two answers, though contradictory on one level are both true if we go to deeper levels. *I am my body, but I am also not my body, for I am more than my body.* What is this "more"? It is my being as a person, my personal identity and uniqueness; it is my consciousness. What is that, my consciousness? It is so real yet so hard to grasp in concepts. Do we wonder enough at this fundamental reality that is ours all the time when we are awake; a reality that accompanies us at every waking moment; that seems to be almost equivalent to our very being?

[2] CONSCIOUSNESS AND THE BODY

What is the relationship between me as a conscious person and my body? Shouldn't this be crystal clear to me since my body is always there wherever I am? What could be closer to me than my own body? What could be more obvious to me than how I'm related to my body? Let's try to see how obvious it is, or whether it is even obvious. Aren't there actually several ways in which I can describe how I am related to my body? Consider some candidates:

- I am my body.
- I am not my body.
- I possess my body.
- I use my body.
- I feel my body.
- I'm in my body.
- I'm one with my body.

Consider the first two: *I am my body,* and *I am not my body.* Both seem to be true, for we can gain insights from our immediate experience to support both. Yet as they stand, they can't both be true as they contradict each other; and two propositions that contradict each other can't both be true. The only way to bring them together is to show that in some respects the first is true and in other respects the second is true. And this is what our wonder journey will try to do.

This chapter explores the ways in which I am *not* my body, the real distinction between a person and his body. The next chapter will explore the ways in which I *am* my body, the unity of person and body, including having a body, using it, feeling it, being in it and being one with it.

THE PHRASE "I AM MY BODY"

The phrase "I am my body" can be taken as meaning that I am simply my body, nothing more; that there is an *identity* between me and my body in that they are one and the same thing. Thus, the destruction of my body at death is the destruction of *me*; there can be no life after death. This is basic materialism.

But the phrase "I am my body" can also be taken as referring to the *unity* of person and body while not denying the distinction between them. I am not only my body; I am something more than my body. Thus, the destruction of my body at death need not be the destruction of *me*; there might be a life after death, a continuation of me as the same person. This is basic dualism.

[3] BASIC MATERIALISM: A PERSON IS HIS BODY, NOTHING MORE

In its core basic materialism is the view that a person simply is his body, or his brain, nothing more. A person's mental life, his consciousness, his thoughts, all that we have sketched above, is not a reality "over and above" the physical. It *is* the physical, even though it does not appear the way physical things usually do. For materialism there is no such thing as a soul distinct from the body, a soul that might continue to live on after the death of the body. There is no such thing as a mind distinct from the body, especially from the brain. Mind is the way the brain functions. Mental events are physical events; consciousness is a brain function.

There are many varieties of materialism. A good representative of all of them, typical of them in its core thesis is the Mind-Brain Identity Theory: mind and brain are one and the same thing; there is an *identity* between them. And mental states are physical states of the brain: every mental state or process is numerically identical with some physical state or process of the brain. The mental state is one and the very same thing as the brain state. Matter can think.

The only kind of causation allowed in materialism is the kind that stems from a physical reality. All my thoughts are effects of brain processes as their causes. I as a person, a center of consciousness distinct from my body can never be a cause; for on materialism there is no such reality. If I am said to be the cause of something such as a decision to perform an action, it is actually my body and especially my brain that is really the cause of that thing.

Why adopt materialism? Four reasons may be mentioned. First, materialism is *simple* compared to its rival theory, dualism. Whenever possible we should adopt a simple theory rather than a complex one. Materialism claims to be able to account for the reality of the human person by postulating just one thing, the body, rather than two, body and something else over and above the body, a soul of some kind.

Second, there is *evolution*. At the beginning we have simple organisms; no spiritual soul. As they evolve, they grow in complexity but no spiritual soul needs to be postulated. When we come to human beings we have maximum complexity, amazing abilities, but again no spiritual soul is needed. Evolution paints a picture of smooth developments and transitions; to hold that a soul enters the scene at some point is to introduce a radical break and a loss of this smoothness.

Third, many people assume that *the real is the physical*. Persons are real; their bodies are real; therefore, persons are simply their bodies. Materialism follows naturally.

Fourth, the *unity* of person and body is easily explained by materialism. I am my body. If my body is 6 feet tall this means that I am 6 feet tall. The same applies to other physical characteristics, such as weight and skin color. When I walk or swim or jump up and down, it's my body that's doing these things. When my body is sick, I'm sick. When you see my body, you see me. When I hug your body, I hug you.

Think of all the activities that constitute your day. You get up in the morning, brush your teeth, have a cup of coffee and go off to work. All these are bodily activities. You type a letter, you pick up the phone; again it's your body. You talk, using your voice, a part of your body. You use your body: that's you in action. Others see your body: they see you. The picture seems pretty clear: I as a person and my body seem to be *one and the same thing*.

But are they really one and the same? Recall the other aspect: *I am not my body*. Let us take another look at these four reasons for adopting materialism. First, a theory may be simple, but is it true? Isn't that the crucial question? Simplicity doesn't guarantee truth. Second, perhaps evolution isn't only a matter of smooth developments. The emergence of consciousness: isn't that a radical break? Couldn't a soul be a similar break? Do we fully understand evolution? As we dig deeper will we perhaps discover new dimensions of reality here? And evolution deals with physical development; whether or not there is a non-physical dimension of a human person is surely a new question, one outside the range of a physical scientific evolution.

Third, there is the assumption that the real is the physical. But an assumption is not an argument, and it is surely not a good logical reason for adopting a position. Philosophy is in the business of questioning assumptions, not simply continuing them. Wonder is especially a matter of questioning assumptions. Fourth, even if the unity of person and body can be explained by materialism it hardly follows that only materialism can do this. What does it really mean to say that I am united to my body? Don't I have to be something other than my body in order to be united to it? The body is not united to the body; only a reality essentially distinct from the body can then also be united to it. Hence unity, far from being explained by materialism really means a denial of materialism and the consequent adoption of basic dualism. To this we now turn.

[4] BASIC DUALISM: A PERSON IS NOT SIMPLY HIS BODY, HE IS MORE

Basic dualism is the view that a person is *not* simply his body or his brain. He *has* a body and that includes his brain, but his being a person is a reality *distinct* from these, irreducible to these. A person as person and the features that make him a person – his personal identity, his personal uniqueness, his consciousness, thinking and feeling -- are realities that exist "over and above" the physical. They are not reducible to the body and to the physical and chemical processes that make up bodily life, as materialism claims. The mind is distinct from the body, especially the brain. Mental events are essentially distinct from physical events.

Basic dualism means the *distinction* between person and body, not a *separation* between them. How they are related and whether there is a substantial soul that can exist separately from the body are matters that go beyond the simple assertion of basic dualism. This theory holds that there is a *real distinction* between person and body, not just a difference of terms that might refer to one and the same thing, such as "Joe" and "the boss" who are really one and the same person.

Let us return to the question of the *unity* of person and body and the relation of unity to the materialist claim of *identity* between person and body. I am so united to my body that we like to say that I am my body. But what does it really mean to say that I am my body? It cannot mean that I am reducible to my body, that I am nothing but my body as materialism claims, for then there would be no real, concrete "I" that is united to my body. As noted, I have to be a reality other than my body in order to be united to it. The body is not united to the body; only a reality that is essentially distinct from the body can then also be united to it. To say that I am my body really means that I identify with my body as a dimension of my being, as something that is in some sense a part of me but is not simply me or the whole of me. *Thus, basic dualism is essential for true unity.* It is a strange paradox that those who denounce all forms of "dualism" in the name of unity actually lose the unity they want to stress because they lose the "I" that must be distinct from the body (basic dualism) in order that it may be intimately united to this body. It is one thing to deny a separatist dualism which makes unity difficult or impossible; it is quite another to deny all forms of dualism or what we have called basic dualism.

The wonder of unity is precisely that a being, the conscious "I" can be so deeply and so intimately united to a thing that is not itself but that nonetheless partakes of its being, as we can see when we say that you touched *me* when you touch my arm or kiss my face. And that *I* walk and *I* swim when it is my body that goes through these motions.

Which should we adopt, basic materialism or basic dualism? Even if materialism could give us a unity between a person and his body, would it do justice to the reality of the person? Basic dualism gives us unity, the unity we know through our immediate experience as persons. The case for dualism against materialism rests on the arguments to be developed below in [5]; arguments which are intended to support the claim that there is real distinction between a person and his body: *I am not my body*; and that the truth in the phrase *I am my body* consists in its expression of the unity of me and my body.

Also, in today's climate the assumption is easily made that the real is the physical; and so, it is important to bring out why this is not so, to show that what makes you a person is not your physical body but other things, which are as fully real as your body and really distinct from it.

In many ways I *am* my body, for I am deeply united to it so as to form *one* human being. But it also true that in other ways I am *not* my body. How can this be? Wonder! Let us now explore some of the many ways in which I am *not* my body; a set of arguments intended to show the essential distinction between a person and his body.

[5] THE DISTINCTION BETWEEN A PERSON AND HIS BODY

#1. I am not my body: consciousness

I am conscious. Is my body as a physical organism conscious? Is any physical organism, just as a biological organism, conscious? Parts of my body as organisms such as my heart and my lungs are not conscious. How could all of them together as a larger organism be conscious? Recall the ten features of the person examined in chapter 1; isn't it clear that none of them apply to my body as such? My body cannot say "I," it cannot be addressed as "you," it cannot understand, and it cannot be morally good or evil. Doesn't this show that I am not my body?

#2. I can oppose my body

I can oppose my body. My body is tired, but I resolve to keep going. I thereby take a distance from my body; it is in this respect not me. I control my body; for example, I move my hand. Or I fail to control it, as a paralysis comes over me. I the one who controls or who fails to control cannot be one and the same thing as this body that *I* control or that *I* don't control.

#3. Loss of body parts does not diminish me as a person

If I lose an arm or a leg to amputation, my body is diminished. But I as a conscious person am not diminished. We can think of "half my body," say my left half. But does it make any sense to speak of "half a person"? Bodies are spatial and can be divided, at least in imagination; aren't persons very different in this respect?

Doesn't his shows the radical difference between person and body? If "I" were simply my body, if I and my body were one and the same thing, then a diminishing of my body would be a diminishing of "me" as a person. Clearly it is not. Therefore, I am not my body.

#4. The argument from death

What happens at the death of a person? The body is radically changed; it is no longer a living body with blood circulation and other active bodily functions. But are these the only changes, or even the most important ones? Isn't the main thing that the person is gone? The body is still there while we mourn the *loss of a person*!

I see and talk to my friend. He is there in front of me, *alive*. Then death strikes. The body is still there, but he is gone! *The person is gone!* Death is the radical separation of a person and his body. In view of my ultimate death, I am not my body.

As I get older my body gets weaker and eventually it wears out and I die. My body dies; but far more important, *I* die. I die: my death is not just the death of a physical organism, a human body; it is above all the death of a person, of *me the person*, the being who can say "I."

At my death my body leaves me; it can no longer support me as my personal being in its present form. I am no longer in that body, which has died; where does that leave *me*, the person?

#5. The radically different characteristics argument

My thoughts as a person and the physical processes in my body such as those in my brain cannot be the same thing because they have radically different characteristics. My thoughts about another person could be loving thoughts; could a brain process be loving? A thought can be rational or irrational; could this apply to a brain process? Brain processes can be measured by scientific instruments; could my desire to know the truth be detected by scientific instruments? My thoughts are my own in a way that brain processes could never be. Since thoughts and physical processes have these radically different characteristics, they cannot be one and the same. My thoughts are mine as a person; physical processes belong to my body. I am a being that can think; my body is not. I am not my body.

I know my thoughts and feelings from the inside in a way that no one else can. No brain process could ever be known in this way. A scientist can examine my brain and its electro-chemical processes; these are part of the public domain, accessible to anyone. But my thoughts are mine, absolutely and exclusively mine. They are part of my inner life as a conscious person, and thus stand in radical contrast to anything public such as a brain and its processes.

Physical things including human bodies are spatially extended but consciousness and all the features of a person rooted in it, such as reasoning, deciding, being grateful and being loving are not. Therefore, they cannot be the same thing. My body may be six feet tall but surely my consciousness is not; so too my personal identity and my uniqueness. My oneness-individuality is especially significant here. For any physical thing, it makes sense to imagine half of it. Thus, my brain has two halves, two hemispheres. But it makes no sense to speak of half a person, half an "I." An "I" is absolutely one. A person has many powers, many mental states; and he may be torn within himself. But these are not literally parts that can be "taken apart," as when a physical object like a machine is taken apart. A physical object is divisible. A person as a center of consciousness is absolutely indivisible. Therefore, a person, an "I" cannot be a physical object such as his brain or his whole body. I am not my body.

#6. *The interiority-being argument*

"I am I" as perfect interiority in my inner being. This can never be true of a physical object. Take a log for example. It has an "outside." Cut it open, and you get more of the same, smaller pieces of wood each with their "outside." Keep this up as long as you like; there will always be only "outsides," never the interiority that I experience when I say "I am I." The same thing is of course true of my body. As a physical body it has only externality; to have interiority one must bring in the person as distinct from the body. I as a person can then know myself as a bodily being, a person intimately united to my body. The body alone, the body as such – the way it exists for materialism – has only externality; not the interiority proper to persons. Interiority thus shows once again: I am not my body. I have interiority, my body does not.

#7. The interiority-knowledge argument

I know myself as myself. I know my own being, the center of consciousness that is me. The remarkable thing here is the *perfect coinciding* of knower and object known. In all other cases the subject that knows and the object that is known are two separate and distinct things. I see a tree, I know my friend, and I know an historical fact. In all these cases there is a duality of knower and known. But a person is radically different. He knows himself in a perfect oneness of the being who knows and the being who is known.

No physical thing could ever be known by its own being as itself. If it is known it is known by another, as an object distinct from the knower. Even my own body can be seen as an example of this. I look at my hand. I can examine it as an object, just as I examine the hand of another person or as a doctor would examine his patient's hand. As an object *out there,* it is not my own being as *I* am my own being; it is known to me only as an object.

This applies with special force to my brain. I am not my brain because I know myself and know myself as a center of consciousness; I generally do not know my brain. And if I do know it, I know it as an object out there and not as myself, and not as a center of consciousness.

Even in my experience of my own body as being me, intimate though it is, we do not find this absolute convergence of knower and known into one. First, I know myself as a center of consciousness, an "I" who thinks and understands and wills and feels, all of which do not refer to any of my body experiences. Second, I know my body as a multiplicity; my right arm, my left arm, my right leg, my left leg, my head, my body as a whole. This multiplicity stands in sharp contrast to the absolute simplicity of "I am I"; I know myself as myself.

I am subject and object in one. In this way I know myself from within and thereby I have true interiority. Only I know myself from the inside. Only I know what it's like to be me.

Chapter 3: Person-Body Distinction

#8. The personal identity argument

Persons have personal identity while physical things like the human body do not, and so they cannot be the same thing. I have personal identity; my body does not; therefore, I am not my body. Let us briefly review each kind of identity, that of persons and that of physical things.

Personal identity is an essential feature of persons. No matter how much you change you are always *you*, the same person. Recall the example of Karl from chapter 2, the cruel Nazi guard who has a dramatic moral conversion where he sees the evil that he committed and now deeply repents it. Though in one sense he is a new person in that his character has changed so dramatically, in another, much deeper sense he is still *the same person*. For the radical change occurred in the life of Karl, one and the same person. He can now truthfully say "I was once a cruel Nazi guard," meaning that I now and the former Nazi guard am one and the same person. The change is meaningful in the way it is only because it involves one and the same person.

Personal identity means *I am always me, the same person*. When I change, I do not change into another person, I do not become another person. I always remain the same person.

The identity of physical things is something else entirely. Recall the example of the wooden ship. Change a few of its planks: it can still be considered the same ship, with no loss of its identity. Change a few more and it is still the same ship. But if you keep changing the planks until you have finally changed all of them you will then no longer have the same original ship. The original ship will have lost its identity, meaning that the identity of a ship is not something definite and clear-cut, but merely something that attaches loosely to the ship. It is something that is mainly of practical use, as in identifying it (and not another ship) as the one legally owned by a certain person. The ship's identity as "the same ship" over a period of time is thus merely a matter of degree, of more or less; and perhaps largely a matter of practical convenience.

The identity of a person, his being "the same person" over a period of time stands in radical contrast to the identity of a ship because it is absolute. A ship can be more or less the same ship as before, but a person is either absolutely the same person as before or he is not at all the same person. For persons there can be no in-between.

Physical things like ships easily lose the "thin" identity they have while persons have a "thick," absolute identity which can never be lost. Physical things around me lose their identity when they change radically – but I don't lose my identity. I remain always the *same person*. This is the basis for my memory of my experiences in the past as *my experiences*. It is the basis for the fact that I can be held accountable for what *I did* in the past.

Do I have the same body now as I had when I was a five year old child? Consider that the cells that make up my body have all replaced themselves several times. In that sense I no longer have the same body, which means that my body as a physical reality has lost its identity since my childhood. But *I* am the same person now as the person who had that child body. So the two – my being as a person and my body – must be essentially different. I have personal identity, my body does not. This means I am not my body; I am distinct from my body.

#9. *The personal uniqueness argument*

Persons have personal uniqueness while physical things like the human body do not, and so they cannot be the same thing. I have personal uniqueness; my body does not; therefore, I am not my body. Compare the two kinds of uniqueness, that of persons and that of physical things.

Personal uniqueness means *there is only one me.* Let us recall and review some of the main points about this from chapter 2. There cannot be another *me* even if there is someone else who is exactly *like me*, and the same for you. Imagine another person who is exactly like you; a person whose personal features exactly duplicate yours, like a photocopy. You and your double appear among your friends; they can't tell the two of you apart. You give a lecture; the next day another lecture is given to the same audience. Was it *you again* or was it *your double*? You know; your double knows. The audience doesn't, for every feature noticeable in one person is present also in the other person. You know perfectly well who you are, and this includes your knowing that that *other* person, your double, is not you. He or she is just as much "not you" as a person who is very different

Chapter 3: Person-Body Distinction

from you in their personal features, such as age, personality, and physical make-up. Imagine a parallel universe where everything in ours is exactly duplicated. There is *another* person in that universe who is feature for feature exactly like you: face, body structure, personality, and everything else. That person is exactly like you but of course he or she isn't you; he is *other* than you. *Only you are you.* This is personal uniqueness; there cannot be *another you* even if there is another person exactly like you. This means that other people are different from you in two different ways: (1) in their *different personal features*; (2) in being *somebody else*; in being *another* person. It is the second that constitutes personal uniqueness.

The uniqueness of physical things is something else entirely. Suppose there is a wooden ship that is really special; it is truly one of a kind, there is no other ship like it. We want to say it is unique. But even here one can *imagine* a second ship "exactly like it," parallel to the example above of another person "exactly like you" whose personal features duplicate yours like a clone. But in the duplicate ship case one would not have the uniqueness noted for the "exactly like you" person case. For physical things like a ship there could only be two things, each a perfect replica of the other; never two beings each of which had the uniqueness proper to persons. For physical things that are entirely alike one can truly say that each is equivalent to the other; there is nothing to choose between them. But for persons the situation is radically different: one person can never be the equivalent of another person. I am me and you are you, *another* person; a world of difference separates us. And this has nothing to do with how similar or different we are in our features. But for ships and other physical things once the features are reduced to exact likeness, the uniqueness these things may have had or could possibly have is entirely eliminated.

Personal uniqueness means *there is only one me*; there can only be one me, even if there is someone else exactly like me, a perfect replica. For physical things there could only be two beings where each is a perfect replica of the other; but never two beings where each had the uniqueness proper to persons. I am unique and unrepeatable, not in my body, not because of my body, but because I am a person. It is my personal being that accounts for my uniqueness. Once again, a person, an "I," cannot be a physical object such as his whole body. I have personal uniqueness, my body does not. This means I am not my body; I am distinct from my body.

#10. I am not my brain

Think of your brain. Here surely, some might say, is a case of "I am my body." Your brain is the central organ essential for all bodily life and functioning. It is essential for rational thought, for all that we noted in chapter 1 under the heading of functioning as a person such as saying "I." It is essential for seeing and hearing, for all the five senses. Surely this is me.

But is it really? Think about it again. What do you know about your brain? How do you even know you have a brain? Isn't everything you know here only what others have told you? In terms of what you know and feel directly as a matter of immediate experience, in particular what you know and feel to be your very self, isn't your brain as far removed from being you, even from being united to you, as an object out there in front of you?

Where do dreams come from? Recall what we saw in chapter 1, section 7. In one way *a dream is very much me*: only I experience it; it exists only for me; any reality it has exists only inside my consciousness. In that sense a dream is very much me. But in another sense *a dream is not at all me*: it comes at me; it is not what I intend and design. It has the character of a thing thrust at me, sometimes unwelcomed, especially a nightmare. It is a foreign reality. Where does it come from? What produces it? Isn't it my brain? If my brain is the producer-inventor of the dreams that are thrust at me, isn't it like another person radically distinct from me? Doesn't this show that my brain is a reality radically distinct from me? My own brain; yet, it is not me!

How strange that the same body that I know so intimately as *my body* and even as *me* should be so far removed from me when it is viewed as a physical organ, especially the brain!

[6] THE IMPORTANT ROLE OF THE BRAIN

THE BRAIN AS NECESSARY CONDITION

Of course, the brain is immensely important, in so many ways. Without my brain I would not even exist as the bodily person that I am. I would not be able to think and feel and act. And if my brain functioning is impaired my abilities to think and feel and act are correspondingly impaired. The ravages of Alzheimer's disease provide a tragic example.

I move my hand; it is not my brain that does so. But, of course, my brain is a necessary condition for this. So too, my brain is a necessary condition for thinking, but it is not that which thinks; it is not the agent of thinking. *I* think; not "my brain thinks." Think of reading a book. To do this you need light; you cannot read in total darkness. Thus, light is a necessary condition for reading, but it is not the agent of reading; you are. You are the one who does the reading. And the light does not actually cause the content of what you read; it only makes possible your access to this content as it is contained in the book.

Again, the brain is immensely important; I depend on my brain. This means I depend on something else to function as a person. To say, "I depend on my brain" is not only not equivalent to "I am my brain," but is even incompatible with it. My seeing depends on my eyes, but it is *I* who see, not my eyes. I see *with* my eyes, *by means of* my eyes. So too, in an analogous though very different way, my thinking depends on my brain. I think with my brain, by means of my brain, but it is *I* who thinks, not my brain.

Again, my brain is a necessary condition for thinking, but it is not that which thinks; it is not the agent of thinking. *I* think; and I do so *with* my brain. How this "with" relation actually works is a deep mystery, though brain science can tell us some things. What we should notice, and make an object of our wonder, is that the relation of thinking and brain processes is at the same time so close, so intimate in terms of actual dependence -- and yet so distant, so utterly removed in terms of my conscious experience. I am conscious of a person I love deeply; I am conscious of that love. I understand the importance of truth, that what I believe should not be what I find convenient, but what is really true, what corresponds to reality, what expresses "how it really is." Compare these clear, lucid conscious experiences, which are parts of my life as a person, a conscious center, an "I" -- with a gray soft piece of matter, chemical processes and electrical impulses. What two sets of realities could be more different?

Wonder: two things so radically different, I as a conscious person and my brain! And yet my brain is so intimately tied in with the "I," my consciousness and its activities. I need my brain to think; but it is *I* who is doing the thinking, not my brain. The role of the brain here, as a necessary condition for thinking but not the agent of thinking, can be seen under four headings:

First, there is the basic and general necessary condition: no brain, no thought; no brain process, no thinking.

Second, there is the more specific necessary condition: no proper functioning brain, no proper thinking. What this means is that damage to the brain or significant alterations to brain chemistry can radically alter a person's consciousness and his ability to think rationally. Think of a drug overdose or brain damage that causes dementia. Other alterations to brain chemistry are not as radical but still significant. Thus, even a normal case of tiredness can slow down our thinking and make it less effective. We can say that a necessary condition for proper thinking is a properly functioning brain.

Put another way, the brain sometimes exerts *negative causal influences* on thinking, in that damage to the brain may prevent thought, or rational thought. But from the possibility of negative causal influences nothing follows for *positive causal agency*. A bomb which can destroy a building cannot bring it into existence. An electric malfunction can impede, distort or prevent a telephone conversation between two people. But the electric equipment that either makes possible a normal conversation or prevents it does not positively cause this conversation. The people do. There is a similar relation between brain process and thinking. The causal relation runs only in one direction: brain processes may prevent normal thinking or make it possible; they cannot positively bring it into existence.

Third, there may also be positive causal influences from brain to thinking, in that certain ways of enhancing brain functioning thereby enhance thinking.

Fourth, if a person's behavior is actually caused by his brain or brain processes, then it is not really his behavior. He is not acting as a person. A deranged person may kill another person. If it is determined that his action was caused by a brain tumor and not by him as a person, we do not hold him responsible. Thus, we can say that *in so far as* a person's behavior is actually caused by his brain or brain processes, it is not really his behavior and he is not responsible for it. We will return to this point below (section 7), Wilder Penfield's causal initiative argument; he manipulates a person's brain causing his hand to move: *"I didn't do that. You did."*

Another comparison to the brain as necessary condition for thinking is the tongue for speaking. *I* speak, not my tongue. I need my tongue; I use my tongue and I would not be able to speak without my tongue. We can use both these comparisons – light for reading and the tongue for speaking – to highlight the four points just made. First, without light there can be no reading and without a tongue there can be no speaking. Second, poor light impairs reading and damage to the tongue impairs speaking. Third, better light allows for more efficient reading and certain medications may enable a speaking-impaired person to improve his speech, perhaps overcome stuttering. Fourth, in the hard-to-imagine case where the agent of speaking is the tongue instead of the person, we would obviously say that the person is not the one who is speaking. Eyes are needed for seeing but eyes are not the agent of seeing; it is the person who sees. Poor eyesight interferes with a person's ability to see while good eyesight enhances it.

THE BRAIN AS COMPUTER

Perhaps a good way to understand the relation between a person and his brain is on the analogy of agent and computer. Not *I am my brain*, but *I have a brain*. I have a brain as a kind of automatic computer. Of course, I do not operate it consciously and deliberately; it works for me automatically. I need only will something and my inner computer works automatically for me to bring it about. Wilder Penfield remarks that "Inasmuch as the brain is a place for newly acquired automatic mechanisms, it is a computer."[1] Mathematical calculations and information processing are operations performed both by human persons and by computers, though of course in essentially different ways; for persons do these consciously and deliberately while computers do not. Persons consciously follow rules while computers merely behave according to rules, as if they were following rules. Still, the comparison is useful in that it suggests that persons do these things by utilizing a tool, their brains.

THE BRAIN AS TRANSMITTER

William James in his book *Human Immortality* offers a striking defense of the person-body distinction. He argues for the possibility of human immortality or life-after-death and thereby for the reality of the conscious person distinct from the brain. His starting point is the doctrine that "thought is a function of the brain." He then asks: "Does this doctrine logically compel us to disbelieve in immortality"[2] and to deny the person-body distinction? His answer is an emphatic *no*. He suggests that there are several different kinds of functions.

One kind of function is *productive*, that is causal. A trumpet produces a sound, the motor of a car produces its motion, and a generator produces electricity. But there are other kinds of functions, and these do not imply that the brain produces thinking in the sense that it causes it, or that thinking just is a brain process. Specifically, there is also a *transmissive* function. That is, when a materialist uses the phrase "thought is a function of the brain" to express his theory, he is using it in only one of its senses. In James' words,

> But in the world of physical nature productive function of this sort is not the only kind of function with which we are familiar. We have also…transmissive function….

---

[1] Wilder Penfield, *The Mystery of the Mind: A Critical Study of Consciousness and the Human Brain* (Princeton, 1975), 60.

[2] William James, *Human Immortality*, 2nd ed., in *The Will to Believe and Human Immortality* (Dover, 1956), 10.

In the case of a colored glass, a prism, or a refracting lens, we have transmissive function. The energy of light, no matter how produced, is by the glass sifted and limited in color, and by the lens or prism determined to a certain path and shape. Similarly, the keys of an organ have only a transmissive function. They open successively the various pipes and let the wind in the air-chest escape in various ways. The voices of the various pipes are constituted by the columns of air trembling as they emerge. But the air is not engendered in the organ. The organ proper, as distinguished from its air-chest, is only an apparatus for letting portions of it loose upon the world in these peculiarly limited shapes.

My thesis now is this: that, when we think of the law that thought is a function of the brain, we are not required to think of productive function only; *we are entitled also to consider...transmissive function.* And this the ordinary psycho-physiologist leaves out of his account.[3]

[7] THE LIMITING ROLE OF THE BRAIN

THE SCHILLER VISION

Clearly there is a close relationship between brain processes and consciousness. When brain processes are affected, consciousness is likewise affected. Brain damage can cause damage to consciousness, especially reasoning ability and memory. But how are they really related? On materialism (the denial of the person-body distinction) the brain and its processes have primacy. Given the brain consciousness follows as a causal effect. Consciousness is caused by the brain; thinking is a brain process.

But suppose we reverse this picture and think of consciousness as having the primacy. Consciousness, and specifically the conscious subject, the "I" exists in its own right, though intimately united with the body and closely dependent on the body. The conscious subject acts *through* the body as a medium of expression. Think of the body, in particular the brain, as a screen or window, and conscious-

---

[3] Ibid., 13-15.

ness as a light. The screen or window lets more light or less light shine through, but the light is there in any case. The light exists in its own right. On this view, the brain acts as a *limit* to consciousness. This is the Schiller vision. Doesn't it provide an interesting and challenging, even an illuminating answer to the materialist thesis that the brain causes consciousness? In Schiller's own words:

> Matter is an admirably calculated machinery for regulating, limiting, and restraining consciousness which it encases. If the material encasement be coarse and simple, as in the lower organisms, it permits only a little intelligence to permeate through it; if it is delicate and complex, it leaves more pores and exits, as it were, for the manifestations of consciousness.
>
> On this analogy, then, we may say that the lower animals are still entranced in the lower stage of brute *lethargy*, while we have passed into the higher phase of *somnambulism*, which already permits us strange glimpses of a lucidity that divines the realities of a transcendent world.
>
> And this gives the final answer to Materialism: it consists in showing in detail that Materialism is a hysteron proteron, a putting of the cart before the horse, which may be rectified by just inverting the connection between Matter and Consciousness. Matter is not that which *produces* Consciousness, but that which *limits* it, and confines its intensity within certain limits: material organization does not construct consciousness out of arrangements of atoms but contracts its manifestation within the sphere which it permits.
>
> This explanation admits the connection of Matter and Consciousness but contends that the course of interpretation must proceed in the contrary direction. Thus, it will fit the facts alleged in favor of Materialism equally well, besides enabling us to understand facts which Materialism rejected as "supernatural." It explains the lower by the higher, Matter by Spirit, instead of *vice versa*, and thereby attains to an explanation which is ultimately tenable, instead of one which is ultimately absurd.

> And it is an explanation the possibility of which no evidence in favor of Materialism can possibly affect. For if, *e.g.*, a man loses consciousness as soon as his brain is injured, it is clearly as good an explanation to say the injury to the brain destroyed the mechanism by which the manifestation of the consciousness was rendered possible [as in the Schiller Vision], as to say that it destroyed the seat of consciousness [as in materialism, where the seat of consciousness is the brain].
>
> On the other hand, there are facts which the former theory suits far better. If, *e.g.*, as sometimes happens, the man, after a time, more or less, recovers the faculties of which the injury to his brain had deprived him, and that not in consequence of a renewal of the injured part, but in consequence of the inhibited functions being performed by the vicarious action of other parts, the easiest explanation certainly is that, after a time, consciousness constitutes the remaining parts into a mechanism capable of acting as a substitute for the lost parts.[4]

Let us note some of Schiller's key points:

- Materialism puts the cart before the horse; this can be rectified by just inverting the connection between matter and consciousness.
- Matter is not that which produces consciousness, but that which limits it, and confines its intensity within certain limits.
- Material organization does not construct consciousness out of arrangements of atoms but contracts its manifestation within the sphere which it permits.

The analogy to my eyes. None of this is meant in any way to deny that I depend on my brain, as was noted above. Precisely, I depend on something else to function as a person. Recall the comparison: my seeing depends on my eyes, but it is *I*

---

[4] F. C. S. Schiller, *Riddles of the Sphinx* (London: Swan Sonnenschein, 1891), 293 ff. Quoted by William James in his *Human Immortality*, 66-68. Ellipses in James' text have been deleted; division into short paragraphs added.

who see, not my eyes. I see *with* my eyes, *by means* of my eyes. So too my thinking depends on my brain: I think with my brain, by means of my brain, but it is *I* who thinks, not my brain. As in Schiller's vision, the better my eyes function, the more clearly I can see. My eyes are "windows" through which I reach reality.

THE BRAIN IS NOT THE SOURCE OF CAUSAL INITIATIVE

Another way to see the limiting role of the brain is to ask: does the brain have a causal role? Surely it does; think of its activity in regulating the heart, the kidneys, body temperature and so much else. But suppose my brain caused my hand to move.

I didn't do that. You did. Wilder Penfield conducted experiments in which we can see the radical contrast between the normal cases where *I* move my hand, and cases where it is really a brain event that causes my hand to move. He tells us:

> When I have caused a conscious patient to move his hand by applying an electrode to the motor cortex of one hemisphere [of the brain], I have often asked him about it. Invariably his response was: "I didn't do that. You did." When I caused him to vocalize, he said: "I didn't make that sound. You pulled it out of me."[5]

What a brain state causes is not my action; it is something that happens to me. If my physical actions were always caused by my brain; if they were the effects of my brain states, my daily life would be just like that of Penfield's patient. Clearly it is not. This means that *I*, as a conscious self, initiate and cause my physical actions, not my brain. Therefore, I am not my brain, and more generally I am not my body.

---

[5] Penfield, 76.

Chapter 3: Person-Body Distinction

THE MANY ASPECTS OF THE BRAIN

The brain: so important, so central; and yet also a limiting force on consciousness. It is central and important as a necessary condition for our being and functioning as persons; it is our inner computer and transmitter. Yet as the Schiller vision shows it also limits us. It is so close to us in making our consciousness possible; yet so far removed from our consciousness itself in that we don't know it directly and hardly think of it as it does its job. We depend on it as we control our lives in moving about and doing things. And yet it also controls us: it determines our body temperature, blood pressure, digestion of food and much more.

[8] FOUR DIMENSIONS OF PERSON-BODY DISTINCTION

We can summarize the case for person-body distinction under four main headings:

1. I am a person; my body is not a person. We can see this by noting the essential capacities proper to persons and totally lacking in all material things including the human body. I am a person: I am conscious, I can say "I," I can think, I can understand, I can act in morally good or morally evil ways, I can "get" a joke, I can appreciate beauty, I can love another person and much more. All these constitute functioning as a person.
2. I am a person; my body is not a person. We can see this also by noting the metaphysical features of being a person. Primary among these are personal identity and uniqueness. I am always me, the same person, over long stretches of time and through radical changes. And there is only one me, even if there is another person exactly like me.
3. I am not my brain. My brain is in fact necessary for my functioning as a person, even for my being a person. But it is not what I am as a person, a thinking and willing and loving being. How often do I even think of my brain and realize I have it? In contrast, I am constantly aware of myself as a person even if only implicitly. My brain is actually very far removed from my consciousness, a world of its own. And the same is really true of

my other bodily organs such heart and liver and bodily processes like blood circulation.

4. I am not my body as a whole even as I feel united to it to form one being. For this unity of person and body to be a reality I as a person have to be something other than the body to which I am united. The body is not united to the body; it just is the body. But I can be united to my body because I am as such not my body. I as a being other than this body I call mine can say "I am united to this body." This unity is the theme of our next chapter.

CHAPTER 4
PERSON-BODY UNITY

[1] INTRODUCTION

In the last chapter we explored the ways in which I am *not* my body, the real *distinction* between a person and his body. In this chapter we explore the ways in which I *am* my body, the *unity* of a person and his body. Part one: how this unity is directly experienced. Part two: a key distinction, two ways in which my body exists for me and in itself, Leib and Körper, two German words; two ways of seeing my body in terms of unity and distinction. Part three: my body exists not only for me and in itself but also for others in personal bodily presence, another form of person-body unity.

PART ONE
THE EXPERIENCED UNITY OF PERSON AND BODY

[2] I HAVE A BODY

We have often expressed the unity of person and body by saying that I am my body. But this should not be taken as meaning that I and my body are one and the same thing, for there is clearly a distinction. Saying "I" belongs to me as a conscious person, not to my body. Saying I am my body is simply a dramatic way of expressing the profound *unity* of me and my body, the profound experienced unity of my consciousness with my body.

One aspect of this unity is that I have a body. But I don't have my body the way I have other things. Many of the other things I have I can give away. I can lose them. I can share them with others. None of these apply to my having my body. The *having* relation is utterly different. Is it even proper to say that I *have* a body, since it is so radically different from "I have a car" or "I have a job" or "I have a friend"? Yet it would be wrong to say that I don't have a body.

[3] I USE MY BODY

There are so many ways in which I use my arms and legs and other parts of my body in my daily activities. I reach into the cupboard to get a cup; I walk over to the table to get a drink; I put food in my mouth; I get up after sitting in a chair; I wash my hands; I wash the dishes. In these and so many other bodily activities all day long do I take my body for granted? But do I not also somehow consciously even if implicitly experience my body, and experience it as me?

Consider again one of the examples above; I wash the dishes. Isn't this bodily activity utterly unlike a crane operator who sits inside the crane and causes the crane to operate, to move a pile of dirt, by pulling on a set of levers? The operator and the crane are completely separate beings. And consciousness, even though distinct from the body, is somehow so completely present in the body as to form one bodily conscious being. In washing the dishes, I move my body; isn't the "I" not only the conscious center of the person but somehow also the body as consciously experienced? As energized from within by consciousness?

[4] I SEE AND FEEL MY BODY

I can see and feel my own body. That is, there is my perception of my own body as me. Doesn't this differ radically from my perception of things out there in front of me, outside me, through my senses? Don't I perceive my own body – in its totality as well as in its parts, such as my hand – in a way essentially different from the way I perceive an apple lying on the table or a tree in my back yard? The apple and the tree: aren't they seen as "out there" in front of me? But my own body: it's not "out there" in front of me; it's me! I feel it from within as being me. The tree is observed as *outside me*; in contrast, my own body is experienced as *being me*. The same body (my body) that another sees as an object out there is something completely different for me! It isn't perceived in the usual sense but is experienced as my very own being!

But can I not also see my own hand in front of me like an object? If so this means that I have a double access to my hand: I feel it from within as part of my body and I also see it in front of me as an object. But even as an object in front of

Chapter 4: Person-Body Unity

me: isn't it different from the other cases? I know it not as "a" hand but as *my hand*, a part of *me*.

[5] WHERE IN MY BODY AM I?

Where in my body am I? I am where my body is, not somewhere else. I am not outside my body, so I am in my body. But then where in my body am I? Am I more in my head than in my toes? Was I even conscious of my toes just now? I am not in my body the way my heart is in my body but in some other, radically different way. What is that way?

If I am more in some parts of my body than in others, in which ones am I more? Am I more in my head or more in my chest? Am I equally in all parts of my head? Or am I more in some parts than in others? If so which ones? How specific can I get, and say this is the spot in my body where I am? Can I say 5 inches from x? Wouldn't such a spot designate only a specific part of my body and not me? Pick any specific spot in your body, and then try to picture yourself without it. Isn't this possible? And if it is, does it show that you are not in that spot?

Doesn't it seem that I am neither all over my body equally nor in a specific spot in my body? Is there something in between? If so, what is it? Where in my body am I? Should we say that to be located in space does not apply to consciousness, that one cannot pinpoint it like a point on a line? And yet, isn't my consciousness where my body is? Doesn't "I am in England" mean not merely that my body is there but that *I* am there, that my conscious being is there? Compare: I am in my body; I am in England. In the latter, I can be more specific: I am in this city, for example London; and I can continue to be more and more specific: section of the city, street, house, floor, room, part of room. I can pinpoint my location in England, or wherever I now happen to be. But what happens when I try this for my location in my body? Where in my body am I? What does *in* mean in the two cases: I am in my body; I am in England? Does *in* mean something different in each of these two cases? Perhaps it does, and yet each use of *in* refers to spatial location; each refers to me, where I am. Is there a solution to this set of puzzles?

What is the relation between consciousness and space? It seems to be very mysterious. Compare these two cases, both involving our notion of being *in*:

- My foot is in my shoe, my shoe is in my room; therefore, my foot is in my room.
- There is a pain in my foot, my foot is in my shoe; therefore, there is a pain in my shoe.

Why is it that the first is true while the second is not? How is a pain spatially located?

[6] AM I ONE WITH MY WHOLE BODY?

Am I one with my whole body? What is included in this body that I am, or that I'm in? My right arm certainly; likewise, my right hand and each of my fingers. How about a fingernail? Surely it is a part of my finger. But now consider the upper one-tenth of the fingernail. Before I cut the nail, it is joined to me. After I cut it, it lies there on the floor, as foreign to me as a toothpick next to it. Was it once part of me? Did I exist in that bit of fingernail now on the floor? It seems not. But then where do we draw the line?

Do I exist in my hair? Surely, I do not exist in my hair after it is cut. But before it is cut: do I feel it as somehow a part of me? If a stranger takes a portion of my hair and holds it will I not feel that I have been touched, and invaded? "Why did you touch me?" Yet doesn't getting a haircut feel radically different from losing a part of my body in an amputation? So, is my hair part of me or not? It seems hard to draw lines here. Do I exist in my teeth? Consider a tooth after it is pulled; I now see it lying on a table, not a part of me. Was it a part of me before it was pulled? Surely it was a part of my mouth; and isn't my mouth a part of me? Suppose I lose a leg by amputation and then see it lying there, a part of me gone, a horrifying thought! Aren't these two cases, the tooth and the leg, radically different? What applies to my leg surely applies also to my hand. Does it apply also to a finger? Also, to a part of a finger? To a whole fingernail? To a tenth of a fingernail? The top tenth is what is cut off when we cut our fingernails. Surely, we do not experience this as a loss of part of our being. But then where do we draw a line? Why can't we seem to be able to draw lines here? What is part of me and what isn't part of me?

How strange this body of mine! What a source of wonder! I know it so well because it is a dimension of my very being. Yet I cannot answer these apparently simple questions. In one way all of my body belongs to me. And yet there is a huge difference between losing a part of a fingernail and losing a hand. Is it a quantitative difference: I lose more if I lose my hand? Is it something else? Does the amount play some role? Is it a question of how deeply I identify myself with a particular part of my body? If so, which parts do I most deeply identify with?

[7] PERSON-BODY UNITY AND THE SOUL

Suppose we say that the soul is what makes you a person, that the soul is the non-physical or spiritual dimension of the person. Then the unity of person and body means that the body is the manifestation of the soul. *The body manifests the soul.* The soul exists through the body. The soul is revealed to others through the body. The soul is like a beam of light; the body is like a rainbow that reveals this light and manifests this light. The beam of light can exist without the rainbow, but the rainbow cannot exist without the light. Even if the soul might exist without the body as basic dualism suggests, the body cannot exist as a human body without the soul. And if the soul can exist without the body it cannot exist in its fullness without the body, as the body is its manifestation. Soul and body are like two sides of the same coin; two sides, not two coins.

The wonder is that in the human person soul and body are essentially distinct and yet also form one being. They need to be distinct to form one being. As noted, I have to be something other than my body in order to be united to it. And so to say that I am my body really means that I identify with my body as a dimension of my being, as something that is in some sense a part of me but is not simply me or the whole of me.

PART TWO
TWO WAYS THE BODY EXISTS: LEIB AND KÖRPER

[8] CONSCIOUSNESS AND THE BODY: TWO PROBLEMS

We have looked at several ways in which I am related to my body. Somehow each of them is already familiar to us, for they are part of our very being as persons. Yet how many of us realized them explicitly? That is the gift of philosophy as wonder: to make us aware of these basic realities in an explicit way, to understand them and appreciate them. One source of wonder is that these ways in which I am related to my body go in opposite directions: in chapter 3, I am *not* my body; now in chapter 4, I *am* my body. How can this be? Is it because "my body" is taken in two very different senses? I want to suggest that this is indeed the reason, or at least a major part of the reason. To this let us now turn.

It is generally assumed that there is one consciousness-body problem, or one mind-body problem, or one person-body problem, with different aspects and theories. But perhaps there are really two different person-body problems; and correspondingly two different relations, referring to two different ways in which I am related to this piece of matter that I call my body.

The first problem initially concerns the question how my consciousness is related to my brain and the many brain processes that accompany it and make it possible. More generally, it is the question of how my being as a person is related to my body as a physical organism. This seems to be the question philosophers engaged in the "mind-body" problem are concerned with. It is the question of how consciousness is related to bodily organs, particularly the brain.

What is noteworthy in this first problem? Isn't it that the body side of the relation in this mind-body problem is mostly unknown to me in my daily life? Isn't it noteworthy that I do not see my brain? That I cannot touch it and observe how it works? As noted, I know that I have a brain only because others have told me about it. My brain is in fact such a vital organ; and yet it is completely unknown to me in any direct way.

Notice how this distance of my brain from my consciousness contrasts sharply with my consciousness of my hand. I know my hand immediately and directly as an integral part of my day-to-day conscious experience. I consciously feel my hand from within; I see it and use it. And I always know at least implicitly that I have it, that it is part of me even when my conscious focus is on other things. My consciousness of my hand leads to the other person-body problem.

The second person-body problem concerns the question how my consciousness is related to my body as directly-immediately and intimately known to me, as felt by me, as "lived" by me. This is both my body as a whole and specific parts of it such as my right hand. Don't I feel my body as a whole to be me? Doesn't feeling tired mean feeling my-body-as-me as being tired? Isn't tiredness a bodily feeling, one quite unlike feeling sorry for a person who is suffering? Isn't tiredness consciously felt in my body as a way my body is "given" to me, experienced by me? I might understand that truth is important even if I didn't have a body; but how could I feel tired if I didn't have a body?

Of course, it isn't just when I'm tired that I feel my body; it is in some way all the time. To be a human person, to act as a person, even when engaged in the most abstract thought that is in some ways removed from the physical realm; even then, I do not lose my awareness that I am a bodily being. At every waking moment I have an immediate experience of my body as me.

The two very different person-body problems are set off from each other by the fact that they view the body so very differently. The first views it as unknown to immediate experience and known only to scientific investigations. The second views it as immediately and intimately known, as felt, as experienced. These two views correspond to two essentially different ways in which the human body exists; two ways in which consciousness is related to the body. For the first my body is an object *outside* my consciousness. For the second my body is somehow *a part of* my consciousness, an essential dimension of my being as human person.

[9] CONSCIOUSNESS AND THE BODY: TWO RELATIONS

The German language has two words for the human body which neatly capture this distinction, Leib and Körper (Leib rhymes with *type*; Körper as in *curve-supper*):

Körper is the human body, any human body, as *an object* that can be studied, mainly by biological and medical science; it is the body as it exists for medical practice. My own body as Körper is largely hidden from me in my immediate experience.

Leib is that same body when it is seen as *my body*; my body as I experience it, as I know it from within, as I live it. It is my body as a dimension of me. It is my body as intimately known to me. It is the human body as known by every human person, small child to adult. To feel it and be conscious of it is not a matter of knowledge based on scientific experiments. Most knowledge of one's Körper has little effect on one's Leib experience. Thus, knowledge about my brain does not give me any Leib experience of my brain, since I don't have that anyway.

I cut my finger and it hurts; a Leib experience. I feel my finger, a part of my body, as painful. This is an immediate experience, felt equally by a small child and a learned adult. Now a doctor examines my finger and sees what the problem is. He looks at the same phenomenon, but what he is aware of is radically different from what I am aware of in my experience. I feel and experience *my body* as my Leib. But he examines and knows only *a body* as a Körper. Leib vs. Körper contrasts *my* body with *a* body. We may see this relation in several ways:

First, Leib-Körper may refer to the two very different ways the human body exists. This refers to *the body itself*. We can say that one and the same thing, a human body, which weighs x pounds, and is y feet tall, is both a Leib and a Körper. It is a Leib to me and to me alone. It is a Körper to anyone when viewed as a biological organism studied by medical science. It is one thing viewed in two different ways.

Second, Leib-Körper may refer to the two very different ways in which *the body presents itself*: to me as Leib and to medical science as Körper.

Third, Leib-Körper may refer to two *types of relations* between a person and his body. The one is an experienced relation: I experience my body as Leib. My body is Leib only in so far as it is experienced by me; my experience of my body as Leib constitutes its being a Leib. If there is no experience, there is no Leib. But Körper exists in itself whether anyone knows it or not. My blood in fact circulates. The immune system wards off disease. As physical processes these things run independently of anyone knowing about them. This is the body as Körper.

Chapter 4: Person-Body Unity

What remains after a person's death is the body. But we can be more specific. It is not the body as Leib for there is no longer a person present to feel his body as Leib. What remains is the body as a Körper, though radically altered in no longer being alive. This is manifested in the root similarity between the German word *Körper* and the English word *corpse*.

Do I have the same body over time? As Körper it would seem that I do not, for the cells replace each other every seven years or so and thus create a new Körper body. But do I not have the same body as Leib? If I feel my body as Leib to be me and if I am the same person over time, then doesn't my body as Leib also continue as the same body over time? That would mean that my identity over time embraces my body as Leib and includes it in its reality, draws it in.

What I know immediately as *myself*, my own person, my own consciousness -- and what I am told is the being of *my body* as Körper are so radically different that they could not possibly be one and the same thing as materialism claims. To see this more clearly consider:

MY BODY AS KÖRPER IS A WORLD OF ITS OWN

I eat my dinner and turn my attention to other things. While I do so my stomach digests my food. How does this happen? Apart from learning about it from science I have no idea. Yet it is happening inside me and it is in some way very close to me. And yet it is so far from me in my total ignorance of it in terms of my immediate experience. It is in a world of its own.

I bruise my hand, and this causes a wound. What does my skin do to heal this wound? It is happening right here in my body; and yet I have no idea how this is happening.

What happens in my brain as I think? I know my thinking intimately, for it is part of my consciousness. But the brain processes that make it possible, that in another way are closely linked to my thinking are utterly removed from my conscious awareness.

How did my body grow and develop from a tiny cell into the developed body I now have, that enables me to reflect on these things, and wonder about them? For the first few years of my life my body grew in height; then it stopped growing.

How did that happen? How did it "know" when it was time to stop growing? How did it bring this about? It happened in me. Yet I have no idea how it happened. I was not aware of it as it was happening.

I move my hand. How do I do that? How do my brain and nervous system command my muscles to move in the appropriate ways? Do I know how to move my hand? Yes and no. As a consciously experienced Leib activity I know very well how to move my hand and thus know what is happening. As a physical process occurring inside my body as Körper I have no idea what is happening.

Digestion, healing, brain activity, growth, bodily movements, and a multitude of other things – such as gland secretions, how oxygen gets from my lungs into my blood stream, how the white blood corpuscles ward off diseases – all happen within me. Yet they are totally removed from me in my conscious awareness. Certainly, I can learn about them through scientific study. But in this respect, they are no different from what I learn about the body of a cat or a dog. Both the body of an animal and my own body as Körper are utterly removed from my immediate awareness. Each one is a world of its own.

How strange that I should be more familiar with what is around me – chairs and tables, cars and houses, the food I eat and the water I drink – than what is inside me, in my body! How amazing my body turns out to be when I do learn about it from science; that I have some 60,000 miles of blood vessels and 60 trillion cells. Each cell in my body is as unknown to me as a cell in any other body. And yet these cells make up the body that is somehow me.

I know my hand; I do not know my brain. Yet my brain is in another sense much more "me," or closer to me, as it is crucial to my functioning as a conscious person. From the Körper perspective my brain is very close to me; from the Leib perspective it is very far from me. It is utterly hidden from my conscious experience; it is a world of its own.

Bottom line: *my being as a person is not my body as Körper*. In this sense I am not my body. Doesn't it follow that a materialism that would identify the person with his body – which must include the body as Körper – cannot be true? And isn't the clear alternative some form of dualism, which we are calling basic dualism?

Chapter 4: Person-Body Unity

MY BODY AS LEIB IS DISTINCT FROM ME AS A CONSCIOUS PERSON

As noted, the phrase *I am my body* should be used only to express the idea of unity, not of identity in the sense of "the same thing as." If I am intimately united to my body as Leib, I cannot just *be* that body. I have to be a person, a center of consciousness, distinct from my body in order to be united to it; both to be united to it in fact and also to experience this unity.

We should also remember that not every experience I have is a Leib experience. When I face a difficult decision, I have the clear sense that it is I who make this decision, no one else and nothing else. Not only is it not my body that decides; my deciding is not at all a Leib experience, such as feeling the cold in my hand as I dip it into cold water.

Even Leib experiences can be used to show the essential distinction between the "I," the conscious person and the body as Leib. Where in my body am I? It seems I am more in my head than in my feet. But still, where am I? Isn't this a sensible question? If not, why not? If it does not admit a standard answer, why not? If it does, how is it to be answered? In all of this wonder at the mystery of "I in my body as Leib" the "I" that is somewhere in this Leib, the "I" whose location is being sought cannot simply be the same thing as the Leib in which it somehow resides. The "I" and the Leib must be distinct to even make sense of the question.

[10] A SUMMARY OF THE LEIB-KÖRPER DISTINCTION

- Leib is my body as I feel it and know it from within.
- Leib is my body as I experience it in daily life: sitting, standing, walking, doing things.
- Leib is my body as "the lived body": personal life, not biological life.
- Leib is my body as a dimension of my being.
- Leib is *my body as me*: to express unity; it is not a denial of distinction.
- Leib means *I am my body*: but not only my body; I am also more than my body.

- Körper is my body as a biological organism; a group of cells, tissues and organs working harmoniously together to constitute one aspect of what I am as a bodily being.
- Körper is my body as a biological organism to support my life as a conscious person.
- Körper is my body as studied by science, as examined by my doctor.
- Körper is my body as a world of its own, biological processes entirely removed from my conscious awareness.
- Körper is *my body as not me*: my body as radically distinct from me.
- Körper means that *I am not my body*: it is radically distinct from me.

KÖRPER	LEIB
1. It is an object out there.	1. It is felt from within, as me or as part of me.
2. It is one of many physical things. It is part of the physical world.	2. It is unique and correlates with my uniqueness as a person. Only I feel my body as me.
3. It is *a* human body, one of many bodies. It is studied by science.	3. It is *my* body, it is unique to me. It cannot be studied by science.
4. It just functions; it is not felt.	4. It exists as felt; it is felt as me.
5. It is mostly unknown to me: like a world of its own; partly known from the outside.	5. It is intimately known: felt from within. It is felt as an aspect of "me."
6. Körper loses its identity over time: baby to adult; cells are replaced over the years.	6. I now have the same Leib I always had; it is drawn into my personal identity.
7. Everyone can see the same Körper.	7. Only I can feel my body as my Leib.
8. I can view any human body as Körper, my own or that of another.	8. Leib is a relation I have only to my own body, not to the body of another person.
Leib and Körper are radically different; and yet they are the same physical body. If my Körper is large, my Leib is large, and feels large. If my Körper is sick, I generally feel that sickness as a Leib experience. If my Körper is healthy, I generally feel that health as a Leib experience.	

Leib and Körper: two very different ways in which the human body exists; basically:

Leib is my body as it exists *for me* while Körper is my body as it *exists in itself*.

Leib is my body as it exists in *unity* with me while Körper is my body as *distinct* from me.

PART THREE
THE WAY THE BODY EXISTS FOR OTHERS

[11] PERSONAL BODILY PRESENCE

So far, we have examined the human body -- as Leib, as Körper and comparisons between the two -- as it exists in itself, especially person-Leib-unity in contrast to Körper-distinction. But there is also the human body as it exists between two persons and among many persons; that is, the human body in inter-personal relations. Occasionally this involves the body as Körper, as when a doctor examines a patient. But the Körper approach is clearly not the way we normally view others and are viewed by them. In fact, our normal views stand in radical contrast to the medical Körper approach. What then are these normal views?

I see my friend. We start talking. What is it that is given to me here? That is present before me here? Not a human body as Körper. But not a human body as Leib either, for this is given only to the person whose body it is. My body is Leib only for me. Only I can feel it from within, as I feel the sensation in my arm when I put it in warm water or feel tired in my body as a whole. What then is it that we have here? Clearly, we need more categories, in addition to Leib and Körper, in order to do justice to the reality of persons in their inter-personal relations. Let us refer to this reality as the *personal bodily presence* of a person.

In the above case where I see my friend the focus is on *another person*, and how that other person is given to me in my seeing him. I see him, another *person*. It would be misleading here to say that I was seeing "another person's body," for this suggests a false abstraction of the body away from the reality of the person, who is not simply his body. What I am seeing, what is present to me is the *personal bodily presence of another*. This bodily presence, which I can perceive with my senses, is both something physical and also something personal, beyond the physical. In seeing your body (especially your face) I see *you*, a person, a consciousness.

But that is only half the story. In the first half the focus is on another person, and how that other person is given to me in my seeing him. The other half of the story is the converse of this, where the focus is on me, on my own personal bodily experience before another. This is the *personal bodily presence of my own being* before another person. I experience my body not only in itself as when I feel cold, but also as it exists before others. Another person sees *me*. "Hello, how are you?" Suppose it was said, "strictly speaking the other person didn't really see me; he only saw my body, or part of the surface of my body. He then inferred that it was me, my conscious self, on the inside." This description seems utterly false to our experience. It is true that another person "sees my body" but when he does so he sees *me*. This is the true description of the experience, an experience of unity, the intimate unity of a person as the union of soul and body. When another person sees my body he sees me, for I feel one with my body. I do not have my body as some kind of external shell, in which I can hide. My body is me, as seen by another. This is of course what underlies our sense of modesty and shame. I do not want to appear in public insufficiently dressed, for the simple reason that when others "see my body" they see *me*, and that could be embarrassing.

The same applies to touching. Someone who experiences inappropriate touching by a stranger in public will say, "Why did you touch me?" Suppose she is told, "I didn't really touch you; I only touched your body." This is absurd, and it is so because of the intimate unity of a person as the union of person and body; for in touching my body you touch *me*, you reach *me*. This unity is experienced equally in the positive cases of touching and the negative ones. The negative cases are those that are unwelcomed. In being touched, I feel exposed to another person; his touch "reaches" me in an inappropriate and distasteful way. The positive cases are those that are welcomed, from a person I love, with whom I feel a spiritual bond and closeness; think of the embrace of lovers. The physical contact of touching between friends and lovers expresses the spiritual unity between them and is therefore a source of joy.

To sum up, in addition to Leib and Körper there is the *personal bodily presence* of a person. This has two forms, or "two halves of the story":

- Where the focus is on another person: the *personal bodily presence of another*.
- Where the focus is on me: the *personal bodily presence of my own being* before others.

This means that the human body as Körper has two contrasts. First, there is the contrast within my own bodily being, the radical difference between my body as I feel it *to be me* and identify with it, my body as Leib – and my body as a group of cells and organs, my body mostly unknown to me, my body as radically *not me*, my body as Körper.

Second, there is the contrast in the realm of the inter-personal, between the usual cases of the *personal bodily presence* of a person – and the special cases where another person's body is seen as Körper, *as an impersonal object* when it is examined by a doctor or a scientist.

[12] THE HUMAN FACE

I am present to you in my face and by my face. Both of these are significant: *in* my face and *by* my face. I am present to you as a bodily being, what we called *personal bodily presence*, which is how a human person exists for others. He is present to others in his body, as a bodily person, not as a soul. For the soul or the person as a center of consciousness and the agent of conscious acts cannot be seen or touched by others. We exist for others and among others in our bodily being, by our personal bodily presence.

A person's face is particularly significant for *personal bodily presence*. Surely the face belongs to the body for it can be seen and it has spatial dimensions. As part of the physical body the face is something physical. And yet isn't the significance of a person's face something that is not primarily physical in the way that seeing an apple is simply seeing something physical? In seeing your face, I see *you*, a person, a being who is conscious, who can say "I," who can be morally good or evil, who can be loving or hateful and so much more. All these are not as such and not primarily physical realities.

The wonder of the human face is largely that it is both physical and non-physical. It is *physical* because it is part of the surface of a person's body; it has physical features and physical dimensions. But is also *non-physical* because it is the presence of consciousness to others: in seeing your face I see *you*, a conscious person. I do not see your consciousness as such, but I see the person who is conscious, whose consciousness is somehow present in his face.

One of the ways in which person-body unity is manifested is by the personal-physical reality of a human face. Conscious person and physical body come together in a person's face. Again, when I see *your face*, I truly see *you*.

I am present to you in my face, and you are present to me in your face. In seeing your face, I see you in a way that is not true if I see the back of your neck. A person is somehow "in" his face in a way in which he or she is not in other surfaces of his body. A person's face and our perception of it present many interesting dimensions; let us note a few:

- The uniqueness of a person's face represents the uniqueness of the person himself.
- I read your face and note whether you are a man or a woman. How is this possible?
- I read your face and note approximately your age. How is this possible?
- I read your face and see that you look sad or happy or surprised or confused. How can these non-physical realities be so clearly and directly expressed in a physical surface?
- I read your face and recognize who you are.
- I know you: a big part of this is to know your face.
- I think of you: I picture you in my mind by picturing your face.
- I have a photo of you: it is a picture of your face.
- If I haven't seen you in a long time and I long to see you again, what I look forward to is once again seeing your face. In seeing your face, I see you.
- If I am ashamed, I hide my face in my hands. I do not want you to see my face because I do not want you to see me. When you see my face, you see me.

- The *personal bodily presence of another* is given to me primarily by his or her face.
- The *personal bodily presence of my own being* before another is primarily by my face.

We communicate by our faces. I see you: you have a warm, beautiful smile; your face "gives" me that smile. It "speaks" to me of your love, your affirmation; and that you are happy now. What power there is in a smile! It is so much more than any physical description can do it justice, no matter how complete that description. And then there are those opposites of a smile: a frown, hostility, an arrogant looking down on others, anger, evil intent and hatred. And then so much more, as when your face says that you are deeply upset; the face that evokes the response "what's the matter?" Or the face that reads boredom, tuning out. How can a physical surface, the human face, have such immense and varied and powerful means of communication?

The human face is a small percentage of the total body skin area; yet it is by far the most significant, going far beyond its physical dimensions. It is somehow where the person is at. Compare the human face and its significance with the back of a person's neck. There is nothing very special about the latter; it is largely just so much flesh and skin. But the face: again, when I see your face I see a *person*, a center of consciousness; I see *you*.

Another dimension of the significance of the human face for a person comes out when we compare punching someone in the stomach and slapping him in the face. The punch may be a very hard one and cause intense physical pain. The slap may be very light and cause hardly any pain. Even so, the slap is in an important sense far more significant and far more hurtful. For the slap is an affront to the person, an attack on the person in a way in which the punch is not. Another person "reaches" me in a hostile hateful way by slapping my face because my face is *me* in a way that other body parts are not. A slap in the face is an insult; the stomach punch is not.

On the positive side diametrically opposite to this is the loving kiss on the face. We kiss a person's face because that's where the person is, not on his left arm or the back of his neck. The lip-to-lip kiss of lovers is an especially intense case of this. They reach each other by this kiss in a way not possible by other forms of body touching. That is also why we want to reserve such a kiss for those other persons to whom we feel a special love and closeness.

Among all living, conscious creatures only human beings make love face-to-face. Surely this says something about our being as persons and how that is manifested in our faces.

The whole human face is an amazing thing. But there is something else, a part of it that has a special significance: a person's eyes. Look into a person's eyes; look squarely and directly and don't flinch. How long can you keep it up? You are not just seeing a physical object. It's not hard to look squarely and directly at a flower for some time. Why is it so different when you look squarely and directly into another person's eyes for some time? Is it because in a person's eyes you see the *person*, the immense reality of a person? The eye is a window into the soul, the conscious person, the reality beyond the outer physical appearance.

Isn't it amazing that your eyes have this dual role? They are *your* windows to the world, the sense organs by which you see the world. And, in the other direction, they are for *other persons* windows to you as a person, to your conscious personal being.

Are humans the only beings who have faces? Picture the dog who has been a victim of cruel abuse by his owner. How utterly sad his face looks! It tears our heart. How can a physical reality say so much: the deep hurt, the sadness, the despair? But more than that, it reveals the dog as a person-like being. Because he is so much like a person, he has a face. You can look into his eyes, and he can look into yours. All this remains even though we don't really know what it feels like to be a dog; and how close and also how far away from being a person a dog is.

The wonder of animals like dogs is that in some ways they are so close to us and in other ways they are so far from us. But the reality of a dog's face helps to bridge the gap a bit. Dogs are surely not impersonal beings like machines. They have faces and their faces speak to us. We are united to them in that we both have faces. The face is a mark of a person, or at least of a person-like being. It reveals that there is something "behind" it; that it is something more than its physical reality.

Think of other higher animals like cats, chimps and elephants; they too have faces. Then consider starfish; there seems to be no face. Consider this generalization: the higher on the scale of animals, the more person-like they are; and, the more they have faces. The two go together: being person-like and having a face. Can we say of animals "the more they have faces"? Does having a face come in degrees? Doesn't a dog have "more of a face" than a fish, which also has a face? Surely a human person has far more of a face than a fish. Could the face of a fish ever "speak" to us in the way a human face can speak to us? "I took one look at her face and realized how deeply upset she was." Isn't it amazing what a human face can tell us? And what the face of a suffering dog can tell us? How can being upset or sad or happy or in pain be contained in a face, and communicated by a face, which on one level is a physical surface? But it is so much more than its physical layer. What is that more? How is it joined to the physical? These are things we meet with every day in our immediate experience; things that are very familiar to us. And yet they are things that turn out to be utterly baffling and mysterious when we turn to them with our philosophical questioning; a questioning that does not end in answers but constitutes wonder at reality.

Trees, like humans and animals, are living things but they have no faces. Isn't this simply because they are in no way person-like? Again, the two go together: being person-like and having a face. Isn't the same true for all other plants? Once we enter the realm of the purely impersonal there are no faces: tools, machines, roads, telephone poles, houses and all the rest. If there are faces, such as one drawn on the front of a car to express anger, it is something we put there, not something which belongs to the object through its nature. We can project faces onto things; but then it is precisely our doing, our imagination and not an objective reality "out there," as in the case of human faces and animal faces.

Wonder at the human face: so close to us in being so familiar, a part of our every-day life and experience -- and yet so distant in its mysteriousness, in being beyond our ability to fully grasp it intellectually with our logical categories and answer seemingly simple questions about it.

[13] THE PROBLEM OF OTHER MINDS

Some philosophers have challenged the kind of analysis of inter-personal relations that we have sketched above, with its basic idea that in seeing you I see not just a physical reality, your body, but I see *you*, a person, a being with consciousness. It is a sceptical challenge, called "the problem of other minds." Briefly, here is how it goes:

I know I'm conscious; how do I know you are? I see you; but what exactly do I see? I see your body, your face, and your physical features. How do I get from seeing these things to your consciousness? I can't see that; it's not a physical reality. How then is it possible for me to know that you are conscious?

Is this a genuine problem? Isn't it true that I can't look into your consciousness and see what is there in the way I can look into an open container and see what is there? But on the other hand, isn't it also true that I can often "read your face" and know with great assurance how you are now disposed towards me, a warm and loving affirmation or a cold and distant "put down" or any number of other attitudes? How can this be? A cause for wonder!

True, I can't see your consciousness; but, of course, I know you are conscious. What I am "given" when I see you is not a mere body but a person. More fully perhaps: what I experience when I see you is a bodily person, *the personal bodily presence* of another human being.

But how do I perceive the personal bodily presence of another person? Doesn't it seem that sense perception is not sufficient here? How does seeing your body reveal that you are conscious? What else is there? How do I perceive other people as *conscious persons*?

Is doubt about other minds a genuine and serious doubt? Or is it just a philosophical game for sceptics, a challenging puzzle but not something to take seriously? Let me suggest that there are several different types of cases here, centering on a basic distinction:

- Claims that other people (and animals) are conscious.
- Claims about what is in that consciousness, the content of that consciousness.

Chapter 4: Person-Body Unity

CLAIMS THAT OTHER PEOPLE (AND ANIMALS) ARE CONSCIOUS

First, there is the general philosophical doubt about all other people, whether or not they are conscious; this is a general scepticism about "other minds" applied to all other persons. "I know I am conscious; how do I know anyone else is?" Can anyone seriously entertain such a doubt? Try living your life without the constant awareness that other people around you are conscious and some of them are observing you. Try looking directly into another person's eyes and doubting that a human consciousness is there behind those eyes. Do some outrageous things; wouldn't you feel embarrassed? That means believing others are looking at you; isn't ***this*** something you necessarily believe? Is it even possible to be a consistent "other minds" sceptic? Isn't this only an academic game? Play it, write out your thoughts about what you come up with and publish it so other people can read it and praise you. Really? Other people?

Second, in stark contrast to the above there are also cases where the doubt can be serious. This applies to individual persons rather than to all other persons. It is a specific and concrete doubt rooted in practical concerns. Thus, in certain coma cases there is real doubt about whether another person is conscious or not. And sometimes we get it wrong, as when a person wakes up after a long coma and announces that he heard everything that was said in his presence; tragically the belief that he was unconscious was mistaken.

Third, there is another area where the doubt can be serious: the large, very complex realm of animal consciousness. Cats, dogs, chimps, and elephants are surely conscious. How about frogs, mice, and mosquitoes? How about sharks, jellyfish, and starfish? Have you ever wondered whether starfish are conscious? Where do we draw the line and say: from here up the creature is conscious and below it is not conscious? Is there a gray area?

Fourth, could there be another area where doubt might become serious? Robots are now being perfected to do more and more of what humans do, such as washing the dishes and guiding blind people and working assembly lines at factories. Suppose they are being made to look more and more like real human persons. Could there ever be a serious doubt whether such a robot is a person? Whether it is conscious? Many people say there could never be such a doubt; that it is impossible to replicate what appears to be a person. Is this correct? Why? Could it be shown?

CLAIMS ABOUT WHAT IS IN THAT CONSCIOUSNESS

First, aren't there some things in another person's consciousness that are clearly given to us in our immediate experience? Think of a person's loving smile or an anxious look on his face. Isn't it true that we learn what love is much more through the loving behavior of others than from our own being loving? Would we even know what love is if we never saw it in others? A baby sees his mother's love; he sees it immediately and directly. If he sees an angry face before him, he will be frightened; the realization is direct and immediate, not an inference.

Second, on the other hand, much of what is in another person's consciousness is not given at all. I attend a lecture. I know how I feel about what is going on. How does the person next to me experience the same event? I have no idea. What are his beliefs? How does he feel about me? So much is secret, deep in the recesses of another person's consciousness. And finally, just as only I know what it's like to be me, only you know what it's like to be you.

Third, some of what is in another person's consciousness is a mixed bag in terms of being given or not given. I think Joe is upset but I'm not sure. What is that look on your face? It is highly ambiguous. You think Beth was kidding; I think she was dead serious. Is Bill telling the truth or is he lying? Generally, only the liar himself knows whether he is lying or not.

Fourth, what is in an animal's consciousness? What does it feel like to be a dog, a cat, a chimp, an elephant? Does this question even make sense for certain other animals, such as mice and frogs, mosquitoes, and jellyfish? How little we know!

Chapter 4: Person-Body Unity

[14] THE MANY ASPECTS OF THE HUMAN BODY

FOUR DIFFERENT ASPECTS OF THE HUMAN BODY

We tend to think of the human body as simply one reality. But we have seen that it is far more than that. There are really at least four realities, or four different aspects:

> *Körper*: **the body of any person,** which exists equally for anyone.

> *Leib*: **my body, which exists only for me,** felt from within as a dimension of my being.

> ***Personal bodily presence of my body as it exists for others, as they see me.***

> ***Personal bodily presence of another's body as it exists for me, as I see that person.***

The second, third and fourth belong together in their stark contrast to Körper, the first. Körper is the body in its non-personal aspect, as a biological organism, an object of science, in many ways similar and comparable to other organisms, especially animals. The other three all belong together and constitute the personal aspects of the human body. It is because of this that we can speak so readily of the oneness of person and body: "I am my body" and "You are your body." One source of wonder is then that one and the same physical reality, a human body, can be two such radically different things: a non-personal Körper and also a highly personal reality. That highly personal reality, though it is a physical reality can almost be identified with a person from the point of view of unity. Yet that person as a conscious being in his essential nature is something radically different from any physical being, as we saw chapter 3.

A DUAL ASPECT OF THE HUMAN BODY: INWARD AND OUTWARD

Here is another source of wonder. Focusing only on the body as a highly personal reality, and thus leaving aside the body as Körper, we can detect another dual aspect. One and the same body as my body, as me in my bodily dimension, exists both *inwardly* to me and for me as my Leib; and also *outwardly* for you as you see me, as you experience me in my bodily presence to you. The same body has this inward and outward aspect. The body you see as me and the body that I feel as me, as my Leib are one and the same body. But what is experienced in the two cases is radically different. You cannot experience my body as Leib, and I cannot experience my body the way you do when you see me. I can get some idea of what you experience when you see me by looking in the mirror, but it is hardly the same. I see a piece of glass; you see a bodily person. I can touch only that glass; you can press flesh. And seeing a face that I know is me and seeing a face that I see as you are radically different.

The duality of *my body-for-me* and *my body-for-you* parallels the duality of persons. I exist for myself in my consciousness, my inner being as a conscious subject. And I exist for you, as the person you know and interact with. I know myself; you know me. One and the same person, me, is experienced in radically different ways. Only I know what it's like to be me; and only you know what it's like to know me as another person. In some ways I know myself better than you know me; I have my inner life, my secrets hidden from others. But you may know me and my character better than I know myself. You may for example know that I am not as loving and generous a person as I think of myself as being.

THE HUMAN BODY AND THE PERSON: UNION BASED ON THEIR DISTINCTION

Another source of wonder concerns the relation between the intimate unity of a person and his body and the essential, sometimes even radical distinction between them. It is that *this unity rests essentially on the distinction*. Unity and distinction seem at first to be simply opposed to each other; so much so that one might be tempted to think of them as logically contradictory, so that if the one is true the other cannot also be true. I hope we have seen enough to see that this is not so, that both are indeed true, two aspects of the reality of the human person. But they do somehow "pull" in opposite directions, so that their joint truth is a profound source of wonder.

Why does unity rest essentially on distinction? Unity means I am united to my body as a whole, my body as Leib; I feel united to it to form one being. For this unity of person and body to be a reality, I as a person have to be something other than the body to which I am united. The body is not united to the body; it just is the body. But I can be united to my body because I am as such not my body; I am distinct from my body. And so, I as a being other than this body I call mine can say "I am united to this body to form one being."

THE UNION OF HUMAN BODIES AND ESPECIALLY THE SEXUAL UNION

Finally, there are the different ways in which human bodies in their highly personal reality can stand in relation to each other; many are forms of unity: a mother holding her child, ballroom dancing, holding hands, hugging, and kissing; some like contact sports are not unity. And then there is a very special case: sexual union. That union is the coming together of the body of each person as Leib and the bodily presence of the other in the deepest and most intimate way. Isn't it also one of the most mysterious ways? In the sexual act doesn't each person exist in and experience his or her body as Leib in an especially intense and unique way? In such moments we are not simply souls, and the body as Körper is completely in the background in terms of our lived experience; it is my personal being as Leib and the personal bodily presence of the other person that constitutes this mysterious reality. Perhaps we should stand back from thinking we know what this is to wonder at the mystery of it!

CHAPTER 5
WHAT IS A PIECE OF MUSIC?

[1] IS THE REALITY OF MUSIC IN THE SCORE OR IN THE PLAYING?

What kind of reality is a piece of music? Compare it to a painting, say the Mona Lisa. A painting has definite physical characteristics. It is so many inches by so many inches, has such and such color patterns and is in a definite location. Essentially the same applies to a statue: size, shape, weight, and a definite physical location.

Now think of a piece of music, Beethoven's Fifth Symphony or a song, the Star Spangled Banner. It has none of the physical characteristics we noted with the painting or the statue. How does it exist? Before it was composed it didn't exist at all. Suppose that for some time it had some kind of preliminary existence in the composer's mind but was not written down. Would we want to say it really existed then? Suppose the composer had died before being able to write it down; "it" would have had died with him. We would never know about it and it would not be included in the list of all the musical works that we say exists.

But in what way do such works exist? Take Beethoven's Fifth Symphony. He's just finished writing it down. The score exists but it has not yet been performed. Does it exist as a piece of music? Yes, certainly it exists; hasn't he just composed it? Hasn't he just finished it? What more could we want? But does the actual piece of music exist as the score, as the notes written down? Isn't the score, the set of notes merely a set of instructions for the musicians, telling them what they have to do to play it? And isn't it the playing of what the score instructs the actual reality of the music? Isn't that what counts? Isn't that what is beautiful, what people love, what they pay to hear, what they take time to hear? If there were just scores of notes but nobody able to play them, what good would that be? Would we then still have pieces of music?

If the music doesn't really exist in the score, if that's merely instructions, let us look at the actual playing of the music to see if we can find its reality there. You attend a concert where the music is played, or you listen to it on the radio or in a CD recording. You marvel at its beauty, the aesthetic power it conveys, and other such experiential factors. Surely that's where the reality of the music lies. That's what you have in mind when you say you love the piece, you know it well and you want your friend to know it and love it as well. And while it doesn't have size and shape and color and physical location, like the painting and the statue, it does have one other significant characteristic: length of time. Some works are 5 minutes long, some 20, some an hour, some longer. So perhaps we can say that the reality of a piece of music is that it is an event of such and such duration. It would then seem to be like other realities that are events, such as a meeting of members of the board of directors, a play like Hamlet or a baseball game. But don't all these seem very different, not only from each other but also and more significantly from the piece of music? The board meeting is a one-time affair; or perhaps such meetings occur often, but, surely, they hardly constitute a reality that one loves and admires such as Beethoven's Fifth. But even if we accept some similarity here by seeing all of these things as events there are further and far more serious problems with seeing the reality of a piece of music as an event.

[2] SOME PROBLEMS WITH THESE PROPOSED ANSWERS

Suppose there is a certain period of time, say two hours on January 1, 2000, when no one was listening to Beethoven's Fifth. During that time period there was no event that constituted Beethoven's Fifth. If we identify the reality of this particular piece of music with an event of its being played and heard by at least one person, we would have to conclude that during this time period it didn't exist. Surely that can't be right; it certainly did exist; it just wasn't being played. When it was played later it didn't come into existence at that point in time. We say it existed before the two-hour time period, during it and after. The same piece of music existed during all three of these periods of time. This shows that the reality of the piece of music is independent of any one or more performances of it. And when we say it is beautiful, that it has a certain power we refer to it, the piece of music that Beethoven composed, not to a particular performance of it in a concert or my playing it on a CD player yesterday afternoon. But that takes us

Chapter 5: What is a Piece of Music

away from what earlier we had thought was its reality: playing it, hearing it; not the score-instructions.

But there are even more problems. There is one Beethoven Fifth Symphony, but many concert performances of it, many listening sessions of it; so they can't be the same thing. One and the same symphony is played many times. One reality is somehow given in many events. Each event is distinct from every other event by time and location. I hear it in my house on Friday while you heard it in a concert the Sunday before. One and the same reality is repeated many times. What is that reality? It's not the score-instructions. It's not any one performance or listening session, since it transcends all of these. What then is it?

Consider a piece of music composed long ago but never performed. The score still exists but no one knows about it; it is gathering dust in some obscure attic. Does this piece of music exist now? Surely it does. It didn't exist before it was composed but now it has been composed. Doesn't that bring it into existence? If we say yes, we seem to be back to identifying the piece of music with the score since that's all that exists now. But the beauty is not in the score; it comes into being in the playing and listening, and that unfortunately doesn't exist in this case.

Worse, consider a piece of music where the score is now lost. It exists because or in so far as it was composed. It doesn't exist because or in so far as there is now neither a score nor any performance or playing of it. We might say it once existed but now no longer exists, like a house built long ago but since then torn down. The problem with this reply is that we have a perfectly clear idea of what it is that once had existence and reality but now no longer does. That is precisely what we don't have with the piece of music. The lost piece of music doesn't exist now while Beethoven's Fifth does exist now. What does that mean? Where does it exist? How does it exist? What is it that exists here even when nobody is listening to it?

Someone might suggest that the piece of music exists in this CD. But that can't be right. The CD is merely a container that holds it. All by itself the CD is useless. Put it into your CD player, turn it on and listen to it. Now you have it! There it is! Unfortunately, that doesn't work. Your experience of hearing it on this particular occasion is just one of many instances of such listening to this piece, which existed before and after this one occasion; and which has existed and will exist for many other people listening to it. You are tapping into something that is already there; that's why you can hear it and enjoy it. But what is this reality that you are tapping into? How does it exist? Where does it exist?

[3] WHERE DOES A PIECE OF MUSIC EXIST?

Where does it exist? Does this question make any sense? Can we say it exists in one city but not in another? Hardly, since it can always and very easily be brought to any city you want, by a CD which you then play or by having an orchestra come to play it. Do we want to say it exists on planet earth but not in some distant galaxy? Perhaps we can answer the question of where it exists by saying it exists in my consciousness as I'm listening to it and of course likewise in yours when you listen to it. We might even want to say that that's the answer to our original question, what kind of reality is a piece of music? That is, the reality of music is the experience of listening to it, of enjoying it.

In one way this is an attractive answer. Isn't it the enjoyment of the music that really counts? What good is the score or the CD if the music is never heard and enjoyed? What good is even a performance if no audience listens to it? But there are serious problems with this answer. There are many instances of listening and enjoying but only one Beethoven Fifth. On a particular performance the music exists once in the concert hall but many times for each of the people attending the concert. And doesn't it exist even when no one is hearing it?

The where question has multiple answers; all of them seem to make sense. But do any of them really capture the reality where the music actually exists? The music exists:

- In the score, the paper with the notes written on it.
- In a CD.
- In a concert performance.
- In a person's consciousness as he listens to it and enjoys it.

[4] DOES MUSIC EXIST IN THREE BASIC COMPONENTS?

Perhaps the problem is that we are looking for a single answer to our original question, what kind of reality is a piece of music? Perhaps there is no single answer, no one thing that constitutes the reality of a piece of music. Perhaps there are several things that together make up the reality of a piece of music, each one being a component of a greater whole. What is crucial then is to see what these components are and how they are related to each other. Here is one way this might be seen:

There are three basic components: (1) the score or a CD; (2) a concert performance or a playing in your room by your CD player; (3) your experience and enjoyment of the music. The really important reality is (3); the other two exist for the sake of (3). We can say:

(1) exists for the sake of (2): (1) makes possible (2).
(2) exists for the sake of (3): (2) makes possible (3).

Thus, the score and CD fail as answers to our original question when seen in isolation; but as parts of a greater whole, they provide elements of answer. They are what allow the concert performance or the CD playing to take place. The concert performance and a playing in your room are key elements; they constitute the objective reality that gives rise to the experience. They are *what* I hear when I listen to the music.

Do we perhaps have something similar in the case of literature? Take Mark Twain's novel, *Tom Sawyer*. Compare Beethoven's Fifth Symphony and Mark Twain's *Tom Sawyer*:

(1) Beethoven composes the score, and Mark Twain writes the text.
(2) A performance or a CD of the music and a copy of the book.
(3) You hear the music and you read the book, in each case experiencing enjoyment.

Consider something different but still manifesting the basic idea of components in a greater whole. Imagine a boy and a girl deeply in love with each other. What is this reality?

(1) His love for her.
(2) Her love for him.
(3) The relation of love that exists objectively between them. This is the greater whole of which the other two realities are components.

Is a piece of music anything like that? That is, is it like that in so far as it is also something whose reality is constituted by other realities distinct from each other?

[5] DOES MUSIC EXIST IN BEING CREATED AND RE-CREATED?

The idea that music exists in three basic components, that it has multiple existence might also be formulated in terms of creation and re-creation. We could say that music exists as:

(1) Its original creation by the composer (leading to the score, the paper).
(2) Its re-creation by an orchestra (in a concert performance).
(3) Its re-creation in a person's consciousness as he experiences it and enjoys it.

On this model the CD is something that holds and preserves the music; it is a transition from (2) to (3). And here again we can say:

(1) exists for the sake of (2): (1) makes possible (2).
(2) exists for the sake of (3): (2) makes possible (3).

If we say that the true reality of music is in its being heard (3) rather than in the score or the performance (1 and 2) – since these exist only to make the hearing possible – then we are left with a remarkable conclusion, namely that music is a reality that isn't just there but needs to be recreated each time to come into existence. A person, a dog, a tree, a machine, a rock: we can say of these realities that they are "just there"; but a piece of music is not "just there" since it needs to be recreated each time in the listener's consciousness. The score is "just there" but that is not the reality of the music; that is not what is sublime and beautiful and can move us deeply.

[6] IS THE REALITY OF MUSIC ONE THING OR SEVERAL?

Perhaps there is an important lesson for us here. Recall our original question, what kind of reality is a piece of music? When we ask questions like this aren't we looking for a single and simple answer, one that would be appropriate for many other questions such as inquiring into the nature of a rock or a tree? But many realities are not like that; they have multiple components related to each other in various ways. A community, a government, mathematics, an ethical system, history and natural science are but a few of the examples that might come to mind.

We have considered the idea that there are several things that together make up the reality of a piece of music, each one being a component of a greater whole. But does this really answer our original question? Is a piece of music really a set of components? In its essence isn't it one reality? When I think of the music and say it is beautiful what am I referring to? Why is it so difficult to get at this reality and understand what it is? Perhaps part of the answer lies in the following. We think in certain categories of reality such as those that apply to a stone or a tree. When confronted with very different kinds of reality our categories fail us and we can't answer the question of what such realities are. There are surely many cases of this. The question of the reality of music is a particularly striking one.

[7] SOME FINAL WONDER THOUGHTS

What is a piece of music? As noted, one important thing about music is that in its very essence it is something extended in time. The Mona Lisa also exists in time but not in the same way; it has simply existed ever since Leonardo da Vinci painted it. In that sense Beethoven's Fifth has also existed ever since Beethoven composed it. But the Mona Lisa is right there all at once in front of you when you're looking at it. The Fifth Symphony is not there all at once but extended over a period of time, about 32 minutes. It does not exist at any one moment, in any one note but in the flow of these notes over a length of time. Its reality, its beauty is how these notes are combined, plus other elements such its force and power and majesty and the rhythm.

Why are these beautiful? Why is one combination of notes beautiful, something that counts as a melody while another doesn't even count as a melody but is merely a set of sounds? Why is one piece of music still more beautiful than another? Why are certain pieces so beautiful that they can even move us to tears? Music can have a power to touch our hearts in ways that perhaps few other things can. Why is that? How can that be? Why does one combination of the notes of the scale touch us so deeply with its beauty while another leaves us cold? There is a tremendous reality in a great piece of music such as Beethoven's Fifth. But what is this reality? Why can't we grasp it fully with our intellects? It speaks to our hearts; our hearts grasp it while our intellects seem to be left largely in the dark, grasping bits and pieces of its reality but falling far short of fully grasping its reality. Our hearts and intellects are left to wonder.

CHAPTER 6
PERCEPTION

[1] WHAT DO WE PERCEIVE? WHAT IS OUT THERE IN THE WORLD?

What do we perceive? What is out there in the world? Perhaps the answers to these questions are not as clear and easy as many of us tend to think. We will see that they are sources of wonder. Let us consider each of the senses, each of the ways we perceive the world:

Feeling. My hand is close to a fire and the fire feels hot. Is the heat in the fire or in me? Is the fire really hot? Or is heat just a sensation in me? Suppose my hand is so close to the fire that I feel the sharp pain of being burned; is the pain in me or in the fire? Surely the pain is in me and not in the fire. But is heat any different? Aren't feeling heat and feeling pain both cases of feeling a sensation? And aren't sensations only in me and not out there in an object? So, is the heat in the fire or in me? Or is it in both? Is the fire itself hot? Or isn't it?

Touching. I touch the surface of the table and feel it to be hard and smooth. What is it that I perceive? Is it the table itself? Or is it only its surface? Or is it only the sensation in me of feeling hardness and smoothness? Is touching a surface all that different from feeling heat? Can I reach a reality out there through touching? Or am I confined to sensations that are only in me?

Smelling. I smell a rose. But is it really the rose I smell, that I perceive? Isn't it rather the odor given off by the rose? Is that odor an object out there? Or is it only a sensation in me?

Tasting. I bite into a steak. It is delicious! Is the taste I experience a feature of the steak itself? Is it a real quality out there actually in the steak? Or is it only a sensation in me?

Hearing. I hear the train. Do I really hear the train? Isn't it the sound made by the train, rather than the train itself? We can see and touch physical objects, but isn't what we hear only sounds? Doesn't "I heard the bell" mean "I heard the sound made by the bell"? But what are sounds? Are they objects existing out there independently of whether anyone perceives them or not? Or are they only sensations in us? We've probably all pondered the question about the tree in the forest that falls when nobody is around. Is there a sound? Many people say no; they seem to be saying that sounds are only sensations in us. Do they mean subjectively "only in us" like a pain? Do they think that when an orchestra comes together to play a Beethoven Symphony, there is nothing in that concert hall but air and physical sound waves, but no real sounds? By "real sounds" I mean sounds as we experience them. In the case of music real sounds are or can be beautiful melodies with various aesthetic qualities. Are such sounds out there in the world?

Seeing. I see the red tomato. Is it really red? Is the red in the tomato there whether anyone sees it or not? Or is redness just an idea in me? Is it just an idea that has no reality apart from my experiencing it? But the size and shape of the tomato, and of course the tomato itself, surely these exist objectively out there in the world. Or are they too just ideas in our minds?

The central puzzle in these thoughts, the occasion for wonder is this: What is *out there* in the world, really there, existing independently of us? And what is merely *within us*, an idea or sensation that has no reality in itself but exists only as experienced by someone?

Here is another thought. We assume there are five senses, but we considered six headings above. How many senses are there? Reflect some more on the first two: feeling and touching. I *touch* the surface of a board of wood and *feel* it to be hard and rough. I touch a piece of marble and feel it to be hard and smooth. I touch the pillow and feel it to be soft. Touching always seems to apply to the surface of things. I put my hand in water. I feel it to be hot. I also feel that it is liquid. This is in some ways akin to touch, for I am touching the water, but note that we use the word *feel*. I feel it to be hot and liquid. This brings us to our question: Do *touch* and *feeling* count as one of the five senses? Or as two, in which case we would have six senses? We touch the surface of the table but feel inside the water. We do both with our hands. But we also feel without our hands, with our whole body. We feel the air as hot on a summer day and cold on a winter day. And we feel the wind; we feel the water when we go swimming. Do touch and feeling go together as one sense or are they separate as two senses?

[2] HOW DO WE PERCEIVE? HOW DO WE REACH OBJECTS?

One puzzle is: What is *out there* in the world, really there, existing independently of us? And what is only *within us,* an idea or sensation? Here's another. Granting that there are things really out there in the world independently of us how do we *reach* them in perception? Later and more radically: do we reach them at all?

Consider external physical objects like chairs and tables and start with seeing. When I see something, I become conscious of it; there is an event *in me*, in my consciousness. Yet that event is supposedly the seeing of an object *out there*, outside me. How is this possible? How do I get from inside me to outside me? Yet that is what I'm claiming when I claim to see an external object. My consciousness of seeing the object is in me and yet it is the consciousness of seeing a tomato out there, outside me. Not only is the object actually out there; it is *perceived as being* out there. It is perceived as being at a distance from me. How is this possible?

How can we possibly see external objects? If we see them, we can do so only by what comes into us: light rays into our eyes, optic nerves, brains and then (somehow!) something in our minds, inside us. How do we get from *inside* us to what is *outside* us? We all believe that we do; but how? If you are imprisoned in a room with a TV screen, how could you possibly go from that TV image *inside* the room to anything *outside*? We see real ball games and ball games on TV, so we can reasonably infer that the TV game we now see faithfully represents a real game out there somewhere. But that's only because we're *not* imprisoned. If we were how could we tell the difference between Mickey Mouse on TV and the Red Sox on TV? Surely our perceptual situation is not like the person imprisoned in the room with only a TV screen. But given the way perception works, why isn't it? How do we get out of our own perceptual "skin"?

There are similar puzzles in the other senses. I touch the surface of a board of wood, and I feel it to be hard and rough. What entitles me to say that the wood is *really* hard and rough, hard and rough in itself? After all what I experience is a sensation of hardness *in me*, and a sensation of roughness *in me*. Yet I claim that the wood itself is hard and rough *in itself*. How do I get from something *in me* to something *out there* independently of me? From a headache-pain-sensation in me I make no jump to any objective reality out there independently of me. But with a sensation like feeling the wood to be hard and rough I do make such a jump. Why is that? And above all, why think it is reasonable and justified?

A pin prick causes a pain *in me*; yet this pain sensation is also the perception of the pin and its quality of sharpness as something *out there*. How can this be? Why is one pain sensation (headache) not an indication of something out there while another pain sensation is (pin prick)?

I feel the water when I'm swimming; I have a certain sensation *in me*. But don't I also perceive the water as *out there*, outside me? How can the one thing be both a sensation in me and also my perceiving something outside me?

[3] HOW DO WE PERCEIVE? THE TRANSITION QUESTION

One question is how we reach objects: how do I get from something *in me* to an object *out there*? Another question is how the something in me gets to be there at all. I see a tomato. How does this happen? Light rays reflected from the object enter the eye, an image forms on the retina, and impulses are sent to the brain, to the center for vision. So far medical science can study the process. But then something radically new happens, which medical science cannot enter: my consciousness, the experience we describe as "I see the tomato." Physical processes are *outside* events, publicly observable. Consciousness is an *inside* reality, accessible only to the person who has the consciousness. And yet the outside physical processes cause the inside conscious events. How is this possible? How does a *brain event* cause a *conscious event*? The two are so utterly different: how can one bring about the other? How can there be a transition from one to the other? Do we wonder enough at this amazing reality: from *outside* to *inside*?

[4] SEEING CONTRASTED TO SMELLING-TASTING-TOUCHING

We usually think of the five (or six?) senses as a single group, a set of "windows" on the world by which we come to know the world. Is this accurate? Let's take another look.

SMELLING-TASTING-TOUCHING ARE BODILY EXPERIENCES

Consider smell, taste and touch. I smell the odor of a rose or of bacon cooking. I taste the bacon, the cheese, the coffee. I touch the surface of the table, my keys, the snow, the water. Aren't all these essentially bodily experiences? I experience the smell in my nose, the taste in my mouth, the feel of the table and of the snow in my hand. Perception here seems to be a contact between parts of my body and the object that I perceive. Perception takes place where the two come together: the object comes to me in taste and smell, or I go to the object in touch.

VISION IS AT A DISTANCE AND IS NOT A BODILY EXPERIENCE

Is all perception like this? Consider vision. Is the role of my eyes similar to what we noted above? The object I see is not in contact with my body but at a distance. Not only is it not in fact in contact with my body; it is also not given to me in my experience as in contact with my body, but at a distance. *To see an object is to see it at a distance*; the object is presented to me as being at a distance. This contrasts sharply to smelling, tasting, and touching, where the object is experienced in its contact with my body.

Isn't the role of the sense organ essentially different in the two types of cases? The eye is an instrument by which I am able to become aware of an object out there. But it is not the place where I experience the object, as it is in the case of smelling, tasting, and touching. The eye is an instrument by which I go beyond myself to reach an object at a distance. But in smelling, tasting, and touching I do not go beyond myself; I stay within myself and feel sensations that are in me.

Suppose a bright light hurts your eyes. Isn't that an experience similar to the three other senses we are considering here, smelling, tasting and touching? Compare the sensation of pain in your eye caused by a bright light with the pain that hot spicy food causes when it burns your mouth. Aren't they basically similar? In contrast, isn't the eye-pain sensation caused by a bright light very different from the normal case of seeing an object at a distance? Now compare spicy food sensations and normal taste sensations. Aren't they basically similar? Isn't spicy food just a painful form of taste sensations?

OUR TOPIC HERE IS ONLY PERCEPTION AS EXPERIENCED

Our topic here is only perception as I experience it, not the physical realities in the world and in my body that make it possible; things such as the light waves that reach my eyes, the odor molecules in the air that drift into my nose, or the nerves in my body that carry the impulses from these to my brain. Our topic does not concern brain processes, which are not at all a part of our normal immediate experience but known to us only indirectly. Our topic is only perceptual consciousness, what it feels like to see, to smell, to taste, to touch, and to hear. In respect to the physical realities whose importance is in making perception possible, the situation is not really different in the two cases we are comparing: seeing in contrast to smelling-tasting-touching.

[5] HEARING COMPARED TO SEEING AND BODILY SENSATIONS

Where does hearing fit in? Is it more like seeing or more like a sensation such as we have in smelling, touching, and tasting? You hear a noise in the next room. What was it? You hear the words I say. You hear beautiful music. In such cases, isn't hearing very much like seeing? It seems to be perception of an object at a distance. Yet isn't hearing experienced in your ears in a way that seeing is not experienced in your eyes? As you drive your car and see the other cars, the signs, the road, and the houses, you pay close attention to what you see; you seem to forget your eyes and that you are seeing with them. Your eyes do not seem to figure prominently in your consciousness, in sharp contrast to your hand when you put it in water or your mouth when you taste chocolate. When you listen intently to what another says, or to beautiful music, or to the birds singing outside, can you also forget your ears? On the other hand, doesn't it seem that you hear in your ears in a way that you don't see in your eyes? It's hard to say, a cause for wonder. And isn't a loud piercing noise that hurts your ears very close to the hot spicy food taste that hurts your mouth? Perhaps we can summarize as follows:

Vision is perception at a distance. I see physical objects including other persons as out there in the space beyond my own body. I see the qualities of objects as on those objects, part of their reality. Thus, I see color as on the object, not as something in me. That the color depends in part on me does not mean that it is in me. What I see is out there, not an idea or image in me.

The objects of touch-feeling, taste and smell are not at a distance; they are experienced up close, in their contact with my body. In this they differ from vision, for there is no bodily contact in vision. Touch-feeling, taste and smell all essentially involve bodily sensations; for example, the sensation of taste in my mouth or the sensation of cold in my whole body as I swim in cold water. There seems to be no bodily sensation corresponding to these in vision.

Hearing: is it at a distance like seeing or is it a sensation in me? Or is it somehow both?

[6] PRIMARY AND SECONDARY QUALITIES

Are all qualities of physical objects of the same kind? Are they all on the same level? Are they all equally real? Are they all equally objective, out there in the real world? Are they all equally parts of the real world? Many of us would probably say yes to these questions. But a little thought will show that matters are not quite so simple. Many thinkers have claimed that there is a distinction, introduced by John Locke, between two very different kinds of qualities:

Primary qualities are shape, size, and extension, as well as solidity or fluidity, as the case may be. Solidity includes or implies rigidity and impenetrability.

Secondary qualities are color, sound, taste, smell, heat and cold, and texture, in the sense of the way the surface of cloth, wood, metal or other things feels to our sense of touch. How do these two kinds of qualities differ?[1]

PRIMARY QUALITIES

(1) Primary qualities are *essential* to physical objects. Such objects must be extended, and they must have some shape and size and certain degrees of solidity and rigidity or fluidity. But they need not have color, (e.g., a mirror) or texture (e.g., a cloud). And, of course, they need not involve any sounds, tastes or smells.

(2) Closely related to this is the fact that primary qualities essentially *constitute* physical objects and define them in their spatiotemporal character; secondary qualities do not. The former are therefore "primary" while the latter are "secondary."

(3) Primary qualities can be *precisely measured*, as the size of a table by a tape measure. Some secondary qualities seem not to be subject to precise measurement; for example, the taste of a steak or the odor of a rose. Others seem to be: heat and sound. But what exactly is capable of being measured? Is it the heat and sound as physical realities? Or is it heat and sound as we experience them? Is that capable of being precisely measured? Perhaps all experiences of qualities, whether primary or secondary, are like taste and odor and so cannot be measured?

SECONDARY QUALITIES

(1) Secondary qualities have a direct, *exclusive link* to a particular sense: colors can only be seen, not heard or touched; odors can only be smelled.

---

[1] This analysis is based on Don Locke, *Perception and our Knowledge of the External World* (London: Allen and Unwin, New York: Humanities Press, 1967), 68-77.

Chapter 6: Perception

But the shape, size and position of an object and its extension can be both seen and touched or felt.

(2) Secondary qualities are *dependent on the senses* we possess, and their nature. Colors appear to us as they do because our eyes are sensitive to certain frequencies of light rays and not to others. If our eyes were structured differently, we would see heat. We would see, for example, the difference between a cold stone and a hot stone. Primary qualities are not dependent on us in this way. A tabletop is square, regardless of what our sense are like.

(3) Are secondary qualities perhaps *only subjective*? Maybe the heat is only in us and not in the fire, and not in the warm room? Maybe the red color of the tomato is only an appearance to us and not a quality really on the surface of the tomato? But it is impossible to deny objectivity to primary qualities. My bed must really be spatially extended to exist at all.

(4) Are secondary qualities perhaps sometimes even *objects themselves*? We say that the music fills the concert hall; does it really? Is it an objective reality "out there" and just as real as the seats in the concert hall? We like to think that we all hear the same music; but do we really? We may interpret it differently, but to make sense of that must we not assume that *what* we hear and interpret is one and the same reality, a piece of music? We say the Beethoven Symphony is heard and enjoyed by everyone in the audience. Is it? Is it an object in its own right?

Music critics will later analyze it; are they all dealing with a real object? Are they all dealing with the same object? Must it not be a real object if it is to be the same object for all of them? Must they not be dealing with the same real object for their work to make any sense? If, in contrast, each of the music critics is dealing only with his own private subjective experience rather than an object common to them all, they would not be talking about the same thing and there would be no basis for their discussion.

Yet music is a set of sounds and sounds were supposed to be mere secondary qualities. We say, "It's cold in here" or "It's very hot today"; do we mean that heat and cold are objects in their own right? "There's a bad odor in this room"; is that a real object, existing independently of being known? Do we all perceive the same object? What seems clear is that all this is never true of primary qualities; they are always qualities of objects, never objects themselves.

(5) Placing *subjectivity* and being *objects themselves* side-by-side: how can it be both of these? Do they not run counter to each other? What is subjective is in us; objects are out there.

[7] AGAIN, WHAT IS OUT THERE IN THE REAL WORLD?

Let us return to our question about what there is in the physical world in the light of the primary-secondary-qualities distinction. What kind of *objects* are there? Some seem clear enough: rocks and rivers, houses and cars, trees and flowers, insects and birds, cats and dogs, other animals and human beings. Are there also *primary qualities of such objects*: size and shape, solidity, and fluidity?

Are there also the *secondary qualities of such objects*? Is there a real red in the surface of the tomato? A real red that is there even at midnight when there's no one around to see it as red? Or is the red of the tomato something that exists only for us, or some of us, ultimately only an idea in our minds? Is the good taste of the chocolate a quality that is really in the chocolate? Or is it only a sensation in our taste buds or in our minds?

Are there also *secondary qualities* that *are themselves objects*? On a hot day is there a real heat in the air around us? In a cold room is there a real cold present in that room the way you and might be present in it? "What a bad stench there is in this room!" Is this odor really there, objectively present? Or is it only a sensation in the minds of all those who are in the room smelling the bad odor?

Perhaps the biggest question here, especially for music lovers, is that of *sounds*. Again, are sounds merely sensations in us? Or do they exist out there, as part of the furniture of the real world? The orchestra is playing a Beethoven Symphony. Is that music really out there? Is it a reality beyond each of the people in the audience listening to it? Do we all hear *the same piece of music*? Or does each person hear his own music, his own private set of audio sensations? If so, how is

Chapter 6: Perception

it that we can talk about the music that we all seemingly hear, if we don't all hear the same thing, the same music, the same object of perception?

If we all hear the same piece of music then must it not be a reality out there, existing independently of us, real whether anyone hears it or not? If the music is there whether anyone hears it or not, doesn't the same apply to that famous tree in the forest? Isn't there a real sound existing out there whether anyone is present to hear it or not?

There seem to be two possible views here; let us apply them to music:

(I) Only sound waves as studied by science exist in the room; the music as you hear and enjoy it is only a set of sensations in you. There is no music as we understand it in the room.

(II) There is the music as we understand it in the room; it fills the room. It's the object of our hearing; we all hear the same piece of music even if we interpret it differently.

On view (II) the music *is* the sound studied by science, the reality that's out there whether anyone hears it or not. The reality as aesthetically experienced *is the same reality* that can also be scientifically studied. That is, science and the aesthetic experience of hearing and enjoying the music are *two approaches to the same reality*. Each is valid in its own way; neither is better than the other; and each has its limitations. Science cannot perceive and appreciate the beauty; aesthetic experience cannot perceive what science detects. What science studies is meaningful because that object is the music we hear and enjoy, the music that's really out there.

So, what is out there in the real world? Three basic views seem to emerge:

(A) Only physical objects with their primary qualities exist out there in the world. There are no secondary qualities of any kind out there; they are purely subjective, ideas and sensations only in individual persons and existing only when they are perceived.

(B) There are physical objects with both primary qualities and secondary qualities, but no objects which are "secondary qualities" such as sounds and odors, heat and cold.

(C) There are physical objects with both primary qualities and secondary qualities, and also objects which are "secondary qualities" such as sounds and odors, heat and cold.

Within (B) and (C) there are variations, such as: Both color and taste; only color but no taste. Both color and sound; only color but no sound; only sound but no color.

[8] EXTERNAL OBJECTS: DO WE REACH THEM AT ALL?

Assuming that there are things really out there in the world independently of us, do we *reach them at all* in perception? Many thinkers have denied that we do; they claim that we perceive only our own ideas and sensations, and from them infer that the corresponding objects and qualities exist out there. The bent stick is a favorite example. When it is half immersed in clear water it looks bent; really of course it is straight. So, they claim, when it is in the water what we really see cannot be the actual stick; what we see is bent, the actual stick is straight, so they cannot be the same thing. What then do we see if it's not the actual stick, the object existing independently of us, out there? It must be an idea in our mind. But if the bent stick is only an idea in our mind how can the straight stick be any different? Isn't it just another idea, merely one that corresponds better with the real stick? If in one case, we perceive only our own idea how can it be any different in other cases? Don't we have an idea in our minds in both cases equally? If so, doesn't it follow that all we really perceive in both cases, in all cases, are our own ideas? That is, we don't really *reach* the actual object in perception; we are stuck in our own ideas. This is the challenge from certain thinkers, philosophers with a subjectivist bent.

Notice that in the bent-stick case it was the primary qualities of the object that eluded our actual perception, its shape and an aspect of its extension. If even primary qualities are beyond our perceptual reach, what will we say of secondary qualities? Consider the color of the tomato, the sweet taste of sugar, the heat of the bath water, the roughness of the raw wood, the sound of the bell. If we follow the logic of the bent-stick argument, what can these be but ideas in our mind? And if we are looking for variation as in the bent-stick/straight-stick case, there is more than enough to go around. The coffee without sugar which tasted just fine to my mother who liked it that way tastes awful to me who likes it only with enough sugar. The sugar is sweet we say; but what can that mean except that it produces a sweet sensation in us? And, of course, the same applies to sound. Compare the sound of the fire engine approaching you and going away: a different sound in each case. Which one is supposed to be the real sound out there that we reach in hearing? Neither can claim that title. Isn't the only solution to say that sound is not a reality out there that we reach in perception but only an idea or sensation in us?

And for vision it isn't just the bent stick that causes a problem. Look at a house, first directly from the front, then a bit to one side, then a bit further to that side, and then from further away; in each case it will appear differently. The critical philosopher with a subjectivist bent will ask: which of these appearances is supposed to be the real one? None can reasonably be selected over the others. Aren't they all "mere appearances"? An appearance can't be the house itself since there are many appearances but only one house. Isn't all we ever see an appearance? But what can an appearance be except an idea in our mind? If, as these reflections seem to show, all we ever see are appearances in our mind can we ever *reach* the object itself?

[9] EXTERNAL OBJECTS: CAN WE REACH THEM AFTER ALL?

A DEFENSE OF DIRECT REALISM: WE CAN REACH EXTERNAL OBJECTS

Hasn't something gone terribly wrong here? Aren't there numerous fallacies in these reasoning processes? If wonder in one direction has left us with doubt or even denial that we can ever reach external objects in perception, is there a wondering in an opposite direction, one that will restore our confidence that we can reach external objects after all? Against a Subjectivist theory that holds that we can't directly perceive external physical objects but only our own ideas which represent them and are caused by them, we can argue in defense of a Direct Realism:

(1) If we can't directly perceive physical objects, do we really perceive them at all? Do we really reach them at all? And if we can't reach them in perception, *how can we know they even exist*? How do we even know the whole external world exists? Including other people? Including even our own bodies, which are external to our minds?

(2) If we don't know external physical objects by reaching them in perception, *how does this whole argument even get started*? It constantly appeals to the reality of physical objects when it contrasts these with "mere appearances." More specifically, the argument appeals to the difference between appearance and reality; recall the bent stick: it really is straight, but it looks bent when half immersed in water. How do we even know that this is so unless we actually see the stick? Must we not see the stick itself just to understand the appearance-reality distinction? How could merely seeing an idea of the stick in our minds be sufficient for this? That is, if we didn't see the stick itself how could we even notice that it appeared in different ways? If we were confronted only with a series of varying—straight stick, then bent stick—how could we even construct this argument? Must we not see the stick itself in order to notice that it varies in appearance in and out of the water? Must we not see the stick itself in order to know that it is one and the same stick in both cases? It seems then that the conclusion of this argument from the bent-stick illusion is incompatible with its premises. This seems to be a decisive refutation.

(3) Doesn't this subjectivist theory -- as based on its challenges in the bent-stick case and the different appearances of the house -- *cut off the branch on which it is sitting*? Doesn't it deny access to the very things it needs to get started? Let us see if we can find an alternative.

Consider the subjectivist theory in its bent-stick argument. Its basic fallacy is the claim that we see appearances *instead of* objects. On the contrary, to see the appearance of x is *to see x itself*; one is not an alternative to the other; and to see x itself is to see it as appearing in a certain way. How else could we see it? Certainly, appearances vary while the object remains the same. But the appearances are not objects themselves. They are *the way an object appears to us*.

When I see the stick half in the water and half out of it, the stick looks bent. But *what I see is still the stick*, the stick itself, not some other object instead of the stick, a "bent-stick-idea." I see the stick itself as it now appears. It now appears bent because of the optics of refraction. But this is only a variation in appearance, in how the stick looks; it does not remove the stick from my visual field, from my power to reach it in perception. It does not hide the stick from me so that I can't get to it with my eyes. *I see the stick itself.*

Thus, the appearance of an external object is not an idea in my mind; *it is the external object itself* as that object now appears to me. In the example of the house, the house itself has many different appearances from different perspectives. If an appearance is said to be what I perceive it is the *house itself* that I perceive, the house itself described in a certain way. To see that appearance of the house *is* to see the house; one is not an alternative to the other. Compare: to sit on a chair *is* to sit on the surface of the chair and to sit on the surface of the chair *is* to sit on the chair. One is not an alternative to the other. I do not see the appearance of the house instead of the house: to see the appearance of the house *is* to see the house. The appearance is not an alternative object of perception as the subjectivist theory claims. That the appearance in part *depends on me* does not mean that it *is in me*. It is not "in" the mind; if it's anywhere it's "in" the object. The appearance is partly constituted by the mind, but it is also and mainly constituted by the object itself and by the conditions of perception, such as light, distance and perspective. *The appearance of an object is that object itself as it now presents itself to me.*

SOME SOURCES OF WONDER

How we reach external objects in perception remains a puzzle, a source of wonder. But this should not lead us to doubt *that* we do, as in the Subjectivist Theory. The wonder can only be there on the basis of the firm conviction that we do really reach objects out there by directly perceiving them; objects beyond our minds and their ideas, as claimed by Direct Realism.

One may also wonder: how do we know that the physical objects out there in the real world are *accurately represented* by their appearances to our minds? We are convinced that the appearances of the house somehow represent to us how the house really looks. But what justifies us in this belief? To know that the picture of a certain person resembles that person we need to know both the picture and the person. Here we have only the "picture." How do we know it accurately represents the object?

But perhaps the comparison to a picture is misleading. The picture and the thing itself, the thing of which the picture is a picture, are on the same level; each is a genuine alternative to the other. In one case you see the house; in another case you see only a picture of the house. In the first case you see the thing itself; in the second case you see only something that represents the thing itself. You see the picture *instead of* the house. All this is precisely what is not the case with the house and the appearance of the house. The appearance of the house is not "another thing" compared to the house; it is *the house itself* as presented to us in vision. And it is surely not an idea "in" our mind but a relation between an objective reality "out there" and a human mind that can know it through the power of perception in vision.

CHAPTER 7
MEMORY

[1] HOW CAN I BE AWARE OF WHAT NO LONGER EXISTS?

What is memory? Isn't part of its essence that it is about the past? I'm aware of you now as I talk to you now. That's not memory: you are now present before me, present in space and in time. Or I'm aware of a timeless truth, say in mathematics, that 4x3 is the same as 3x4. That too seems to be in the present and not as such about the past. But if I recall a childhood experience, call it before my mind, "see" it in my mind, that is memory. How is this possible? What I now "see" in my memory or by my memory no longer exists. How then can I be aware of it? Or should we say that in some sense a past event does exist? It doesn't have present existence, but it does have past existence; these are two ways something can exist.

Past existence seems to be something we must necessarily assume, else there would be no object for memory to refer to. And yet wouldn't past existence be a strange form of existence? I can enter a presently existing house; I cannot enter a house which existed in the past but has been torn down. Isn't the only "real" house a presently existing house? If a realtor sold you a house that turned out to be a merely "past" house, wouldn't you feel cheated? Wouldn't his claim that it has some kind of existence and is therefore worth something ring hollow?

Despite this, let us assume the past does have some kind of reality, the reality we reach in memory experiences. How do we reach it? How do we go back in time to reach it in awareness? We can't literally go back in time and relive a beautiful experience; we can't go back and undo a mistake we made. How then can we go back in memory?

When we remember a past experience, we remember it *as past*. There is a feeling of the past about what we remember. What is that? What we remember somehow wears the mark of pastness on its face. What is that? There are also different feelings of pastness depending on how far back the event remembered is. I remember the visit to the medical lab this morning, a few hours ago; I remember an experience in third grade, many years ago. How different these two feelings of pastness are! Where does this difference lie? How is it that I can tell right off the memory experience itself that the one is very recent, and the other is long ago? The one just happened while the other is ancient, far back in time.

[2] TWO THEORIES OF MEMORY

Impressed by the idea that we can't really reach into the past because it no longer exists some philosophers have proposed a Representative Theory of memory. What we are directly and immediately aware of in memory is not the past event itself since that doesn't exist now, but an image of it that represents it, somehow along the lines of a picture of a person that represents that person. The image resembles the event and being aware of it is what gives us access to the past event. This theory seems to solve the problem of how we can "see" what no longer exists.

But is the theory successful? It holds that what is present to our awareness in memory is not the past event itself but only an image of it; we seem to be cut off from the past event itself, being left with merely a kind of picture of it. But then how do we know it really is a picture *of it* and not just a picture? How do we know it was produced by the past event? How do we know it resembles the past event, that it is not just any representation of it but a faithful representation? Being cut off from the past itself we can never make a comparison between the image of the past event and that event itself. We seem to be imprisoned in our own mind. We seem to have lost what we started out with: awareness of the past. Far from explaining what memory is and how it is possible, the Representative Theory seems to make memory impossible.

The alternative theory is the Direct Realist Theory of memory. What we are really aware of in memory, directly and immediately, is the past event itself, not some picture of it. How strange: a past event, therefore no longer in existence and yet a direct object of our awareness! A source of wonder! But isn't that the reality of memory and what we mean by memory? And isn't anything else, such as the rep theory a fraudulent substitute, taking away memory and substituting something else in its place? The rep theory gives us a *present* reality as the object of awareness in memory. But isn't the whole point of memory that we are aware of a *past* reality, a past event? What we have before us in memory is not a present reality but a past reality as it now appears to us. There is a certain parallel here to the Direct Realist Theory of perception. It holds that we do not see ideas of a house instead of the house itself; we see the house itself as it now appears to us. So too we remember the past event itself as it now appears to us. The fact of its appearing to us is precisely what constitutes our memory of it.

Isn't the pastness of what we remember directly given to us in our memory experience? The event I remember is not just given to me as part of my awareness; it is given *as past*. The rep theory loses that. It makes the object of awareness a present image. But such an image can never be what memory really gives us. Memory must be, and be experienced as being, a direct link to the past. What we are aware of in memory is not just a certain content, what an event was like, but that this content, this event was a past reality. Its pastness is part of what is given to us.

[3] DIFFERENT FORMS OF MEMORY

Consider these two cases of memory: (A) I remember a past experience in my life. I call it to mind, I "see" it clearly before me. (B) I remember something I learned in the past. This gives us our first important distinction:

- (A) Memory of the past and retained in the present.
- (B) Memory that refers to what is acquired in the past and retained in the present.

As an example of (A) I remember a memorable trip to the Greek Islands over 50 years ago. In particular, I remember being in Delos and seeing the sunset over the Aegean Sea, an incredibly beautiful sight! The key features of this form of memory are that it is directly about *the past* and about *my experience* in the past. As an example of (B) I remember most of the important things I learned in a Physics class I had in college. Both are called memory and yet they are very different:

- Form (A) is specifically about the past. Form (B) may be about any time period, as when I learn and then remember that there will be a meeting tomorrow; or timeless truths, as when I remember my arithmetic.
- Form (A) is specifically about me; it has one type of object: an event in my own past. Form (B) is usually not about me; it has many different kinds of objects: historical facts, geographical facts, scientific facts, mathematical truths and so much more.
- Form (A) constitutes memories. Among my many memories is the sunset at Delos. Form (B) is never called memories; its objects are radically different from memories.
- Form (A) is a "reaching into" the past, "reliving" the past, "seeing" a past event. Form (B) as noted is not specifically about the past and therefore lacks this feature.

I remember the sunset in Delos; I remember the physics I learned in school. But usually, I don't think of these explicitly. I "have" them in my memory, but I don't usually have either of them before me in my present consciousness. This gives us our second important distinction:

(C) Occurrent memory: what is explicitly before me in my present consciousness.

(D) Non-occurrent memory: what is stored but not explicitly present in consciousness.

In one sense I remember the Delos experience even when I'm thinking of something else. It is there in my memory because I have not forgotten it. The same applies to the physics I learned in school. At any one moment almost all of what I remember is of this type, (D). Thus, memory can refer both to an actual present experience when something is explicitly before my consciousness, occurrent memory (C); and to a capacity or storehouse available to me for use but not part of an actual experience explicitly before my consciousness, non-occurrent memory (D).

Are these two distinctions enough to cover the whole vast field of memory? Consider some examples of memory statements. Can they be fitted neatly into the categories above or do we need to expand our list? If so, how should we do so?

- I just remembered that I left the lights on in the basement yesterday.
- I just remembered that my friend's birthday is tomorrow.
- I just remembered that today is Sunday.
- I remember how to tie a square knot.
- I remember where I parked my car.
- I remember when it happened.
- I remember how that tune goes.
- Please remember to mail the letters for me on your way to town.
- Please remember me to your wife; please remember me to your husband.

An interesting type of case is when I recall particular persons, places or things without remembering any particular occasions when I saw them. I remember Paris because I visited it several times. I have certain memory images of it before me, but I cannot recall any particular event as I can with the sunset on Delos. Such memory is in some way like (A), about the past and about my experience in the past. But it is also different in that (A) is essentially about a specific event actually remembered while the Paris case is not.

[4] MEMORY AND KNOWLEDGE

Are memory and knowledge the same? Is it true that if I remember something, I know it, and if I know it, I remember it? If I remember the results of all the national elections for the last 100 years, I know these results. And if we say that memory is the retention of knowledge acquired in the past, aren't we saying that the two go together?

But there are other cases where the two seem to diverge. Consider:

- Doesn't knowledge also include what I'm observing right now and not only what I know because I've acquired in the past and now remember it?
- "I know his name; I just can't remember it right now." I have non-occurrent knowledge of his name but not occurrent.
- "You knew you were expecting visitors; you should have remembered it."
- Suppose that as a child you visited Niagara Falls. You know you did because you were told about this, but you do not remember it. (See also the case below about walking among the flowers in the field.)
- Suppose I have images of some event that I seem to have experienced in early childhood but don't know if this event really happened or if I'm only imagining it; and suppose further that it did really happen. Do I in fact remember it without realizing this?

[5] IS MEMORY BASICALLY RELIABLE?

Aren't we sometimes deceived by our memory? I say that I remember an event in my very early childhood. "I remember walking among the flowers in the field and noting that they were taller than I was." At one time I claimed to remember this. Then my mother told me there is a picture of little me in the field surrounded by the tall flowers and it must be my recalling this picture that accounts for my "memory" and not my actually remembering the event itself as I experienced it, for I was much too young to really remember it. If I can be mistaken once, why can't I be mistaken again and again? Can I rely on my memory? How can I distinguish actual memory from imagination? I seem to remember a past experience; did it really happen? Or is it just something I'm imagining? I seem to remember a discussion with another person long ago. Did it really happen the way I remember it? Or am I reading into this "memory" ideas that are foreign to it, that stem from me and do not belong to the past event as it really happened.

The memory sceptic seems to have a case. How do you know your memory is basically valid and reliable? Perhaps it is always deceiving you? Or, short of that, is it deceiving you so often that you shouldn't trust it if you are interested in believing only what is true? The basic problem seems to be that in order to validate memory you need to get outside it so that you can compare what it reveals with the original datum. But, of course, you can't do that. The past event you claim to remember is passed and gone; you can't get back to it. You can ask someone else, as I asked my mother about the field of flowers, but then she has to rely on her memory. Doesn't every attempt to validate a particular memory item rely on further appeals to memory? Doesn't this just raise the problem of the reliability of memory all over again? Aren't we stuck in our memory beliefs without any recourse to something outside them that could validate them?

But hasn't memory been shown so often to be reliable? And doesn't that count heavily in favor of memory being basically reliable? The sceptic will reply that you have to remember that memory has been shown so often to be reliable. And that is again an appeal to the very memory we were supposed to be establishing.

Can the memory sceptic be answered? Here are some replies to consider:

1. ***We cannot show that memory is sometimes unreliable without relying on memory and on its being basically reliable.*** So the sceptic's case against memory itself appeals to the very reliability of memory that he claims to challenge. Doesn't this show that memory as basically reliable is absolutely indispensable for human reasoning?
2. ***If memory as basically reliable is absolutely indispensable for human reasoning can we not accept its basic reliability as a first principle?*** Isn't it similar in this respect to the basic reliability of human reasoning itself? That too can't be proved without assuming it. Nor can it be questioned and challenged without also assuming it. We seem to hit a rock bottom here in human thinking, a basis which cannot itself be established by appeal to something beyond it, but which must be assumed for any thinking at all.
3. ***Without relying on memory and trusting it as basically valid we couldn't even have any present knowledge or belief. "This is a table."*** How can I know this unless I recognize it as a table? And how can I recognize it as a table unless I rely on my memory?

4. *Without relying on memory as basically valid we couldn't speak.* Speaking relies on having the right words at our disposal, which in turn relies on memory of those words.

5. *Speaking also relies on remembering the beginning of the sentence that I am now uttering in order to finish it, again relying on memory.*

6. *Without relying on memory and trusting it as basically valid we couldn't read.* That too relies on memory of words and on remembering the beginning of the sentence I'm now reading in order to finish reading it and understanding it.

7. *We raised the question above whether every attempt to validate a particular memory item doesn't rely on further appeals to memory and whether we aren't stuck in our memory beliefs without any recourse to something outside them that could validate them.* Isn't there a simple answer to this? We can check photographs, videos and perhaps records such as documents, books and newspapers. Doesn't this give us an immediate access to the past to verify our memory claims?

[6] THE INDISPENSABILITY OF MEMORY

We can see from items 1-6 above how absolutely indispensable memory is. Without memory we could not function as persons. Isn't that why amnesia is such a terrible thing, such a tragic loss? We realize that something of immense importance is missing. Our memories of childhood, of friends, of important events in our lives are such vital parts of our being as persons that their loss is such a heavy blow. We want to remember the big picture, the essential features; the details are much less important. I remember *that* I went to Greece in 1963; that's what's important. Perhaps I'm not entirely clear about some of the *details*, such as which events came before or after certain other ones. The indispensability of memory and the opposite phenomenon of its loss in amnesia raise other wonder questions. We remember some things and forget others. Why do I remember the sunset at Delos and not other sunsets?

CHAPTER 8
LANGUAGE

[1] INITIAL WONDERING

HOW IS LANGUAGE POSSIBLE? HOW CAN WE BRIDGE THE GAP?

I speak to you and you hear me and understand me. How is that possible? How can something inside me, my thoughts, what I want to say to you, get inside you? It is of course inside me, inside my consciousness, and not on the surface of my body. And it gets inside you, inside your consciousness, not to the outside of your body. How is it possible to bridge this gap?

How is it that by making certain sounds I can transfer what is in my mind to your mind? That seems to be a huge gap; yet it is bridged by the simple act of making a sound. But making a word-sound is not a simple act like saying "ah" as the doctor looks into my throat. The word-sound is different because it has a meaning. But how can a sound get this additional reality attached to it, that it has a meaning? The word I utter has a meaning; but it is also the case that *I* mean something when I speak. There is *my* meaning and the *word* meaning. The two are not the same but they are closely connected, for it is by the use of word meaning that I am able to mean something. By word meaning I convey what I mean.

By speaking to you I can transfer what is in my mind to your mind. And so, the same thing that was in my mind is now in yours. That is strange enough. But that same thing, existing in the form of words with meaning also seems to exist in the space between us. Suppose I say something I shouldn't have said, something I now very much regret saying. I try to deny that I said it. But then I am challenged: "you said that!" Doesn't this mean that my offensive words are now somehow out there, in the public domain? "You heard what he just said!" For my words to be out there in the public domain does seem to mean that they are in the space out there. But words do not exist in space the way chairs and tables exist in space. For one thing words have a very fleeting existence. They are said; then they're gone.

But, in another way, many of them are not gone; far from being gone, they still exist in the memory of those who heard them.

By speaking to you I can transfer what is in my mind to your mind. Of course, what is in my mind is still there; it is duplicated in your mind. We now share the same reality. How is this possible? It's not like sharing a room where we share because we are in the same space. In speaking the two things shared are separated, one is in one person the other in another person.

HOW IS LANGUAGE POSSIBLE? OTHER SOURCES OF WONDER

How do I form the words inside my mouth? I cannot possibly describe how I do it. I just do it. Do *I* know how to do this? Or is it my brain and nervous system that "knows" how to do this? I am not my brain and nervous system; I hardly know how they function. So how is it that I can get them to do this for me?

I speak to you. This is a bond between you and me. How is this possible? Why should what I say be the same thing as what you hear? We are all confident that these two things are generally the same. How can we be so sure? Usually what I mean when I say something to you is the same thing as what you understand as my meaning; I successfully convey my meaning to you. Again, how can we be so sure that this connection is successfully made? When it isn't we usually realize it, but not always.

When you hear my voice you hear *me*. But do you really hear me? You hear a set of tones or sounds that my vocal chords produce. That's hardly *me*. Yet we confidently say, "you heard me"; or "did you hear me?" In getting those sounds into your ear and brain and mind you somehow get something of *me*. They are my words. I reach you through them. They can be neutral in their impact, or good; or they can hurt. Suppose a person is hurt by an offensive remark; later he exclaims "you said that!" These bitter words assign responsibility to the other for what he said. Doesn't this show that a person's words are his own in a deeply significant way?

How does a child acquire his native language? He hears it and "gets" it; he somehow comes to understand that it is language, a form of communication, a bond between persons; and not just another set of noises. He also "gets" it in the sense that he will be able to do the same thing: speak the language. He gets all this automatically. In the sense of intentional action, he doesn't have to "do" anything; it happens for him, it is somehow done for him. No one has to teach him how to form words in his mouth. No one would be able to do this anyway. How do you say "mama"? It has been noted that babies babble differently when surrounded by different languages as early as three months.

Language is a bond between persons. Imagine losing this capacity. People still spoke to you, but you couldn't understand them anymore. You couldn't form your words to speak to them anymore. And you couldn't read or write anymore. Don't we take these amazing capacities for granted? Try to imagine how utterly isolated you would be if you lost them.

[2] WHAT IS LANGUAGE?

WHAT IS THE ESSENCE OF LANGUAGE?

What is language? What is its essence? By language I can *mean* something. Think of the times you've said, "No, that's not what I mean." What did you mean? What sort of thing were you doing when you meant something? You were using language. The same point can be made in thinking of another person. "What did you mean?" To get the other person's meaning, and to convey your meaning to him is to communicate successfully by language. Meaning in this sense, actively *meaning* something shows that language is intentional communication.

It seems tempting to identify language and meaning in this way. But perhaps this is not the whole story. Here is another way to look at what language is. Let us distinguish:

1. **Language in itself.** It is there to be used, in the ways described in 2 and 3 below. But what does it mean that it is there? How does it exist in itself, there to be used? Isn't this what we refer to when we speak of the different languages, English, French, German, Italian and so many more? There are so many languages in the world! Estimates are that there are

well over 6,000 living languages in the world, close to and perhaps over 7,000.
2. ***Language as used by persons in speaking and hearing:*** *the spoken word*, or rather the many spoken words, in conversations, lectures, classrooms, speeches and much more.
3. ***Language as used by persons in writing and reading:*** *the written word*, or rather the many written words, in notes, letters, books, articles, newspapers, fliers and much more.

For language in itself we have *the meaning* of a word or phrase; for speaking-hearing and writing-reading the crucial thing is what a person means, what *I mean* and what *you mean*.

The written word is somehow preserved as such. It is there on paper and remains in existence unless destroyed. The spoken word has a very fleeting existence and is mostly lost and gone after being uttered. But some of it is remembered, and, in that way, it somehow continues to exist. Think of your memories of words of love given to you long ago that touched your heart then and still do so now. Your memories become part of your being as a person. The words "I love you" are poured into a child; he doesn't remember any particular time of hearing them, but their profound effect remains and become part of who he is as a person.

The spoken word can be part of a one-on-one conversation. I talk to you, and you listen. You talk to me, and I listen. There are the spoken words, the eye contact and the body language. It is happening all at once, a reality of the present moment. None of this applies to the written word. I write you a letter at one time and you read it at a later time.

Very important for the spoken word is tone of voice; this is especially true for one-on-one conversations. Tone of voice is either entirely absent in the written word or very hard to include. To try to compensate for this some of us now use emoticons in texts and e-mails. For the spoken word pronunciation is crucial; for the written word spelling is important.

We have noted that actively *meaning* something shows that language is intentional communication. But is it really always intentional? We will return to this question shortly.

WHAT IS INCLUDED UNDER LANGUAGE?

What is included in the broad category of language? Is sign language a real language? It has nouns, verbs, adjectives, and adverbs. It has grammar rules. These would seem to be quite sufficient to make sign language a real language. After all people communicate by the signs of sign language when the usual forms of language are not possible; and so sign language serves the same purpose as regular language. I can *mean* something and *understand* another's meaning in sign language just as I can in written and spoken language.

Does a system of smoke signals count as a language? It might seem so because it is intentional communication; I can *mean* something by that signal. But that doesn't seem to be sufficient to make it a language since a smoke signal system is so primitive and limited in what it is capable of conveying that it seems best not to include it as a form of language. Intentional communication, even where it is a necessary feature for language is not a sufficient one. We will see shortly that intentional communication is not always a necessary feature for language.

How about a red light meaning *stop* and a white flag meaning *surrender*? Do they count as languages; that is, language systems? They are each forms of intentional communication and in a broad sense of the term they mean something. But they hardly constitute language systems because they are so primitive and limited in scope. Each is a symbol, and in that sense each is similar to a word; but a single word does not constitute a language system.

We speak of body language but is this really a form of language? Isn't being intentional a necessary feature of language? But body language is often not intentional. "He gave it away by his body language; surely he didn't mean to and he didn't realize it." And yet non-intentional body language is language in the sense that we communicate by it. Eyes which stay focused signal attraction to the other person and to the subject. Widening of the eyes indicates interest; it is an opening and welcoming expression. Head held high and also forward and upright expresses attentiveness and a positive response. Head held down means disapproval or dejection or shame. Chin up means confidence. While talking with another person we often smile and nod, a positive signaling; frowning is a typical negative one. Consider some of these points further:

The natural and spontaneous smile and the welcoming-loving-affirming eyes: these occur spontaneously. As gestures of body language, they are not intentional, and not even consciously experienced. What they convey, the love and affirmation of one person to another is intentional. The message is intentional; the mode of communicating it is not. Other examples of non-intentional elements in language include how a person says what he says, as in a tone of anger without realizing it; and cases where something "slips out" during a conversation, something the person had meant to keep to himself. In this broader sense of language, it refers basically to communication: we can and do communicate beyond what we mean to communicate.

So much of this is not intentional, and often not conscious. But it is a powerful form of communication. Perhaps we should re-evaluate the idea that being intentional is essential to language. That is, there are different forms of language, some intentional and some not. I see you and immediately I like you; it is clearly written on my face. You see it and you "get it."

In one respect language is intentional: when it refers to actively *meaning* something it is intentional communication. But in another respect, there is also language in a broader sense which includes elements that are non-intentional. Much and perhaps most of body language comes under this heading.

SENTENCES AND PROPOSITIONS

Words have meanings but it is also sentences that have meanings. For many sentences their meaning is a proposition. The two form interesting comparisons and contrasts:

- Different sentences may express the same proposition. The English sentence "I love you" and the German sentence "Ich liebe dich" express one and the same proposition. Each is a translation of the other because the same meaning is carried over in the translation from one language to the other. We have two languages, two sentences but one proposition.

- One and the same sentence may express different propositions. The one sentence "Jim rents his room" can express two different propositions. It has potentially two different meanings: one, that Jim is a landlord who rents his room out to someone else; two, that Jim himself lives in that room for which he pays rent. Another example is from Harvard philosopher Quine: "Our mothers bore us." In both these cases we have two propositions potentially contained in one sentence; one sentence with two different meanings.

[3] WHAT IS A WORD?

Consider the spoken word. How can a certain sound be something so much more than a mere sound? It can have a meaning, and in many cases several meanings. Shall we say it has its meaning because it is given this meaning? But how is that done? Who does it? The same applies to the written word. Why is one set of letters a meaningful word while another is not?

Think of the power of words. A word can sting, it can hurt. Another word can be the source of deep joy or consolation or encouragement. A word or two can save my life. "Watch out!" By someone uttering these two little words and my hearing them my life is saved.

Where do words exist? They seem to have some location. They are here on planet earth and not in outer space. A given language exists more among the people who speak it than among others who don't speak it. Yet it doesn't seem to be totally absent even among those who do not speak it. Maybe nobody around here speaks Hungarian, but we all know that this language exists, and we know a little about it, so it has some existence even here. If no one speaks a given language, does it still exist? Is an extinct language still a language?

Where do words exist? Can we say written words exist in dictionaries, on printed pages, on handwritten pages and in other forms such as on computer screens? Can we say that spoken words exist where they are uttered, by a speaker in a lecture and between you and me when we have a one-on-one conversation? Do they exist in the space of the lecture hall and the space that is between you and me?

How do words exist? They don't exist the way rocks exist but are they equally real? Words seem to have an objective existence as much as rocks and yet their mode of existence seems utterly different from that of rocks. They are not like ideas in the minds of individual persons for they exist essentially between persons, parts of the great communication process that exists between persons. Are they perhaps even more real than rocks? And more important?

What counts as the same word as opposed to a different word? The same letters and the same sounds can correlate with the same or different words. Here are three important categories:

1. Same letters—different word. That gold mine belongs to me and so it is mine. What I mean is that she was very mean to him. I long to see her; it's been a long time. To bear a pain is very different from seeing a picture of a black bear. Tell me in one sentence what his jail sentence is. Did you lie down? Tell me the truth, don't lie to me.
2. Same sound—different word or word phrase. J. L. Austin gives the example: iced ink sounds just like I stink.[1] Another example: let us eat lettuce. This point applies only to spoken words while the other two apply equally to spoken and written words.
3. Same word—different meanings, senses and uses. I fall down the stairs; I fall in love; I fall in grace. You can make progress, make amends, make it clear, make it a career, make something like a work of art, make a living and make love.

---

[1] J. L. Austin, *How to do Things with Words*, ed. J. O. Urmson (Oxford University Press, 1962), 123.

[4] HOW DO WORDS GET THEIR MEANING?

WHAT IS LANGUAGE MEANING?

A parrot makes a noise that sounds exactly like the word "go." He utters the sound, but he does not *say* the word in the sense of meaning it; for words are by their very nature connected to meaning. He was making language-sounding noises, but he wasn't using language. He didn't *mean* anything. There was no meaning. Compare:

1. What does this word mean?
2. What does this phrase or this sentence mean?
3. What do you mean?

For #1 consult the dictionary. For #2 a single phrase or sentence can have different meanings. "I'll be there." Is that a promise? Or is it only the expression of an intention? For #3 different people mean different things at different times.

Word meaning (#1) and personal meaning (#3) are closely related. I use words with the meaning they have (#1) to perform the activity designated by "I mean" (a variant of #3). Word meaning is independent of me; personal meaning is dependent on me.

THE REFERENT THEORY OF MEANING

How do words get their meaning? One answer is reference, the referent theory. The word "rock" means what it refers to, those things we call by that word. But this answer doesn't always work. Consider some examples where meaning and reference cannot be identified:

1. The words "morning star" and the words "evening star" have different meanings but they have the same referent, the planet Venus. Meaning and referent do not always coincide.

2. Objective denotation and personal connotation: the word hospital has a single, objective denotation, its reference to a hospital. It has a positive, good personal connotation as a place for a doctor who finds his work there challenging and enjoyable. It has a negative, bad personal connotation for a patient who suffered there; two very different meanings.
3. Words such as if, and, is, whereas, however and therefore have meanings but none of them refer to anything; that's not how they get their meaning.
4. "There are no round squares." "There are no unicorns." These are true and meaningful, but the key terms do not refer to anything. In fact, the whole point is to state this fact. The first is necessarily true, logically true; the second only happens to be true. There are no unicorns in our world but there could be another world where such creatures do exist.

Does Hamlet exist? Shakespeare's play *Hamlet* obviously exists; it is often performed on stage. Does the person referred to by this name actually exist? No, there is no such historical figure. But when the name appears in the play it has the *referring function*; to whom then does it refer? Is there a realm of fictional entities to which terms like "Hamlet" refer? If so how would such entities exist? How would such a realm be related to the real world, the realm of actually existing persons and things? Is there another, perhaps a better way of dealing with terms like *Hamlet*? If so, what is it?

THE USE THEORY OF MEANING

It is often suggested that meaning is use. Words have meaning because they can be used to do things in their role in language. Words get their meaning from their use. Is this how we should handle the problems considered above in #1-4? Should we say that the *referring function* of a word or phrase can have a legitimate *use* even when there is no really existing object to refer to, no actual *referent*?

And if you are asked the meaning of a word or phrase you might reply by providing another one which has the same use. You help a person understand the meaning of a term by showing him how it is used. And to know the meaning of a term is to be able to use it correctly.

The use theory sounds attractive, and it seems to get us out of the hole that the referent theory put us in. But consider this case. A schoolboy is in the third grade in a foreign country; he has limited knowledge of the local language. One day he is called in by the teacher and punished for using a certain word, a local swear word. He comes home in tears exclaiming that he has no idea why he was punished. His parents ask him what he did or said. Finally, he comes out with the offending word, protesting he doesn't know what it means, and especially that he doesn't know it is a bad word. But he had picked it up from the other boys and he knew how to use it. In fact, he used it correctly, as an expression of anger at having to do a chore that was not legitimately required of the schoolboys. He knew the *use* of the word, but he did not know its *meaning*. This seems to show that they cannot simply be equated.

[5] LANGUAGE AS SPEECH ACTS

SPEECH ACTS

There are many ways of looking at language: as a *bond* between persons; as *meaning*, both what a person means and what a word/phrase means; as *used* by persons. Here is another:

It has been said that the fundamental reality in language is the *speech act*.[2] When we use language we perform an act, a speech act. "I warned him!" Words and phrases are used to do things: to communicate by means of various speech acts. Words alone do not communicate; they need to be used in speech acts. Consider the sentence "you may lose your job." Was that a threat? Or was it a warning? Or was it just a statement of fact? How was that

---

[2] Based on John R. Searle, *Speech Acts: an Essay in the Philosophy of Language* (Cambridge University Press, 1969), 16. In his words, "speaking a language is performing speech acts."

sentence used? What did it mean? Sentences may have different meanings not only by virtue of their word meanings but also by virtue of their force, where *force* refers to the type of speech act in terms of things like threats, warnings and statements of fact. Every speech act has some force; here is an example of a particularly significant force.

THE POWERFUL WORDS OF THE JUDGE

Can saying it make it so? "Of course not," we might say. "Things are what they are and our saying what we say doesn't change anything." Certainly, if it's raining, then saying the sun is shining doesn't make it so. But now consider another type of case. The jury has just found the defendant guilty as charged. It is time for the judge to speak: "Five years."

Here is the remarkable thing: his saying these two words *makes it so* that the defendant is now facing a five year jail sentence. Here saying it does make it so! When the judge pronounces his sentence, he is not describing anything or simply stating a fact. He is *doing* something in a much stronger sense than when I tell you about my trip to Italy and describe what happened. The judge -- by saying these words, by this speech act -- is *creating a new reality*. He is making it the case that the convicted person will now have to spend five years in jail. He is bringing into existence something which did not exist before, a jail sentence for the person found guilty.

Compare the case of the speech act of the judge when he says, "five years," which creates a new reality, with the case where the defendant is hard of hearing and asks the person next to him to tell him what the sentence is. That person then utters the exact same words "five years"; but now it is a very different kind of speech act, one with an essentially different and diminished force. The second speech act merely informs the defendant; it describes it, it states a fact. Here the old dictum that saying it doesn't make it so fully applies.

Of course, the judge's words also inform the defendant. But this is merely part of his act of sentencing, while the second speech act is entirely that of informing.

Chapter 8: Language

DO ALL SPEECH ACTS CREATE NEW REALITIES?

As we saw, in the jail sentence case, a speech act creates a new reality. Before the words of the judge the defendant was not facing jail time; now and as a result he is facing jail time.

Does this apply across the board to all speech acts? Do they all function by *creating a new reality*? Consider a set of further cases:

1. I promise you: I will be there.
2. I'm informing you: I will be there.
3. I'm warning you: the bull is charging!
4. I'm ordering you: get out!
5. I'm threatening you: get out or I'll kill you!
6. I'm informing you: your car is not safe to drive.
7. I apologize to you: I'm so sorry for what I did.
8. I thank you for the loving thing you did for me; I express my gratitude.
9. I order you: forward, march! (a command given to troops to march in formation).
10. I name this ship The Spirit of America.
11. I do (said as part of a marriage ceremony).
12. I bequeath my stamp collection to my son.
13. I appoint you ambassador to France.
14. I announce: there will be a quiz today (said by a teacher to the class).
15. I yell: out! (said by an umpire in a baseball game).

This list gives us some idea of how many different kinds of speech acts there are. It seems that each of them creates a new reality. By promising you something I create an obligation for myself to carry out that promise. By informing you I bring about the reality that you now know something you didn't know before. By warning you a new reality is created: "You are warned." Similarly: "You are ordered." And threatening creates the reality of a threat hanging over you.

Suppose I am your car mechanic and I inform you that your car is not safe to drive. Despite this you drive it anyway. You have a terrible accident caused by the unsafe condition you were informed of in which two other people are seriously injured. Someone can then rightly say to you: *you were informed*. The words of the mechanic created a reality: that you knew about the unsafe condition of the car. This kind of informing is very different from the case where I tell you about my trip to Italy. One can equally say to you: *you were warned* that your car is not safe to drive.

If I say to you that I am sorry for what I did our relationship is significantly changed. Something odious has now been removed and thereby a new bond created. At the other end of a spectrum, by thanking you I acknowledge the reality of the loving deed you created for me, and that recognition is then itself a new reality: your deed is recognized and appreciated. We can see the force of the reality of the deed created by the act of thanking by thinking of its absence where it should have taken place: the shock we feel when a deed of love is ignored. You save my life at great cost to you, and I simply ignore it, walk away without recognizing it, without thanking you.

The military order places the troops under an order, a new reality. If I name the ship, it now has a name. By saying "I do" I make it the case that I am now a married person; I become a spouse; the new reality of a marriage bond has been created. If I bequeath my stamp collection it becomes the property of another person. If I appoint you ambassador, you are now an ambassador. By my words to the class the quiz comes into being. Does my saying "out" create a new reality? Or does it just affirm a reality that is already there, that the runner is in fact out? But suppose it is a mistaken call; the runner is in fact safe. If the bad call stands the runner is out; that does seem to be a new reality, one which would not have existed except for the bad call.

Do *all* speech acts create new realities? Or only some, perhaps most, including all those we have considered here? Think of other speech acts like praising and blaming and insulting.

ANOTHER WAY SPEECH ACTS CREATE NEW REALITIES

We can distinguish *the speech act itself* and *the results* of the of the speech act, where the results are seen as new realities created by the speech act. The results of the speech act itself are basically two kinds: the spoken word and the written word:

1. The spoken word now exists in the space between persons; and it is (usually) taken in by the person or persons who hear it. "I heard you." Its existence is limited to a specific time and place.
2. The written word now exists on paper or some other medium. Its existence is not limited to a specific time and place but can be spread far and wide.

A *person* does something by his speech act: he says x or he writes y. But there is also a sense in which *words* (spoken and written) do something as the results of speech acts. Consider first the *person* who does something: a speaker at a train station announces over the PA system, passengers are warned to cross the tracks only at the bridge. Second, by this speech act it is also the *spoken words* which do something: warn the passengers. Third, the same words of warning can also be written as a sign for all to see. Now it is the *written words* which do something: warn the passengers.

SAME SET OF WORDS: DIFFERENT SPEECH ACTS

Another source of wonder is that the same set of words may have different meanings as speech acts. Consider some of the examples used above:

1. "I will be there." Is that a promise or only a statement of intention, perhaps a prediction?
2. "Five years." When the judge utters these words, they create a new reality: the defendant is facing jail time. And in hearing them the defendant is also informed; the speech act is a case of both together. But when his neighbor repeats the words to him the speech act is only one of informing in contrast to the judge creating.
3. "The bull is charging." Both a warning and an informing; or only an informing?

4. "Your car is not safe to drive." Both a warning and an informing; or only an informing?
5. "You may lose your job." A threat? A warning? Or only a statement of fact?

ARE SPEECH ACTS TRUE OR FALSE?

On the one hand, some speech acts are neither true nor false. The judge's saying "five years" is initially neither true nor false. Rather, it is his saying these words that *makes* the prison sentence to be what it is. Only later when it is repeated as a report is it true or false. The initial speech act of the judge itself may be evaluated in other ways: just or unjust, appropriate or not.

On the other hand, some speech acts do come under the true-false evaluation. Consider:

- I'm warning you: "the bull is charging!" (Maybe he's not: it's not true.)
- I yell: "out!" (Maybe it's a bad call; the runner is really safe: it's not true.)
- I announce: "there will be a quiz today" (Maybe it's only a bluff: it's not true.)
- I'm informing you: "your car is not safe to drive" (Maybe I'm mistaken: it is safe.)
- I promise you: I will be there. (Wouldn't this be a false statement if I couldn't be there?)

Consider some other cases. Am I authorized to name this ship? Or perhaps it has already been named? Is the stamp collection mine to give away? How would we evaluate these speech acts and others such as thanking, apologizing, questioning, ordering and threatening?

HATE SPEECH

Words can be extremely powerful. Think of a mean word said to you that stings you. Doesn't that hurt more than some physical pains? Think of words whose only function is to express and convey hatred, animosity, meanness, the desire to cause pain and humiliation. They may be directed at another individual or they may target a whole group, such as racial slurs. They create a new reality, but in ways that are very different from what we have examined so far. The new reality created by the judge is somehow out there, existing objectively, independently of the words that brought it into existence. The same seems to be true for all the others: promising, informing, warning, threatening, naming a ship, ordering, thanking, apologizing, etc. But in hate speech isn't it the words themselves that are the new reality? And isn't that what makes them so terrible? The words themselves somehow incorporate the hate; and they mark that person as being hated. They are intended to penetrate the victim and hurt him. When it is said that words *do* something this seems never to apply more aptly than in hate speech.

LOVE SPEECH

While hate speech pours hatred into another person, love speech does the opposite: it pours love into another person. No two realities could be more at polar ends of a spectrum than these two. Words of love are also a new reality themselves. They express and convey the love of one person to another. They may be words of affirmation, closeness, encouragement, consolation, gratitude, forgiveness and much else. Here too words *do* something, something wonderful!

[6] SOME MAIN POINTS OF WONDER

1. I speak to you, and you hear me. How is that possible? How can something inside me, my thoughts, what I want to say to you, get inside you?
2. How do I form words in my mouth when I speak to you? I can't say how; I just do it.
3. You hear my words. Or do you hear me? Or is it both? How is that possible?

4. Where does meaning lie? In a person: I mean something, this and not that. Or does it lie in the word? Words have meaning. Or does it lie in phrases? In all of these?
5. If I mean something I intend that something. Does that show that language is essentially intentional? But body language is also language, and it can be largely non-intentional.
6. Where do words exist? Spoken words? Written words?
7. Where does the meaning of words and phrases come from? One answer is reference. Words and phrases derive their meaning from what they refer to. But often the things they refer to don't exist; for example, round squares and unicorns.
8. Another answer here is use; words and phrases derive their meaning from how they are used. But I can know the use of a word without knowing its meaning, as in a swear word.
9. Same words: different meanings and different uses. "I will be there." Does this mean that I informing you of a fact, that this is what I will do? Or is it a promise?
10. Words have power: the judge says, "five years" and that speech act, saying those words is what sends the poor defendant off to prison for five long years. Think of the power of certain phrases: "I'm so sorry!" and "Thank you so much!" The power of warnings, threats, and insults. The power of hate speech, of love speech.

CHAPTER 9
WHAT IS TIME?

"What is time? If no one asks me, I know what it is. But if someone does ask me and I want to explain it, I don't know what it is."[1]

This quote is from St. Augustine who was a great philosopher. Why was he puzzled about something so familiar to us, so elementary and constantly with us? Why isn't time something clear and obvious? Why is it a cause for wonder? As we explore time, we will come to understand why St. Augustine was puzzled by it, why time isn't something clear and obvious.

The topic of time has fascinated philosophers since St. Augustine wondered about it and actually before his time as well. It is safe to say, (a) that no one has really solved the puzzles he raised, and (b) that there are even more puzzles than those he points to. Surely the topic of time is a source of philosophic wonder. Part of this is that there are so many "wonder topics" under the heading of time, distinct but also related to each other and overlapping. Let us examine some of these topics of time, starting with the flow of time.

[1] THE FLOW OF TIME

What is the flow of time? Does time flow like a river? There seem to be two views in which time may be seen as flowing like a river. Both involve the future, the present and the past.

In the first *events move in time*. They move from the future, to the present and to the past. What is now future moves closer and closer to the present, briefly becomes the present, and then moves into the past, moving further and further away from the present as it becomes more and more past. As of this writing January 1, 2030, is in the distant future. A year from now it will be a bit closer, a year

---

[1] St. Augustine, Confessions, Book 11, "Time and Eternity," Chapter 14, "What is Time?"

later still closer, until it becomes the present. For one day it is the present. Then it moves into the past, yesterday, the day before, and then further and further into the past.

The first view may be seen in terms of events that have a personal meaning. A child eagerly awaits his next birthday. It is now two months away; what a long wait! Then it is one month away, one week, then one day. Finally, it is here! We celebrate it; but then it goes on its journey into the past. In forty years, the no-longer-child will surely have forgotten it. But, on this view of time, it still exists, in the distant past.

If we accept this view, do we want to say that time flows objectively? That is, that it is time itself that flows, irrespective of our experiencing it? Would time still flow in the way we described it if there were no conscious beings to experience it? Do we experience it as flowing because it really is flowing, that our experience is a perception of temporal reality? Or do we want to say that this flow of time essentially involves us as conscious beings? This would mean that events move from my future, to my present and then on to my past. And the same would be true of your future, your present and your past.

If the flow of time essentially involves us as conscious beings, is it one flow that we all share in? Or do we each have our own time? Of course, we share a common time as part of our common shared human experience. "I'll meet you tomorrow at 10:00AM" only makes sense if we share a common time that includes both of our "tomorrow at 10:00AM" moments. And yet do we not experience time differently? For me the time went by fast while for you it dragged on. But doesn't this confuse our experience of time with time itself? But how can we think about time except as we experience it? Let us then (for now) consider time as it relates to us.

In the second view *we move through time*. On the first view events flow past us; we are as it were stationary. On the second view it is each person who moves through time. You proceed from your beginning to your childhood, your later years, and your present moment. From the present moment you move into your future. Here the river is our moving in time.

But don't all things move through time in this way? They start at their beginning, pass through their past, exist in the present and then continue into their future. The difference is that human beings not only undergo this movement through time but also experience it. As each of us gets older we realize that our past existence, what we've already had in our lives is steadily growing and our future existence, what's left of our lives is constantly shrinking. We realize that our death is approaching. Doesn't this make time something eminently real? We have only a certain amount of it left in our lives. How much do we have left? Will we use it profitably?

Most of us I think don't want to know how much time we have left. It may be less than we think. Why don't we want to know? Surely it is an important fact. Don't we want to know what is important? Why is this case different? Are we perhaps in denial here?

We noted a moment ago that you proceed from your beginning to later years and then to the present. But when is your beginning? Is at birth? Or is it earlier, so that it includes time in your mother's womb? Is it true to say, "I was once a baby in my mother's womb"?

Are the first and second points of view on the flow of time compatible with each other? Each by itself seems to be true to our lived experience. But now consider both together, lay them side by side. The flow of time is in opposite directions. In the first it goes from future to past; in the second it goes from past to future. How can both be true together? If I first tell you I'm now travelling from New York City to Boston and then tell you I'm now travelling from Boston to New York, you'll probably think I've made a U-turn. That would be fine. But if I insist it's one and the same journey you will say it can't be both; one of my statements must be false. Why doesn't the same apply to the flow of time? If time flows from future to past (first) how can it also flow from past to future (second)? Can we say that events flow in one direction and we go in the opposite direction? Are there two realities that flow when we say that time flows? If not, what is the flow of time?

[2] IS THERE A PRESENT MOMENT WITHOUT US?

In both the first and the second points of view above, time seems to be seen as relating to us. Thus, in the second point of view we move through time; clearly this refers to us. And in the first point of view, the flow of events from the future through the present and on into the past, it is our present moment that is meant by "the present." *Is there also a present moment without us?* Is there time without us? Or does it exist only for us? Some people think so.

But don't we want to say that one ice age came before another, and perhaps lasted twice as long? Doesn't that involve time? Surely if time is real now, and if the reality of time is its flow, then time was real and flowed back then. But there was no present moment back then that was "our present moment." Shall we then say there was simply a present moment, existing in its own right even without anyone there to experience it? Shall we say that there is always a real, objective present moment, an "objective now"? Suppose we say there is. Is it this objective "now" moving through time which really constitutes the second point of view, from the past through the present and on into the future? *Is there an objective now without us?*

If there is, isn't it a strange being, a "now" that no one experiences? If there is not, if it is only "our now" that constitutes the flow of time, how can we account for time as flowing before there were any human beings on this earth? Was there time then that didn't flow?

[3] TIME AS NOT FLOWING

Time flows. Or does it? Is the idea of time flowing correct, especially the image of time as a river? Many people think so. Yet many philosophers have seriously questioned it, even denied it, calling the flow of time a myth. Here are some reasons why.

(1) *Future events don't exist.* This applies particularly to the first view. You can't attend a party that only will exist; if it isn't going on right now in the present you can't attend. Future existence doesn't count as real existence. But if future events don't exist how then can they move through time? How can they be moving towards us?

Chapter 9: What is Time?

(2) If time flows like a river, *how fast does it flow*? Does it even make any sense to ask this question? If we do, don't we need a second order of time by which to answer our question of how fast time flows? And then how fast does that second order of time flow? We need a third order for that. And then we need a fourth order, and so on and on, an infinite regress. But if don't ask this question, if we say it can't be asked without getting us into the absurdity of an infinite regress, can we still say that time flows? It doesn't seem to flow like a river. In what sense can we still say that it flows? Or maybe it doesn't?

(3) A river can be *slowed down or speeded up*. Can this be true of time? Movement in time can be slowed down or speeded up, as in the case of a car; and our sense of time passing can seem slower or faster. But can any of this be applied to time itself? Does this make any sense?

(4) We can think of the flow of the river being *stopped altogether*, as by a dam. We may say "time stands still" but what do we mean by this? Do we perhaps mean that everything, but time stands still? Do we mean that changes have ceased? Can any sense be attached to the idea that time itself stands still? There are three things one might say: (i) time exists with changes; (ii) time exists without changes; (iii) time itself ceases to exist; it stands still. Here (i) is the actual reality and (ii) might be a theoretical possibility, but (iii) seems utterly impossible. Don't we think time itself could never stand still? Aren't we convinced that, no matter what, time will continue to exist; that it will never cease or stand still? Thus, it seems that time cannot be like a river because a river may cease to flow, but time could never cease to flow. Doesn't this mean that time doesn't flow like a river?

(5) On the second view it is each person who moves through time. You proceed from your beginning to your present moment and from there you move into your future. But *do you really move into the future*? If you, do it would seem that at some point you get there, you arrive. But do you ever arrive in the future? Aren't you always in the present? Isn't it always now, today, never tomorrow? What is the second view then? Do we move towards things that are now future but will

become present? Do we move towards them (second view)? Or do they move towards us (first view)? Does anything "move" at all? Does time flow like a river?

(6) Perhaps the whole idea of trying to explain time as a movement such as a river is basically misguided. Doesn't *movement already presuppose time*? Movement means change in time. The car moves at 55 miles per hour; an hour is a unit of time. If we don't already grasp the idea of time, what sense could we make of the car moving? For it to move means it goes across a certain distance of space (55 miles) in a certain amount of time (60 minutes). Thus, we must already understand time in order to understand movement. We seem to have things backwards: the river image doesn't explain time; time explains the river image. Perhaps time is too basic a reality to be explainable by an image as simple as a flowing river.

[4] TWO BASIC WAYS OF SEEING TIME

Thus, there are problems with seeing time as flowing, especially like a river but perhaps in other ways as well. Fortunately, time can also be seen in a very different way. That is, there are two fundamentally different ways of seeing time:

- **Events in time can be ordered dynamically**, as the river of time flowing past us or as our movement through time from our past, through our present and into our future.
- **Events in time can also be ordered statically**, like beads on a string eternally fixed in their location, related to each other in terms of before and after and simultaneous.

To illustrate the latter: in American history the Revolutionary War came before the Civil War. This is now true, has always been true and will always be true; it is simply and timelessly true, like the truth that 2+2 equals 4. Here there is no flowing of time; there is just a constant and static relation between events. My mother's birth came before my birth; my birth comes before my death. This is time; it is part of the essence of time; yet there is no flow, no movement.

These two ways of ordering time are the stuff of much of the discussion of time among philosophers. They have been given labels:

- ***The A-series: time as ordered dynamically.*** For example, events moving from the future, becoming briefly present, and then moving into the past, and continuously moving further and further into the more and more distant past.
- ***The B-series: time as ordered statically like beads on a string.*** Event x occurs earlier than event y. And event x occurs simultaneously with event z. There is no flow of time.

In the A-series what is now future will become present then past. Events change their temporal location. And statements about them change their truth value. "The birthday party is tomorrow"; if that is true today it will be false tomorrow and every day thereafter. In contrast, in the B-series events never change their temporal location. The birth of Bach is before the birth of Mozart which is before the birth of Beethoven. This is always true; it is timelessly true even though it is about events in time.

These two ways of ordering time: Is one fundamental and the other derived from it? If so which one is fundamental? Or perhaps they are equally basic, neither fundamental to the other.

Does time flow? Doesn't it seem to? And yet, aren't there huge difficulties in seeing it as flowing? That's one reason time is a source of wonder.

[5] SPACE AND TIME

Space and time are often spoken about together. And they do go together. "I'll meet you in the park (space location) at 3:00PM (time location)." Indeed, time is sometimes seen as the fourth dimension of "spacetime." Yet they are very different. We can see this -- as well as raise some interesting questions and note a similarity -- by focusing on the two terms that characterize where we are: we exist *here* and we exist *now*.

1. We can pick our here, simply by moving around; we cannot pick our now, that is a given.
2. We are all together at the same now; but we are mostly in different here's.
3. There is no here without consciousness; is there a now where there is no consciousness?
4. Here is relative to each of us; there is no objective here that exists in itself. Is the now also relative? Or is it objective? That is, is there a present moment really occurring now whether anyone realizes it or not? Was there a series of nows during ice ages when no one was there to experience them?
5. Both the here and the now have indefinite boundaries, or perhaps no boundaries. It is now 4:35PM; it is now Wednesday; it is now August; it is now 2014. And similarly, I'm here at my computer; I'm here in this room; I'm here in this house; here in this town; here in this county; here in this country; here on planet earth; here in the solar system.

[6] THE PAST

Is the past real? No, the past is gone, no more, and therefore not real. You cannot attend yesterday's party; it's over, it's no longer a reality. Remember that house you once lived in: it's been demolished; it no longer exists; it's a "past house," not a real, present house.

Is the past real? Of course, it is! My birth: is that a reality? If it's not it means I wasn't born! My birth is immensely real; without it I wouldn't be here now. But, of course, it's a past event; so past events have a reality; hence, the past must have a reality. So many more examples could be given. What is history? It is of course a study of the past. A subject of such immense importance as history cannot be about nothing. It studies something, the past; therefore, the past is real. And every other human subject – math, physics, chemistry, psychology, sociology and so many more – has a past history of discoveries, developments and theories without which it wouldn't exist now. Nations, religions, cultures, etc. all have a past.

It is helpful to make a distinction between two possible claims:

(A) *"Past things do not exist."*

(B) *"The past does not exist."*

Statement (A) is partly true and partly false. True, the demolished house does not exist anymore. But, of course, many other past things still do exist. In fact, virtually everything that now exists including the house you now live in has a past existence; it came into existence in the past. Present things would not exist, would not be real, if they didn't have a past. The partial truth of (A) can then be seen as meaning, "Some past things do not exist now."

Some past things do not exist now. That's the key point: they don't exist *now*. The claim of statement (B) that the past is unreal seems to be based on the assumption that only present existence is real existence. The past doesn't have present existence; that shouldn't be a surprise. There are different ways a thing can exist, can be real. A word is something very real; a mean word spoken by another causes pain; a word of love gives joy. The reality of a word is very different from the reality of a stone; and there are many other similar examples. Can we say this: both present existence and past existence are real; they are just different as realities?

The past certainly appears to us as being very real. First, there is the objective existence of all past times, all past events, stretching all the back to the beginning of time, or infinitely. (Which is it?) This includes the many, many times before my birth: the Civil War, Ancient Greece, the ice ages, etc. Second, there is what is of the greatest importance for me: my past. Much of it I don't remember, such as my birth, my early bonding with my mother, the moment I came to realize that humankind comes in two forms, male and female, and which of these I am.

What is striking for bringing out the reality of the past as it applies to me are the vivid memories of past experiences that I carry in my consciousness. Here truly is a source of wonder. I now remember the summer house in Wallingford, Vermont, where I spent the summer of 1948. I remember it vividly; I have a picture of the house in my consciousness. I have it now. But the reality that I picture now before me is something past. I remember the past time spent there. How is it possible for me to reach from the present into the past? How is memory of past experiences possible? We can only wonder! But what should be clear from this is that what I remember must in some way be real for me in order for me to have a valid memory of it, as opposed to an illusion or simply the workings of my imagination.

Here is a final point of reflection. Don't we at every moment live out of the past and into the future? To see this try imagining a present moment that doesn't come out of the past, that exists entirely on its own as a brand new beginning. Isn't this impossible? At every moment we live on our experiences of the past; not only what we remember but also much else, such as all the things we have learned and how we came to be socialized to be the way we are now. Isn't this clear and evident testimony to the reality of the past?

[7] THE FUTURE

Is the future real? Isn't it real at least in some way? Don't we live into the future? At every moment our conscious life is future-directed. I start a project, small or large, anticipating that I will finish it: in the future. I start a sentence anticipating that I will finish it: in the future. I take my bags home from the airport because I will want to have what's in them: in the future. Anticipating, planning, hoping and fearing; all these look to the future.

A friend asks me, "Do you have some time?" I reply, "Yes, I have some time." What I have is future time, certainly not past time. What I have is precious and is appreciated by my friend. Doesn't this show that future time is somehow real and so the future is also real?

The idea, "Yes, I have some time" is a bright and cheerful viewpoint on my future. But there is also a dark and somber one. As we get older our past existence, what we have already had in our lives is constantly growing; and our future existence, what is left of our lives, is constantly shrinking. Yes, I have a future, but it is one that keeps getting smaller and smaller. In this frightening way, isn't the reality of the future vividly impressed on us?

In the image of the river of time, future events are seen as being ahead of us, first in a distant future, then in a nearer future, then in a very near future; then becoming present; then slipping into the past. For this to make any sense the future must have some kind of reality.

Chapter 9: What is Time?

We make predictions about future events, such as who will win an election, what team will win a game. Consider those that turn out to be correct; they are true statements. What is it that makes them true? Isn't the only answer that it is the reality of the future event predicted?

Is the future real? There are at least two points of view under which the future seems not to be real. First, future events haven't happened yet. Doesn't saying "haven't happened yet" imply "haven't happened" at all? And doesn't saying that imply saying they are not real? Can the future be real if future events are not real?

Second, is the future open? Consider deliberation. For example, I have two job offers, A and B. I weigh the pros and cons of each; I deliberate which one to accept. This means I envision two possible futures, one with my holding job A and one with my holding job B. To say that both futures are possible is to say that the future is open between them. Isn't it clear that deliberation makes sense only to the extent that the future is open? If it isn't, if it's already fixed and therefore inevitable that one course of events will occur, I cannot deliberate about choosing one of these courses of events. If I believe that deliberation makes sense, that it is sometimes up to me to choose one possible future over another, then I must believe that the future is open. But to say that the future is open seems to be saying that it is empty with respect to the two possibilities. And to say it is empty seems to imply non-being, or that it is not real.

On the other hand, some things are fixed and inevitable; they are beyond our control, and in this respect the future is not open. Is that part of it therefore real? Is the future partly real and partly not real? Can the real and the not real co-exist in one realm, the future?

Is the future real? It seems hard to give a clear-cut answer to this. Future events haven't happened, so they seem not to be real. Yet we can plan for them; so maybe in some sense they are real. Many things that will exist in the future exist already now; if they didn't exist now, they wouldn't exist in the future either. Other future things don't exist now; they will come into being only in the future. Future events and future things are one part of the question.

The other part is the future itself or the future as such. What does it mean to say that is real? Or that it is unreal? When it is conceived as a kind of empty container that will be filled with events, is it unreal because it is empty? Or is it real because it is a container? If this container didn't exist it couldn't be filled with events as the future unfolds. And isn't the future all too real when seen as my future, the time I have remaining in this life before it ends at death? Here it seems rather that it is the absence of a future that lacks reality and the presence of it that has reality. Is the future real? It is certainly a cause for wonder.

[8] THE PAST AND THE FUTURE COMPARED

The past and the future are often spoken of together as if they were two similar realms, like two islands or two rivers. But a closer look through the lenses of philosophical wonder lets us see that they are in fact very different from each other. To bring this out let us note some of the asymmetries between the past and the future:

1. We have knowledge of the past: much of our own past life, what we have experienced during our life, the history of the world. We have nothing comparable for the future, only certain beliefs, speculations, hopes and fears.
2. I can remember some of my past experiences, such as my summertime in Vermont; I have nothing comparable for the future.
3. I know the length of time of my past; I don't know this for my future.
4. Much of my past I have forgotten; there is nothing comparable for my future.
5. My past is essential for my present being; if I wasn't born (in the past) I wouldn't exist now; again, there is nothing comparable for the future.
6. I live out of my past, my past experiences, what I've learned, etc.; I also live into the future in anticipations, and in some respects these two are comparable. But they are also radically different in that the living out of the past is essential for my present experiences, while the corresponding living into the future is not; I could die at any moment!
7. A huge difference is that the past is fixed, unalterable, while the future is to some extent open, what we implicitly assume whenever we deliberate about what to do in the future.

8. The past is lost and gone, apparently never to be retrieved. It seems to be this in its very essence and is thus necessarily lost and gone. This does not apply to the future, which in its essence is what awaits us, and is therefore the opposite of lost and gone. In some respects, there may be loss in the future. First, I may lose a particular possible future, as when adversity strikes; for example, the loss of a limb means the loss of a future career as an athlete. Second, and much more dramatically and tragically, the moment of my death means the loss of all my future as it would have been had I not died at that moment.
9. In so far as both past and future represent what is not, there is an ultimate, irreducible difference between the no longer of the loss of the past, and the not yet of the future that lies ahead.

[9] THE PRESENT: NOW!

Is the present real? Of course, it is! It is the past and the future where doubts can be raised: the past is gone; it is no more and so in a sense is not real; and the future is not yet and so again in a sense is not real. But the present: that's where we are now! Still, we must raise the big questions: when is now? What is the present? How long does it last? Does it last at all?

This year is the present year. As I write this it is 2014; 2013 is a past year and 2015 is a future year, so 2014 is the present. But most of 2014 has already gone by and so it is really past and not present; and some of it is still to come and so it is really future and not present. August is the present month; but again part of it is past and gone and the rest of it is future and not yet. The same is true of this week, this day, this hour, this minute; in each case we have the familiar idea: part of it is past and gone and is therefore not the present, and the rest is future and not yet and again therefore is not the present. We can continue but we will see the same thing, for even the present second has tiny parts, milliseconds. We then come to mathematically significant lengths of time, but not to anything we can actually experience. Whatever unit of time we take will always have its past and its future, with the present squeezed out between them, and so reduced to a mere boundary line between the past that is no more and the future that is not yet.

Is the present then only a boundary line? Such a line seems to be a mere abstraction, lacking the full reality of something concrete. You can live in a particular country, or you can live in the neighboring country; but you can't live in the abstract boundary line that marks where the one country ends and the other one begins. Don't we live in the now? But does this mean we live in a boundary line? The now, the present moment seems to have a fullness of reality that a mere abstraction like a boundary line doesn't have.

What is the now? We can't catch it with our mind; it constantly slips away as we try to pin it down to see what it is. Yet, in terms of time, it seems to be the most important thing. The past is important because it leads up to and makes possible the now. And the future is significant because we are always living into it and doing so from the now. If the now loses its grip on reality, how would that affect the past and future? Could time be real if only the past and the future had real concrete existence, with the present reduced to a mere abstraction?

Perhaps we can conceive of the now as in some way reaching into and including the immediately preceding past and the immediately following future. Try to think about this while listening to a piece of music. What is it that you hear? Isn't it somehow a small set of notes just past and anticipating similar notes just ahead, the latter especially if you know the piece well?

Is the present, the now real? To be real it seems that it must have some sort of temporal extension; and for this to be so it must somehow reach backwards and forwards, into the past and into the future. And if that is so, both the past and the future would seem to take on a new look. It would no longer be quite true that the past is gone: part of it would be here in the present. And it would no longer be quite true that the future is not yet: part of it would be here in the present.

Is the present real? One of the strongest factors speaking in favor of its absolute reality is that we so often want to hold on to it and not have it taken away by it slipping into the past. Many years ago, I brought my father and mother to Logan Airport in Boston. They had been with us for a visit and now it was time for them to go back to their home in Austria. I was very close to them and hated to see them leave, though I knew it was necessary. I remember the clock saying 7:00PM; they would be boarding at 7:30. We had a half hour; I wanted to hold on to that half hour. Then it was 7:10, 20 minutes; 7:20, 10 minutes; 7:30, no time left, time to leave and board the plane. What was I trying to hold onto? The time with my parents. But that was an extension of time, not a tiny, short moment of now. Was the whole of the original 30 minutes a now? In some way it was. But if we say this we are back to an extended now, an hour, a day, a week, a month, a year. We examined this and found it not to be the now, the present, but always a two-part extension of time divided between a past that is gone and a future that is not yet.

So, what is this now that we live in, that we often try to hold on to, though we know we can't? Is it a mere boundary? No, for it is the concrete lived moment of experience in time. Does it then include some of the past? If so, how much of the past? And is there a boundary line between the past that is part of the present and the past that is not, that is really past, passed and gone? Parallel questions arise in regard to the future: how much of it; is there a boundary line? Try as we may, we cannot seem to get an intellectual grip on the now, the present. And yet it is something we experience at every moment. And we have been doing so for our whole life. Why can't we answer these seemingly simply questions: what is the present, the now? How long does it last? Does it last at all? If not, what does it do?

We try to hold on to the now, but we can't; it slips away into the past. What we seem to want is a full now. It is sometimes suggested that eternity is such a now, one that really stays and doesn't go away into the past. It is a now where the Logan Airport clock stays at 7:00 and does not proceed mercilessly to 7:30 and signal that the beautiful time with my parents is over, finished, taken away from me. It is a full now where all that I experience is packed into a single moment rather being scattered and spread out over long periods of time.

But if that Logan Airport clock really stays at 7:00, and stays there forever, won't you get bored after a while? Of course, I don't mean an eternity at an airport! The significant point here is that eternity is in its essence a perfect fullness of time while boredom is the opposite of this, emptiness. Time with persons you love and enjoying beauty are examples of fullness of time.

Perhaps one could simply say that it is the essence of time that it passes. If we try to divide time into separate parts – past, present and future – we will run into the insoluble problem of trying to capture the now. We cannot capture it because it is fleeting; time passes, it is a smooth movement. To exist in time means to experience reality dynamically. It is hard to put this into words, because our language and ways of thinking are rooted in what is fixed, permanent and not moving. Time is precisely not that, and so we have a hard time understanding it, and our categories fail us. What I'm suggesting here is a turn in our thoughts in a different direction, an exploration along different lines. I think this is what French philosopher Henri Bergson was trying to get at.[2] I think he's on the right track. Perhaps we think in terms of the not-fleeting because we have a deep, inner longing for the eternal; if so, could it be because this is our true home?

[10] SOME THEORIES ABOUT TIME

Another source of wonder is that philosophers and scientists have come up with so many different and conflicting views about time, something which in itself is so familiar and seemingly clear and obvious. Their theories center on a number of key issues and questions:

First, there is the static-dynamic issue about the nature of time. This has its roots in a paper by J. E. McTaggart, "The Unreality of Time."[3] How could anyone deny something as obvious and clearly given as time? Here, in a nutshell, is McTaggart's argument. He is the one who introduced the two series about how time may be ordered that we saw earlier:

- **The A-series: time as ordered dynamically.** For example, events moving from the future, becoming briefly present, and then moving into the past, and continuously moving further and further into the more and more distant past.
- **The B-series: time as ordered statically like beads on a string.** Event x occurs earlier than event y. And event x occurs simultaneously with event z. There is no flow of time.

---

[2] See his *Time and Free Will: An Essay on the Immediate Data of Consciousness* (New York: 1910, 1960), Chap. II.

[3] *Mind* 17, 1908, 457-74.

Chapter 9: What is Time?

McTaggart argues (a) that time is in its nature dynamic and therefore needs the A-series so that without this series there could be no time; but (b) that the A-series is logically incoherent and so cannot exist. The logical conclusion is that time does not exist! Philosophers have come to the rescue of time and tried to answer McTaggart's challenge. Two basic theories developed out of this. One is the dynamic theory which defends the logical coherence of the A-series and thereby saves time; it includes both the A-series and the B-series.

The other is the static theory which agrees with McTaggart that the A-series is incoherent but differs from him in claiming that the analysis of time doesn't need the A-series; it needs only the B-series. It essentially depicts time as being like space. On this theory, "there is no moving present, and there is no flow of time….Events are not intrinsically past, present or future, and they do not change with respect to being past, present and future…The static view denies that there is a present at all."[4] That is, events are not as such or in themselves past, present or future; they are related only in being earlier or later or simultaneous with each other. We say Chicago is west of New York; but there is no such property as "westness"[5]; so too, it is claimed, there is no such property as being past or being future or being present. Events simply occur before and after and simultaneously. And just as there is no absolute "here" so too there is no absolute "now"; there is no time that is really now just as there is no place that is really here. Both the here and the now are purely relative to different persons. As noted, time is like space: "time and space are analogous. Space is tenseless and so is time."[6]

Does the static theory do justice to the nature of time as we experience it? Doesn't it fall short in at least three ways: the *now*, the *past and future*, and the *flowing or passing* of time?

Isn't there a present moment that really exists *now*? Isn't that moment, the "now" unique and absolute in the way that the "here" where I now happen to be is not? Isn't it so that there are many "here's" all relative to where different people

---

[4] From Keith Seddon, *Time: A Philosophical Treatment* (Kent, UK and New York: Croom Helm, 1987), 7.

[5] Ibid., see 33.

[6] Ibid., 62.

happen to be, while all of us exist in the one "now" that is a unique moment in the course of time?

Aren't *past and future* radically different? The past is fixed, the future is largely open.

Isn't it clear that time *flows or passes* at least in some sense? Perhaps there are problems with taking the image of the river too literally. But consider these two typical experiences. You want to go for a swim, but the pool closes at 8:00PM. It's now 7:00. If you don't go now or very soon you will miss your chance to have a swim because the hour from 7:00 to 8:00 will have gone by; it will have *passed*. You are spending an hour with a person you love; it has just begun. Before you know it the time will be over; the time will have *passed*.

Perhaps we cannot solve all the logical problems associated with the dynamic view of time. Even so, couldn't we just accept the clearly given of time as involving the *now*, the *past and future*, and the *flowing or passing* of time and make it an object of wonder? Do we really need a theory?

Perhaps one of the problems with some theories is that they take things like the flowing or passing of time too literally along the lines of a flowing river. Perhaps the reality is that time flows or passes in some deeper, ultimate sense, one that cannot be captured by our familiar images such as the flow of a river. The flow of time would be the ultimate, the original reality. The flow of a river would be a kind of copy or imitation, or a distant reflection of it. We would explain the flow of the river by reference to the flow of time, not the flow of time by trying to explain it by appeal to the flow of a river.

Second, there is the past-present-future reality issue. We have seen that there are reasons both to affirm and to doubt the real existence of the past and the future. This leads to a number of different possibilities:

1. The Block Universe, standard view: all three, past-present-future, are real. And they are essentially the same. This corresponds to the Static Theory discussed above.
2. The Block Universe, alternative view: again, all three parts of time are real but there is an essential difference between past and future, and each of

these and the present. This view is one version of the Dynamic Theory; it is suggested by our analysis in earlier sections.

3. The Growing Universe: only the past and present are real; the future is not; it is an empty space into which we are all moving. This is another version of the Dynamic Theory.
4. Futurism: only the present and the future are real; the past is not. The past is gone and so it is unreal but the future is where we are heading and so it is important and real.
5. Presentism: only the present is real; the past and the future are both unreal.

Theories 3-5 all affirm the reality of the present but deny either the past or the future or both. But is it really possible for any of these three parts to exist without the other two? Isn't it rather that time cannot really exist at all unless all three really exist? That is, the present can only exist at the end of the past and at the beginning of the future.

Third, is time something in itself or is it only a set of relations among events? This is the issue between the substantival theory and the relational theory. A good test case for deciding between them is this: could there be time without events? For example, could 5 minutes go by with absolutely nothing happening? Could a year go by with nothing happening? What would be the difference between them? We wouldn't know of such a time vacuum; could it still exist?

Fourth, there is the issue between those who believe in Einstein's Relativity Theory and those who question it. Einstein's theory conflicts with our ordinary experience of time in three main ways: (1) It denies that time always flows at the same rate; it claims that as you move faster time slows down for you. (2) It denies that one can speak of time as a reality in itself; it claims that there is only a four-dimensional whole, "time-space," and that this has no absolute existence but is relative to different frames of reference. (3) It denies absolute simultaneity; whether two events are simultaneous or not will be judged differently by two observers and neither of them is objectively correct or incorrect; there is no truth to the matter, it's relative to frames of reference.

Fifth, did time have a beginning or does it stretch back infinitely into the past? Both are hard to imagine. If time had a beginning one is still tempted to ask what was happening before then; but, of course, that would be a meaningless question. If time stretches back infinitely does this include some empty time? (See the third issue.) Or would all of it contain actual events? Could there be an infinite number of actual realities? There are decisive objections to this idea.

Sixth, is time objective or subjective? Objective time exists in any case, whether we experience it or not. Subjectivism says time is in us; it is merely how we experience the world. Yet we all exist in the same time world; "I'll meet you at 11:00," the real, objective 11:00, not your subjective one or mine. The ice ages occurred at a certain time long ago, before any of us were around; they existed in the real, objective time. A piece of music exists essentially in objective time; a time all of us share; a definite and objective amount of time, say 30 minutes.

Clearly time is an amazing source of wonder! If only we had more of it to use for wonder.

CHAPTER 10
CAUSALITY

[1] WHAT IS A CAUSE?

We often look for the causes of things. Why did the plane crash? That is, what was the cause of its crashing? We could also ask of another plane why it didn't crash: what causes a normal plane to be able to fly? Why doesn't it fall down like most other heavy objects? What caused this strange rash on my arm? How can I lose weight? What could cause me to lose weight? These are all practical questions that we are all familiar with, that we ask all the time.

But in addition to the practical question in the form, *what is the cause of x?* there is also another deeper question, *what is a cause?* This is the philosophical question, *what is the nature of causality?* Or, *what does it mean to say that one thing is the cause of another?* It seems like it should be easy enough to answer this question since we are familiar with examples of causality all around us all the time; we shall see. Pressing down on the piano keys causes the music to be played. Practicing playing the piano causes you to become more skilled. Certain atmospheric conditions cause rain to fall. The hammer pounding the nail causes it to go into the wood. The sharp knife pressing down on the piece of meat causes it to be cut.

HUME'S THEORY OF CAUSALITY

What is the nature of causality? What does it mean to say that one thing is the cause of another? The philosopher David Hume offered us an answer to these questions. Let's examine it and see if it squares with our experience. Here is Hume's analysis of the nature of causality:

Causes and effects are changes in the world that have we seen as constantly conjoined. Press down on the knife and the meat is cut; the second always follows the first, they always go together. Causality is regularity: the cause is regularly followed by the effect. Causality means constant conjunction: they are always joined together. One event always follows another; that is the nature of causality.

Is that all there is to it? Isn't there a connection between cause and effect? Doesn't the cause somehow necessitate the effect? Beheading is always followed by death. It *is* followed? Or it *must be* followed? Hume will answer as follows:

All I can ever see or observe is regular sequence or constant conjunction. I see that death always does follow beheading. I can't see any necessity. I can't see any connection. What is necessity supposed to look like? What is the connection supposed to look like? They are nowhere to be found in the world out there. What you take to be necessity and connection is only in us. When we have seen events of type x constantly followed by events of type y and we then we see a particular x, we come to expect to see also a particular y that follows it. As we witness a beheading, we expect the poor person to die immediately afterwards. That's because this type of event, this x (beheading) is always followed by another, a y (death). Now we could go into more detail and examine exactly what happens in the body after beheading. But all we will find is regular sequence. When the brain no longer gets oxygen certain other events follow in the body, one of them being that state we call death. Look as hard and long as you like, use any scientific instrument you can get your hands on, you will never find those elusive properties you call necessity and connection. All events are separate and loose; none are connected.

Does Hume have a point? Surely, he does. Has he seen something? Surely, he has. Consider the following experiences. I have a headache; I take pill x and the headache is gone. I repeat this; *after* I take pill x my headache is gone, every time. All of Hume's ideas are verified here: regularity or constant conjunction. And after taking x I come to *expect* the headache to be gone. I conclude that x is the cause of the headache being gone. But what do I really know about this causal story? Do I know anything more than the Hume ideas just mentioned: regularity and expectation? So, isn't that what constitutes the causal relation? I find that when I put my hand in the flame of a candle it burns. Why should this be? What more do I know besides our Humean ideas, regularity-expectation? I eat what I call a banana; every time I do so I get a certain taste in my mouth. I eat an orange and get a different taste. For each item there is a regularity of taste sensations. It is invariable. The orange never tastes like the banana and the banana never tastes like the orange. What do we have but regularity-expectation?

Isn't there more than regularity in the world? Hume challenges us: if there is more what is it? Many people would say there is a *connection* between cause and effect and a *necessity* in the causal relation; that given the cause the effect doesn't just occur but must occur. But Hume will challenge us: can you see this connection? Can you see this necessity? Can you touch them? Can you perceive them with any of your other senses? Can you reason to them? Don't we have to admit that we can't do any of these things? How then do we know that connection and necessity are parts of the causal relation? Perhaps they're not; perhaps Hume is correct in claiming that in the world there is only regularity; and that the only other part of the causal picture is merely in us, a subjective factor; that given our past experience of regularity we come to expect the next case to be similar.

Surely Hume has seen something. What he says is certainly an invitation to wonder. Before hearing of Hume, didn't we take causality for granted? Didn't we assume it's just obvious that there is a connection between cause and effect? And that the effect doesn't just follow the cause as a matter of fact but that it must do so? Hume gets us to see that things are not so simple and obvious and easy. Hume is surely correct that causality is something interesting and problematic; but is he correct in the theory he adopts as a result of his reflections on causality?

A KEY DISTINCTION

We shall have to test Hume's theory, in part by looking at the consequences of adopting it to see if it is correct. For now, a key distinction needs to be made:

What the plausible story above shows is that we often come to know what effects *specific causes* have through observing regularity. But this tells us nothing about the real question, which concerns what a cause is, the *nature of causality itself*. If Hume were merely telling us that we come to know what causes what by observing regularity it wouldn't be anything very dramatic. He would hardly have become famous because of this. Rather Hume is offering us a theory about what it is that constitutes the causal relation: it is nothing more than regularity. Is that all it is? Or is there something more? If so what is it? Hume says he doesn't know but perhaps we can figure it out by reflecting on our immediate experience.

The plausible story also reveals that we often don't understand why a given cause has the particular effect it has. Why should fire cause pain? What connects the flame we see with the pain we feel? Isn't Hume correct when he says we can't see any connection, we can't see any reason why this should be so? But the fact that I don't understand a *particular causal relation* does not mean that I don't understand something about the *causal relation as such*, the nature of causality. I don't understand what this cause is. But don't I understand what causality is?

TESTING HUME'S THEORY

Is Hume's theory correct? To test it consider an experiment in imagination. I have a charm bracelet and whenever I wear it while playing the games at the casino I win. And whenever I don't wear it I lose all my money. Just for fun, and because I am a philosopher more interested in Hume on causality than in winning money, I wear it about half the time and don't wear it the other half. I continue this for 20 years. For all the 2,000 trips *with* the bracelet I win big; for the 2,000 trips *without* it, I lose all the money I brought. If I told you this story with a straight face you surely wouldn't believe me! Why not? It would be too much of a coincidence, far more than what we know is actually possible. You do it twice with and twice without, and the results are as described above; that's a story we might be able to accept. But if you start adding to it we will warn you not to push your luck. We will stop believing you long before your 2,000 plus 2,000 trips. We can refer to this as the *incredible coincidence* idea.

But now let us reflect on this story with Hume's eyes. Doesn't it all fit into his analysis of what causality means? Each wearing of the bracelet is followed by a win and each not wearing it is followed by a loss. We have a perfect regularity, a constant conjunction. So, what's the difference between the actual world as Hume describes it and the bizarre sequences of our bracelet-gambling story? In each we have mere regularity, one thing just following another, with no connection between events and no necessity. Where is the difference? The way Hume describes our world of "cause" and "effect" and the way the casino events unfold are exactly the same: one thing follows another with no connection and no necessity.

What is the moral of the casino story? If that story represents an impossible account of how things happen, and if another story (Hume's) says essentially the same thing, then doesn't that other story also represent an impossible account of how things happen? Doesn't the comparison to the casino story show that Hume's theory doesn't do justice to reality? Actually, there are several closely related even overlapping points that come to mind from the casino story, as well as other things from our experience, beginning with incredible coincidence:

1. ***Rejection of incredible coincidence.*** You let go of a rock and it falls to the ground. You repeat this, over and over and over. It happens every time. Hume says it is a mere constant conjunction; there is no causal force that makes it happen (gravity). Really?
2. ***Explaining regularity.*** Hume says causality is constant conjunction or regularity. He explains causality by regularity. Isn't it just the other way around: we explain regularity by causality? How else could the amazing and universal regularity we see be explained or accounted for except as representing causal connections and causal necessity?
3. ***Scientific laws.*** They tell us not merely what does happen but what must happen. Rocks must fall and water must freeze when the temperature drops. But Hume can give us only what does happen. A scientific law allows us to make inferences; given the weakness of the dam and the strength of the current you can infer that the dam must break. But if we have only a series of events that have occurred regularly in the past we could not make any valid inferences. We need the necessary connection that Hume denies.
4. ***Induction.*** Don't touch that stove; it's hot and it will burn you! How do you know that it will burn you? All you know is that in the past such stoves have burned you. What allows you to make an inference from a past regularity to a future regularity? Why think that such an inference is valid? Without a causal connection it would seem that such inferences are not valid.

5. **Control.** You want to have control of your life. To drive your car you need to be able to control it. Turn the steering wheel left and the car goes left. Step on the left pedal and the car stops. Step on the right pedal and the car moves ahead. Without the assurance that these involve causal connections would you be confident that you have control of your car? If there is only regular sequence in the past, what assurance do you have that this regularity will continue in the future? If you don't then the next time you step on the brake the car might zoom ahead at full speed! How's that for control?

6. **Necessity.** Hume denied necessity in causality. Let go of a rock and it always falls. But suppose you deny this; you are surely not guilty of a logical contradiction as if you were to deny that 2+2=4. Here there is a logical necessity; 2+2 must equal 4, while it is not the case that the rock must fall in that sense. True, there is no logical necessity in causality in the way there is with 2+2=4. But surely there is another kind of necessity: causal necessity. The force of the hammer makes the nail sink into the wood; it necessitates this. Given the blow of the hammer the nail must sink in. This is the necessary connection which is part of the very essence of the causal relation. Hume rightly denied logical necessity in the causal relation; he wrongly concluded that there could be no other kind of necessity.

7. **Intelligibility.** Can we understand why a causal relation is what it is? Can we see why x must cause y or why the latter must be the effect of the former? Very often we cannot, a point Hume was fond of stressing. The small white pill makes my headache go away; we say it causes this change, but at least for most of us there is no intelligibility here, no seeing why it must do so. But there are other cases where we do see the necessary connection, why the cause must have the effect, this exact effect. The case of the two cogwheels provides the perfect example. Cogwheel A has 20 cogs, and it is attached to cogwheel B which has 10 cogs. One revolution of wheel A causes two revolutions of wheel B. We see that it does, and that it must do so; it could not be otherwise. Here we have a causal relation with full intelligibility; we understand why the effect must be as it is.

Through cases such as this we come to understand causality as such and can then apply this more generally to other cases as well. Another example of where we seem to be able to see why a cause has the particular effect it has, why it must have this effect, is the hammer-nail example. Don't we grasp the necessity here, that the nail must sink into the wood? Don't we grasp the connection between hammer action and nail result?

8. ***Does Hume contradict his own theory?*** His theory is that all events are loose and separate; there are no connections. He also says that observing a regularity in the past makes us expect a similar regularity in the future. A blow to the head is painful. As I see another one coming, I'm frightened; I expect pain again. What can this mean but that the experience of past blows to the head being painful causes me to expect pain in the future? And that the idea of such causing means the past experience produces the expectation of future pain, and that it is therefore connected to it? In practice, in his actual contact with reality Hume saw this clearly. Why then did he deny it in his theory?

[2] DOES EVERY EVENT REQUIRE A CAUSE?

Every event, every change, every coming into existence requires a cause. This is often called the Causal Principle. Is it true? Let us examine some possible replies to this question.

Yes, the causal principle is surely true. As we often say, things don't just happen; there is always a cause or a reason why they happen. You have a strange skin rash on your right arm. You go to your doctor; after carefully examining it and running some tests, he comes to you with his diagnosis: your rash is a most unusual one because it has no cause! Wouldn't you protest: doctor, you may not *know* what the cause is but surely there must *be* a cause? It may even be the case that it is impossible ever to determine what the cause is; but, again, don't we all clearly understand that there must be some cause? Must there not be something that produced this rash, that brought it about?

Yes, don't our reflections on how Hume's theory fails to do justice to reality as we know it from our immediate experience show that the causal principle must be true? What is missing in Hume is connection and necessity; and these are just the things the causal principle makes explicit. It states that every event must have a cause: necessity. And, of course, that cause, in order to be the cause of the effect must be connected to the effect: connection.

If it is true, how do we know it? Can we get it from experience? Doesn't experience merely tell us what causes what? What *does* cause what? But here we have necessity: that there *must be* some cause. Hume will say that experience never gives us necessity, only facts; never a *must* but always only a *that*. On this point isn't he correct? How then do we come to our understanding of the causal principle? Shall we say it is by our intellectual powers of insight? That we have the capacity to see not only that certain things are in fact the case, but that others must be the case? For example, we see by insight that if the angles of a triangle on a flat surface are equal the sides must also be equal, and vice versa. It cannot be otherwise.

If these reflections are correct, we could say that causality as connection and necessity is not something we *get from experience*, but something we *bring to experience*. At the beginning we often don't know what the cause is but we know that there must be some cause.

Despite all this there is occasionally some doubt about the causal principle. One area involves quantum mechanics where it is claimed that elementary particles move in ways that are uncaused. Their behavior is "indeterministic," meaning it is not "determined" by causal necessity. There is much discussion and controversy about this. One possibility often discussed is that we are unable to determine what the cause is but that this leaves open the possibility (even the necessity) that there is some cause; indeed, that there must be some cause even if we can never find it.

Another area where there is doubt about the validity of the causal principle is free will. If I freely choose to do x doesn't this mean that nothing caused me to do it? If something did cause my action wouldn't that imply necessity? And doesn't necessity mean the opposite of freedom? On the other hand, doesn't the denial of the causal principle mean the claim that some things "just happen"? And isn't there something strange, even irrational, in that claim?

In addition to the two replies considered so far (yes and doubts), let us look at a third possibility. Some people say the causal principle is not something that is either true or false but a guide or injunction to always look for a cause. It is a recommendation that we should always assume there is a cause and keep looking for it until we find it. Is this a reasonable position? Could it be a valid or useful guide if it were not also true? Suppose it was said that it is a useful guide *because* it is true? Its importance as a guide would be preserved; but we would also be returning to the first answer that says it is true.

Two key distinctions emerge from our analysis so far:

1. How we know this cause – how we know there must be some cause.
2. What this cause is – what causality as such is, what it is in its nature.

[3] MUST A CAUSE ALWAYS PRECEDE IT EFFECT?

It is often claimed that a cause must precede its effect in time. You catch a disease and then you feel sick. You hit the ball and then it sails out of the park for a home run. But does a cause always precede its effect? A car is pulling a trailer; they are locked tightly together so that as soon as the car moves the trailer also moves. Surely the motion of the car is the cause of the motion of the trailer. But don't they occur precisely at the same time? The car cannot move unless the trailer also moves; the trailer cannot move unless the car also moves. Isn't this a clear case of simultaneous causation? So, the cause need not precede the effect. Wonder!

Can the effect precede the cause, so that the effect comes first, and the cause comes after it? Can a cause work backwards in time? Interesting tales are spun around this idea. Suppose you decide to kill your grandmother. Why not if causes can work backwards? But if you kill your grandmother, she will not bear the child who is your mother; so you won't exist to do any causing, whether in the present or the past. Isn't the past forever fixed so it cannot be changed?

HUME AND THE QUESTION OF TEMPORAL ORDER

It is part of Hume's analysis of causation that the cause must precede the effect. Hume claims that it is part of the very meaning of a cause that it precedes its effect. Perhaps we can now see why he would say this. If cause and effect are constantly conjoined and we say only this, how could we ever distinguish between them? The hammer strikes the nail and the nail sinks into the wood. Why say the hammer motion is the cause and the nail sinking is the effect? Why not say the nail sinking is the cause and the hammer motion is the effect? The nail sinking is what causes the hammer motion. That's of course absurd, and Hume must have known it was absurd. But think carefully: what is Hume's reason why the order is not the way just described? Why isn't the nail sinking the cause and the hammer motion the effect? Is it really because of the time order, that the hammer motion has to come first? Isn't it rather because the hammer acts on the nail while the nail doesn't act on the hammer? Isn't it because the two events are connected in this way, that the hammer motion produces the nail sinking into the wood? But, of course, these are just the things Hume wants to deny. So, he has to find some other way of distinguishing cause and effect, and the temporal priority of cause over effect seems like a convenient way to do this.

But doesn't the car-trailer example refute this? The motion of the car and the motion of the trailer are tightly linked. Consider each of these relations:

- The motion of the car is necessary for the motion of the trailer.
- The motion of the trailer is necessary for the motion of the car.
- The motion of the car is sufficient for the motion of the trailer.
- The motion of the trailer is sufficient for the motion of the car.

In short, neither can move without the other also moving. The motion of one is both necessary and sufficient for the motion of the other. How then are we to tell them apart and say which one is the cause and which one is the effect? Hume would like to say the cause comes first in time; but we have seen that in fact it doesn't. The car-motion is the cause of the trailer-motion, not because it comes first (it doesn't) but because it produces the trailer-motion while the trailer-motion doesn't produce the car-motion; it just comes about as the result of the car-motion, as its effect. Without temporal priority Hume's theory would allow the trailer motion to be the cause and the car motion to be the effect. Why not on Hume's theory of mere regularity?

Is the hammer-nail case similar in this respect? Doesn't the nail sink into the wood at the precise instant that the hammer strikes it? Other examples of simultaneous causation come easily to mind. The sun causes your sun-burn at the very same time as you suffer this effect. The functioning of the motor in your car occurs at the same time as the motion of the car which it causes. Surely there may always be further effects later in time; so that acknowledging that there are causes simultaneous with their effects, and even lots of them, doesn't in any way rule out many other effects later in time. What seems to happen in many cases, perhaps all cases, is that a given cause has one or more simultaneous effects and a whole array of later effects. An assassination means the causing of a person's death. The person dies when the bullet has its effect. The later effects of the killing ripple down through history, including a world war.

[4] WHAT KINDS OF REALITIES CAN BE CAUSES?

Somebody throws a brick at a window, and it breaks. What was the cause of the window breaking? The immediate answer: the brick. But another answer is possible and perhaps more accurate: the brick hitting the window, or the motion of the brick through the air and into the window. The first answer names a *thing*, the brick; the second answer names an *event*, the brick hitting the window. The idea of the second answer is that it isn't the brick all by itself that causes the window to break, but an event, the brick flying through the air. Are all causes events? A virus causes an illness. But isn't it really the event of the virus entering the body that causes the illness? A bullet kills a man. But a bullet all by itself cannot kill a man; it has to be shot in a certain way from a gun. Again, we have an event or perhaps a series of them. So, once again: are all causes events? Can you think of any causal activity, any cause-effect relation that cannot be formulated as one event being the cause of another event?

In all these cases the events described as causes and as effects are changes. Is this always so? A rock placed on a pillow causes a dent in the pillow. The rock doesn't move; it doesn't change. The same applies to the pillow. A beam supports the ceiling in a house. Does it cause the ceiling to stay in place? If so we seem to have another case of causation without change.

Go back to the case of the bullet that kills a man. We would also say that the person who did the shooting killed the man. Compare these two statements:

1. This person killed the man.
2. This bullet killed the man.

Superficially these two statements are very similar and grammatically they are parallel. But let us examine them closely; we will see significant differences.

First, the person performed an *action* in doing the killing; the bullet did not. We can say that the person killed the man by means of the bullet and that the bullet was used by the person to kill the man. None of this works in reverse.

Second, let us assume the killing was deliberate and not accidental. Then the person *intended* to kill the man and did so for a reason. Intentions and reasons are totally out of place in regard to the bullet.

Third, the person is *responsible* for what he did; the bullet is not.

Fourth, the bullet is part of a whole process that includes it being placed in the gun, the gun being in proper working order, the trigger being pulled and the bullet flying through the air. The bullet is part of a long causal chain, with various events preceding it and others following it. In contrast, the person *initiates* his action of killing the man; the action *starts with him*, originates in him. Isn't that why we say he is responsible? If the role of the person were like that of the bullet, with causes coming before him could we still say he is responsible? If there is a further cause beyond him that made him do it, that somehow pushed him in his movements we would not say that *he* did it. If someone grabs my hand and pushes it the hand motion is not my act; it is not the case that I did it. Thus, the person is, in the sense just explained, an *original cause*; the bullet is not.

How can this be? Don't we generally assume that every cause needs some further cause to bring it about? The strong wind causes the branch to break; but something else had to be there to cause the wind. A cause is or involves an event; and didn't we just note that every event needs a cause to bring it about? But the action of the person killing seems to defy this. If it is a part of a causal chain, brought about by other perhaps previous causes, is it still his action? Is it still something we can hold him responsible for? It seems not.

What kinds of realities can be causes? We have noted three:

- Things like bricks.
- Events like bricks flying and bullets hitting people.
- Persons like the one who killed another with a bullet.

For the first and the second: the second is a more accurate and complete account than the first; the brick by itself is only a part of the cause. In a sense the third is also not a complete account in that the person uses something (a bullet) to do what he does, to perform his action. And yet isn't there a more important sense in which the person is a complete account? He did it, he is responsible; he did it alone and so he alone is responsible. He did it, he initiated the action; it came from him, hence his being responsible. He did it; he did it alone as no cause lies behind his doing it that would then be the ultimate or real cause.

[5] CAN PERSONS BE CAUSES?

We seem to have uncovered two main kinds of realities that can be causes: events and persons. These are the second and third items above; the first, a thing like a brick, is really best seen as part of the second, events. But can a person really be a cause in a true and literal sense?

No, only events can be causes. When persons are involved in causation it is really events that are the cause, with persons part of this event-causal process.

Yes, persons can be causes. *I am the cause of my actions.* That's what it means to say that they are *my* actions, that I am *responsible* for them. Think of the many things you do, your actions. Some are weighty and significant, and for some of these we attribute responsibility, such as when a person deliberately kills another. Many are not significant, but routine daily activities such as putting things away and the many actions that form parts of our work. Perhaps we can come to see what it means to say that persons can be causes when *I am the cause of my actions* by considering two very simple, even mundane examples; and then contrasting them with cases that are direct opposites of persons as causes, or agent causality as it is often called. The two examples are: *I move my hand* and *I jump into the water*. What is significant about these that make them occasions for wonder? For each we can say:

- I initiate the action.
- I originate it.
- I produce it.
- I make it happen.
- I bring it about.
- The action starts with me.

None of this ever applies to event causation; none of it ever could apply to it. A fire destroys a house. The fire is really an event; like all events it occurs at a definite time and place and for a certain period of time. When such an event takes place, we naturally ask for its cause. What caused the fire? Suppose we were told that nothing beyond the fire caused it; that the fire was a case of initiating, originating and the other items in the list just above. For one thing we would protest that in the list above there is a person essentially involved, an "I" and that each of them would make no sense without the person as agent. Events cannot be originators; they must always be the effects of other events, or perhaps persons.

WONDER AT PERSONS BEING CAUSES

Now here is our occasion for wonder: how can there be such things as persons being causes when this involves persons as *beginning* a causal chain, as *originators* of their actions? Didn't we note that events, to be causes, must themselves have causes to bring them about? Didn't we claim that everything that happens requires a sufficient cause to make it happen, and thus to explain it? But now we seem to have a radical exception to this. Persons are causes which are not the effect of previous causes; they are causal beginnings, causal originators.

And yet, don't we experience ourselves as just such causal originators? *I* did that, it was *my* action, it *stemmed from* me; and (in some cases) it is something that I am *responsible* for. If I feel an intense guilt for something I did that I recognize as seriously wrong, isn't that feeling of guilt essentially rooted in my sense that I did it, that it was my action, stemming from me?

Let us return to our two examples: *I move my hand* and *I jump into the water*. Consider for each its contrasting case where it is not my initiative that brings about the effect; where I am not the cause of the action, where it does not originate with me; where it is not a case of *I did it*. For the first we would have *something moves my hand*. This is a typical case of event causation. My hand moves but I don't move it. The reality, and the significance of agent causation, where the action stems from me, originates from me is precisely that this contrasting case is not the typical situation. The amazing thing is that my hand can move without it being the case that *something moves my hand*. How is that possible? I originate its motion without that action being itself the result of prior causes.

In the second contrasting case *someone pushes me into the water*. In both the original and the contrasting case I fall into the water. In the original I am active; it is my doing; in the second I am a passive victim. My being pushed into the water is again a typical case of event causation, coming under the usual description of such causation as itself requiring a cause. But, clearly, I can end up in the water not only when I am being pushed from behind, but also and much more usually when I jump in of my own accord. I do it; it is my action, from my own initiative; in contrast to my behavior being the effect of a previous cause.

I move my hand: *I do it*, I act; I initiate the action. When something moves my hand: *it happens to me*. The same applies to my jumping into the water and my being pushed in.

Suppose I am pushing a small but heavy carriage up a hill. I need to exert power in order to accomplish this. Reflect on this simple action. I experience myself as the cause of the motion of the carriage. And in my exerting power, my muscular power in doing the pushing I experience the power that is part of causality. Hume claimed he could never detect power in causality, only regular sequence. Well, here is a case of experiencing power, my own causal power in pushing the carriage up the hill. Or if a boxer hits his opponent in the face with a powerful blow, he too experiences the causal power he exerts in his action.

GRASPING WHAT CAUSALITY IS BY BEING A CAUSE MYSELF

There is another important point in relation to Hume that we can draw from the heavy carriage example, and indeed all the other cases of human action as agency. Hume claimed we have no experience of causality except regular sequence for past cases and expectation of similar results for future cases. But don't we have an experience of something else that is even more significant for causality than regular sequence and expectation? That would be the experience of power. Briefly: causality essentially involves power; a cause is something that has the power to bring about its effect. A hammer blow is the power that makes the nail sink into the wood, a poison that kills you does so because it has the power to do so. A small and weak tractor cannot cause a very large and heavy trailer to move up the hill; it lacks the power to do so. Indeed, we measure causality by power: can x cause y? Yes, if it has the power to do so; otherwise not. Thus, I grasp what causality is in its nature, as a connection between things where the cause is what has the power to bring about the effect; I grasp this by the experience of my own being as a cause, when I exert power in pushing the carriage up a hill and a host of other similar cases.

Can persons be causes? Indeed, they can. *I am the cause of my actions.* Wonder at that! That it must be so in order to say that they are *my* actions and that I can be *responsible* for them. Notice another significant thing. Only human actions can be commanded or requested or forbidden. Compare human actions to various events that occur in me, such as that my hair grows, that I sweat and that I get tired. These are all things that happen to me, in contrast to human actions where the key idea is that I do them, that I am active as a human agent. Why would it be nonsensical to command me to sweat or to grow my hair? Isn't it because these are things that are not in my power to bring about, that are not up to me? They are not human actions. The very fact that other things can be commanded or forbidden further testifies to the reality of human agency and the causal power that it essentially involves; and, thus, brings out again the reality of the causal relation as a real connection between things and one thing having the power to bring about or produce an effect in another thing.

[6] ARE CAUSES AND REASONS DIFFERENT?

There are different kinds of reasons:

1. Conscious reasons for a free act. I help you out of love.
2. Conscious reasons for non-free behavior: emotions. I feel anger, sadness, joy; I am touched and moved by the beauty of music.
3. Conscious reasons for non-free behavior: belief and doubt.
4. Non-conscious reasons for an act. He thinks the reason he did x was y; but the actual reason is really something quite different, z. He thinks he did it out of love; the real reason is resentment.

Reasons and causes seem to be different: a reason can be a good reason or a bad reason. This seems not to apply to causes. But how do we distinguish between reasons and causes?

You see the angry bear charging you. Why do you feel fear? Is it a reason or a cause? Does an insult cause anger? Or is it a reason? You grieve at the death of a loved one: cause or reason? You are moved by the beauty of music: cause or reason?

I'm on a ski lift and I grasp my seat tightly. We can say that my fear causes me to grasp my seat tightly. Or should we say that my fear is my reason for grasping it tightly?

Perhaps there are different kinds of causes, as there are for reasons. What are they? Do they overlap? Cold causes water to freeze; an assassination causes a world war. These seem to be very different: causality in nature vs. causality in human affairs. "She made me feel very uncomfortable" is very different from "the bad food made me feel sick." The second is a cause. Is the first a cause or a reason?

Bibliographical Note: Hume's theory of causality is in his A Treatise of Human Nature (1739), Book I, Part III, Sections II, III, IV, VI, XIV and XV; and in his An Enquiry Concerning Human Understanding (1748), Section VII. This chapter is greatly indebted to Richard Taylor's superb analysis of causation and human agency in his Action and Purpose (Prentice Hall, 1966; Humanities Press, 1973), especially Chapters 1-9; and to Brand Blanchard, Reason and Analysis (La Salle, IL: Open Court Publishing Company, 1962, 1973), Chapter XI.

CHAPTER 11
FREEDOM

PART ONE
FREEDOM IN GENERAL

[1] CASES THAT SEEM TO BE BOTH FREE AND NOT FREE

Wonder: do we always know what freedom means? Is it always clear whether an act is free or not? There are cases that seem to be free and also not free. Consider: a thief points a gun at me and demands my money. I am forced to give it to him and so in that sense it's *not* free. Yet I choose to give it to him rather than suffer the consequences. It is my choice and I act upon it. Doesn't that make it a free act? In this sense it *is* a free act. And isn't this the deeper and more important sense? But there is more: the case of a martyr who doesn't give in to a gun-point type of threat. He freely says *no* and chooses to die rather than betray his faith or do wrong.

Consider another wonder case. Is Danielle Free? She has been scarred by an early childhood experience of which she has no conscious memory, one involving a blond-haired dog. In a strange way this has left her psychologically incapable of wanting to touch any light-colored dog. She is totally unaware of her condition. On her sixteenth birthday she is offered two puppies, a black one and blond one. She is given a choice, and she selects the black one, thinking it was a free choice, that she could have chosen either one.[1] Was it a free choice?

Yes, she wanted a black dog, and she chose accordingly. Her choice came from her own desires. Her behavior was uncoerced and unimpeded. Doesn't that make it free? Or was she not free because she was, unknowingly, not really in

---

[1] Taken from Robert Kane, *A Contemporary Introduction to Free Will* (New York and Oxford: Oxford University Press, 2005), 29. This book is an excellent introduction to freedom, including the freedom-determinism issue.

control of the situation? It was not up to her how she would choose, for that was already predetermined by her psychological condition. She felt free but she was not really free. She believed that she could have chosen otherwise, and that her freedom consisted in this. We know this is an illusion. Is it the *illusory* character of her situation that makes her behavior unfree? Or is it the fact that her choice was *determined* by a factor other than the one she thinks was operative here? Is this the reason it was not free? Or is it perhaps both factors in combination? And, which is here deeper and more important, the sense in which she was free or the sense in which she was not free?

What can we conclude for this? Taken in isolation *free* and *not free* logically contradict each other and so it cannot be that they are simply both true of a given act. Must it then not be that an act is free in one sense but not free in another sense? And that this means there are different kinds of freedom or different ways of exercising freedom; that freedom is not simply one thing but a variety of things? Let us now explore this in our wonder about freedom.

[2] DIFFERENT KINDS OF FREEDOM

The idea that freedom can mean different things, that there are different kinds of freedom leads to some important distinctions, some implied by our two cases, some going beyond them.

OUTER FREEDOM AND INNER FREEDOM

We have outer freedom when we are not in jail and live in a "free" country. Being free in this sense is often called *liberty*. But in another sense, even persons free in these ways may be unfree because they are imprisoned in their own inner being by severe inhibitions that literally prevent them from outwardly doing what they inwardly want to do; what they would otherwise freely choose to do. We can be outwardly free and inwardly unfree; for example, a person who is very shy. We can also be outwardly unfree and inwardly free. While in jail I still have inner freedom in that I'm still free in how I respond to those who have unjustly imprisoned me: by hatred and a desire for bloody revenge; or by a humble and loving readiness to forgive as we see in St. Francis of Assisi and Martin Luther King in his essay, "Loving your Enemies."[2] That is one way of drawing the distinction between *outer* freedom and *inner* freedom.

The distinction between outer freedom and inner freedom can also be drawn in another way: inner referring to choosing and outer referring to physical act. I see a person in need of help. My immediate response is to help him, an *inner act of choosing* to help him; I then actually do help him by an action, an *outer physical act*, such as pulling him out of the water if he is drowning. These usually go together and are so closely linked as to be experienced as one thing. But there are tragic cases where they pull apart. Imagine a person who is suddenly and to him inexplicably afflicted with physical paralysis. He is capable of making the inner act of choosing to move his limbs in order to get up and walk; but he then discovers to his horror that he is unable to do so, that the outer physical act does not follow upon the inner act of choosing. To be free to choose is not the same thing as to be free to carry out this choice by the movements of our limbs. *Inner* freedom does not guarantee *outer* freedom.

INNER FREEDOM: FOUR DISTINCTIONS

Inner freedom is especially important. How is it exercised? When we turn our wonder gaze at this freedom, we come to see some important further distinctions:

First, there is an inner *choosing without any outer action*, as when I freely respond in love to another person, including situations where I would like to act by a deed of love but cannot. This contrasts with inner *choosing to perform an outer action*; the inner choosing forms the basis for the outer action. I choose to help you and then actually do so by my action.

Second, there is inner freedom as the capacity to choose among two or more realistic options. "Take your pick." You can choose either one of the two prizes. Or you have two job offers and you can choose either one of them. This kind of

---

[2] Martin Luther King, *Strength to Love*, chapter 5 (New York: Pocket Books, 1968), 42-49.

case contrasts with cases where we have no choice in the sense that only one path is realistically open to us, so that we are not really free to choose anything else. Let us call the freedom to choose among options *decision freedom*.

Is freedom always like this? Is freedom to be identified with decision freedom? Many people think so; they think freedom just means being able to freely decide among options, and when you don't have freedom to choose among options you don't have freedom. But is this really so? What does our wonder reveal? Consider an example. You ask me a favor. You are my friend; it is a small favor, and I am a loving person. So, I say "of course I'll help you; of course, I'll do this favor for you!" I never seriously consider not helping you. I choose to help you and then I actually do it; I carry out my response in an action. Is this a case of freedom?

It doesn't seem to be a case of choosing between possible meaningful alternatives and so it doesn't seem to be decision freedom. Isn't it still freedom? Don't I freely choose to help you? The act is my own, it stems from me; I do it willingly. Doesn't this show that I do it freely? Why do I need more than one path of choosing and acting in order to act freely?

Can we go even further? Not only is it a case of freedom; isn't it actually an even better kind of freedom than the decision freedom of choosing among alternatives, where the decision could go either way? Decision freedom says, "maybe I'll help you and maybe I won't." Isn't the spontaneous "of course" response better? Isn't it even the only true response worthy of a real friend? Surely the "of course" response is a case of freedom; let us call it *spontaneous freedom*.

Our second distinction then is between *decision freedom* and *spontaneous freedom*.

Third, there is another significant element in this example, "of course I'll do this favor for you!" In choosing to help you I choose the good. Is choosing the good perhaps a mark of true freedom? Is the hardened criminal who spontaneously chooses evil not really free but as it is often expressed "a slave of sin" and hence not really free? He is unfree because he is in the grip of evil. To be truly free one must be free of this grip, which means being ordered to the good.

What we can draw out of this is our third important distinction within freedom: the *ability to choose* between good and evil and the *commitment to the good*.

For example, I am tempted to do something wrong. I have the ability to choose honesty or dishonesty. If I choose dishonesty, I am not really free; I am not free in that deeper sense of freedom which is freedom for the good. Choosing evil is then another case of both freedom and not freedom: I am free in the sense that I have the ability to choose evil; but I am not free in the sense that choosing evil makes me not free, because true freedom comes only by choosing the good and thus being in the good.

Can we combine two elements from the second and the third? That would be the idea that spontaneous freedom (second) for the good (third) is the ideal freedom, the true freedom? This seems to be the conclusion our wonder has led us to. But freedom is generally depicted in the literature as the ability to do or choose in more than one way; to choose among alternatives that exclude each other. "I could have done otherwise" or "I could have chosen otherwise." In one way this does seem characteristic of freedom. In another way it seems not to be, for spontaneous freedom seems to be the exclusion of such an "otherwise": of course, I'll help you, I could not realistically have done anything else, I could not really have chosen otherwise. Again, we have our wonder: freedom as *including* an "otherwise" and freedom as *excluding* it.

Fourth, there is another category of freedom, *free will*. This is the capacity to choose among alternatives such that having chosen one way I could also have chosen another way *under exactly the same conditions*. Clearly there are cases where, if conditions had been different, I could have chosen differently. If the criminal had been in a situation where no one was in his way he could have chosen not to kill. Thus, it is important to keep in mind the qualifying phrase *under exactly the same conditions*. The capacity to choose among alternatives such that having chosen one way I could have chosen another way *under different conditions* does not constitute free will. That would be freedom but not a clear example of free will.

Our fourth distinction is between *free will* and *freedom without free will*.

Do we ever act with free will? Do we have this power? Many thinkers deny free will. If you had good reasons to choose one way under certain conditions, why would you ever choose otherwise *under exactly the same conditions*? Free will is an important and controversial issue which we will take up in the next chapter. It is important largely because of its bearing on the question of moral responsibility. If we hold a criminal morally responsible for his crime, are we assuming he acted with free will? Does moral responsibility require free will? Wonder!

OUTER AND INNER FREEDOM: A LIST OF ALL THE DISTINCTIONS

It might be helpful to pull all these items together into one list of six distinctions:

1. **Outer freedom as liberty,** as not in jail and in a free country – inner freedom as the inner response of love or hatred, forgiveness or revenge.
2. **Outer freedom as action** – inner freedom as choosing what action to take.
3. **Inner choosing without any outer action – inner choosing to perform an outer action.**
4. **Inner decision freedom** as choosing among several options – **inner spontaneous freedom** as simply choosing the one clear path. "Maybe I'll help you and maybe I won't"; as opposed to the response of spontaneous freedom: "of course I'll help you!"
5. **Inner freedom as commitment to the good** – as the ability to choose good or evil.
6. **Inner freedom as free will** – as choosing in ways other than free will.

The first three distinctions go together, having to do with the difference between *outer* freedom and *inner* freedom. The last three stand alone, each bringing out a key difference in the idea of freedom; and each concerned only with inner freedom.

Comparing the first two distinctions we note that in #1 the significance of the distinction is to see the *contrast*, how inner and outer freedom can be at odds with each other; that we may have inner freedom *despite* not having outer freedom. But in #2 the point of the distinction is to see the two kinds of freedom *united into one*, having inner freedom *together with* outer freedom.

Note that *freedom* does not necessarily imply or include *free will*. All cases of free will are also cases of freedom but not all cases of freedom are also cases of free will. We will return to this point shortly, at the end of the next section.

[3] WHAT IS FREEDOM?

THE ACTIVE DIMENENSION OF FREEDOM

For the remainder of our analysis in this chapter and in the next, we will be concerned exclusively with inner freedom, which is the dominant theme of traditional writings in this area.

The different kinds of freedom analyzed in the previous section may all be seen under a single heading which we may call *the active dimension of freedom*. The basic idea is that in each case the person is doing something, he is acting, he is causing something, he is in control, and he is responsible for what he causes. What is freedom in this sense, or in this dimension?

An example may be useful to get us started. I'm walking in the park, and I see a person lying by the side of the path. He's been badly injured. I'm horrified! I go over to him, bandage or assess his wounds and then take the necessary steps to get him medical attention. Isn't this a clear case of a free act? Doesn't it show that I'm free? But what does it mean to say that I'm free here, that my action is a free act? Let me suggest three essential features of a free act:

1. It is my act, it stems from me, I initiate it, I cause it; it is in my control; it was up to me.
2. I did it with some thought and attention.
3. I had a reason or motive for why I acted as I did. "I did it out of love"; "I did it in order to ensure that this person received the help he needed; that was my purpose." It wasn't without reason or in any way mindless.

First, a free act is one that is up to me, one that is in my control. This contrasts with my initial reaction of horror, a feeling that came to me, which was not something that was in my control or up to me, hence not a free act.

Consider responsibility. A child is seriously injured by an adult, and we say to the adult, "You are responsible for this!" Or, in another case, "I am responsible for this!" The reality and seriousness of responsibility are clearly rooted in this first feature. I can be responsible for causing something only if it was somehow in my power, in my control, up to me to either cause it or not cause it. And I can of course also be responsible for what doesn't happen; where I am responsible for an omission, for not doing something I could have done and should have done, as when I let a child drown who could have been saved by me.

Second, if I turn unconsciously in my sleep, this is also in some sense an act of mine but hardly a case of a free act. It is not in my control, and it is not done with any conscious thought and attention.

Third, turning unconsciously in my sleep fails the test of freedom also because there is no motive or reason involved. That the third element is part of freedom comes out clearly when we consider that my action towards the injured person would not have taken place had I not been motivated to help him. My motives were my concern for him, my compassion, my sense of duty, and my wanting to do the right thing.

Consider another case: anger comes over me in response to what someone does to me. The anger response stems from me (like a free act); but it is not something that is up to me (unlike a free act). The anger comes over me, and for that I am not at the moment responsible. But how I deal with the anger is up to me. It is a free act, one that I initiate, that I cause, that I control, and for which I am therefore responsible.

THE RECEPTIVE DIMENENSION OF FREEDOM

Do these three features define freedom? Let me suggest that they define only one of the two dimensions of freedom, the active. What is the other dimension? Consider some examples.

- Gratefully receiving the gifts of my life, such as the gift of being loved, the gift of beauty.

- Humbly accepting a correction that I realize is fully justified and helpful for me.
- Open-minded and open-hearted inner listening to ideas that I find foreign and distasteful but that I realize may be correct or at least have some element of truth in them.

Receiving, accepting, and listening point to the receptive dimension of freedom. But they are also connected to something that has an active character: cooperation. In each of these three cases isn't it also true that I should actively cooperate with what has been given to me in order to make it fully my own, to integrate it into my character? If I don't do this, would these gifts seem to remain somehow dormant and at least partly ineffective in us? Wonder!

FREE WILL AND A FURTHER KIND OF FREEDOM

We noted that *freedom* does not necessarily imply or include *free will*. All cases of free will are also cases of freedom but not all cases of freedom are also cases of free will. Consider the free response expressed by "of course I will help you!" Implicit in this is the idea that I could not realistically have done otherwise, in contrast to free will which is precisely the idea that I could have done otherwise, in the same situation. The *of course* response is characterized by spontaneity; let us then call the freedom embodied here *spontaneous freedom*.

PART TWO
SPONTANEOUS FREEDOM

[4] SPONTANEOUS FREEDOM AS BASIC FREEDOM

Is spontaneous freedom really freedom? To answer this question, recall the three features just noted as the essence of freedom. An act of spontaneous freedom is my own act, it stems from me, I initiate it, I cause it; it is in my control; it was up to me. It is done with some thought and attention. And there is a reason or motive for doing it. Hence it is free.

But the deepest answer to this question is that spontaneous freedom is *basic freedom* or *basic choosing*, which means it is basic to decision freedom. I cannot freely choose between x and y unless I can first and more fundamentally simply and freely choose x, or simply choose y, by the power of free basic choosing which is what I exercise in spontaneous freedom.

What this means is that if I choose x in a situation where nothing else attracts me, I choose x freely. I manifest freedom, without choosing between alternatives. Recall our example where a friend asks me a simple favor. "Of course, I'll do it! I'll be happy to do it!" I choose the loving response without ever considering any other alternative. I do not choose x over y for I simply choose x and I do so because I want to do so. The choosing is a free act: as noted, it is my act, it stems from me, I initiate it; I cause it. It was up to me; it was done with some thought; and for a reason.

A corollary of the fact that spontaneous freedom is really freedom and basic freedom is that we are equally responsible whether we act by decision freedom or by spontaneous freedom. A teacher yells at a student in anger. Does it make any difference for responsibility whether she made a decision to yell after considering not yelling; or yelled at the poor student by spontaneous freedom, perhaps as a natural response stemming from her character as an angry person?

[5] IS SPONTANEOUS FREEDOM THE IDEAL FREEDOM?

Which is better, decision freedom or spontaneous freedom? Which is the ideal freedom? Consider some examples to help answer these questions. I have a chance to steal some money that I desperately need, and I know I can get away with it. Consider the two basic possibilities: "Of course I won't steal it! I'm an honest person." Or, "maybe I will and maybe I won't; I hesitate, I have to make a decision." It is a free decision that could go either way. Isn't the first better, the ideal freedom? Whom would you prefer as your friend, the *fully honest* person who is able to respond with spontaneous freedom? Or the *half honest* person who needs to make a free decision between two attractive alternatives, who wavers between these alternatives?

In a parallel way, whom would you prefer as your friend, the person who will of course stand by you in your time of need, even at some sacrifice to himself? Or a person who might stand by you and probably will, but who needs to make a decision to do so? Which one is your true friend? Isn't it is the one who is faithful to you by spontaneous freedom? And if we want to say that the response of your faithful friend is an expression of freedom, then true freedom, the ideal freedom lies not in a decision between two options, where the outcome could go either way but in spontaneous freedom which exemplifies freedom in its core reality: I do it; it stems from me, it is my act; and I do it with some thought, for a reason and a with a motive.

What does possessing a moral virtue mean? Consider a person who has the virtue of generosity. Doesn't this mean that he gives generously and does so easily? That it does not cost him a painful decision? Doesn't this mean that his choosing to give is by spontaneous freedom? And doesn't the same apply to all moral virtues? That to have a virtue means the corresponding behavior flows with the ease of spontaneous freedom? And isn't this is the freedom of the saints, a freedom we should all strive to attain? Again, isn't being able to respond with spontaneous freedom for the good better than having to exercise decision freedom which could go either way?

One more example: I'm playing chess and trying to decide between two possible moves. Which one is the better move? Certain factors speak in favor of move A while others speak in favor of move B. I have to make a decision; I exercise decision freedom. If I were a better chess player, I would immediately see that move A is the right move, the better move. I wouldn't have to make a decision, I wouldn't hesitate; I could choose immediately and directly, by spontaneous freedom. Again, isn't it clear that spontaneous freedom is the better way, the ideal freedom?

It is important to note that only *spontaneous freedom for the good* is an ideal; either a moral good like honesty and love or a practical good. The spontaneous freedom of a hardened criminal is the very antithesis of the ideal freedom.

[6] IS SPONTANEOUS FREEDOM THE PRIMARY FREEDOM?

I am looking for a job and I have two offers, job A and job B. Both attract me; each has its good side and its bad side. One has higher pay but the other is in a nicer location. How do I decide between them? Isn't it by mentally sorting out the factors on each side in order to weigh their relative importance? As long as the factors are evenly divided, I feel I can't decide; I feel I'm in a bind. As I reflect some more on these factors the picture starts to clarify; for example, the factors for job A override those for job B. What is the goal? Isn't it to reach a point where I clearly see that these factors so obviously override the competing factors that I say, "Of course I'll take job A; it is clearly the one I want, the one I prefer." But when that happens, haven't we reached spontaneous freedom? And doesn't this mean that even decision freedom is somehow secondary to spontaneous freedom in the sense that the goal of decision freedom is reaching spontaneous freedom? Again, doesn't this mean that the ideal freedom is not decision freedom, a hesitating between several possible options with each having some attraction – but rather spontaneous freedom, where I'm "simply free," free to choose the one clear thing to do? Doesn't this suggest that the core reality of freedom is spontaneous freedom, with decision freedom being derivative from it in the way the job-offer decision is made? And that spontaneous freedom is primary freedom, with decision freedom sometimes a way of reaching it? Briefly, as noted earlier, I would not be able to choose between A and B in decision freedom if I did not already have the power of simply choosing; that is, *basic choosing* as spontaneous freedom.

[7] SPONTANEOUS FREEDOM AND POSSIBLE ALTERNATIVES

Spontaneous freedom means choosing something without realistically considering any alternatives. Is the choosing of one of these alternatives possible? "Of course, I will help you!" I do not even consider not helping you. In that sense I do not really choose between two options, A and B, helping you and not helping you; I simply choose A. Could I have chosen B instead? Could I have done otherwise? Here we must make a distinction.

In one sense I *could not have* done otherwise. That's the kind of person I am; that's what spontaneous freedom means. But there is another sense in which I *could have* done otherwise. The B option of not helping you was in some sense open to me; it was physically possible. Had there been a weighty reason not to help you, such as an emergency where I had to save a person from imminent danger, I would have chosen option B. More generally, option B must be open and possible for spontaneous freedom to even exist. If I cannot help you because I am bound hand and foot, the free response of spontaneous freedom is not even possible, since freedom is not possible. Thus, the occasion for exercising spontaneous freedom does not even arise.

The term *spontaneous* in spontaneous freedom means only that the choosing was done without seriously considering any realistic alternatives. "Of course, I will help you." It does not mean "spontaneous" in the sense of immediate or instantaneous, especially when this refers to the action performed with spontaneous freedom. Nor does "spontaneous" imply an absence of necessary effort in overcoming difficulties. My helping you may cost me great effort and be quite burdensome, but of course I'll do it; I would never consider not doing it.

Spontaneous freedom functions on different levels of significance for us as persons. Here are a few of the many cases that exist:

- Routine practical matters (Of course I'll put away the food after I'm finished eating).
- Serious practical matters (Of course I'll buy liability insurance for my car).
- Simple, momentary acts of love and kindness (Of course I'll help you).
- Deeper commitments of love and friendship (Of course I'll remain faithful to you).
- Deeper moral commitments of honesty (Of course I'll tell the truth).

[8] IS SPONTANEOUS FREEDOM FOR EVIL AN ACTUAL FREEDOM?

Imagine a person who is the direct antithesis of the *fully honest* person; a person who habitually responds dishonestly with spontaneous freedom, the *fully dis-*

honest person. Given a chance to defraud someone for personal gain his response is "of course I'll defraud him; why do anything else?" Is this spontaneous freedom for evil an actual freedom? Our wonder takes us in two directions:

On the one hand we want to answer *no*: spontaneous freedom for evil is not an actual freedom. Think of a hardened criminal, a serial killer, liar or thief who will *of course* choose to kill or lie or steal when it suits him. Doesn't his spontaneously choosing evil make him "a slave of sin" and hence not really free? Isn't he unfree because he is in the grip of evil? To be truly free, must one not be free of this grip, which means being ordered to the good? And doesn't the same apply to the "fully dishonest" person? He is not truly free because he is in the grip of his habit of dishonesty; he is a slave to this habit. His "of course" response is not truly freedom, for at its core freedom is for the good. No one says of a hardened criminal that he is free!

If we go with the *no* answer immediately above, wouldn't it apply equally to an addict? Superficially his behavior is spontaneous freedom, but, in reality, he is unfree because he is in the grip of his addiction, a slave to it. No one says of an addict that he is free!

On the other hand, we must also answer *yes*: spontaneous freedom for evil is an actual freedom. In the above we considered freedom in the context of the good, in that freedom is essentially ordered to the good. Now we must consider freedom in its basic nature as choosing, either by decision freedom or by spontaneous freedom. We then see that spontaneous freedom for evil is still an actual freedom; it meets the three requirements for freedom that we have noted. That is: (1) I did it, it stems from me, it is my act; (2) I do it with attention and thought; (3) I do it for a reason and a with a motive, usually some subjective good or pleasure I think I will get from this evil.

In a word: spontaneous freedom for evil, as in the case of the hardened criminal, still counts as freedom, as the evil is freely chosen, usually as an apparent good or pleasure, and the person is or can be morally responsible. Such freedom fails in its "calling" to be ordered to the good; it is a misuse of freedom; it deforms one's character rather than forming it. It thus represents a significant failure, but it does not negate it as a form of actual freedom. Freely choosing evil is still freely choosing, hence a case of freedom.

[9] DECISION FREEDOM AND SPONTANEOUS FREEDOM

If spontaneous freedom for the good is the ideal freedom and the primary freedom, where does this leave decision freedom? And how are decision freedom and spontaneous freedom related to each other? I suggest four significant relations between these two types of freedom:

First, *spontaneous freedom for the good is the ideal and better than decision freedom.* Recall our examples: loyalty to a friend, honesty, moral virtues like generosity and being a good chess player; these either require spontaneous freedom or find their highest form in it.

Second, *spontaneous freedom is basic to decision freedom.* Decision freedom is possible only because we have the power of freedom as *basic choosing*, which is what we exercise in spontaneous freedom. I cannot freely choose between x and y in decision freedom unless I can first and fundamentally simply choose x or y by the basic choosing of spontaneous freedom.

Third, *spontaneous freedom is sometimes not enough; we also need decision freedom.* We need decision freedom to say *no* to moral evil. All of us are occasionally tempted to evil, for example dishonesty. We need decision freedom to choose between honesty and dishonesty when they are both live options. And if we say a criminal is morally responsible for his crime, aren't we assuming that he could have chosen otherwise, and meaning that he could have exercised his decision freedom to say *no* to moral evil? In such cases spontaneous responses are wrong; we need decision freedom exercised for the good in order to do the right thing. Another type of case where we need decision freedom is when confronted with complex situations that call for careful deliberation, sorting out all the factors involved in order to arrive at the right decision. Marriage, career, and a head of state deciding whether or not to declare war, are a few of the many instances where a quick spontaneous response is out of order; where a careful decision is what is needed.

Fourth, there is spontaneous freedom for the *end* and decision freedom for the *means*. Of course, I will liberate you; how I do it requires a decision. Conversely, there is decision freedom for the *end* and spontaneous freedom for the *means*. I decide between being generous and being selfish. Having decided to be generous, how I carry this out comes by spontaneous freedom.

CHAPTER 12
DETERMINISM AND FREE WILL

PART ONE
DETERMINISM

Are we free or determined? We have examined what it means to be free; now let us try to see what it means to be determined. Does being determined always mean not being free? Aren't we at least partly determined in that heredity and environment determines our character? Is the theory of determinism correct when it says we are completely determined? In parts one to three we examine determinism and being determined; in part four we examine free will.

What is the significance of this issue? Why is it a source of wonder? There are several reasons. One is about what we are as persons. Are we free to be our own persons, to determine our own path in life? Or is that determined for us by factors outside of our being and beyond our control? Another following closely on this is the question of moral responsibility. If we are completely determined, can we still be morally responsible? To get started on this issue here is a little story that takes us inside the determinist's mind-set, his world-view:

[1] DETERMINISM: A LITTLE STORY

Imagine a group of people living happily together in a peaceful community. There are no jails, and no one harasses anyone else. It seems like a utopia. The people are free to do whatever they want. But their wants are strictly determined by a small group of conditioners who produce in them certain beliefs and desires which in turn completely determine their choices and actions. Are these people free? They certainly have liberty, for they are not in jail and not coerced at gunpoint. Doesn't that give them freedom of action? They can act on all their desires. Do they not have an inner freedom to choose how they will act? In one sense they seem to be free; but in another sense they seem to be unfree since they are at the mercy of their conditioners. Are they free or determined? Could it be both? Should we say they have a *surface freedom* to choose and act as they want but lack a *deeper freedom* since the springs of their choosing and acting are not their own but determined for them by others? But what would it be like to have this deeper freedom or freedom on a deeper level? Is this even possible and meaningful? Wonder!

The determinist now asks you to suppose that the conditioners are removed, but that the process of bringing about the beliefs and desires in the people is still one of determination. Now these beliefs and desires are brought about in the more usual ways. Each person is born with a certain genetic endowment of physical characteristics, temperament and character traits. He is born into an environment of family, a local cultural setting and a larger cultural setting. Later education, life experiences, and other factors are added to the mix. All these factors make up the *given* in each person's life. This given, heredity and environment, determines his behavior. The big question is: does it do so completely? That it does so partly, that the given has a significant influence on behavior seems evident and can easily be granted. But is it the whole story? The theory of determinism claims that it is. What else could there be? This is its challenge.

The point of the story about the conditioners should now be clear. What the determinist claims is that this is our story! Where is the difference except for the conditioners? Their role has now been taken over by heredity and environment; is anything essential really changed? Yes, we are free to choose and to act. Yes, we have *surface freedom*; but do we have the *deeper freedom* that would allow us to claim that we are our own person? Determinism can be seen as the view that we have surface freedom but don't have the deeper freedom.[1]

[2] DETERMINISM AND TWO LEVELS OF OUR EXISTENCE

We exist on two levels, an *upper level,* and a *lower level*:

---

[1] The peaceful community story is based on B. F. Skinner's *Walden Two*.

The *upper level* is where I have the feeling of freedom because I have *surface freedom*. I am free to act on what I choose, and I am free to choose as I want, either by decision freedom or spontaneous freedom. I feel free and I am free because I am in control. What I choose and what I do stem from me; they are up to me.

But why do I choose as I do? This brings us to the *lower level*. One person chooses honesty and another dishonesty. Isn't this usually and largely because of their character? One is an honest person and the other a dishonest one. And isn't this in turn because of their past, their heredity and how they were brought up? Perhaps their own free choosing played a significant role in making them the one kind of person or the other. But then that choosing needed a motive. And again, we must ask: was that motive *sufficient* to account for the choosing? If not, the motive was not effective; hence there really was no motive. If it was sufficient doesn't this mean that determinism reigns on the *lower level*? And doesn't this destroy the *deeper freedom*?

Determinism says we are unfree to choose the factors that account for how we choose and act on the upper level in our surface freedom; and that this makes us ultimately not free. The determinist Schopenhauer captures this idea in a simple formula:

> "A man can surely do what he wills to do, but he cannot determine what he wills."[2]

A man can surely do what he wills: we are free on the *upper level* with *surface freedom*. But he cannot determine what he wills: we are not free on the *lower level*; no *deeper freedom*.

We can do what we want; but where do our wants come from? We did not freely create them; they were ultimately all given to us by our heredity and environment. We can *do* what we want but we cannot *choose* the wants that go into

---

[2] Quoted by Paul Edwards in Sidney Hook (ed.), *Determinism and Freedom in the Age of Modern Science* (New York: Collier Books, 1961), 121.

this choosing; they are given to us, not freely chosen. This is determinism. In summary:

- **Upper level** – yes surface freedom – determinism asserts freedom – they are *allies*.
- **Lower level** – no deeper freedom – determinism denies freedom – they are *enemies*.

Determinism is the view that the lower level where freedom is denied is the crucial reality.

[3] THE CASE FOR DETERMINISM

TWO FORMS OF DETERMINISM

Determinism may be seen as a *general theory*. This is the idea that everything in the universe is the necessary and inevitable outcome of various factors including earlier events; that everything is completely determined by these factors. When determinism is applied to physical things including our bodies it seems to be true and, in many respects, unproblematic. It is when it is *applied to human beings* in the formation of their character and in its claim that their behavior flows necessarily from that character, that its truth becomes a matter of controversy, and that the freedom-determinism issue arises; and with it problems and occasions for wonder.

Determinism says human character formation and the choosing and acting that flow from character are completely determined. Some people reject determinism because they understand *determined* as meaning *caused* in a physical sense. Water pressure causes the dam to break. Someone pushes me and I fall down. The push is the cause of my falling down, which is something that happens to me. When *determined* is understood as a cause in this sense I am of course not free and determinism in this form is clearly an enemy of freedom and human dignity.

But *determined* can also be used in a broad sense to mean *brought about;* couldn't it then be seen as including not only causes like being pushed but also factors like reasons and motives? Thus, that my behavior is determined means that it is brought about by my beliefs, desires, reasons and motives, which are rooted ultimately my character. These things then explain why I chose as I did, and they make my choosing intelligible and meaningful. Since these things are *my* beliefs and motives, aren't they part of my being as a person? And wouldn't being determined by them be consistent with my dignity as a person and my freedom? Being determined in this sense leads to a very different form of determinism, one that does not destroy freedom.

Let us then distinguish two forms of *determinism*:

- Physical determinism: human behavior as completely determined by physical causes.
- Personal determinism: human behavior as completely determined, but where a significant part of this is determined as brought about by personal factors like reasons and motives.

We will be concerned exclusively with personal determinism, the far more plausible view and probably the dominant one in most discussions of this issue.

SOME ARGUMENTS FOR DETERMINISM

First, we have already noted that motives are always necessary for human choosing and acting and that these motives must be *sufficient* to account for the act in order to be effective; in order to function as motives at all. And if a motive is sufficient to account for how we choose, doesn't it then determine that choosing? And if this is always so, isn't determinism established?

This is simply an instance of the general idea that *every event has a cause.* That is, things don't just happen; there is always some cause to account for why they happen, or why they exist. The term *cause* in this context should be understood in a broad sense to include motives, reasons and other factors such as character that account for human choosing and acting.

Second, in the past we often claimed people were free in cases where we now realize the behavior is determined in a way that denies freedom and therefore removes moral responsibility. In the past a child in school was often blamed and punished for poor work because it was thought that he was being lazy. Now we know the real story: he suffers from a learning disability. He can't help behaving in the way he does; it is completely determined; he is absolutely innocent. We who blame him are wrong for punishing him unjustly. But then we didn't know any better; so how could we have acted any differently under these conditions? If there are further cases similar to this, isn't determinism supported?

Third, don't we generally assume determinism in daily life? Joe has an outburst of violent anger and acts accordingly. We ask: *why did he do that?* Aren't we assuming there was some sufficient reason or motive that determined his behavior, and thus explains it? We try to bring up our children so that they behave properly, according to the rules. Don't we hope that their behavior will be regular and consistent with these rules? And if it is, doesn't this mean that it is determined by motives sufficient for the children to want to observe these rules?

Fourth, recall the story about the conditioners. I am free to choose and to act because I have *surface freedom,* but I do not have the *deeper freedom* that would allow me to be my own person. Determinism is simply the idea that I have surface freedom but not the deeper freedom. But what could it mean for me to "be my own person" in a way that escapes determinism when it says that my heredity and environment make me who I am? Would I have to freely choose my heredity and environment? How could I do that? Wouldn't it be impossible if not meaningless? If so doesn't this show that determinism is true of us?

Wonder. When our behavior is determined by other persons, the conditioners, we feel we are not free; we are puppets in their hands. But when the conditioners are removed, and the same process of determinism occurs in the usual ways we accept it as natural. Why is that?

[4] THE CASE AGAINST DETERMINISM

The case for determinism that we just examined claims that personal determinism, which is the idea human behavior is *determined* or *brought about* by personal factors such as reasons and motives, is consistent with our dignity as persons and perhaps even with our freedom. The case against determinism claims that, despite initial appearances, *any* determinism is contrary to our dignity as persons and certainly to our freedom. Why is this so? What is determinism?

Determinism is an enemy of humanity; it destroys human freedom and dignity. Surely, we feel free and we think we are free, but this is an illusion. We are not free because everything we do is determined by outside factors stemming from our given heredity and environment. We think we are free because we are unaware of these factors that pull at us like hidden strings and thereby determine our choosing.

Recall the case of Danielle, the girl scarred by her early experience of a blond-haired dog which left her incapable of choosing any light-colored dog. Unaware of her condition and given a choice between a black dog and a blond one she selects the black one, thinking it was a free choice, that she could have chosen either. But determinism says it was not a free choice because it was not up to her how she would choose; that was already predetermined by her psychological condition. She felt free but she was not really free. Determinism then generalizes this kind of case to all human behavior, claiming that such factors are always operative when we choose and act. A thinker who adopts this view is Baron Holbach:

> You will say that I am free. This is an illusion which may be compared to that of the fly in the fable, who, lighting upon the pole of a heavy carriage, applauded himself for directing its course. Man, who thinks himself free, is a fly who imagines he has power to move the universe, while he is himself unknowingly carried along by it.[3]

Another thinker taking this view is Mark Twain:

> Man is not to blame for what he is. He didn't make himself. He has no control over himself. All the control is vested in his temperament – which he did not create – and in circumstances which hedge him round from the cradle to

---

[3] Baron Holbach, quoted in Hook, 120.

the grave and which he did not devise. He is a subject for pity, not blame – and not contempt.[4]

Thus, determinism destroys human freedom and dignity by making us mere puppets at the hands of forces outside of us, our heredity and environment, as these two writers and the story of the conditioners bring out. Let us now examine some reasons for rejecting determinism.

First, if determinism is true why are we determined to feel free, to believe in free will, a freedom that negates determinism? Why internally do I think I have free will if determinism is true? Is it because though an illusion belief in free will makes human functioning run more smoothly? Is it because belief in free will is at the root of holding persons accountable, which is necessary for the proper functioning of society? Most people hold to free will, believing in its reality. If free will is an illusion it would be a massive illusion, since we presuppose our own free will and that of others all the time. How could such a massive illusion provide this proper functioning? Belief in the reality of free will serves us well. But the determinist will have us believe it's a big illusion? Why is he determined to do that?

Second, if determinism is true our status as persons with its inherent dignity is destroyed. But isn't this dignity more evident and clearly given to us than any theory such as determinism? If so, isn't this a good reason for rejecting determinism? And why believe that we are victims of a massive illusion? Isn't it more reasonable to believe that we really are the persons we think we are with our freedom and dignity?

Third, does determinism destroy moral responsibility as we know it? If so, wouldn't this be a good reason for rejecting it? This is a large question which we will pursue in part three.

---

[4] Mark Twain, "Reflections on Religion" (written in 1906, published in 1963). Quoted in Paul Edwards and Arthur Pap, *A Modern Introduction to Philosophy* (New York: The Free Press, 1973), 5.

[5] A KEY DISTINCTION: DETERMINISM AND BEING DETERMINED

Wonder: there seems to be a strong case to be made *for* determinism and also a strong case to be made *against* determinism. In the *for* case determinism does not seem to destroy freedom while in the *against* case it does seem to destroy freedom. How can that be? And where does it leave us? Perhaps a key distinction can be of help:

- Being determined as meaning brought about. My behavior is determined in so far as it is brought about by my beliefs, desires, reasons and motives.
- Determinism as the theory that human character formation and the choosing and acting that flow from character are completely determined. A person's behavior is completely determined by his beliefs, desires, reasons and motives.

Where *determinism* seems to destroy freedom could it be that the reason for this is that it is really *being determined* that destroys freedom? But being determined does not always destroy freedom. It seems to be a matter of *how* we are determined, the kind of being determined that is crucial. Let us now examine this idea, that there are different ways of being determined.

PART TWO
BEING DETERMINED

[6] BEING DETERMINED AS A BAD THING

BEING DETERMINED THROUGH SPONTANEOUS FREEDOM FOR EVIL

Consider a hardened criminal. His heredity gives him an angry temperament. He is born into a dysfunctional family. His mother never bonds with him, and he feels rejected and unloved. He learns that to stay afloat and to get ahead one has to do "whatever needs to be done." He drifts into a life of hard drugs. He comes to a point where the only way to sustain his habit is by committing a robbery. But it gets worse. In order to pull it off and get away with it he has to kill another human being. Being determined means that his heredity, his childhood environment and his present beliefs and desires necessarily lead to only one thing: murder. It is being determined as directed to evil, spontaneous freedom for evil, a horrendous picture of human existence.

The hardened criminal is one example of being determined as directed to evil. There are others. The drug addict is born with an addictive personality; his early childhood environment and the addicted friends he grows up with do the rest. He does not freely choose his addiction; it is foisted on him, he is made into an addict, determined to be one by factors outside his control.

One of the people you know is friendly, warm, and loving, pleasant to be with. Another is the exact opposite: unfriendly, grouchy, and not easy to get along with. Why is that? Did they freely choose to be that way? Or was their personality formed by heredity and environment? If so, we have more examples of being determined and the corresponding spontaneous freedom; in the first case for good and in the second case for evil; a lesser evil certainly than the criminal but still an evil on the good-evil scale. For each of these, which explanation is more likely, freely chosen or being determined?

AN OBJECTION AND REPLY

But is it really all a matter of being determined? For each of these – the criminal, the addict, and the grouchy person – don't many such people overcome their evil ways? They realize how bad their situation is and they resolve to turn away from the past and start a new life. They make a strong effort of will; often they are successful. Why do some succeed while others fail? Those who succeed have it in them to do so; they have the strength and the skill, and these were given to them – being determined again! John Hospers explains:

> If we *can* overcome the effects of early environment, the ability to
> do so is itself a product of the early environment. We did not

give ourselves this ability; and if we lack it we cannot be blamed for not having it.[5]

[7] BEING DETERMINED AS A GOOD THING

BEING DETERMINED THROUGH SPONTANEOUS FREEDOM FOR THE GOOD

Is being determined always a bad thing? No, everything depends on the *kind* of being determined. One kind is being determined through spontaneous freedom for evil. But there is also its diametric opposite: being determined through spontaneous freedom for the good.

I'm born with a happy and peaceful disposition, into a family that loves me and teaches me love, honesty, generosity, faithfulness, good work habits and other true values. These factors make me who I am; they form my character. That character is the source of moral virtues:

Honesty: I'm in a situation where I could easily steal some money. But I am an honest person and so my response is: "Of course I won't steal it!" I do not seriously consider stealing although I know I could. Isn't part of the very meaning of the virtue of honesty that my response of honesty is by way of spontaneous freedom? Isn't it so that to the extent that I hesitate and seriously consider both honesty and dishonesty I do not possess the virtue of honesty? If I need decision freedom, I lack the virtue; if spontaneous freedom for honesty suffices, I possess it.

Generosity: Isn't a generous person one who gives generously and does so easily? It doesn't cost him a painful decision for his choosing to give is by spontaneous freedom. And doesn't the same apply to all moral virtues? That to have a virtue means the corresponding behavior flows with the ease of spontaneous freedom. And isn't this the freedom of the saints, a freedom we should all strive

---

[5] John Hospers, "What Means This Freedom," in Hook, 138. Italics in original.

to attain? Again, isn't being able to respond with spontaneous freedom for the good better than having to exercise decision freedom which could go either way?

Faithfulness: Here too there is spontaneous freedom. Think again of your faithful friend[6] who will of course stand by you, who doesn't need to make a *yes* or *no* decision for this. In an important sense he can't even make such a decision because of his unshakable commitment to you. He is determined to be faithful to you, to stand by you. And he is "determined" not only in the usual sense that he is resolute, but also in the philosophical sense that his loving and faithful character determine his action, so that any alternative is realistically impossible because his response to you is spontaneous freedom. He is determined to the good, so clearly and strongly that he responds by spontaneous freedom.

What is true of faithfulness is true of the other virtues as well: the spontaneous freedom that is proper to them flows naturally and even necessarily from the person's character and so we can say it is determined by it. And with this we reach being determined for the good. And isn't this the best possible state of affairs? What could be better? Not a choosing the good that depends on a decision freedom which could go either way; and surely not a spontaneous freedom that is not committed to the good. Far from destroying human dignity, being determined for the good is what human dignity calls for: a character where the person is determined *by* the good and because of this is determined *to do* the good.

BEING DETERMINED AS GOOD AND NECESSARY

Being determined is not such a bad thing as some people fear, something to be rejected and overcome. It is only being determined for evil that is bad; and the badness lies in the evil, not in the being determined. In fact, being determined is largely a good thing, sometimes even a necessary thing. Some important examples:

1. ***Being determined in the form of being given the gift of the capacity for rational thinking.***

---

[6] Chapter 11, section 5.

Chapter 12: Determinism and Free Will

2. ***Being determined in the formation of our character.*** Of course, we did not create our own character; how could we possibly do this? It was given to us; it was determined for us by our heredity and early environment. This being determined is something that is necessary and could not possibly be otherwise. It is absurd to reject it or to try to overcome it.

3. ***Choosing flows from character.*** We choose according to the kind of person we are. In the simplest type of case a loving person will choose to act lovingly. Is this a case of being determined? Suppose it is; would that matter as long as the choosing wasn't evil? Being determined simply means the choosing is necessitated, guaranteed. If that is for the good or for something neutral, does it matter? What's wrong with it being guaranteed, as it is by being determined? What's wrong with it being explained and made intelligible, as it is by being determined? In short: there seems to be nothing in being determined as such and by itself that is objectionable.

4. ***Choosing flows from character where one chooses evil.*** This is bad, but not because of the being determined; it is bad because one chooses evil. Any other way of choosing evil would also be bad. Again, there is nothing in being determined as such and by itself that is objectionable.

5. ***Choosing flows from character where one chooses the good.*** This is good. And here being determined even adds to the good since being determined guarantees the choice of good and other ways don't.

6. ***Choosing flows from character where one chooses something practical.*** I choose steak on the menu because I like it more than the other entries. Let's say my choice was a case of being determined. Why would that matter? Suppose it was a choice made in some other way; why would that be better? There is nothing in being determined as such and by itself that is objectionable.

7. ***Being determined is sometimes rejected because of an implicit and false identification of being determined with materialism; or the related idea that being determined needs to be imbedded in materialism. On the contrary, being determined can be imbedded in the rejection of materialism.*** Think of a spontaneous response of love which is determined by

the loving character of the person and is thus a form of being determined or something akin to being determined and stems from the spiritual reality of love.

8. ***A major point: to be loved and shown love is a great gift.*** You are blessed in this way! This is being determined as the given in life, and in this case being determined at its best. To see this as reducing you to a mere puppet is a serious distortion and misrepresentation.

9. ***A corollary to this: to be denied love is a terrible misfortune.*** But the evil here lies not in the fact of being determined but in how the person was determined.

[8] BEING DETERMINED: SOME KEY POINTS

1. Being determined seems to be a two-sided thing. It is a bad thing and an enemy of freedom when it takes away free choosing and when it is a spontaneous response to evil.

2. But it is a good thing and an ally of freedom when it refers to spontaneous freedom for the good; and it is a necessary thing for formation of character, which is necessarily a given and thus cannot be a matter of free choosing. **Wonder**: that it is both!

3. What is important is not that we are determined but how we are determined. If I am determined by brain-washing or in some other way pushed by irrational forces, that is a terrible thing. But if I am loved as a child and shown what love is, that is a being determined of an altogether different kind and a wonderful thing.

4. So much of reality and our experience of reality is a matter of the given and therefore of our being determined, in contrast to our free choosing.

5. Among the many examples of reality that are a matter of the given are the nature of good and evil and our being as persons. We don't get to freely choose that love is good and hatred is evil; we don't make good to be good and evil to be evil. These are givens that lie in the very nature of reality, that are a necessary and essential part of reality.

6. And we didn't make ourselves persons. We find ourselves existing as persons, the ultimate given! Wonder!
7. Being determined is not the same thing as determinism. Recall the crucial distinction:
8. Being determined is a fact; it is the fact that our character is determined or brought about by influences such as heredity and environment; that our choosing flows from our being determined at least in part by our character; and other similar things. This can be a good thing or a bad thing depending on how we are determined.
9. Determinism is a theory, that this being determined is total, leaving no room for anything else; specifically, no room for free will.

PART THREE
DETERMINISM AND MORAL RESPONSIBILITY

[9] TWO LEVELS OF MORAL RESPONSIBILITY

First, there is *practical* responsibility. If I accidentally back my car into your fence I am responsible for getting it fixed. It was not even an intentional, free act but an accident. Still, because I am the cause of the damage, I am responsible for making up for it.

Causing things is one form of practical responsibility. Omissions are another. If I fail to pay sufficient attention while driving a car, I am responsible for a resulting accident. We will return to this point later under the heading of "the texting girl."

Practical responsibility remains untouched by determinism. It is something everyone is familiar with and accepts, determinists and their opponents alike.

Second, there is a deeper, *ultimate* responsibility. What does determinism say about it?

[10] ULTIMATE MORAL RESPONSIBILITY

WHAT DETERMINISM SAYS ABOUT ULTIMATE MORAL RESPONSIBILITY

Consider the hardened criminal again. We say that he should have chosen otherwise; he should have chosen not to kill the person, and to accept the consequences of not killing him. These consequences are very bad for him. But *determinism will say that he didn't have it in him to choose otherwise.* In order to be able to choose otherwise he would have had to have a motive to do so, a motive or reason along the lines of compassion or a sense of moral rightness, a desire to do the right thing. Given the person he is (shaped by his heredity and environment) he simply didn't have the motive to refrain from murder. And without a sufficient motive, as we have seen, it is impossible to choose freely. He seems to be stuck, determined to do evil.

And yet, don't we want to hold him morally responsible for what he did? But can we if his behavior is completely determined by the factors involved? If realistically he could not have done otherwise than he did being the person, he is? That we cannot hold him morally responsible in such cases seems to be a necessary consequence of determinism. Paul Edwards explains why: "our actions are caused by our desires and choices"; and then:

> We must go on to ask where *they* come from; and if determinism is true there can be no doubt about the answer to this question. Ultimately our desires and our whole character are derived from our inherited equipment and the environmental influences to which we were subjected at the beginning of our lives. It is clear that we had no hand in shaping either of these.[7]

---

[7] Paul Edwards, "Hard and Soft Determinism," in Hook, 121. Italics in original. Edwards defends "Hard Determinism" in opposition to "Soft Determinism" which claims that determinism does not rule out moral responsibility.

Edwards concludes: "From the fact that human beings do not ultimately shape their own character, I said, it *follows* that they are never morally responsible."[8]

John Hospers argues for the same conclusion:

> There remains a question in our minds whether we are, in the final analysis, *responsible for any of our actions at all*. The issue may be put in this way: How can anyone be responsible for his actions, since they grow out of his character, which is shaped and molded and made what it is by influences – some hereditary, but most of them stemming from early parental environment – that were not of his own making or choosing? This question...troubles many people who...have the uneasy suspicion that there is [an] ultimate sense, a "deeper" sense, in which we are not responsible for our actions, since we are not responsible for the character out of which those actions spring.[9]

Hospers asks us to consider a criminal who commits a monstrous crime.

> But now we find out how it all came about; we learn of parents who rejected him from babyhood, of the childhood spent in one foster home after another, where it was always plain to him that he was not wanted; or the constantly frustrated early desire for affection,...and his subsequent attempt to heal these wounds to his shattered ego through defensive aggression.[10]
>
> The poor victim is not conscious of the inner forces that exact from him this ghastly toll; he battles, he schemes, he revels in pseudo-aggression, he is miserable, but he does not know what works in him to produce catastrophic acts of crime. His aggres-

---

[8] Ibid., 125. Italics in original.

[9] John Hospers, "What Means This Freedom," in Hook, 131. Italics in original.

[10] Ibid., 132.

> sive actions are the wriggling of a worm on a fisherman's hook. And if this is so, it seems difficult to say any longer, "He is responsible." Rather, we shall put him behind bars for the protection of society, but we shall no longer flatter our feeling of moral superiority by calling him personally responsible for what he did.[11]
>
> Someone commits a crime and is punished by the state; "he deserves it," we say self-righteously – as if we were moral and he immoral, when in fact we are lucky and he is unlucky – forgetting that there but for the grace of God and a fortunate early environment, go we.[12]

Hospers also argues that the less we know about another person especially a criminal, the more likely we are to attribute his behavior to his freedom and deny necessity, and say he is morally responsible and guilty – while the more we know about him (his horrible childhood), the more likely we are to say that his behavior is determined and necessary rather than being free and then say that this takes away his moral responsibility.[13]

MORAL RESPONSIBILITY IN THE CONTEXT OF MORAL RIGHT AND WRONG

It is important to note that the claim here is that determinism rules out ultimate moral *responsibility*; not the basic categories of moral *good and evil* and *right and wrong*. These remain intact with and without determinism. Determinism is in part a theory about moral good and evil and moral right and wrong. It cannot be both a theory about these and also their denial. The determinism-free will question hinges largely on whether we can be responsible for bringing about these moral realities. They must therefore already be real in their own right before this question can be raised; and in order for it to make sense. Finally, this

---

[11] Ibid.

[12] Ibid., 138.

[13] Ibid., 133-34.

question is significant mainly because of our moral choosing; not our choosing which clothes to wear today.

This is related to a crucial point: the distinction between *judging actions* and *judging persons*. I am horrified by the crime committed by a criminal: I judge his *action* as wrong. Then I read the Edwards-Hospers accounts about why the criminal acted as he did, what factors brought about such behavior, and I pull back a bit and say that I shouldn't judge. But now it is not the action but the *person* that is in question. Not judging the person as guilty does not mean judging the action as not wrong. On the contrary, only because the action is wrong and seen to be wrong does the question of judging the person as guilty or not guilty even arise. If the action were morally good or neutral, there would be no question of whether to judge the person's guilt.

PART FOUR
FREE WILL

[11] A CONTEXT FOR FREE WILL: THE TEXTING GIRL

A recent video tells the following story. A young girl is having a great time with two friends in her car, and she is texting another friend. And, she is also driving the car. In order to text she has to take her eyes off the road, just for a few seconds. But a few seconds is an eternity in such a situation. Sure enough, a moment later she sees that her car is about to smash into another car head-on. A horrific crash ensues. Other cars come crashing into her car. Then the scene quiets down. We see her alive in the front seat, two dead girls lying on the back seat. She screams uncontrollably as she realizes what has happened, what she has done. For the sake of a stupid texting message which could easily have waited a few minutes, I have caused the death of my two friends! She screams and screams and screams! "Let me go back to the time before I texted. I would not have texted! I would have done otherwise!" She is absolutely convinced: I *should* have done otherwise, which means that I *could* have done otherwise, and done so in exactly the same situation: free will. Given the person I am, with all that I know and care about, I could have not texted. "Oh, how I wish now that I had not texted! I would give anything to be able to repeat this earlier moment, to go back to it, and this time to do it differently: regret!"

Doesn't determinism fail us here? According to determinism, given the person she was at that moment, with all that she knew and cared about, she could not have done otherwise. Given all that existed at that moment her texting while driving was inevitable. Given the weak condition of the dam, a certain pressure of the water behind it will determine that it breaks; it's inevitable. The poor girl is no different if determinism is correct. Her behavior follows with the same necessity as the breaking of the dam when the pressure is great enough. Her regret, no matter how powerful psychologically, is all in vain, a monumental illusion. She could not have done otherwise. So, isn't it pointless for her to beat herself so mercilessly? What happened is what happened; it could not have been otherwise.

So says determinism. But is it true? The opposing view says that the realities we see here, the powerful realities of regret and moral responsibility are more certainly given to us than any theory such as determinism. Deep down in her soul she knows she is ultimately responsible because she acted freely. She brought about the action which caused the horrific accident resulting in the needless death of her two friends. It was her action; she brought it into being and so she owns it and she is responsible for it. She intended the action even though she did not of course intend its tragic consequences. But she must have known that these consequences were possible, even somewhat likely, and so she is responsible for them. She knows she could have acted differently, hence that she should have acted differently. She had free will. She had reasons to text, she had reasons not to text; she freely chose the former. It may have been free will by decision freedom; it may have been free will by spontaneous freedom, a quick and careless act. Either way it was her free will; she put herself into it and made it her own. And for this she is responsible.

Doesn't determinism fail us when we reflect on the texting girl? It cannot account for her ultimate moral responsibility in causing the deaths of her two friends, a responsibility that comes upon her with an anguish that tears her soul apart. It cannot account for her regret.

There is an important final point about the texting girl. The horror of this story is the actual result of her texting while driving, the horrific crash and the death of the two other girls. But the moral lesson and its implication for the question of free will and ultimate responsibility lie not in the actual result but in her choosing to text and drive. She acted irresponsibly. That remains true even if she had been lucky and no accident had resulted. She knew an accident could occur, she willingly risked it; and for this she is morally responsible.

[12] FREE WILL: WHAT IT IS AND ISN'T

As noted in the previous chapter, free will is the capacity to choose among alternatives such that, having chosen one way I could also have chosen another way, *under exactly the same conditions*. This qualification is crucial. I choose not to eat something because I'm not hungry. Change the conditions: now I am hungry, so I do eat it. Hence in the first case where I didn't eat, it remains true that I could have eaten if the conditions had been different, as they were in the second case where I was hungry. So this ability, to be able to choose otherwise under different conditions, does not involve free will; it does not require free will. It is something clear and obvious, acknowledged by all people, on both sides of the free will debate.

There are several things that free will is not. Here are some of them:

One, free will is *not a further kind of freedom*, not another category of freedom alongside spontaneous freedom and decision freedom. Rather it is a new element; it may or may not accompany these. As noted, the texting girl may well have acted with spontaneous freedom. If she did then she *didn't* consider alternatives; this doesn't mean that she *couldn't* have considered alternatives. If she could have and acted on one of them then she acted with free will and her sense of regret and being morally responsible is justified. Her acting spontaneous is perfectly compatible with her acting freely and thus being responsible.

It is especially important not to confuse free will and decision freedom. Both have to do with the idea of "could have chosen otherwise" but they are as such distinct. They may come together in one act, but they may also exist separately. First, free will may be exercised without decision freedom; the texting girl choosing with free will and spontaneously. Second, decision freedom may be exercised without free will; where decision freedom means sorting out the factors to see which is clearly the best, thereby trying to reduce it to spontaneous freedom. In such cases it is not correct to say, "I could have chosen otherwise under the same conditions."

As noted, free will is not another category alongside decision freedom and spontaneous freedom. Free will combines or doesn't combine with the other two in four ways:

1. *Decision freedom with free will:* I decide between A and B and I could have decided the other way under the same conditions.
2. *Decision freedom without free will:* I decide between A and B and but I couldn't really have decided the other way under the same conditions. After sorting out the factors I come to see which one is clearly the best, thereby reducing it to spontaneous freedom.
3. *Spontaneous freedom without free will:* the usual case of spontaneous freedom.
4. *Spontaneous freedom with free will:* choosing spontaneously but where it is still true that I could have chosen otherwise under the same conditions.

Spontaneous freedom and decision freedom represent psychological categories; free will is a metaphysical thesis about the nature of freedom, what it includes. Spontaneous freedom and decision freedom are obvious, clearly given realities that we all experience; free will is a difficult and controversial topic: what it is, how it functions and even whether it exists at all.

Two, free will does *not in itself imply hesitation* in the way decision freedom sometimes involves hesitation. Consider again the case where I can easily help you in your need. It is better if I act with spontaneous freedom than if I hesitate. "Of course, I will help you!" This is better than the hesitation of "maybe I will and maybe I won't." The point is that hesitation can apply to decision freedom but not to free will. What should be avoided is the hesitation of some forms of decision freedom, not free will. As noted, spontaneous freedom is perfectly compatible with free will, for the good as in cheerful giving and for evil as in texting while driving.

Three, free will is *not the rejection of being determined.* It is the rejection of the theory of determinism, that our behavior is totally determined by factors beyond our control. Being determined is the idea that much is given to us and that this given plays a significant role in our behavior. If I am a kind and loving person this is largely because this character trait was given to me by my heredity and environment especially my parents who loved me and showed me what love is in their behavior. If I see another person who is grouchy and unloving isn't this probably because the given in his life was so different? Perhaps he was not really loved, or never felt that he was loved, perhaps even felt rejected? It is all too easy to judge him harshly and blame it all on his "free will." Shouldn't the fact of being determined be given a role along with free will? In the end who can really know the relative part played by each element?

Being determined is the idea that the given plays an essential role in our behavior. Part of this is that the ability to exercise free will must be in us. This refers first to the basic power of free will that is part of our essential nature as persons; and second to the occasions in life where free will can come into play. We cannot just exercise free will for we must always have a motive. But where do our motives come from? Must they not be given to us? And doesn't this given mean being determined?

Again, we cannot just exercise free will for we must be given what it takes to exercise free will. Recall the criminal strongly inclined to lie and to murder. Does he have it in him to do what is right? Does he have some goodness in him that he can tap into? If not, it seems he cannot make an act of free will for the good. If he does have it in him, it must be given to him, and this seems to mean being determined in this way.

Suppose a criminal does not have the goodness in him that he can tap into. Then would he not be determined to do wrong, to lie and to murder if his inclinations led him there? If free will is a reality doesn't it simply mean that free will exists in some cases? It does not mean that it exists in any one particular case; or that is the decisive factor in accounting for a behavior. Wonder!

Free will to do the good must stem from the good a person has; he must *have it in him* to choose the good; only if you have love in you can you give love to others.

Four, free will does *not mean that we can shape our own characters*. This is obviously impossible; our character is something clearly given to us. The issue lies elsewhere. Not in the creating of character but in the "flow" from character to behavior. Is this flow always and necessarily determined as the theory of determinism holds? Or does it allow for the operation of free will? If I find myself with an impatient temperament as part of my character, am I free to either give in to it and behave impatiently or else resist it with inner *no* and behave accordingly?

Five, free will is not *indeterminism* in the sense of what is random, arbitrary, capricious and just happens, for no cause or reason. On the contrary it is highly meaningful in opposition to these. One might say that free will means self-determination or self-determinism: *I choose.*

The notion of choosing and choice calls for a clarification; it can be used in two senses:

- *Choosing among options by decision freedom;* choosing A rather than B.
- *Choosing in a basic sense common to both decision freedom and spontaneous freedom.*

[13] FREE WILL: ITS IMPORTANCE AND VALUE

FREE WILL FOR MORALITY

Recall the texting girl; her quick and careless choosing to text while driving causes the needless death of her two young friends. "What did I do? I am *responsible*! I could have done otherwise! I could have done so in exactly this same situation! How I wish I could do it over, roll back the clock and this time not text while I drive! I *regret* what I did in the strong sense." Regret in the strong sense refers to evils that I've done where I know perfectly well that I *could have not done them under the same conditions*; this is regret based on free will.

As we saw, determinism holds that I am ultimately not responsible for the evil I do. In contrast free will is the denial of determinism mainly because it leaves out *ultimate moral responsibility*. Doesn't it come into play in cases like the following? I realize that I have done something wrong, something seriously wrong; and I did it knowingly and willingly. When I later look back at it and realize what I have done, I feel an intense guilt, a deep remorse and sorrow. I realize: *I did it*! I did it in a deeper sense than the more common form of "I did it" that applies to surface freedom. Perhaps this sense of ultimate responsibility affords us not only an insight into the meaning of free will but also evidence for its reality. If ultimate moral responsibility is real, must it not lie on a level deeper than the interplay of factors typical of surface freedom? For ultimate moral responsibility to be real don't these factors, though playing an essential role, fall short of being the whole story? What is more? Isn't it free will?

Free will is important also because it is often needed as the ability to say *no* to moral evil. Ideally, we should have the total commitment to the good of spontaneous freedom. "Of course, I'll do the loving thing." "Of course, I'll act honestly." But practically we have tendencies not only for the good but for evil as well. Free will is something that can stop us from falling into evil. Say no to moral evil! By consistently using our free will to say *no* to moral evil we may be able to "determine" ourselves towards a spontaneous freedom for the good for much of our lives.

FREE WILL FOR DELIBERATION

According to determinism the future is completely determined by what has happened in the past. Given the past, and the laws governing all of reality, only one future is possible. But as we lead our lives, we invariably assume that the future contains alternative possibilities, that it is open and not rigidly fixed. When I deliberate between x and y I do so on the assumption that both are open to me. Deliberation, to make sense, needs an open future, one where both x and y are possible; and where it is thus *up to me to make one of them real*, by choosing it and acting on it. But if determinism is true isn't this an illusion? Given the past, only one of these possibilities is actually open. Is it reasonable to believe that something so basic to human life, something that we constantly take for granted is a monumental illusion? Isn't the reality of our experience of deliberation more evident than any theory such as total determinism? Could we lead our lives at all if we were not convinced of a largely open future which we can affect it by our deliberations? And doesn't deliberation require free will?

[14] FREE WILL: SOME LIMITATIONS AND DIFFICULTIES

Despite its importance there are also some difficulties with free will. Two come to mind:

The first has to do with *free will in itself*, its nature, and even whether it exists at all. On the one hand, free will seems to be a clearly given reality. Am I not my own person, in control of myself rather than being merely the product of factors outside me? And isn't free will a clearly given reality when we consider ultimate moral responsibility, regret especially for moral evils committed, the ability to say *no* to doing moral evil and deliberations for future actions?

On the other hand, free will seems to be impossible. Isn't there always a sufficient motive for how I choose? And to be effective must it not determine my behavior? If I choose A rather than B by an act of free will, it means I could have chosen B under exactly the same conditions. Is this really possible? Doesn't it seem that to have chosen B the scales must have tipped in favor of B in some even slight way? Else how could I have chosen B? Yet if it was a matter of the scales tipping in favor of B however slightly in order to ensure that B is actually chosen then it would not have been an act of free will?

Wonder: free will seems to be both a clearly given reality and also something impossible!

The second difficulty has to do with our *knowledge of free will*. This divides into free will in my own case; and free will attributed to another person, as when I

Chapter 12: Determinism and Free Will   207

blame someone for a wrong he committed on the assumption that he acted with free will.

My own case: I believe I acted with free will; that I could have chosen otherwise under exactly the same conditions. Can I ever really know this? How can I rule out the possibility that there were factors in place, perhaps unconscious, that determined my choosing with necessity?

The case of another person: the same concerns apply here too. First, how can I ever really know that another person could have chosen otherwise under exactly the same conditions? Second, how can I ever know in a given case of wrongdoing whether or not the offender had the sufficient goodness in him that he could tap into so that he could make a free will decision for the good? Don't both of these seem to be things one could never know?

If one could never know that another person acted with free will, does it follow that one should always refrain from judging others? That is an idea often advanced. Two examples come to mind: the injunction *do not judge* and the saying *there but for the grace of God go I*.

But can a policy of never judging be carried out in real life? Must we not be able to hold others accountable? To do this must we not judge them? Must this practice not be justifiable in at least some and probably most cases? Doesn't it necessarily require free will? Isn't judging others and holding them accountable necessary for the infliction of punishment?

Wonder: judging others seems to be both unjustified and also justified and necessary.

[15] DO WE HAVE FREE WILL?

FREE WILL MUST BE SEEN FROM WITHIN

If we view human behavior from the outside, in a manner typical of science, we are likely to look for explanations in a way similar to the way we look for explanations in other areas. Why did the dam break? Why did the plane crash? And why did he leave the party suddenly in a fit of anger? We look for something that explains the behavior completely, that leaves no gap. This implies that, given the same conditions again, our friend would again leave the party in a fit of anger. Same conditions, same factors, same result. This is of course determinism. And to a large extent this works well. Recall the cases where spontaneous freedom is the ideal: of course, I'll help you; and, of course, I'll take job A over job B because I now see clearly that it is the one I really want. In such cases determinism and spontaneous freedom work well together.

That is all well and good. But there are other cases where this approach doesn't work. Deliberation is one; ultimate moral responsibility and strong regret are others. To understand and do justice to these cases we must abandon the external-scientific-deterministic approach and see the behavior from within. This is what I have tried to bring out in the past-looking reflections on the texting girl. The explanation for her behavior is visible only to her from within her own person and to us as we empathize with her and try to replicate in our own minds what she went through as an *internal experience*: *I did that, I need not have done that, I could have done otherwise, and done so in exactly the same situation*. It is not visible from an outside point of view as an object of scientific inquiry.

For an example of seeing free will from within, recall the case where I am tempted to steal, strongly tempted. I need the money and I know I can get away with it. I deliberate. I decide not to steal. I choose honesty over dishonesty, and I do so just because I now want to do what is right and good. There is no further reason, no further factor that "explains" it, one that would be accessible to an outside viewpoint. It is my decision, a decision for the good; a decision for the good just because it is good. It is my decision in an ultimate and irreducible sense, not one that is explainable by something else.

FREE WILL AS CHOOSING AMONG DIFFERENT KINDS OF GOOD

Many cases of choosing among alternatives are *quantitative*; which course of action is likely to give me more of something: more money, more security or more pleasure. But some are not like that; they are *qualitative*; they involve not more or less good, but essentially different kinds of good. They appeal to different centers in a person. Why act dishonestly? It will give me a subjective pleasure.

Why act honestly? It is a good that stands on its own, objectively and independently of my subjective states. It is an intrinsic value. Such a value and my subjective pleasure represent – not two goods of the same kind, one more good than the other – but rather two *essentially different kinds of good*. One important kind of free will choosing is between two essentially different kinds of good. And understanding this kind of choosing is a good way of understanding what free will is and that it is real by seeing its reality from within.

[16] THE LARGER PICTURE

FREE WILL AND DETERMINISM: THREE POSSIBILITIES

The larger picture concerns first, the relative places given to free will and to determinism in one's overall view of reality; and second, to the role of being determined. Let me begin with the first, a brief outline of three possibilities:

1. **Free will is real and is the dominant reality.** Free will is an essential part of our nature as persons. The will is in its very nature free. Determinism is either rejected as an error; or if it is allowed in, it is given only a small place, a minor role in human behavior in the form of being determined. Often no distinction is made between freedom in general and free will.
2. **Free will is real but determinism as represented by being determined looms large.** Being determined is given a prominent place in human behavior; and it may even seem that it is the whole picture so that free will must be established by careful analysis in order to gain its rightful place. Being determined is taken seriously while determinism is rejected.
3. **Free will is not real; determinism reigns supreme.** What seems like free will choosing has its sufficient reasons in the being of a person; and is therefore completely determined by it. I may think I could have chosen otherwise under the same conditions, but this is an illusion; I am simply unaware of the factors "tugging" at me to choose as I do.

HOW BEING DETERMINED IS PRIMARY

1. ***Being determined is primary in four senses. First, metaphysically.*** We are what we are because we are determined to be that way. Heredity and environment make us the persons we are; they form our character, determine it. Then character largely determines our choosings. An honest person will generally choose honestly. Deviations generally result from other factors in a situation, factors that operate deterministically, for example, bad luck.

2. ***Second, in terms of value.*** Spontaneous freedom for the good is the ideal. Ideally there should only be this spontaneous freedom for the good where being determined is dominant. Where this is realized there is no need and no room for free will.

3. ***Unfortunately, this ideal is not realized: we are prone to evil, and so we need free will.*** As noted, we need it at the beginning so that we don't choose evil when tempted to do evil. And we need it afterwards if we have done evil: regret, repentance, reparations, forgiveness.

4. ***Here is a beautiful boat; ideally this should be the end of the story. But the boat is prone to leaks, so we need a pump to bail out the water. It would be much better if we didn't need the pump. We are the boat in our capacity for choosing the good; its being prone to leaks is our being prone to do evil; the pump is free will, which is a means and not an end.***

5. ***Third, in terms of context***: free will exists in a context of being determined. Here is a partial list of things that are what they are because they are determined to be so: the nature of the human person, the nature of the world, the nature of good, the nature of evil, that certain actions like driving while texting are wrong, that certain actions like lovingly caring for a sick person are good, that certain melodies are beautiful, that some of these melodies can move some people very deeply, that there is love in the world and that love can make us deeply happy. We don't get to choose any of this; all of it is already determined. Wonder!

6. ***Free will exists in a context of being determined.*** Particularly significant is the fact that where free will exists and can be effective it must be given

Chapter 12: Determinism and Free Will 211

to the person exercising it. Being given means being determined. Basically he must be given free will as a capacity of his being as a person; and then practically he must be given what it takes to exercise it.

7. *If he is to have a chance to choose the good when tempted to do evil, he must have it in him to be able to choose the good.* Was he given the necessary love as a child so that he now does have it in him to choose the good? Or was he denied this so that he cannot now choose the good? If so, free will cannot come into play and an unfortunate being determined rules.

8. *Fourth, being determined is primary epistemologically, in terms of what we know and don't know.* It is more clear and more certain that a criminal is at least partly determined in his behavior than that free will plays any role at all; or if it does to what extent. The being determined part is obvious and certain; the free will part is far from obvious and certain.

9. *No one doubts that being determined plays at least some role. Many people doubt that free will plays any role because they doubt that it even exists.* Can you freely wonder?!

[17] SIGNIFICANT FEATURES OF THIS ANALYSIS

A WORD ON THE ANALYSIS PRESENTED HERE

The analysis here differs significantly from some of the traditional accounts that defend human freedom and moral responsibility against determinism, which is seen as a mortal threat to the important values contained in human freedom and moral responsibility. Some key points:

1. *Free will:* it is not the most important and prominent reality. Its place is in a much larger context that includes the given-being determined and spontaneous freedom.
2. *Spontaneous freedom*: it is far more important and significant than free will. "Of course, I will help you!" Isn't this response of spontaneous free-

dom far better than free will which could go either way? If so, spontaneous freedom should be given a prominent place.

3. ***Being determined:*** the key distinction is made between the fact of being determined and a common theory about it. Being determined is usually neglected and overlooked because of its close association with the theory of determinism which one is determined to avoid at all costs; one fears that being determined could be confused with determinism and be an open door to let it in. Being determined is also more important and significant than free will and should be given its rightful prominent place.

SPONTANEOUS FREEDOM AND DETERMINISM

Spontaneous freedom is not given its due place in some traditional accounts because one fears it is too close to determinism; it seems to have an affinity to it; and like determinism stands in contrast to the idea expressed by the phrase *I could have done otherwise*. But, in fact, the two are essentially different:

1. *Determinism does not imply spontaneous freedom but applies also to decision freedom, with two or more live options. Thus, determinism goes beyond spontaneous freedom.*
2. *Spontaneous freedom does not imply determinism. Perhaps the texting girl (who caused a massive accident by her texting-driving) acted with spontaneous freedom but is still morally responsible because she had free will. She could have done otherwise (free will) even though she did not in fact consider doing otherwise (spontaneous freedom).*
3. *Determinism is a theory; spontaneous freedom is a fact of human behavior.*

BEING DETERMINED: SOME BASIC POINTS

1. ***Being determined should not be confused with determinism.*** Again, determinism is a theory while being determined is a fact of the human situation.

Chapter 12: Determinism and Free Will

2. ***Being determined stands to determinism as matter stands to materialism.*** We can readily say yes to the former in each case while saying no to the latter in each case.
3. ***We can give a prominent place to being determined without adopting determinism.***
4. ***The key point is not that I am determined but how I am determined; that I am determined at least in part is clear.*** How am I determined? Is it to the good and the rational? Or is it to evil and the irrational?
5. ***To a large extent we can identify being determined with the given.***

BEING DETERMINED: SO MUCH IS GIVEN

Being determined means that so much is *given* to me; things that are not up to me, not in my control, not in my power; these are the hallmarks of freedom. Here are some examples of the given in life, of many different kinds and on many different levels:

1. That I am a person.
2. That I am this particular person.
3. What I have been given: through my heredity.
4. What I have been given: through my environment.
5. My character, hopefully that I am basically a good person; this is largely presupposed for choosing the good, including choosing the good by free will.
6. My spiritual powers of intellect, will, and heart.
7. My knowledge.
8. My memory.
9. My powers of logical analysis and reasoning.
10. My powers of sense perception: seeing, hearing, etc.
11. What is given to me through the senses: the objects I see, the tones I hear, etc.
12. My skills and my ability to develop them, such as my ability to learn a language.

13. What I can be grateful for: important persons in my life and the relations of mutual love.
14. Gratitude: food, shelter, physical health, mental health, living in a free country, etc.
15. Gratitude: sensitivity to beauty.
16. Gratitude: beautiful things especially beautiful music, nature, etc. There is so much else.
17. My power of free will (assuming free will is a reality).
18. My motives for free choosing, by free will and other ways of freely choosing.
19. "It just occurred to me…"; "the name of the person I was searching for just came to me."
20. My moods come over me, they are given to me.
21. My dreams are given to me. Why did I dream this? Where did it come from? **Wonder**:

- On the one hand dreams are so much me and so deeply in me; they are only in me so that it is impossible to really share them with others; descriptions always seem to fall short.
- On the other hand, dreams are not at all me but somehow completely foreign to me in that I did not freely choose to dream this; I cannot control my dream, it is a totally given.

[18] THREE CORE POINTS OF WONDER

ONE: BEING FREE SEEMS TO BE OPPOSED TO BEING DETERMINED AND YET BOTH SEEM TO BE AN INTEGRAL PART OF REALITY

- I am free, I can choose and act of my own accord; what I do is up to me.
- But how I choose is determined by my motives, my character, ultimately by my heredity and early childhood environment. I did not feely choose these; they were given to me.

TWO: DOES BEING DETERMINED DESTROY FREEDOM?

Closely related to the above but calling for a more extensive elaboration is the question whether being determined does or does not destroy freedom. Suggested reply:

It all depends on *how* one is determined; here are several ways it does destroy freedom:

- *The story of the conditioners.* If being determined takes the form of conditioning, is it not a way of destroying our freedom?
- *The story of Danielle.* Wasn't her being determined to always avoid choosing any light-haired dog a destruction of her freedom in this respect?
- *The drug addict.* His addiction is foisted on him and deprives him of true freedom.
- *The theories of Holbach and Mark Twain.* Freedom is an illusion; we are unknowingly carried along by the universe of which we are a part. A person did not make himself; he has no control over himself; he is a subject for pity, not responsibility and blame.
- *The theories of Edwards and Hospers.* Our actions flow from our character, which was given to us, determined for us; this destroys our freedom.

Here are several ways that being determined does not destroy freedom:

- Being determined is good and necessary in many ways especially formation of character; choosing freely then naturally flows from this character.
- Being loved is a way of being determined and a great gift; one that leads to much freedom.
- Being determined is primary and necessary for free will: where free will exists, it must be given to the person exercising it.

- Being determined is primary and necessary for free will: does the person have it in him to make a genuine free will choice? If so this must be given to him. Free will is always exercised in terms of the given for a person which is a matter of being determined.
- This is especially significant in the case of being able to say no to evil and choose good by free will; does the person have it in him to be able to do this? If so, it must be given.

THREE: ARE WE ULTIMATELY MORALLY RESPONSIBLE FOR WHAT WE DO?

- **No. Edwards and Hospers:** we are not responsible for the formation of our character and therefore we are also not responsible for the behavior that flows from it necessarily.
- **Yes.** There is the deep conviction when I have done something wrong that I did it freely and so could have done otherwise; and that therefore I own it and I am responsible for it.

Take time to wonder at the subtle realities of determinism, freedom, and free will and their interplay in your own life! When do you believe you are most free or most determined? Wonder at moments of spontaneous freedom and what they reveal about your character.

CHAPTER 13
TRUTH

[1] WHAT IS TRUTH?

TRUTH AND REALITY

Wonder: what is truth? We hold truth in high esteem when we realize how important it is to know the truth on important matters, to get at the truth and only the truth by "getting it right"; and to honor the truth by not lying. But what is this reality that we call the "the truth"?

The truth is not a thing like a tree or any other "substantial" reality like a person or a dog. What is it then? We often speak of "the truth"; but, actually, there are many truths, an infinite number of them; consider the truths of arithmetic that 1+1=2, 1+2=3, and 1+3=4 and so on.

What then is a single, specific truth? Consider an example where the phrase *the truth* might come up. Mother and daughter are having a conversation. "Where were you at 2:00AM last night?" The reply isn't very convincing. The dialogue goes back and forth. Finally, Mom says with lots of emotion and emphasis: "OK, just tell me the truth!" Doesn't *the truth* simply mean "Tell me what really happened"? "Tell me how it really is, or really was at that time." Isn't the urgent request for the truth the request to be able to come to an awareness of *reality*, how it really is? If so we seem to have an important clue to the nature of truth: reality.

Consider another example. I have a friend, John, who is accused of a serious crime. I look into the matter, carefully consider all the evidence and conclude that it clearly shows that he is innocent. I form the belief "John is innocent." I claim that he really is innocent, that this is the truth of the matter. Suppose I am correct, that in fact he really is innocent. Then my belief is what it is because it is about *truth*; it is about the *reality* that he actually is innocent.

Can we then simply say that truth is reality? The *reality* is that John is innocent. Doesn't *truth* pertain to something else? To something that is true? If so, we move from considering *the truth* to *true*. What then is that something that is true; true in some cases and false in others?

WHAT IS IT THAT IS TRUE?

What is it that is true? True cannot exist all by itself; there is always something that is true. What is that something? As noted, it is not a thing. For example, a table cannot be true or false; so too, a person, a place, an event, etc. These exist or do not exist, but they cannot be true or false. Consider our example *John is innocent*. Assume it is true. What is the "it"? It is not John; it is not innocence; it is not even the reality that John is innocent.

Is it the *belief* that John is innocent? Whose belief? Why pick one person rather than another? If 40 people believe he is innocent are there 40 things that are true? That doesn't seem right. But perhaps the most telling objection is this. Suppose no one believes he is innocent, not even John himself; he has been brainwashed into believing that he is guilty. Still, isn't it so that John actually is innocent; that it remains *true* that he is innocent? What is it that remains true when all beliefs fail? What is the "it" that is true when there are no true beliefs?

PROPOSITIONS

If beliefs don't work, let us try something else: it is the *proposition* asserting that John is innocent that is true. It is propositions and not beliefs that are bearers of truth or falsity. If John really is innocent then it is the proposition *John is innocent* that is true, really true, whether anyone believes it or not. Perhaps as noted no one believes it, not even John. The proposition is still true if it asserts what is really the case. Surely truth may exist without beliefs for there are truths which no one knows, which no one believes. But this can be so only if the propositions expressing these truths exist in themselves, independently of any beliefs.

True beliefs cannot exist without true propositions, for it is true propositions which make these beliefs true beliefs. But true propositions may exist without beliefs. Thus, it is not beliefs that are true or false, but propositions. Beliefs may be called true or false derivatively in that a true belief expresses a true proposition.

More generally, beliefs cannot exist without propositions for propositions are the *contents* of beliefs. I cannot just believe; I can only believe *that something is the case*, and this refers to a proposition. I can believe that John is innocent; I can believe that he is guilty. Further, you and I can have the same belief in the sense that we believe the same proposition. In an important sense your belief is not my belief, for we each have our own beliefs. How then is it possible that we can speak meaningfully of having the same beliefs? For of course we do say this; we say it when we agree on something. We say this when we "believe the same thing"; and to believe the same thing means to believe the same proposition. So once again, what is true or false is not the belief as such, but *what* is believed, the *content* of the belief, which is a proposition.

But do we really need propositions? Why can't we just say that it is *sentences* that are true or false? That won't work either; like beliefs they are not exactly what we are looking for.

SENTENCES AND PROPOSITIONS

To see this, consider the sentence "I love you." That can mean different things: romantic love, the love of a parent for a child, the love of a child for her parents, and more. But this gives us a hint of what we are looking for: a proposition as the meaning of a sentence; and a sentence as expressing a proposition. Consider how the two are related:

- One sentence may express several different propositions: "I love you" in the ways just indicated. Another example is the sentence "Jim rents his room" which can mean either that Jim is a landlord who rents his room out to someone else or that Jim lives in a room for which he pays rent; two different propositions, with two different meanings.
- Several sentences may all express one and the same proposition. The English sentence "I love you" and the German sentence "Ich liebe dich" may express the same proposition.

- Basically, a proposition is the meaning of a sentence.
- Alternatively, a sentence expresses a proposition; or more precisely, a given proposition is what a given sentence may be expressing.

Just as we ask for the meaning of a word, we can also ask for the meaning of a sentence. We may ask: what does the word *culture* mean? And we often ask: what do you mean? This is typically the request for the meaning of a sentence. "I'm leaving"; and we wonder what that means. Are you leaving for a short while? Are you leaving permanently? We wonder about the meaning of this sentence; we wonder: what is the proposition that it expresses?

The key thing is that when we look to a sentence as the something that is true or false it is really the proposition that stands behind the sentence that we are looking for; the proposition that is the meaning of the sentence and that is the actual bearer of *true* and *false*.

All this means that it is really only propositions that are true or false, not sentences. A sentence is true or false only derivatively in that it expresses a true or false proposition. The essential difference between a proposition and a declarative sentence may become obscured by terms that are ambiguous. One example is the word *statement* which can refer to a declarative sentence, a proposition, or both taken together. The same applies to the word *assertion*.

We have seen that beliefs are true or false only derivatively. They are true or false in a secondary sense, namely if the propositions that form their content – *what* is believed – are true or false. What is primarily true or false is a proposition. In a parallel way, sentences are true or false only derivatively. They are true or false in a secondary sense, namely if the propositions which the sentences express or convey, are true or false.

Chapter 13: Truth

WONDER: PROPOSITIONS AS SAYING SOMETHING

When we consider the idea of saying something, don't we generally have in mind some person who is doing the saying? How else could there be the reality that is saying something? Wonder invites us to take another look.

Truth pertains to the statement or proposition that asserts, or "says," that something is true when it really is true; that, for example, "says" *John is innocent* when in fact he is innocent. This asserting or "saying" is not something which is done by a person; it is something done by the proposition itself. It is in the very nature of a proposition to "say" something. When we want to know what a proposition is, we want to know what it "says"; they are one and the same thing, or at least two sides of the same coin. When we want try to understand what a proposition means, we want to understand what it "says"; again, they are one and the same thing or two sides of the same coin. This distinction, between the way in which a person "says" something and the way a proposition "says" something, is one we are all familiar with in everyday life. Compare:

It says here that the store is closed.
He says that the store is closed.

The first is a sign on the wall that expresses a proposition, and it refers to the way a proposition "says" something. The second is a verbal utterance, something "said" by a person. It refers to the way a person "says" something.

The two are distinct but also closely related, and also call for our **wonder**: a *person* can say something only by using a *proposition* that says something. When *he* says that the store is closed, he is doing so by uttering the *proposition* that says the store is closed.

WONDER: WHERE DO PROPOSITIONS EXIST?

Where do propositions exist? Surely, they don't exist "out there" in the physical world along with sticks and stones. Do they then exist in us, in our minds? It seems they do not:

We want to be able to say that during the ice age it was true that ice covered much of the world, even though there were no persons at the time who knew it to be true. Doesn't this mean that this truth existed at that time without any mind grasping it? And if this truth existed must there not have been a proposition that existed and was true? How could this truth exist without a proposition, since it is always propositions that are bearers of truth? Doesn't this mean that in addition to the ice and other physical objects existing at that time something else also existed at that time, namely propositions? That surely seems strange; but how else could it be?

- *Ice covered* much of the world, but it wasn't true that it did so?
- It was true that it did so but there was no true proposition saying that it was so?
- There was a true proposition saying that it was so, but it didn't exist at that time?

Wonder: none of these three options seems to work well; are we then back to holding that a proposition existed at that time and was true? We might say that propositions exist timelessly like numbers; but wouldn't that include that they also existed somehow back then?

Wonder: if propositions don't exist in minds, does it mean that they exist independently of any minds? How can they exist in this way? But if they exist, they must exist in some way.

Wonder: propositions are very puzzling entities, so much so that one may be tempted to deny that they exist. But if they don't exist, what is it that is true? Not beliefs and not sentences; it seems nothing is left except propositions. Surely truth exists and, if so, there must be something that is true. As we saw truth cannot exist all by itself and typical things like tables, persons and places cannot be the something that is true. What then is that *something*? What can it be but a proposition? Surely, they are puzzling but are they really any more puzzling than, say, numbers?

If no physical reality existed and no persons, would numbers still exist? Wouldn't it still be true that 2 + 2 = 4? And that 100 is larger than 50? Wouldn't the laws of logic still hold, especially the principle of non-contradiction, that something cannot be both true and false, in the same respect? If we say that numbers and the laws of logic exist, can we not say with equal plausibility that propositions exist?

Some people say numbers are human creations and wouldn't exist if we didn't exist. But then how would it be possible that we discover new things about numbers? And that some puzzles about numbers remain unsolved by mathematicians? Numbers somehow seem to lie beyond us in their nature and being, and so they are not reducible to something in our minds.

[2] WHAT MAKES TRUE PROPOSITIONS TRUE?

This brings us to the next big question: what is it that makes true propositions true? One answer is *coherence*: a true proposition is one that coheres or fits in with other true propositions to form one grand totality of The Truth. But what makes that true? And couldn't there be a set of propositions that all cohere with one another to form one big lie? Think of a person who is really guilty but who spins a plausible tale, a story consisting entirely of coherent propositions.

CORRESPONDENCE

What is it that makes a true proposition true? Another answer, the traditional answer and the one I want to suggest as the correct one is *correspondence*; correspondence with reality.

Go back to our example of John who is accused of a crime. I claim he is innocent. I am correct because he really is innocent. We can then say that the reality is that he is innocent and that this is the truth of the matter. Can we then also say that truth is reality? No, the *reality* is that John is innocent while *truth* pertains to something else, namely a proposition "saying" that this is so, asserting that it is so. And this brings us to the relation between truth and reality: a proposition is true when and because it asserts what is really the case. This is what it means to say that it corresponds to reality. In short, truth means correspondence to reality or with reality.

The idea that the nature of truth is correspondence with reality goes back to Aristotle. In his words "To say of what is that it is, or of what is not that it is not, is true."[1] Basically, it means that to say that something is true is to say that it asserts what is really the case; that what it asserts is the case corresponds to what is really the case. The key idea is *corresponds*.

Wonder: what is this relation expressed by *corresponds*? Consider the correspondence between the true proposition *John is innocent* and the reality *that John really is innocent*. Can it be explained by something else? It is, for example, not the relation of picturing. A picture of Mary in some way "corresponds" to Mary herself, but this is a "correspondence" in an altogether different sense; it is a completely different relation. The picture may be more like Mary, it may resemble her more closely; or it may be less like her. But the picture is not literally "true" as the proposition *John is innocent* is true or can be true. A true picture is a good picture, an accurate picture; it is "true" in a very different sense, one merely analogous to the truth of propositions, as when we say that John is innocent is true, that it really is so that he is innocent.

There are other relations of correspondence that we may consider:

> A key may correspond with its keyhole and one half of a stamp with the other half, while an entry in a ledger may correspond to a sale and one rank in the army to another in the navy.[2]

Each of these relations seems to be essentially and radically different from the relation of correspondence between a true proposition and the reality that it refers to and that makes it true. Perhaps focusing on them can help us see more clearly the unique character of correspondence.

---

[1] *Metaphysics,* 1011b, 25-28.

[2] Alan R. White, *Truth* (Garden City, New York: Doubleday Anchor Books, 1970), 105. Italics in original.

Wonder: what is this relation of correspondence? We seem to know perfectly well what it is even though we cannot articulate it in words. Is it something we grasp immediately in its intrinsic intelligibility? Is it something that cannot be explained or defined in terms of anything else because it is something ultimate and irreducible? We are left with wonder.

REALITY

Truth means correspondence with reality. But what is that reality? Take the proposition *John is innocent*. Does it correspond to John as an individual person? Does it correspond to the idea of innocence as such? Doesn't it correspond to a very different kind of reality: *that* John is innocent? This is generally called a state of affairs or a fact. Thus, the reality to which a true proposition corresponds is a state of affairs or a fact: *that* such and such is the case. We can also say that a state of affairs or a fact is the referent of a proposition.

Reality is what makes propositions true; the reality that John is innocent is what makes the proposition *John is innocent* true. In the other direction we can say that a true proposition is one that asserts what is the case; for example, that says "John is innocent" when in fact he is innocent. This is the relation of correspondence. That the *proposition* "John is innocent" is true means that what it asserts really is so, that it corresponds to the *reality* "that John is innocent."

WONDER AT REALITY

Wonder: is there a future reality? "There will be a sea battle tomorrow." Can this be true already today? Both a *yes* and a *no* answer seem to be plausible. No: as of now there is no sea battle for this to refer to, no actual reality to which a true proposition could correspond. Yes: someone who correctly predicts that a sea battle will take place tomorrow is speaking the truth; hence the proposition can be true today. Several other considerations seem to bear this out:

1. Truth is timeless. What is true is true regardless of the time it refers to. It is simply true that World War I started in 1914. The event of its starting

is in the past. That it started then is simply true because it is simply the case; it is timelessly true, not a past truth.

2. What has to await the future is not the truth of a true proposition about the future but rather our coming to know this or to confirm it.
3. We should not confuse "x is not true unless y" and "x is not true until y." Here x refers to the proposition that the sea battle will take place and y refers to its actually taking place. "To say that 'there will be a naval battle tomorrow' cannot be true unless there is a naval battle tomorrow is not to say, nor does it imply, that what is said cannot be true until there is such a battle."[3]
4. We should not confuse the fact that there will be a naval battle tomorrow, which is what the truth of the proposition depends on and what it corresponds to – and the existence of the battle, the battle itself.[4]
5. Quite generally, can't a proposition refer to something that doesn't exist? I hope to take a vacation next year. That vacation doesn't exist now, but doesn't it make perfectly good sense to think about it, to talk about it and take steps to ensure that it will become real?[5]

Wonder: what kind of reality does a true proposition correspond to when it is expressed by a counter-factual statement? Such a statement takes the form: if x had occurred y would have occurred. When such a statement is true what is it that makes it true? By hypothesis there is no actual state of affairs that it can correspond to. It is about what would have happened but didn't actually happen. Consider some examples. In each case if the statement is true what is the reality that makes it true? What is the reality to which it corresponds?

- If he had walked out on the thin ice he would have fallen into the water.
- If he had fallen into the water, he would have gotten wet.
- If she had left her house at 7:00PM before the tornado she would still be alive today.

---

[3] White, 47.

[4] Based on White, 47.

[5] Also based on White, 47.

- If she had taken her medications regularly, she would still be alive today.
- If you had told your joke when Harry was present, he would have gotten very upset.

Wonder: what kind of reality does a true negative proposition correspond to? Negative propositions are those that assert what is not the case. Again, consider some examples. And in each case if the proposition is true what is the reality to which it corresponds?

- There are no snakes in this room now.
- There were no snowflakes in Florida on July 4th, 2015.
- Jack has no chance of making the basketball team.
- Mother Teresa never robbed a bank.
- Aristotle never talked on a cell phone.

For both of these two types of cases, counter-factuals and negatives, there seems to be no reality to which true propositions correspond. Does this mean that the idea of correspondence has to be abandoned or modified? Or if it is kept, are there certain facts or states of affairs to which they do correspond? Are there perhaps negative states of affairs? An example would be that there are no snakes in this room. The truth of this proposition seems to be clear and obvious, and to present no problems. But when we look for the reality that this true proposition supposedly corresponds to we seem to find nothing or nothing actual. But then non-actuality is just what such propositions are meant to convey. "Don't worry, there are no snakes in this room; you can enter it safely." The hearer is then reassured by the good news. And this is the reality that there are no snakes here. What kind of reality is that? Do we always understand this term *reality* when we use it? When we think we understand what it means? Wonder again!

The ultimate wonder puzzle: if nothing existed would it be *true* that nothing exists?

[3] FALSEHOODS, ERRORS AND LIES

A false proposition is one that asserts what is not really the case. Thus, if John really is innocent, then "John is guilty" is a false proposition. Alternatively, a false proposition is one that does not correspond to any actual state of affairs. For example, that Santa Claus is coming is not an actual state of affairs so the proposition "Santa Claus is coming" is a false proposition. The contradictory of a true proposition is always a false proposition, and the contradictory of a false proposition is always a true proposition.

The truth of true propositions is independent of our believing them; in the same way the falseness of false propositions is independent of our disbelieving them or considering them or believing them. What is false is *already false* before we come upon it and consider it; it does not have to be *seen as* false in order to *be* false.

It is *propositions* that are true or false and *persons* who can be in error. To be in error means to be convinced of a proposition that is false; to think it is true while in fact it is false. A proposition by itself can only be false, not an error. And if I consider a proposition that is false, or use it as an example, or doubt it, I am not in error. It is when I *believe* a false proposition that I am in error. It is this further point, this relation of a proposition to *belief* that makes it an error.

A proposition by itself cannot be an error, nor can it be a lie. It is only persons who can be in error or lie. What then are the differences between the two, errors and lies? First, an error involves only *one* person, the one who errs. A lie involves *two* persons, the liar and the victim.

Second, the liar believes the false proposition that is the content of the lie to be *false*, while the person in error believes the false proposition that is the content of the error to be *true*.

Third, an error means that a certain person *in fact* believes a false proposition. A lie is an *attempt* to cause another person to believe a false proposition, for not all lies cause false beliefs; some lies are unsuccessful in their attempts to cause false beliefs in other persons.

Fourth, a lie has a *moral* significance that an error as such doesn't have. Generally, lies are morally wrong while errors are morally neutral. Closely related to this is that you *decide* to lie but you do not decide to be in error; you fall into error.

The stark contrast between errors and lies, even though both have an essential relation to falsehoods, can be brought out by defining a lie through an A-B-C-D analysis. In a lie a person:

(A) Asserts what he
(B) Believes to be false, so as to
(C) Cause a false belief in another person, in order to
(D) Deceive him.

The C and D parts bring out the crucial difference between lies and several other things that can also include the A and B parts; things such as jokes, lines in a play, stories and using a false proposition as an example to make a point.

[4] IS TRUTH OBJECTIVE?

THE OBJECTIVITY OF TRUTH

Wonder: is truth objective? If so, what does this mean? If it is subjective what would this mean? One common meaning of truth as objective and not subjective is that it is not dependent on individual beliefs. What is true is true whether I believe it or not. A patient is given the bad news that he has cancer. The doctor's diagnosis is correct: he really has cancer. Then this is the truth of the matter. If the patient cannot bring himself to accept this, if he refuses to believe it, it is still true. He is in denial of truth, of reality; for truth is the expression of reality.

Doesn't this example bring out the objectivity of truth as absolutely obvious and evident? And yet some people seem to deny that truth is objective and thus independent of us. We hear the phrases *true for me* and *true for you*. Thus, some people will say "If you believe in God, then God's existence is true for you; if you don't then His existence is not true for you."

No one applies *true for me* and *true for you* to matters like having cancer or not having it. Why then do they apply it to matters like the existence of God? The typical reply is that in matters like the cancer case we have or can get answers to our questions while in matters like the existence of God we cannot get answers; the claim is that each person has his own opinion and no one can say who is really correct; that is, who "has the truth." Why then say that there is a truth, an objective truth? "If there were an objective truth about God who's to say what it is? Since no one can say what it is, it makes no sense to say that this truth exists."

Wonder: what lies behind this? Why is objective truth affirmed in one case (cancer) and denied in another (God)? Reflect on the idea *who's to say what it is?* Why is this seen as so important? Does it really matter whether anyone can *say* what is true? Isn't the crucial question what *is* true, what is really the case, what is objectively the case? That is the question of truth, ultimately of reality; of objective truth and reality whether anyone can say it or not. Saying what is true is only important because there really is a truth, an objective truth existing independently of whether anyone is in the position of saying what this truth is.

RELATIVISM AS A THEORY OF TRUTH

The claim that truth is not objective in matters like the question of the existence of God; that in such cases it is relative to persons is a form of relativism. It is a theory about the meaning of truth; the claim that truth is relative to individuals, that there is no objective truth; no truth independent of persons, no *how it really is*. Its basic idea, as noted is: "Who's to say what is objectively true? Since no one can say what it is it makes no sense to say that it exists."

Wonder: can this view be held consistently? It is the claim that in matters where people disagree, where there are no agreed-upon "answers" no one is correct; there is no objective truth. But this is itself a matter where people disagree. So, no one is correct? There is no objective truth? But now consider those who propose this idea: are they claiming that what they say is the truth, the objective truth? If they are not claiming this, why propose it? But if they are claiming it, isn't there a clear contradiction: *it is really true that there is no really true?*

In the cancer case isn't there clearly an absolute, non-relative truth of the matter? Here the *true for me* theory is too absurd to be taken seriously. But I want to suggest that it is false on a much deeper level; that it is mistaken at its very core because it is mistaken about the very nature of truth. The mistake of denying the objectivity of truth applies across the board for it includes matters such as whether God exists and other matters that people disagree about, such as politics and ethics.

The difference between matters like the cancer case and whether or not God exists lies, not in the nature of truth but in how or whether we can get at such truth. Truth is the same in all cases: objective. What differs in the two types of cases concerns reaching it in our knowledge and belief or not reaching it and remaining in doubt, ignorance, or error. The one seems easier, more obvious and commands universal agreement. The other about God is deeper and more challenging.

SOME CRITICAL QUESTIONS ABOUT RELATIVISM AS A THEORY OF TRUTH

1. Doesn't it confuse *I don't know* with *there is nothing there to be known*? A denial of objective truth means a denial of the corresponding reality, and this is what relativism intends. But surely *something is the case* about God, about life after death, even if some people do not know what it is, or are mistaken in what they believe about it. Something is the case means that there is some reality there, known or not known; and truth is whatever corresponds to this reality.

2. In a similar way doesn't it confuse *I can't prove this to be true* with *it isn't really true*? But can't something be true without my being able to prove this, or show it? Can't John really be innocent even if he can't prove it? We will return to this point in the next section.

3. Doesn't relativism fail by not having adequate room for being mistaken? We are mistaken when we hold a *false belief*. Consider a male chauvinist who believes "women are inferior to men" or a sadist who believes "torturing people for fun is morally acceptable." Are these beliefs not clearly

false? Are such people not clearly mistaken? Who could seriously say to them, "that's true – it's true for you"?

And suppose someone said, "Relativism regarding truth is a false theory." Wouldn't the relativist want to say he is mistaken? Yet he couldn't without contradicting his theory; for to be consistent, he would have to say "if you believe that, then it's true for you." If he says of someone that he is mistaken, that what he believes is false, he is abandoning his position that "if you believe it, it's true – it's true for you."

4. Is relativism *itself true*? How is the relativistic theory that there is no truth supposed to be really true? Is it supposed to be objectively true, true whether we realize it or not? If the claim is made that it is, isn't the contradiction obvious? The denial that there is an objective truth is put forward as a claim to be itself an objective truth: it is really true that nothing is true! If relativism acknowledges that its own theory is not really true, can't we simply say: yes, agreed, it's not true? But if it's not true, shouldn't we reject it?

EVERY THEORY RESTS ON OBJECTIVE TRUTH

Isn't there an important lesson here? That is, *every theory rests on the notion of objective truth*. Every theory, to be meaningful, must be put forth as the claim *so it really is*; the claim to be objectively true. Lacking this claim, it cannot be a meaningful theory. But relativism, to be consistent, must lack this claim; doesn't this mean that it cannot be a meaningful theory?

Take any theory put forth by one of the sciences: Newton's theory of gravity, Einstein's theory of time, theories about climate change, theories of personality type, and many others. Don't they all make claims that such-and-such is really the case? Some are more established, so that one might claim they are really facts; others are less established. But even here there is an essential reference to objective truth. Doesn't *established* mean shown to be true or likely true?

GENUINE RELATIVITY

Some things really are relative: what is on the right and what is on the left are relative to your point of view; up and down are relative to the center of the earth. Rules about touching the ball are relative to specific games: in football touching is allowed but in soccer (except for the goalie) it is not allowed. None of these cases show that truth is relative; on the contrary they are further examples of truth as objective. In each of these cases, *that* such and such is relative to this framework and not to another, that it is relative in this way and not in another – all these are *really the case*, they are all *objectively the case*. And so, propositions stating such relativities are themselves absolutely true, objectively true; or false. They are true if the relativity they express is in fact the case; false if it is not. Thus, all genuine relativity depends ultimately on an absolute or objective basis. *It is really so, it is objectively so, that such and such is relative.* The relativist theory of truth fails to capture this fundamental fact. The nature of truth as objective, as stating what is really the case underlies absolutely everything, including all relativity and all theories. Relativism of truth is thus self-contradictory at the most fundamental level.

THE RELATIONAL AND THE RELATIVE

It is important to clearly distinguish these two different propositions:

- Truth is *relational*.
- Truth is *relative*.

Truth is *relational* asserts the *objectivity* view of truth; truth means correspondence with reality and correspondence is the relation between a true proposition and the reality it refers to.

The claim that truth is *relative* means the *denial of the objectivity* of truth; it is the idea that truth is somehow relative, as in "true for me" and "true for you" rather than objectively true, true independently of you and me.

ANOTHER LOOK AT "TRUE FOR ME"

Perhaps what is sometimes meant by "true for me" is simply that I believe something to be true while you may not believe it to be true. That is something very different. Note that here the "for me" part refers to my belief system as opposed to someone else's. It is not an attack on the objectivity of truth as in the original "true for me." Rather, *for me* is simply a misleading way of saying something very clear and simple: my belief belongs to me and not to you. Surely this does not contradict the objectivity of truth. My belief is *about* something, a reality independent of it; a claim that something is the case; that it is true, objectively true.

And if it is such a claim, surely my belief may be correct in that what I believe to be true *really is true*, that it is *the truth*. If so, then opinions and beliefs do not contradict objective truth; on the contrary they appeal to it and really would not make any sense without it. All this clearly points to the objectivity of truth.

Recall our example of John who is accused of a serious crime. I carefully consider all the evidence and conclude that it clearly shows that he is innocent. And so I form the opinion "John is innocent." I claim that he really is innocent, that this is the truth of the matter, the objective truth. Now suppose I am correct: in fact he really is innocent. Then my opinion is what it is because it is about an objective truth, the objective truth that he really is innocent.

But suppose I am mistaken: he is not innocent, he is guilty. Then something else is the truth of the matter, his being guilty. This is equally an objective truth. So the objectivity of truth remains. *Something* is the case; something is the truth of the matter, the objective truth.

And so opinions, far from suggesting that truth is subjective, show that it is objective. Opinions are striving to reach an objective reality and may be in conformity to it.

THE OBJECTIVITY OF TRUTH AS A ROCK BOTTOM

The cancer example brings out the objectivity of truth as something we can know with an absolute certainty. Here is another point of view on this. We can see it as forming part of the rock bottom of our whole intellectual life: it cannot be denied without self-contradiction. To see this, consider the claim "Truth is not objective." If someone says this, we can ask: is *that* true? If the answer is *no* we can say: correct, it is not true, for truth is objective. If the answer is *yes*, "truth is not objective" we can again ask: is *that* true? Presumably one will claim it is true. What else could one reasonably do? But what can this mean except the claim "so it really is"? Is it supposedly *really true* that truth is not objective? Isn't this "is" the same as saying it is *objectively true* that *truth is not objective*? Isn't this a blatant contradiction?

Anyone who tries to claim that truth is not objective can do so only by claiming that truth is not really objective but is really something else. But to say it is "really something else" is simply to reintroduce the very objectivity of truth that one tried to deny. To deny the objectivity of truth is to claim, "There is no objective truth." Is *that* true? Is it really true? Suppose the reply is "yes, that's true, it is really true." And that amounts to saying, "It's really true that there is no real truth." Again, we can see the blatant contradiction.

The objectivity of truth is a rock bottom, first in the sense that it is something absolutely certain in that any attempt to deny it must necessarily presuppose it and appeal to it and thereby reintroduce it. And second, in the sense that it forms the basis for all thinking, a *belief* is a claim that such and such is the case, meaning that it is really the case, that it is objectively so. If I believe John is innocent, I claim that so it really is, that this is objectively true. And *knowledge* means grasping how it really is. If I know that John is innocent, I grasp that he really is innocent. If I *wonder* whether John is innocent, I wonder what the reality here is. To ask a *question* is to inquire into how it really is, as in "what really happened?" Every *theory* can be meaningfully put forth only in the name of objective truth. Thus, the theory of evolution claims to describe what really happened in the matter of biological development. Einstein's theories claim to describe what is really the case in regard to the basic nature of physical reality.

SCEPTICISM

Is scepticism an exception to this? On the contrary, isn't it a typical example of this? If scepticism claims "we cannot know anything about x" isn't it appealing to truth, objective truth? And isn't it doing so in two ways?

- First, isn't it claiming we cannot know how x really is: *the truth* about x?
- Second, isn't it claiming that it is really *true:* we cannot know anything about x?

Isn't scepticism a theory that begins with and builds on the unmistakable fact that we cannot always reach truth? Isn't it a theory that then moves beyond this and puts forth a further thesis, "we can never reach truth"? That is: "we can never get at reality as it really is." So, isn't the very thesis of scepticism necessarily expressed in terms of objective truth, namely the claim that objective truth is always beyond our reach?

[5] DOES TRUTH DEPEND ON PROOF?

Another way to deny the objectivity of truth is to say that truth depends on proof. "If it hasn't been proved it's not true." Is *that* true? Has *that* been proved? Surely it has not been proved, nor can it be proved. By its own logic it cannot be true; it falls by its own weight; it refutes itself. It is an idea that cannot be advanced without falling into self-contradiction.

Truth does not depend on proof; proof is not necessary for truth. Consider these points:

1. Proof does not make something true. It is *reality* that makes propositions true; or we can say it is the correspondence between a proposition and reality that makes a proposition true. It is the reality that John is innocent that makes the proposition "John is innocent" true. Whether it is proved or not may be very important to John; but proof does not affect reality nor the truth that depends on reality.

2. Truth is *independent* of proof. If a proposition is true, it is so independently of whether anyone can prove it. If John is in fact innocent, then the proposition "John is innocent" is true even though no one can prove it. John may not be able to prove his innocence, even though he is in fact innocent. I can prove to you that I know how to ride a bicycle by actually doing it. Now the proposition "I know how to ride a bicycle" has been proved. But it was true before the proof and it would be true even if it were not proved, even if I didn't have a bicycle to prove it true, to show you that it is true.
3. Proof means *showing* that something is true. But this is possible only if it is already true, true before any proof. The proposition must *be* true before it can be *shown to be* true, or displayed as true, which is what proof means.
4. Proof is *a form of evidence.* To prove something means to give conclusive evidence that it is true. Proof is therefore relevant to the reasonableness or justification of belief; it is not necessary for the truth of a proposition. Evidence refers not to what makes a proposition true but to our grasp of it; our knowing it or having good reasons to believe it.

Truth does not depend on proof; it does not require proof. *If it's true it's true, whether it has been proved or not.* Truth depends only on reality; it is independent of proof. Proof simply means showing conclusively that something is true; it is irrelevant to whether or not it is true.

[6] ARE THERE DIFFERENT KINDS OF TRUTH?

THE MULTIPLE MEANINGS THEORY OF TRUTH

A somewhat different challenge to the objectivity of truth is the claim that while there is an objective truth, not all truth is objective; that is, that there are two or more kinds of truth. It is a denial that *all truth* is objective, that it belongs to the *very nature of truth* to be objective, that truth is *necessarily* objective, that there cannot be any other kind. It is the claim that there are two or more kinds of truth, that truth has multiple meanings:

There are two ways for something to be true: it can be subjectively true or it can be objectively true. If I say "Butter pecan ice cream is delicious" I have said something true because this statement accurately reflects my personal taste; my statement about the taste of the ice cream is a *subjective* truth. It is true for me, the subject, but not for the object, the ice cream itself. I'm talking about something true about me, not about the ice cream; subjective not objective. If I say that the sum of two plus two is four, I'm making a different sort of claim than stating my taste in ice cream. I'm communicating a belief that I hold about an external, *objective* truth.[6]

The alternative to this is that truth is one: there is only one kind of truth, objective truth. Objective truth, though one, refers to many different kinds of realities.

A CRITICISM OF THE MULTIPLE MEANINGS THEORY OF TRUTH

1. The theory confuses the *nature* of truth, the meaning of truth with the kinds of *subject matter* that true statements are about. Subjective tastes about ice cream are simply one of many kinds of subject matter or kinds of objects or realms of reality that true propositions are about. That the subject matter or kind of object or realm of reality is something subjective does not mean that propositions and truths about it are also subjective.
2. That Frank likes butter pecan ice cream is a fact or state of affairs, the way things really are; just as the fact that 2 + 2 = 4 is a fact or state of affairs. Propositions which assert these states of affairs, which correspond to them, are objectively true because they state *what is really the case*. They are true in the only way that something can be true: *objectively true*. There is no such thing as a subjective truth – only an objective truth about subjective matters.

---

[6] Based on Francis Beckwith and Gregory Koukl, *Relativism,* (Grand Rapids MI: Baker books, 1998), 27.

3. Frank likes butter pecan ice cream. Susan doesn't; she likes chocolate ice cream instead. And for Frank the right shoe size is 12; for Susan it isn't, she has size 9. If the first of these is supposed to be a "subjective truth" why wouldn't the second one also be a subjective truth? In both cases, the person may say "I'm talking about something true about me." If truths about individual tastes and preferences, different shoe sizes, heights, weights and ages are all "subjective," why wouldn't this also apply to truths about different houses, namely that some are made of wood and some are made of brick? Wouldn't then all truths be "subjective"?

4. What differs from one realm of reality to another is not "kinds of truth" but other matters. These other matters include how we come to know truths, different kinds of evidence and how we can show something to be true. How I come to know that you are a loving person differs significantly from how your doctor comes to know that you have high blood pressure. But both of these are equally matters of *objective truth.*

5. The confused idea that some truths are subjective may be due to the fact that some truths are known or experienced subjectively while others are not. Frank's liking for butter pecan ice cream is experienced internally only by Frank. Others cannot experience Frank's liking for this particular ice cream. But we can all still know that it is a fact, a reality that this is his experience. While the experience itself is subjective, that Frank has a particular subjective experience is objectively true.

TRUTH IS ONE: THERE IS ONLY ONE KIND OF TRUTH

The key point noted above is that truth is one: there is only one kind of truth, objective truth. Objective truth, though one, refers to many different kinds of realities. The unity of truth applies not only to the denial that there is such a thing as subjective truth but also to a denial that there is such a thing as religious truth and scientific truth; that *true* means something different when one is talking about God and about molecules.

On the contrary, *true* has exactly the same meaning in both cases, objective truth, what corresponds to objective reality. What varies in the two cases are the different kinds of objective realities that true propositions are about.

There is only one truth, objective truth; not a subjective truth, not a scientific truth, not an ethical truth, not a religious truth; one kind of truth about many different kinds of realities.

CHAPTER 14
KNOWLEDGE AND BELIEF

In chapter 13 we pursued the question of the *meaning* of truth: what does it mean to say that something is true? Now let us turn to the question of our *reaching* truth.

Can we reach truth? The short answer is that sometimes we can and sometimes we can't. When we can, we have knowledge or belief. For *knowledge* means knowledge of truth and *belief* means an inner claim to truth, the claim that what we believe is true. Let us examine knowledge and belief in [1]-[6]; then turn to some related topics in [7]-[12]: doubt, tending to think, the negation of belief, cases where we fail to reach truth and the question of partial truth.

[1] THREE TYPES OF KNOWLEDGE

We speak of knowledge all the time. Do we know what we mean? Perhaps we assume that knowledge is always one and the same thing. Wonder invites us to take another look.

Consider a first set of cases. I know my mother; I know my friend. I know the place where I live, a piece of music, a painting, a poem and a novel. I know my physical aches and pains and other sensations. I know my inner psychological states of love, fear, desire, hope, etc. I know what I see and hear and smell and taste. I know my past experiences of persons, places, and events through memory.

Here is a second set. I know how to ride a bicycle, how to swim, how to drive a car, how to solve easy math problems and how to get around town. I know how to speak English. Some people know how to play the piano; some know how to pilot an airplane. These are all skills, physical and mental and combinations of the two.

We have a third set. I know that there is much that I don't know, that to err is human. I also know many facts of common sense, current events, science, history and geography. I know that some people are trustworthy and that others are not.

I know that water is H2O, that in World War II the Allies won and that Rhode Island is on the east coast of the USA.

Wonder: we see that knowledge is really several different things:

- *First, there is knowledge by acquaintance, called kennen in German.* It takes as its object a thing in a broad sense. To know means to know something. I know my friend.
- *Second, there is competence knowledge, können in German.* It takes as its object a skill. To know means to know how to do something. I know how to ride a bicycle.
- *Third, there is propositional knowledge, wissen in German.* Its object is a proposition. To know means to know that something is the case. I know that water is H2O.

The main focus in the philosophy of knowledge is propositional knowledge. Within this type there is an important distinction, knowledge in the strict sense and in a loose sense.

[2] KNOWLEDGE: STRICT AND LOOSE

Wonder: what do we mean when we say *I know it*? Do we always mean the same thing?

Case one: I am on a quiz program. "Do you know the answer to this question?" If I get it right, I can then say *Yes, I knew it*. I was correct in my answer. But suppose I'm asked *were you sure it's correct*? I have to admit I wasn't sure. It wasn't a guess for I had good reasons for my answer. But what I really meant by saying I knew it was that I was convinced of it, along with the realization that I could have been mistaken. So, I knew it in a *loose* sense of knowledge; I had an awareness of it; it was part of my storehouse of information; I wasn't ignorant of it.

Case two: I am a witness in a court of law. "Did you see the defendant leave the house?" I reply that I did. "Are you sure it was really the defendant?" *Yes, I know it.* That means that I'm sure; I *know* it was him. Here my claim is essentially different, significantly stronger. I am claiming more than that I was convinced of it, that I had an awareness of it. I am claiming certainty, for I am claiming that I really *knew* it; that I knew it in the *strict* sense of knowledge.

Thus, propositional knowledge can be understood either in the strict sense or in a loose sense. When I have knowledge-strict I really *know*: I'm certain, I have a full grasp of it. Is John innocent? "Absolutely! I *know* he is innocent! No question about it!" When I have knowledge-loose I don't really *know* in this absolute and full sense. I claim to know he is innocent only in the sense that I'm convinced of it. I realize I could be mistaken, however unlikely this might be. Knowledge-loose is knowledge without certainty.

Here is the basic contrast:

- ***Knowledge-strict sense:*** I know it! I'm certain of it. I can vouch for it.
- ***Knowledge-loose sense:*** I am informed of it; I am convinced of it.

What I know in the strict sense must really be the case: strict knowledge implies truth. I can know that Albany is the capital of New York State; I can only believe (falsely) that New York City is the capital. It is impossible to know this, since it is not the case. Since knowledge in the strict sense implies truth, it must also include a certain degree of assurance and confidence on the part of the person knowing. I *know* that something is the case only if I have a sufficient grasp of it to be able to reasonably exclude the possibility that it is false. Thus knowledge-strict includes certainty. If I'm uncertain, my knowledge can only be knowledge-loose. Even a high degree of probability does not suffice for knowledge-strict. "Do you really *know* this?" we ask. "Well, I *don't know* it, but I am convinced of it." My knowing is knowledge-loose.

In summary: knowledge in the strict sense implies truth, and a corresponding assurance or certainty that one has grasped the truth. It stands in contrast to knowledge in the loose sense where this assurance of having grasped the truth is missing. The two categories are mutually exclusive. What I know in the strict sense I don't know in the merely loose sense; and what I know in the loose sense I don't know in the strict sense. An overview may be helpful:

KNOWLEDGE	
KNOWLEDGE-STRICT I *know* it. I really know it! I have full confidence it really is so. I am certain of it; I have a right to be certain. I have the compelling evidence to justify this.	KNOWLEDGE-LOOSE I know the answer to the question. I'm informed of it; I'm not ignorant of it. But I don't *know* it in the strict sense. I have a *mere belief*.

The two lower boxes are intended to indicate that the two categories are mutually exclusive. Where I have knowledge-loose I don't have knowledge-strict; and vice-versa. Unless otherwise noted here *knowledge* will henceforth always be used in the strict sense.

[3] TWO KINDS OF BELIEFS

Wonder: do we always use *belief* in the same way? It seems we use in two ways:

- *Mere belief*: "You just believe it; you don't really know it." Thus, I believe the bridge is safe to drive over on my way to work each morning, but I can't claim to be certain of it. Mere belief stands in contrast to knowledge. I believe it but don't claim to know it.

- *Basic belief*: "I don't just believe it; I know it as well." Thus, I believe that I live in the United States, and I would also claim to know it full well. Here belief is not in contrast to knowledge but included within it. I believe and claim to know!

Consider this: you know that 2+2=4. Do you also believe this? Wouldn't it be strange to say, "I know this but I don't believe it"? Isn't this one of your beliefs? Yes, it is surely one of your basic beliefs. If saying "I believe 2+2=4" sounds strange it is because one thinks of *belief* as mere belief; that of course is strange. But if it means basic belief which includes knowledge it is perfectly in order. If I know I also believe in that I'm informed and convinced. Here we find that belief and knowledge are wedded, so to speak.

Thus, we see that there are two different ways in which we use the term *belief*. First, we use it *in contrast to knowledge*. I merely believe it; I don't know it, I'm not certain of it. "I believe the bridge is safe." Second, we use it *as part of knowledge* or *wedded to knowledge*. If I know that 2+2=4, I also believe this in the sense that I am convinced it is true. Thus, we have:

- *Mere belief:* you believe it but you don't know it. Belief in contrast to knowledge.
- *Basic belief:* you know it and so you also believe it. Belief as part of knowledge. Here belief means being convinced. When you know you are convinced: you believe.

  There is also a corresponding two-fold contrast involving *knowing* and *believing*:
- *Knowing as believing:* to know is to believe. Here belief is basic belief, an ingredient in knowledge; belief wedded to knowledge. If I don't believe something (in this sense) I also don't know it. Basic belief means being convinced.
- *Knowing separate from believing:* to know is not to believe, in the mere belief understanding of belief. Here belief is mere belief, in contrast to knowledge. I merely believe instead of knowing. I believe the bridge is safe but I don't know it; I'm not sure of it since I could be wrong.

Mere beliefs are all the beliefs which refer to things we believe but are not certain. We believe them but we do not know them; we *merely* believe them. They are "mere" only in the sense that we do *not know* them. We merely believe them in that we "*only*" believe them; we do not know them. The term *mere* as used here does not mean trivial, foolish, false, or unjustified, although a particular belief may be any of these things.

Thus, when you believe but don't know, the belief is a *mere belief*. I believe my team will win, but of course I don't know it. I believe it, but I am not sure, I could be wrong. It is not knowledge. It lacks the conclusive evidence that guarantees it really is so, the evidence required for it to be knowledge. But I still believe it, I am convinced of it. It is a *mere belief*. I believe that the bridge is safe. Do you know it? Well, no, I don't *know* it, but I do believe it. Probably I believe it with a very firm conviction else I would not cross the bridge. But still, since I'm not certain I don't know it; I merely believe it. Do I believe that my trustworthy friend will come when he said he would come? Yes of course I believe this, he is a person of his word; I am convinced he will come. Am I certain of this? No, I can't be certain, because I can't rule out the possibility that something will happen to prevent his coming. And so I can't say in this more precise philosophical language that I *know* he will come. I lack knowledge, but I do not lack conviction; I am convinced to a degree less than knowledge. I believe he will come; I have the *mere belief* that he will come.

[4] MERE BELIEF IN CONTRAST TO KNOWLEDGE-STRICT

Despite these distinctions mere belief and knowledge-strict have much in common. Both stand opposed to ignorance and doubt. Both aim at truth. But they also contrast in several ways:

1. Falsity: I can believe falsely or mistakenly, but I cannot know falsely or mistakenly. I cannot have false knowledge; I cannot know that x is the case when it is not the case. I cannot know that John is guilty when he is in fact not guilty. I might *think* that I know; that is possible, but in reality I don't know. There is no such thing as false knowledge. But there is such a thing as false belief; there are unfortunately many examples of this.
2. Withdrawing claims: If I claim to know something and then that claim turns out to be false, I must withdraw my claim to know. "I know he's guilty!" But then it turns out that he is innocent. I have to retreat and say,

"I thought I knew, but I guess I didn't." This does not apply to mere belief. If I had said "I believe he's guilty" and then learned of his innocence, I would not have had to withdraw my claim to believe. I believed erroneously but I still believed. My belief was mistaken but it was still a belief. It was a mere belief. In short, I have to withdraw claims to *know* when shown to be mistaken; but not claims to *merely believe* when shown to be mistaken.

3. Success term: knowledge is essentially a success term; mere belief is not. Really knowing means getting it right; believing does not always get it right for there are false beliefs.

4. Varying degrees: mere belief comes in many varying degrees of strength of conviction. "I think so, but I'm not at all sure." I believe with a very low degree of conviction. I would not be too surprised if I turned out to be mistaken. "Yes, I think we'll win" as we are only slightly ahead and there is still a lot of time to play. But in contrast to this, I may also believe with a high degree of conviction, one that seems to border on knowledge. "Yes of course he's reliable, I have no doubt. He's proven his reliability many times." "Are you absolutely sure he will be reliable on his next assignment? Do you *know* it?" "No, I can't say I know it for I don't have certainty; but I believe it with a very strong and assured conviction."

Wonder: does knowledge also have many varying degrees of strength of conviction? Or is there just simply knowledge, all of it equal in strength and certainty? I know I exist. I know there is a world of physical objects outside of and independent of my consciousness. Are these on the same level, equal in strength and certainty? Or am I more certain of my own existence?

[5] A BRIEF SUMMARY OF KNOWLEDGE AND BELIEF

1. Knowledge strict sense: I *know* it; I don't just believe it as a mere belief. I can know only truth, what is actually the case; knowledge implies truth. I am convinced of it, and I am certain of it.

2. Knowledge loose sense: I'm *informed* of it; I'm not ignorant (I know the answer). But it also includes mere beliefs, where it could turn out that I'm mistaken. I am convinced of it but not certain of it.
3. Mere belief: I think it's so but I could be mistaken. I *merely believe* it, I only believe it; I don't know it in the strict sense. I am convinced of it but not certain of it.
4. Basic belief: I believe it in the sense that I'm *convinced* of it. If I know it strict sense, I also believe it as a basic belief. It is the whole package: knowledge-strict and mere belief. It is my *entire belief system* which guides me through my life.

Wonder: does knowledge-loose cover the same ground as mere belief? If I know it in the loose sense (being informed of it) do I not also believe it as mere belief (being convinced of it)? If I'm convinced of it as mere belief, am I not also informed of it as knowledge-loose? If what I have is knowledge-strict then of course I don't have mere belief. Assuming that knowledge-loose and mere belief cover the same ground, we can reformulate our list as follows:

1. ***Knowledge-strict***: I know it; I am certain of it. I don't just believe it as a mere belief.
2. **Knowledge-loose or mere belief:** I'm *informed* of it; I know the answer. I *think* so but I could be mistaken. I am convinced of it but not certain of it.
3. **Basic belief:** I believe it: I'm *convinced* of it.

Basic belief underlies both mere belief and knowledge-strict.

Again, an overview may be helpful:

THE WHOLE BOX IS BASIC BELIEF	
KNOWLEDGE-LOOSE or MERE BELIEF

Belief which is not knowledge-strict. It lacks the conclusive evidence that guarantees it really is so; it lacks the evidence required for knowledge-strict.
I believe it but I don't *know* it.
I *merely* believe it.
I could be mistaken. | KNOWLEDGE-STRICT

The knowledge that contrasts to mere belief.
Knowledge-strict has the conclusive evidence that guarantees it really is so. This is the compelling evidence necessary and sufficient for knowledge-strict.
I *don't merely* believe it. I *know* it.
I am certain and I have the right to be certain. |
| BASIC BELIEF UNDERLIES BOTH MERE BELIEF AND KNOWLEDGE-STRICT

Basic belief = I'm convinced of it, so I believe it. ||

The two middle boxes indicate that the two categories are mutually exclusive. Where I have mere belief, I don't have knowledge-strict; and vice-versa.

[6] BELIEVING A PERSON

Wonder: what is the object of our beliefs? What is it that I believe? Is it always and simply a proposition? I believe John is innocent; I believe the proposition "John is innocent"; I believe this to be a true proposition. But now consider the expression "I believe you." Here *belief* can refer either to a mere belief, or to a strong and assured conviction, a basic belief which claims to be knowledge. This is brought out in the phrases "Yes, I *believe* you, I *trust* you completely; I have absolutely no doubt; I know that what you say is true." That is, the "believe" in "I believe you" expresses trust in the person, not merely in the proposition; and the phrase "I believe you" is almost equivalent to "I trust you": I trust you to be telling me the truth. The corresponding denial "I don't believe you" means "I don't trust you" in the sense of "I don't trust you to be telling me the truth."

So, we cannot simply say that what we believe is always and simply a proposition. There are also cases of dual objects: a person and a proposition, as in the phrase "I believe you":

- *Person:* the term "you" is one object of the verb "believe": I believe you.
- *Proposition*: this is the other object: I believe what you are telling me, that it is true.

The two go essentially together. I believe the proposition because you have said it; you vouch for it; you have given me your word for it. When expanded the phrase "I believe you" means "I believe *you* to be telling me the truth, and so I also believe that *what* you say is true.

Having surveyed knowledge and belief let us turn now to some related topics.

[7] DOUBT

Wonder: what is doubt? What does it mean to say, "I doubt it"?

First, isn't doubt always the opposite of belief? If I doubt something I don't believe it; and if I believe it, I don't doubt it. This is believing as basic belief and so includes knowledge.

Second, does doubt always mean the same thing? It seems not. Sometimes doubt means withholding belief; not taking a position. "Is John guilty?" I have no idea; I don't take a position one way or the other. But sometimes doubt means taking a position, one that tends in the direction of denial. "I doubt that he can do it" seems very close to "I tend to think he cannot do it." We have then two senses of doubt:

Doubt-1: withholding belief, not taking a position, neither affirming nor denying. Doubt in this sense is a way of not believing something that is offered for possible belief. "This is a great buy," the salesperson says to me, hoping I will accept it and believe it. But I don't believe it; I'm wary, I'm sceptical. "I don't buy it" where *buy* means *believe*. That is, I doubt what the salesperson says. I do not deny it; it might be true. But I'm not convinced it's true. I withhold belief, neither believing it is true nor believing it is not true. Since I just don't know I doubt it.

Doubt-2: mild suggestion of denial. Here doubt means taking a position, that of tending to think it's not so. "Is he coming back?" To reply, "I doubt it" is to say "I tend to think he's not coming back." Or, "I'm afraid he's not coming back." I tend to think this but of course I'm not sure; I don't know it and I don't believe it; I only tend to think so.

The common element in both of these is that doubt is the opposite of belief, as noted. If I say to a person "Yes, I believe you" I mean that I accept what he or she says as true, in contrast both to the withholding of belief of doubt-1 and the mild suggestion of denial of doubt-2.

Third, is doubt the same thing as lack of certainty? If I doubt, I am not certain and if I am certain I don't doubt. But they are not the same; they are in fact essentially different.

There are innumerable things that I believe without being certain about them. These are the things that I hold to be really so, that I am convinced of; that I believe to be so in the sense of mere belief. That I am not certain of them does not mean that I doubt them. "Do you believe the bridge is safe, that it will support the weight of the car?" "Yes, I certainly believe this, I do not doubt it. If I did I would not go on it!" "Are you absolutely certain of it?" "No, I can't say that, for I realize there is the slim possibility that it will collapse; but I certainly do not believe this." Hence "I do not doubt that the bridge is safe; I believe it is safe, I trust that it is safe."

My faithful, trusted friend tells me something. I believe him, I believe what he tells me; I trust him. Am I certain that what he tells me is true? Perhaps I'm not;

my belief is a mere belief, not a certainty. But I do not doubt him, else I would not say that I believed him.

There is a huge difference between *mere belief* which includes a lack of certainty and *doubt*. To believe, even without being certain, is to be convinced; to doubt is to be unconvinced.

[8] TENDING TO THINK

Wonder: we have used the phrases *I tend to think* and *tending to think*. What is *tending to think*? We seem to know what it means when we use the phrase. But what is it? It is not believing, but something short of that; a holding back of the commitment to claiming truth that is involved in belief. "I can't say I believe he's innocent for I'm not convinced of it. But I'm more inclined in that direction than in the opposite; I *tend to think* he is innocent." It is not believing for it does not involve being convinced. But it is something stronger than "I just don't know" or "I have no idea" meant as a total withholding of any commitment. It seems to lie about halfway in-between these two other positions. Thus, we have:

- *Believing*: being convinced and saying that it is so without being certain (mere belief).
- *Tending to think:* being inclined towards saying that it so without being convinced.
- *Total withholding of any commitment:* not being convinced and not being inclined.

Wonder: established usage has categories like believing and knowing; why doesn't it also have the category *tending to think*? Isn't it also of some importance? Note that *tending to think* applies not only in negative cases like our examples here, *I tend to think it's not so*; but, also, and equally in positive cases, *I tend to think it is so*; as in *I tend to think he is innocent*. That is, all doubt-2 involves tending to think but not all tending to think involves doubt-2.

Chapter 14: Knowledge and Belief

[9] THE NEGATION OF BELIEF

Wonder: what is the negation of belief? What does it mean to say, "I don't believe it"? I suggest it is ambiguous between two very different things:

(1) *Denial*: I believe that it's not the case; I deny that it is so. "It's not true."
(2) *Doubt-1*: withholding belief; I neither believe it nor deny it. "I just don't know."

For example, the report comes in that John has been found guilty by the court. You say, "I don't believe it." What do you mean? There are two distinct possibilities:

(1) *Denial:* you deny that he is guilty; you continue to believe he is innocent: "I don't believe it! I believe he is innocent." You take a position: not guilty.

(2) *Doubt-1*: you withhold belief since you are not convinced he is guilty, nor that he is innocent: "I don't believe either way, I just don't know." You don't take a position.

In (1) you *do* believe something: the opposite of what was proposed to you, the negation of the "it." You believe "not-it." In contrast, in (2) you *don't* believe, you withhold belief; you don't believe either way. You say, "I just don't know."

In (1) the negation applies to the *proposition* which forms the content of the belief: I deny p, I claim that not-p, where p stands for the proposition. In contrast, in (2) the negation applies to the *psychological act* or state of belief: I don't believe it, I'm withholding judgment since I can't decide one way or the other.

[10] CASES WHERE WE FAIL TO REACH TRUTH

Can we reach truth? We have been examining cases where we can: knowledge or belief. For *knowledge* means knowledge of truth and *belief* means a claim to truth, a claim that what we believe is true. More precisely for belief, we reach truth when we have *true beliefs*. Let us now turn to cases where we fail to reach truth. Here are some:

1. **Error:** holding false beliefs, the most drastic case of failing to reach truth.
2. **Ignorance:** simply being cut off from awareness of truth, the most widespread case.
3. **Not understanding something in practical matters;** for example, how this machine works.
4. **Not understanding something in deeper matters;** mysteries such as how consciousness is related to the brain, or how physical tones can have such sublime beauty in music.
5. **Doubt-1: a withholding of belief; not taking a position.** "I just don't know."
6. **Doubt-2: a mild suggestion of denial; also, not believing.** "I tend to think it's not so."
7. **Basic scepticism**: the claim "we can't know" applied to a specific ream or universally.
8. **Radical scepticism:** the stronger claim "we can't even have reasonable beliefs." We are always in the dark.

These cases may be seen as dividing into two groups:

(A) Cases where we *in fact* don't reach truth: 1-4.
(B) Cases where we believe or *claim* that we don't or can't reach truth: 5-8.

[11] A SUMMARY OF KEY TERMS

Some key terms are included in the list just above, especially the two forms of doubt. In addition, we may note the following key terms of our analysis:

1. *Knowledge by acquaintance:* I know my friend.
2. *Competence knowledge:* I know how to ride a bicycle.
3. *Propositional knowledge:* I know that water is H2O.

Chapter 14: Knowledge and Belief

4. ***Knowledge in the strict sense:*** I know I exist.
5. ***Knowledge in the loose sense:*** I know where you live (I'm informed but not certain).
6. ***Mere belief:*** I think our team will win but of course I'm not sure.
   Mere belief seems to be equivalent in scope to knowledge-loose.
7. ***Basic belief:*** I'm convinced; includes both knowledge-strict and mere belief.
8. ***Believing a person***: I believe you and I believe what you are telling me, that it is true.
9. ***Tending to think***: I am inclined towards saying it is so or not so without being convinced.
10. ***Denial as negation of belief:*** "I don't believe it!" I deny it; I believe it's not the case.

These terms also divide into two groups:

(C) Terms dealing with knowledge: 1-5.
(D) Terms dealing with belief and the related notion of tending to think: 6-10.

We are often so quick to claim to *know* many things which in fact we merely *believe*. Furthermore, our levels of knowledge and belief vary in their strengths. Start to look at your own claims to knowledge and beliefs and reexamine them. What do you really know? Believe? Both?! Wonder!

CHAPTER 15
OPINIONS

[1] WONDER: WHAT IS AN OPINION?

Wonder: what is an opinion? How is the term used? Is it always used in one way with one meaning? Or are there several meanings, several ways in which the term is used? I want to suggest it is the latter. And that part of the wonder here is that the term *opinion* is used in very different and even opposing ways. Here are three:

Sometimes it is used in a dismissive way in opposition to truth: *that's just your opinion.*

Sometimes it is used in a way that is not dismissive but actually very positive; not at all in opposition to truth but rather as a claim to truth: *getting an expert's opinion in a court of law.*

Sometimes it is used as part of a contrast: *just the facts, not opinions.*

Let us examine each of these, beginning with the positive way, as a claim to truth.

PART ONE
OPINIONS AS CLAIMS AS TO TRUTH

[2] OPINIONS AS BELIEFS

Doesn't *opinion* sometimes simply mean *belief*? Using the term *wrong* to mean morally wrong, suppose I say *in my opinion this is wrong*. Doesn't this mean the same thing as the phrase *I believe this is wrong*? If it's my opinion, isn't it my belief? And if it's my belief, isn't it also my opinion? The two terms are interchangeable in this context. And if beliefs are claims to truth, then opinions are also claims to truth.

Consider three more examples. If I say *in my opinion John is innocent,* do I not mean the same thing as when I say *I believe John is innocent*? The two are interchangeable.

When a doctor gives you a second *opinion,* he tells you what he *believes* is the truth.

Think of two people having a vigorous argument about politics or religion. What makes it an argument is that they have opposing opinions, each person claiming the truth: "I'm right"; "I'm correct because I have the truth on my side." Each person's opinion is his claim to truth. And each person's claim is opposed to that of the other. An argument is a clash of *opinions*, a clash of opposing claims to truth because it is a clash of opposing *beliefs* about what is true.

If opinions are beliefs, then what applies to one applies to the other as well. A look at our experience confirms this:

- Opinions can be reasonable or unreasonable, the same holds for beliefs.
- Opinions can be correct or incorrect; the same applies to beliefs.
- You and I can hold the same opinion; for example, that capital punishment is wrong or that it is right. If so, we hold the same belief, we believe the same thing.
- That *same thing* is the content of the opinion-belief, *what* we believe, the proposition we hold to be true. Opinions have a content; beliefs have a content.
- Beliefs are claims to truth. To say *I believe John is innocent* means I claim he really is innocent, that the proposition expressing this is true. The same applies to opinions.
- Opinions are claims to truth. Their meaning, their function, their role in our lives can be understood only in terms of their relation to truth. Opinions are important because truth is important.

[3] OPINIONS AS KNOWLEDGE

Wonder: if opinions are beliefs does this mean they are mere beliefs? Some surely are. If I say *that's just your opinion,* I surely don't mean to credit you with having knowledge. What I often mean is that you have a mere belief: you don't *know* that; you just *believe* it.

This correlates with the idea that knowledge is usually seen in contrast to opinions. I say *I know that 2+2 is 4*. Wouldn't it be strange if I had said *in my opinion 2+2 is 4*? And isn't the reason why it's strange simply the fact that I *know* that 2+2 is 4?

Wonder: does this mean that are all opinions are excluded from the realm of knowledge, that opinions are never cases of knowledge? Or can some opinions be knowledge? Consider:

An expert is called to testify in a court of law. He is asked "to give his opinion." He tells the court, for example, that the bullet that killed the victim could not have been fired from the gun in exhibit A. He is an expert; he has studied the matter carefully; he *knows* this is so.

So, we have a case of something that is both an opinion and knowledge. Let me suggest there are others. I hold the ethical opinion that torturing a suspect in order to elicit a confession from him is morally wrong. I hold the ethical opinion that slavery is morally wrong. In both these cases and others, I claim that I have knowledge. I *know* torture is wrong. I *know* slavery is wrong. Calling it an opinion does not negate its being knowledge.

A court of law hands down a juridical opinion; for example, that racial segregation is wrong, that it violates basic human rights. Doesn't this opinion express knowledge? Surely it does. I submit we can justifiably say that we *know* that racial segregation is wrong.

Suppose I find myself in a very difficult personal situation. I'm unsure what to do. You are my trusted friend. I have great respect for your opinions in such matters. So, I come to you and ask you for your opinion regarding what I should do. *Please give me your opinion.* You do so. I listen, I think about it, I decide that your advice is sound, and I act upon it. My situation improves dramatically. *Of course, that's what I should do!* Clearly you were right. Could this not be a case of knowledge? I know you are right. The evidence for this is clear and compelling. Again, calling something an opinion does not preclude its being knowledge.

Here is a final type of case that shows opinions can be knowledge. To return to one of the examples above, I claim to *know* that racial discrimination, racial segregation and racial bias against minorities are morally wrong. But, to my surprise, I find myself one day in "mixed company"; that is, among some people who are explicitly racist. I hate their opinions, but I do not hate them as persons. Hate the sin, love the sinner. Hate the error, love the one who errs. Or at least respect such persons. So, out of respect for them as persons and with the view of possibly winning them over to my side I express my firm conviction (my knowledge) that racism is wrong as "my opinion" that it is wrong. I say to them, "No, I have a different opinion." Here *opinion* is nothing more than an expression of respect. It is in no way a diminishing of the claim to know; or still less, a taking back of this claim. I can say with perfect consistency that in my *opinion* racism is wrong and that I *know* this to be so. Again, opinions can be knowledge.

So, we have at least five types of cases where opinions are or can be knowledge:

1. **Expert opinions.**
2. **Ethical opinions.**
3. **Juridical opinions.**
4. **Personal advice and counseling.**
5. **Respect and politeness:** the use of the term *opinion* as a gesture of respect, an expression of politeness towards a person who holds an opposing view.

[4] OPINIONS AS MERE BELIEFS

We have looked at cases where *opinion* simply means *belief* and where the suggestion is that it is a strong and well-founded belief. Some cases could even be knowledge, so that *belief* in this context should be read as *basic belief*, meaning both mere belief and knowledge. Thus, when I say *in my opinion this is wrong* meaning that *I believe this is wrong* I may well be claiming that I actually know it is wrong.

At other times *belief* as applied to opinions is used in a narrow sense to mean *mere belief*. Clearly, some opinions are not knowledge but mere beliefs. Some of my ethical opinions are mere beliefs. I believe x is wrong but I'm not sure; I merely believe it. The same applies to the other categories. The expert testifying in a court of law may not be certain about a particular point. He may say *in my opinion the victim could not have survived more than 6 hours under these conditions, but I'm not sure*. Here "in my opinion" means a mere belief.

Some mere beliefs are well-grounded in solid evidence; they are *justified* beliefs. Others are not well-grounded in solid evidence; they are *unjustified* beliefs. Still others are in a gray area where it is difficult to put them neatly in the one or the other box. An excellent doctor with many years of experience runs a series of tests according to standard procedures and tells you the results. You believe that what he tells you is true; your belief counts as a justified belief. On the other hand, the medical opinion of someone with no medical training and experience probably doesn't count for much. If you believe him your belief would surely be unjustified. But it could still be true.

[5] THREE TYPES OF OPINIONS AS BELIEFS

Putting these things together, we see three ways in which the term *opinion* may be used:

One: *basic* belief. Here *opinion* ranges over a wide area that includes both mere beliefs and knowledge; some expert opinions and some cases of ethical opinions might be knowledge.

Two: *mere* belief. Other expert opinions are mere beliefs. Recall the court of law. *In my opinion the victim could not have survived more than 6 hours, but*

I'm not sure. In general, when we say "You don't know that; it's just your opinion" we are using *opinion* to mean mere belief.

Three: *unjustified mere* beliefs. Recall the medical opinion of the person with no medical training and experience. Believing him results in an unjustified belief. Unjustified mere beliefs are unsupported beliefs, lacking in adequate evidence or not based on good evidence. "You have no good reason to believe that." Another example: rumor has it that the factory will shut down. Is this really true? Is there any solid evidence for this? If not, it's "just an opinion" some people have; an unsupported, unjustified belief, unwarranted belief; hence an unreasonable belief.

Given that an opinion is a mere belief all we know is that it's not a case of knowledge. Whether it is justified or not is an entirely new question. My doctor gives me his opinion and adds that "it's only an opinion," meaning that he's not sure of it. But what he tells me may well be correct and supported by all his knowledge and expertise and experience; in other words, a well-grounded belief, an opinion based on solid evidence, a clearly justified belief. Opinion as mere belief need not be, and very often is not, unjustified belief.

Category one includes a wide range of cases; two and three, progressively narrower ones. What is in a later category is also in each of the earlier ones, but not vice versa.

These categories are fluid: a particular opinion as a *basic* belief may start out as a *mere* belief but then with the addition of substantial further evidence turn into *knowledge*. But in terms of its content, what is believed, it is the same opinion in both cases.

Likewise, a particular opinion as a *mere* belief may at first be unjustified and then with the addition of solid evidence become a justified belief.

It is important to keep in mind the important distinction between the question of truth and the question of justification. Is this a true belief? Is it a justified belief? They do not always go together. An unjustified belief may still turn out to be true; and a justified belief may still turn out to be false. Justification does not guarantee truth though it implies *likely to be true*. And being unjustified does not in itself mean that the belief is false. We have four kinds of cases:

1. Justified and true.
2. Unjustified and false.
3. Unjustified but true.
4. Justified but false.

PART TWO
OPINIONS IN OPPOSITION TO TRUTH

[6] OPINIONS SEEN IN DISMISSIVE WAYS

"NO OBJECTIVELY RIGHT OR WRONG ANSWERS"

The term *opinion* is sometimes used in a dismissive way suggesting an opposition to truth, as is brought out the following statement:

> Whether or not the swap of U.S. Army Sgt. Bowe Bergdahl for five high-level Taliban leaders was a wise move is strictly a matter of opinion. There is no objectively right or wrong answer.[1]

Consider the phrase "there is no objectively right or wrong answer." Doesn't this mean the claim that there is no truth to the matter, for an objectively right answer would be the truth? And an objectively wrong answer would be a mistake, a claim that something is the truth which is in fact not the truth because something else is the real truth? In either case there would be a real truth, which is what the phrase wants to deny. It seems clear then that *opinion* is set off here against *truth*: we have an opinion *instead of* the truth. Note how this stands in radical contrast to what we pursued above, that opinions are claims to truth and therefore would make no sense apart from truth.

---

[1] Theodore L. Gatchel, "Straight answers are still needed." *The Providence Sunday Journal*, July 6, 2014, F7.

Also, the claim is that "there *is* no objectively right or wrong answer"; not merely that we have not successfully attained it, for that would be to acknowledge that there *is* a truth here.

What is meant by the statement quoted above is often expressed by the phrase *that's just your opinion*. It is worth taking a close look at this phrase. It is very common; people use it freely. But what does it really mean? How is it used?

"THAT'S JUST YOUR OPINION"

The phrase *that's just your opinion* or *that's just an opinion* is often used in dismissive ways in attempts to try to deny the reality of objective truth. Three of these ways are:

1. *The use of opinion as being merely an expression of feelings instead of a claim to truth.*
2. *The use of opinion in the theory of relativism as a denial of objective truth.*
3. *The use of opinion as a conversation stopper.*

Wonder: we saw earlier in section 2 that the terms *opinion* and *belief* can often be used interchangeably. *In my opinion he is innocent* means the same as *I believe he is innocent*. But when we speak of *just your opinion* things change. Would we ever say *that's just your belief*? If not, why not? The term *opinion* has a different ring from the term *belief* in this context. Why?

Let us now examine each of the three items listed above.

[7] JUST AN OPINION AS AN EXPRESSION OF FEELINGS

One way the phrase *that's just your opinion* is used in a dismissive way to try to deny the reality of objective truth is by the claim that *opinion* is merely an expression of feelings instead of a claim to truth. For example, consider expressions such as: *This is great! This is exciting! This is dull! This is scary!* Each is often taken as merely an expression of subjective feelings.

Wonder: are these purely subjective or do they have an element of objectivity in them?

On the one hand, one could claim that they are purely subjective and are often labeled *merely opinions* precisely in order to contrast them to expressions that are objective because they are objectively true or false. The phrases *merely opinions* and *that's just your opinion* are used precisely to contrast them to what is taken seriously as being true or at least possibly true.

On the other hand, one could also reasonably claim that these phrases are not purely subjective. They are expressions of feelings, but these feelings have an objective referent. The phrase *this is exciting* is meant to pick out something about the object ("this") which really has a certain quality, or perhaps a set of qualities that is properly labeled exciting. The object cannot be entirely neutral in its objective nature if someone is to call it exciting. This is not to deny that there are subjective elements in the total picture, that we bring certain things to our experience without which the events and objects in our experience would not be seen as exciting or dull or scary. It is only to say that these feeling and their expressions in words are not entirely subjective but have a significant objective component. And it is this objective component which enables us to use the term *opinion* legitimately to apply to phrases such as *this is exciting,* and *this is scary.* Thus, *in my opinion this is scary* means "I claim there really is something about this that, given who I am and other variables, understandably arouses fear in me."

Wonder: what conclusion should we draw from this?

The claim that expressions of feelings are not purely subjective but genuine opinions with a claim to truth can be tested very easily. Whenever a genuine opinion is held by one person it is always possible and usually meaningful for another person to disagree with it. "No, I have a different opinion;" meaning an opposing opinion. And it is then common for the two persons to discuss the matter; to advance reasons for their position in order to see which one of them is correct. But this means that each of the two opinions is a claim to truth, that it is a belief. One person makes one claim to truth, another makes an opposing claim; this is their disagreement.

So, if their disagreement is a clash of opinions, it must be that these opinions are claims to truth, which means they are beliefs, and therefore that opinions are beliefs. It follows that the attempt to dismiss objective truth by an appeal to opinions as expressions of feelings fails, for such an attempt rests ultimately on opinions as claims to truth.

[8] JUST AN OPINION AS RELATIVISM

A DENIAL OF OBJECTIVE TRUTH

There are still two further uses of the phrase *that's just an opinion* that we must consider. The first and more important of the two is when the phrase is used as a denial of objective truth. This often occurs in an ethical context. For example, person A expresses the opinion *abortion is morally wrong*. How does person B reply? He or she might agree or disagree or perhaps say something like *I don't know, I haven't made up my mind on this issue*. But instead of any of these, person B replies with the phrase *that's just your opinion*. What B means to say by this is: *it's just your opinion; it can't be really true, or false. For there is no truth in this matter since it's all just a matter of opinion*. This is one way of expressing the theory of ethical relativism or one version of it.

The core idea here is this: what was said about abortion is an "opinion" *instead of* the truth. What is meant is not that it was false, which would mean that something else was the truth. What is meant is rather that there is no truth about this matter; "it's all subjective or relative." The phrase *it's just your opinion* is intended to set opinion off against truth. There are truths (say about arithmetic and geography) and there are opinions, and "never the twain shall meet." It is an explicit denial of the central thesis here, that opinions are in their very nature opinions about what is true; that without truth there could be no opinions. An opinion is a claim that something is true.

The phrase *it's just an opinion* is meant to convey the idea that what was said ("abortion is wrong") is neither true nor false, because such a statement cannot be true, or false, since there is no truth about this subject. There is no truth, only *opinions*; and opinions are not true or false, they cannot be true or false, since they are nothing but expressions of feelings, of attitudes, or of how one "looks at it."

This relativistic view might be called the "opinion instead of truth" view since it denies the very existence of truth in a certain realm, and not just that a particular statement is true. As noted, it often appears in the context of ethics where it is ethical relativism.

ETHICAL RELATIVISM

What does ethical relativism mean? Wouldn't it mean that there is no subject matter in ethics, that we can never do the right thing, or do something wrong, since nothing *really is* right, and nothing *really is* wrong? Any statement saying x is right or y is wrong is "just an opinion," just an expression of feeling or sentiment which has no validity beyond the individual expressing it. Why bother with ethics then? Isn't ethical relativism really the death of ethics? We will return to this important topic as the theme of chapter 17.

Wonder: is relativism an attack on truth? Or is it an attack on the reality of ethics, a real and objective right and wrong and good and evil? Or is it an attack on the two together?

[9] JUST AN OPINION AS A CONVERSATION STOPPER

Let us turn to the second of the two further uses of the phrase *that's just your opinion*. This is where the phrase is used as a conversation stopper, or discussion stopper, or argument stopper. It is a signal that the speaker wants to end the discussion, especially an argument. The stopper use of the phrase has in common with the relativistic-subjectivist-denial-of-truth use that both express a disdain for the truth question. Both are ways of not pursuing the truth question, not desiring to know or reasonably believe what is true.

The difference is that relativism is a general theory about truth, the claim of its non-existence in a certain realm, often ethics. *There is no truth here, there are only opinions.* Or, *where you think there is a truth, there are really only opinions, opinions instead of truth.* The stopper does not represent a theory. It is simply a device used by a person at a particular time, with reference to a particular topic; it is a way of saying that he is not in the mood to continue it. It means "Let's stop" or "I want to stop" or (rudely) "You need to stop."

Both use the term *opinion,* not as an expression of the desire to pursue the truth, but in a way that is contrary to this, a way of blocking our access to truth. That is how the term *just* functions here; roughly: "it's just an opinion -- forget truth."

[10] THE DIFFERENT MEANINGS OF JUST AN OPINION

We have noted five different meanings of the phrase *just an opinion*, including *it's just an opinion* and *that's just your opinion*. It will be useful to draw them all together:

1. Mere belief. It's just an opinion; we don't know it (Opinions as claims to truth).
2. Unjustified mere belief. It's just an opinion; it needs justification to support it before we can reasonably believe it (Opinions as claims to truth).
3. Merely a subjective feeling. It's just an opinion, not a statement that is true or that can be true. It's just your opinion; it's not how it really is. It's not really exciting, it's not really scary; it's just how you feel about it (Opinions in opposition to truth).
4. Ethical relativism. That's just your opinion, it's not really so. It's an opinion instead of the truth, for there is no truth here (Opinions in opposition to truth).
5. Conversation stopper. That's just your opinion; that's all I'll grant you, not that your opinion is true. End of discussion (Opinions in opposition to truth).

Chapter 15: Opinions

Wonder: note the radical contrast between 1-2 and 3-4 indicated by the key contrasting terms *claims to truth* and *opposition to truth*. This means that items 1 and 2 fall under the broad banner of objective truth. They are, where appropriate, valid responses to truth and the call to be truthful, to take truth seriously. Each says in effect: *be careful, that's just an opinion; it does not or it may not fully reach the truth.* In sharp contrast, items 3 and 4 are antithetical to truth; they are attempts to deny truth. And they say in effect: *this is just an opinion instead of the truth.* Or, *there are only opinions, there is no truth.*

In the first two *this is just an opinion* means *it somehow falls short of reaching the fullness of truth.* But it is an opinion in the great realm of truth. In the second two *this is just an opinion* means *that's all there are, opinions; there is no truth*; opinions trying to replace truth.

Item 5 is very different from the other four. It is essentially a device used by a person to steer a conversation away from one topic to another. It is not, like 1 and 2, a theoretical label put on an opinion in an attempt to describe it accurately. It has something of the spirit of 3 and 4; it seems to be a disdain for truth or the question of truth. But it is not a general theory like ethical relativism or the claim that opinions are merely expressions of feelings with no truth content.

The first two are perhaps valid and legitimate uses of the phrase *just an opinion*. Where used appropriately, where the description actually fits, it really is *just an opinion*, in contrast to being knowledge (for #1) or justified mere belief (for #2). In contrast, the last three, especially 3 and 4, are not valid because each one is in one way or another a falling short of what should be our commitment to truth.

The first two look *towards* truth and imply a desire to reach it. The other three look *away from* truth and even imply a disdain for truth and the desire to reach it.

[11] WHAT THEN IS AN OPINION?

Wonder: what, then, is an opinion? Why do we use this word when we have other words and expressions -- such as knowledge, basic belief, and mere belief --

that cover the same area as opinions? Does *opinion* refer to any one thing that has a clearly given essence?

These are difficult questions. Let me suggest a direction for an exploration of this topic. The term *opinion* seems to combine two ideas, which do not really seem to fit together very well.

First, the term *opinion* seems to connote the idea of something personal. "This is my own personal opinion." We want others to respect our opinions, to listen to them and to take them seriously. People feel hurt when their opinions are slighted, ridiculed, or ignored. People insist on the right to have and to express their own personal opinions. It almost seems as if an opinion is a belief that has been personalized. This is surely not entirely accurate, but it might contain an interesting and significant grain of truth.

Second, the term *opinion* is often used to convey the idea that the basic belief in question is something less than the ideal of knowledge. "It's only an opinion." Or "it's only my opinion, I don't know." Often an opinion is even dismissed as "just an opinion" in one of the ways this expression can be used.

These two ideas are not easily reconciled. The first is positive and valuable; the second is negative, a falling short of full value. Why then does the one term *opinion* combine them both?

PART THREE
FACTS AND OPINIONS

[12] IS THERE A CONTRAST BETWEEN FACTS AND OPINIONS?

Wonder: is there a contrast between facts and opinions? Yes and no; we can distinguish three different kinds of cases, on different levels:

WHERE THERE IS A CONTRAST BETWEEN FACTS AND OPINIONS

1. An epistemological level: the relation between *knowledge* and *belief*. Consider the claim: "That he died is a fact; that he was murdered is just an opinion." Why would we say this? Calling his death a fact presumably means that we know this

to be a fact and calling the other an opinion means it is a mere belief. We have then a contrast between knowledge and mere belief, facts and opinions; facts representing knowledge, opinions representing mere beliefs.

WHERE THERE IS NO CONTRAST BETWEEN FACTS AND OPINIONS

2. Another epistemological level: the relation between *facts* and *beliefs*. But sometimes there is no real contrast between facts and opinions because opinions are beliefs about the facts. The two terms come together in a single meaningful whole. In my opinion, John is innocent of the charges against him. This opinion is either true or false, depending on whether or not it corresponds to reality or to the facts. In this kind of case there is no contrast between facts and opinions because they are two sides of the same coin; facts refer to reality and opinions refer to our relation to reality, to our beliefs about it.

Could such opinions actually be knowledge? Recall the use of *opinion* to describe the testimony of an expert in a court of law who offers his opinion about the case and justifiably claims this as an item of knowledge. This seems to be a striking case of no fact-opinion contrast.

3. A *metaphysical* level: the relation between *reality* and *moral qualities*. Consider the phrase: "That slavery existed in the USA prior to the Civil War is a fact; that it is morally wrong is just an opinion." Often this is meant as claiming there is a contrast: the existence of slavery is a reality while its moral wrongness is not a reality but "just an opinion." In this claim of a contrast between facts and opinions, facts represent reality while opinions non-reality, the non-factual. What is "just an opinion" is seen as not real in contrast to what is real.

Wonder: is this claim of a contrast between facts and opinions valid? Let me suggest that it is not. Rather, both sides of this comparison represent facts; that is, realities. Recall the two sides: the reality of slavery and its moral wrongness. The one is a historical fact, the other is a moral fact; both are equally facts. And both are equally well known; we can be as certain that slavery is wrong as that it took place. We have then another case where there is no contrast between facts and opinions but a bringing them together.

Wonder: we sometimes restrict the term *fact* to empirical facts like the historical fact of the existence of slavery, geographic facts like the size of a continent and scientific facts like water is H2O. But is this restriction warranted? If facts are significant because they are real, shouldn't we also say that the wrongness of slavery and the goodness of gratitude are facts? Surely, they are just as real and some of them are more significant than some empirical facts. What is more significant: that your friend loves you deeply and is faithful to you? Or that he or she is so many feet tall?

THE THEORY OF ETHICAL RELATIVISM AND THE FACT-OPINION CONTRAST

We may note another use of the fact-opinion distinction: ethical relativism. Consider the claim: "Facts are real; we can know them, and we can test claims made about them. But moral good and evil, right, and wrong are just opinions; they are not real, not knowable and not testable. Facts are objective; opinions are purely subjective." This is a typical way of formulating and trying to advance the theory of ethical relativism which we met earlier in section 8 of the current chapter and will take up again in chapter 17. The denial of ethical relativism means holding that moral good and evil, right, and wrong are not just opinions but realities like all other facts.

Wonder: could it be that when there is an objection to the fact-opinion distinction, the deepest reason for this is the suspicion that it is at bottom a disguised form of ethical relativism? Is this heightened by the fact that *opinion* is so often read, and read almost automatically as *mere opinion* or *just an opinion*? When ethics is put into the category of *mere opinion* it seems that the suggestion of ethical relativism might become almost irresistible. If we are to avoid ethical relativism, we must also avoid stating the fact-opinion distinction in this context as a contrast. Once again, we note a case where there is no contrast between facts and opinions.

Chapter 15: Opinions

FACTS AND OPINIONS:
A BRIEF SUMMARY OF THE THREE KINDS OF CASES

1. *A contrast on an epistemological level*: facts as knowledge and opinions as mere beliefs.
2. *No contrast on another epistemological level*: brought together when opinions are beliefs about facts.
3. *No contrast on a metaphysical level*: reality and moral qualities; the reality of slavery and its wrongness are equally facts, just different kinds of facts. Neither is just an opinion in contrast to a fact. Recognizing this means avoiding of the theory of ethical relativism.

[13] A BRIEF SUMMARY OF OPINIONS

PART ONE: OPINIONS AS CLAIMS TO TRUTH

When opinions are claims to truth this can take various partly overlapping forms:

1. Opinions as basic beliefs.
2. Opinions as mere beliefs.
3. Opinions as unjustified mere beliefs.
4. Opinions as knowledge, as in the term expert opinion.

PART TWO: OPINIONS IN OPPOSITION TO TRUTH

When opinions are set off in opposition to truth this is often done by the use of the phrase *that's just your opinion* or *that's just an opinion*. Three of these ways are:

5. Opinions as merely expressions of feelings instead of claims to truth.
6. Opinions as used in the theory of relativism in its denial of objective truth.
7. Opinions as used for conversation stoppers.

PART THREE: FACTS AND OPINIONS

Is there a contrast between facts and opinions? Yes and no, in three kinds of cases:

8. Yes: facts as knowledge and opinions as mere beliefs.
9. No: beliefs about facts.
10. No: slavery exists, and it is wrong; both are equally facts, just different kinds of facts.

Wonder at the many ways in which opinions can be referred to. How do you tend to use the word in everyday life? Wonder at the power of an opinion! Wonder at how often we dismiss an opinion.

CHAPTER 16
THE LOVE OF TRUTH

[1] ORIGINAL WONDER

SOME BASIC WONDER QUESTIONS

Wonder: what is love of truth? How can we come to a grasp of what this love is? Isn't part of the answer our deep desire to know? Don't we all have, deep down, a desire to know the truth, how it really is, especially in regard to the most important questions. Pascal captures this:[1]

1. When I consider the short duration of my life, swallowed up in the eternity before and after, the little space which I fill and even can see, engulfed in the infinite immensity of spaces of which I am ignorant and which know me not, I am frightened and am astonished at being here rather than there; for there is no reason why here rather than there, why now rather than then. Who has put me here? By whose order and direction have this place and time been allotted to me? (#205)
2. This is what I see and what troubles me. I look on all sides, and I see only darkness everywhere. Nature presents to me nothing which is not matter of doubt and concern. If I saw nothing there which revealed a Divinity, I would come to a negative conclusion; if I saw everywhere the signs of a Creator, I would remain peacefully in faith. But, seeing too much to deny and too little to be sure, I am in a state to be pitied. (#229)
3. Wherefore I have a hundred times wished that if a God maintains Nature, she should testify to Him unequivocally, and that, if the signs she gives are deceptive, she should suppress them altogether; that she should

---

[1] These passages and others below are from the *Pensées* (*Thoughts*), published posthumously. Blaise Pascal, 1623-1650, was a French philosopher, mathematician, scientist, and inventor.

say everything or nothing, that I might see which cause I ought to follow. Whereas in my present state, ignorant of what I am or of what I ought to do, I know neither my condition nor my duty. (#229)
4. It is incomprehensible that God should exist, and it is incomprehensible that He should not exist; that the soul should be joined to the body, and that we should have no soul. (#230)
5. My heart inclines wholly to know where the truth is, the true good, in order to follow it; nothing would be too dear to me for eternity. (#229)

My heart inclines wholly to know the truth: the ultimate expression of love of truth!

Wonder: on the one hand don't we all have, deep down, a desire to know the truth, how it really is, especially in regard to the most important questions? On the other hand, do we always live up to this calling? Or do we sometimes fall short, as in believing what we want to believe?

SOME FURTHER WONDER QUESTIONS

Wonder: What kind of love is the love of truth? It seems to be different from other kinds of love: love of persons, love of music, love of country; how is it different? How is it similar? In what ways are all these joined together as forms of one thing, love?

Wonder: should we love all truth equally? If it is true that my house is 30 feet from the road is that a truth we should love? If so in what way should we love it? Or should love only significant truths because of their significance?

Wonder: part of loving truth seems to be getting it right. Is that enough or does love of truth call for more? If so, what is that *more*? Getting it right seems to be part of all cases where the truth question enters, including the seemingly minor case of the house-road distance.

Wonder: what is getting it right? Is it the right response to truth? Or is it the truth itself? Is it perhaps both?

Wonder: why should we love truth? Is it because of its intrinsic value? Is it because of its practical value? Isn't it both? We see the intrinsic value when we correct a small mistake as in *it happened in 1950, not in 1951*. The mistake is of no real account but the error as a violation of truth should not stay uncorrected. We see the practical value of truth in its violations, such as: a medical diagnosis that falls short of the truth and turns out to be deadly; a lie as an attack on truth that hurts a person; Clifford's shipowner whose negligence with truth cost many lives, a story to which we will turn shortly.

Wonder: how do we fail to love truth? Two ways come to mind. The first is indifference to the truth question. *This is what I want to believe; never mind whether it is true.* It need not be as direct and blunt as this but when people's attitude towards the truth question has something of this character there is a definite falling short of the love of truth. Included in this is carelessness in ascertaining the facts correctly and accurately. The second is telling a lie where one prefers an advantage to be gained by the lie to giving the right response to truth. Are there other ways?

Wonder: how do we live up to the call to love truth? I suggest we look at the writings of three famous thinkers, Clifford, James[2] and Pascal. Reflecting on each can I think help guide our thoughts as we ponder the call to love truth. Clifford's love of truth leads him to urge us to be careful not to lose it by failing to take the question of evidence seriously. Pascal's love of truth leads him to wonder about the nature of the human person. Clifford and Pascal each seem clearly to be motivated by a deep love of truth. Is this equally clear in James? Or is his appeal to pragmatic reasons for belief a falling short of the response called for by genuine love of truth? Perhaps James has an equal love of truth but views the response to truth

---

[2] William Kingdon Clifford, 1845-1879, was an English mathematician, scientist and philosopher. William James, 1842-1910 was an American scientist and philosopher.

differently from Clifford and Pascal. Let us begin with Clifford, what he offers us in his essay, "The Ethics of Belief."

[2] CLIFFORD

CLIFFORD'S "THE ETHICS OF BELIEF": OUR DUTY IN THE REALM OF BELIEFS

Wonder: How do I realize love of truth in my life? Do I strive to believe only what is true? If so how I do I accomplish that? Isn't it largely and perhaps exclusively in terms of what I believe and don't believe; my belief system, the realm of my beliefs? Is it oriented to truth?

For Clifford this means an emphasis on my *duty* in the realm of my beliefs, in contrast to my *right* as in James. That duty is to always believe only on sufficient or adequate evidence. This implies my duty to withhold belief if I lack sufficient or adequate evidence. Clifford's core thesis, his basic idea in "The Ethics of Belief" is captured in his succinct phrase:

> "It is wrong always, everywhere, and for anyone, to believe anything upon insufficient evidence."

> "If a man, holding a belief which he was taught in childhood or persuaded of afterwards, keeps down and pushes away any doubts which arise about it in his mind, purposely avoids the reading of books and the company of men that call into question or discuss it, and regards as impious those questions which cannot easily be asked without disturbing it—the life of that man is one long sin against mankind."[3]

---

[3] William Kingdon Clifford, "The Ethics of Belief." *Contemporary Review*, 1877.

Chapter 16: The Love of Truth

Wonder: why is it wrong to believe anything on insufficient evidence? Clifford answers this question with a vivid example, the case of the ship owner.

Summarizing and paraphrasing:

A ship owner was about to send out a ship. He knew that she was old and not very well built and needed repairs. He had doubts that she was seaworthy; doubts which preyed upon him and made him unhappy. He thought that perhaps he should have her thoroughly overhauled and refitted. But he succeeded in overcoming these doubts and thereby dismissed from his mind all ungenerous suspicions. In this way he acquired a sincere and comfortable belief that his ship was sufficiently safe and seaworthy. He watched her departure with a light heart and wishes for success; and he got his insurance money when she went down in mid-ocean and told no tales.

What shall we say of him? Surely this, that he was guilty of the death of these men. No doubt he sincerely believed in the soundness of his ship; but the sincerity of his belief is not enough and it cannot not save him because *he had no right to believe on such evidence as was before him.* He had acquired his belief not by honestly earning it in patient investigation but by stifling his doubts. In the end he felt so sure about it that he could not think otherwise; yet he had knowingly and willingly worked himself into holding that belief and so he must be held responsible for it and for all its tragic consequences.

But suppose the ship was not unsound after all. Would that take away his guilt? No, he would have been lucky, not innocent. The question of right or wrong in regard to belief is not a matter of whether the belief turns out to be true or false but only whether the person had a right to believe on the evidence that was available to him. Was it sufficient to justify his belief?

One could object that what is really wrong is not the belief but the action which follows from it. But if the action is wrong then surely a belief which naturally leads to it is thereby also wrong. The two go logically together; they cannot be separated. The owner who acted wrongly did so because he first believed wrongly; he believed on insufficient evidence.

Wonder again: why is it wrong to believe anything on insufficient evidence? Clifford provides one answer, the case of the ship owner, the *practical* value and importance of truth. But there is also a deeper answer, the *intrinsic* value and importance of truth.

SOME KEY POINTS IN CLIFFORD'S "THE ETHICS OF BELIEF"

*The *practical* value and importance of truth: the shipowner.

*He had no right to believe on such evidence; he is guilty of the death of these people.

*It is always wrong to ignore evidence: honest and open-minded inquiry is always called for.

*It is always wrong to stifle our doubts: honest and open-minded inquiry is always called for.

*Actions stem from beliefs; the two go together. It is not possible to separate belief from action.

*The deeper importance of truth: each person should revere truth for its *intrinsic* value.

*Clifford's Rule: it is always wrong for anyone to believe anything on insufficient evidence.

BASIC BELIEF, MERE BELIEF AND KNOWING IN CLIFFORD

When Clifford speaks of *belief* and *believing* what is he is referring to? I suggest it is *basic belief*. As noted, this includes both claims to knowledge and mere belief. That is:

We can claim to *know* x only when we have compelling evidence for x that is necessary and sufficient for a justified claim to know x. I can claim to *know* that this is my house since I've lived in it for many years. We can claim to *merely believe* y only when we have evidence necessary and sufficient to justify the belief that y is true with a high degree of probability. I *believe* that this is your house because I remember recently being told it is on good authority.

AN OBJECTION AND REPLY

Wonder: is following Clifford's Rule that it is wrong to believe on insufficient evidence always the right thing to do? In one way it surely seems so. But consider an objection that might be raised against this and that seems reasonable. Imagine it is Europe around the time of the Second World War. And imagine further:

> The Nazis are coming! We have very little time to escape! The only way to escape is by getting on the ship immediately and heading out. But then someone reminds us of Clifford and warns us: do you know the ship is safe? Do you have sufficient evidence to justifiably believe it is safe? Remember: it is always wrong to believe anything on insufficient evidence.

What shall we do? Obey this application of Clifford and take the time to have the ship checked out? The Nazis will have caught up with us and it will be too late!

Surely this would be a very foolish thing to do and not what Clifford had in mind. And we don't need to do this to live up to Clifford's injunction about staying with the evidence. We need to ask: what does following Clifford in this case call on us to do? Clearly it is to get on the ship as quickly as possible and head out as quickly as possible. That is precisely what going with the evidence calls for: the way to save your life is to head out immediately. That is, the evidence here is that the probability of saving your life by getting on the ship immediately is far greater than stopping to do a careful examination of its seaworthiness. Consider:

If you stop to check the ship you will *certainly lose* your life. Getting on the ship carries the risk that it is not safe and will sink. But it also offers *the only chance of saving* your life if it is safe. Surely getting on the ship is a good bargain. Clifford himself recognizes exactly this point when he remarks:

> Moreover there are many cases in which it is our duty to act upon probabilities, although the evidence is not such as to justify present belief; because it is precisely by such action, and by observation of its fruits, that evidence is got which may justify fu-

ture belief. So that we have no reason to fear lest a habit of conscientious inquiry should paralyze the actions of our daily life.

Wonder: should we conclude from this that it is indeed always right to follow Clifford's Rule? That is, what seemed to be an objection to Clifford actually turns out to be an application of Clifford and his Rule. But perhaps there are other objections that could reasonably be raised; are there such objections?

SOME REFLECTIONS ON CLIFFORD

Wonder: how does following Clifford's Rule function on the psychological level? I suggest there are two kinds of cases regarding our psychological acts:

One is a natural and spontaneous withholding of belief where we do not have adequate evidence. Consider the person sitting across from me in the subway train. Where was he born? I have no idea. And so I naturally and spontaneously withhold any belief about this. There is no inclination to form any belief because the total lack of any evidence is so clear and apparent.

Two is where the withholding of belief or giving our assent is not spontaneous, where we must make a decision. In some cases we must make an effort to withhold belief in order to avoid believing something merely because we want to believe it. I find myself liking a certain person and wanting very much to believe that he is trustworthy, and wanting to entrust him in some very important matter. But is he really trustworthy? Do I have sufficient evidence for this? I should not believe he is trustworthy merely because I want to believe this.

Surely Clifford's Rule comes into play here. How do we follow it? Let me suggest:

Make a conscious and deliberate effort to avoid believing only what you want to believe. Positively, make a conscious and deliberate effort to believe and claim to know only in accordance with the available evidence. This means:

1. Avoid selectivity: selecting what supports your cherished belief and ignoring what is contrary to it.
2. Avoid having an agenda: if you set out to prove something you may well be able to find enough data to support it, to believe it to be true. But is it really true? Does an objective inquiry lead to the conclusion that it is really true, that the evidence supports this?

One important thing we can take from Clifford is the virtue of intellectual humility by following Socrates in the *Apology*: a person is wise if he realizes how much he doesn't know and understand in comparison to what there is, to what fullness of truth consists in.

APPLICATIONS OF CLIFFORD'S RULE IN EVERYDAY LIFE

How does Clifford's Rule that we should never believe anything on insufficient evidence apply in everyday life? Let us consider some instructive applications:

1. Doctor Allen believes he should do the surgery which he sees necessary.
2. Doctor Benson believes he should not do the surgery which he sees as too risky.
3. Carl is a member of the jury; he votes to find the defendant guilty as charged.
4. Diane hears a bad rumor about a co-worker and wonders whether or not to believe it.
5. Edward is faced with a difficult, life-changing decision which will be based largely on the facts of the case as he sees them; what are his beliefs about this matter?
6. Francesca is about to sign on the dotted line; what are her beliefs about this matter?
7. George believes the gun is not loaded.
8. Helen believes the old bridge is safe for her and her family to cross.
9. Ivan is asked by the police to identify a suspect: "Yes, that's him, I'm sure!"
10. Jihadist Joe believes it is God's will that he kills the infidels (that's us!).

CLIFFORD'S RULE: PROPORTION YOUR BELIEF TO THE EVIDENCE

Clifford's Rule may be read as consisting of three parts and expressed as follows:

1. If you have insufficient evidence: you should suspend belief.
2. If you have strong evidence: you may have a mere belief.
3. If you have compelling evidence: you may claim to know.

Wonder: when is the evidence sufficient? When is it insufficient? When can we say it is strong? Does it need to be strong in order to be sufficient? When can we say it is compelling? Often the answers to these questions are obvious; often they are not. Can we always tell when we have the compelling evidence that entitles us to claim that we know; as opposed to having only the strong evidence that entitles us to say we have a mere belief? Do you know that your trusted friend will stand by you? Or do you really have only a mere belief? If asked you would most likely say you know he will stand by you. Is that because you feel this is expected of you and that anything less would be a sign of failure in you? Or do you really know this in the sense that your claim to know and not merely to believe is a justified one?

[3] JAMES

JAMES' "THE WILL TO BELIEVE": A CLAIM THAT WE HAVE A RIGHT TO BELIEVE

Wonder: what motivates our beliefs? Is it always the love of truth? Do we sometimes believe something for pragmatic reasons because it pays to do so in some way? Could this ever be defended as rationally justified?

Consider the famous essay of William James "The Will to Believe." Does he endorse the idea of pragmatic reasons for beliefs, not only as what we in fact do but also as what we are sometimes justified in doing?

Consider that his essay is largely a reply to Clifford, and it is intended as a refutation of Clifford's main point that it is always wrong to believe anything on insufficient evidence; and as providing an alternative view of our right to believe. He describes it as "an essay in justification of faith, a defence of our right to adopt a believing attitude in religious matters, in spite of the fact that our merely logical intellect may not have been coerced."

Doesn't this amount to an endorsement of pragmatic reasons for beliefs? Doesn't it stand in sharp contrast to Clifford's Rule: stay with the evidence? Doesn't believing by staying with the evidence stand in opposition to believing for pragmatic reasons?

How does James defend his endorsement of pragmatic reasons for beliefs? How does he justify his departure from Clifford's Rule? It has to do with the question of neutrality, the fact that neutrality is not always possible. To see this, let us distinguish two very different kinds cases where *not believing* comes into play:

- Where neutrality is possible. Is John guilty or innocent? I have no idea. And I also have no stake in the case. I don't know John and my only interest in the case is that justice be done; that all involved may believe the truth of the matter. So I simply withhold belief; I don't believe one way or the other; I stay neutral. Pragmatic reasons for believing never come into play because they are not relevant.

- Where neutrality is not possible. Again, is John guilty or innocent? But now John is my very close friend and so I do have a stake in the case. He is in serious difficulty because the charges against him are very serious, and they seem to be based on good evidence. He comes to me to ask for my support. Will you defend me? More basically, do you believe in me? Do you believe the charges are false? Do you believe I am innocent? Neutrality is now impossible. I must take a stand, for him or against him. Now pragmatic reasons for believing do come into play; they are highly relevant. But are they justified? For the sake of our friendship, it surely pays for me to believe in his innocence. But is this a valid reason for doing so? James would say yes, Clifford would say no; who is correct?

GENUINE OPTIONS: WHERE NEUTRALITY IS IMPOSSIBLE

James is concerned only with the second of these two cases. It concerns what he calls *our passional nature* which refers to our desires, our hopes and fears; to what we love and what we hate; to what we like and what we dislike; in a word, to the voice of our hearts.

Among the things proposed to our belief, things we may end up either believing or not believing there is one kind that is particularly important. James calls it a *genuine option* and defines it as: (a) *living*, where both possibilities have some attraction for us; (b) *momentous*, one of great importance; and (c) *forced*, one where there is no middle ground between the two possibilities; hence where neutrality is impossible, as explained in the following passages:

> "The thesis I defend is, briefly stated, this: *Our passional nature not only lawfully may, but must, decide an option between propositions*, whenever it is a genuine option that cannot by its nature be decided on intellectual grounds; for to say, under such circumstances, "Do not decide, but leave the question open," is itself a passional decision – just like saying yes or no – and is attended with the same risk of losing the truth."

> "Neutrality is not only inwardly difficult; it is also outwardly unrealizable, where our relations to an alternative are practical and vital. This is because belief and doubt are living attitudes and involve conduct on our part. The only way of doubting, or refusing to believe, that a certain thing is, is to act as if it were not. If I doubt that you are worthy of my confidence, I keep you uninformed of all my secrets just as if you were unworthy of the same."

> "There are inevitable occasions in life when inaction is a kind of action, and must count as action, and when not to be for is to be practically against; and in all such cases strict and consistent neutrality is an unattainable thing."

> "Suppose you are climbing a mountain and have worked yourself into a position from which the only escape is by a terrible leap.

Chapter 16: The Love of Truth

Have faith that you can successfully make it, and your feet are nerved to its accomplishment. But mistrust yourself and think of all the sweet things you have heard the scientists say of maybes, and you will hesitate so long that, at last, all unstrung and trembling, and launching yourself in a moment of despair, you roll in the abyss. In such a case, the part of wisdom is to believe what is in the line of your needs, for only by such belief is the need fulfilled. Refuse to believe, and you shall indeed be right, for you shall irretrievably perish. But believe, and again you shall be right, for you shall save yourself."

"It is as if a man should hesitate indefinitely to ask a certain woman to marry him because he was not perfectly sure that she would prove an angel after he brought her home. Would he not cut himself off from that particular angel-possibility as decisively as if he went and married someone else?"

Wonder: is it really true that *wisdom is to believe what is in the line of your needs*? Doesn't wisdom rather urge us to strive to believe what is true? Truth and our needs do not always coincide; where they don't isn't it the truth that we should choose? Isn't that what love of truth means? And surely the man should not hesitate to ask the woman to marry him. But isn't this easily understood by pointing out that it concerns action and not necessarily belief?

KNOWING THE TRUTH AND AVOIDING ERROR

"When we give up the doctrine of objective certitude, we do not thereby give up the quest or hope of truth itself. We still pin our faith on its existence, and still believe that we gain an ever better position towards it by systematically continuing to roll up experiences and think."

"There are two ways of looking at our duty in the matter of opinion: *We must know the truth*; and *we must avoid error*. These are our first and great commandments as would-be knowers."

"Clifford exhorts us to treat the avoidance of error as more imperative and let truth take its chance. Believe nothing, he tells us, keep your mind in suspense forever, rather than by closing it on insufficient evidence you incur the awful risk of believing lies."

"You, on the other hand, may think that the risk of being in error is a very small matter when compared with the blessings of real knowledge, and be ready to be duped many times in your investigation rather than postpone indefinitely the chance of guessing true."

"I myself find it impossible to go with Clifford. For my own part, I have also a horror of being duped; but I can believe that worse things than being duped may happen to a man in this world. So Clifford's exhortation has to my ears a thoroughly fantastic sound."

"It is like a general informing his soldiers that it is better to keep out of battle forever than to risk a single wound. Not so are victories over enemies or over nature gained. Our errors are surely not such awfully solemn things."

"In a world where we are so certain to incur them in spite of all our caution, a certain lightness of heart seems healthier than this excessive nervousness on their behalf."

"*Moral questions* immediately present themselves as questions whose solution cannot wait for sensible proof. A moral question is a question not of what sensibly exists, but of what is good, or would be good if it did exist. Science can tell us what exists; but to compare the *worths*, both of what exists and what does not exist, we must consult not science, but what Pascal calls our heart."

"Science herself consults her heart when she lays it down that the infinite ascertainment of fact and correction of false belief are the supreme goods for man."

[4] COMPARING CLIFFORD AND JAMES

Wonder: Clifford and James are united in their concern for truth but they differ in their concrete responses. Both say *don't lose the truth*:

- Clifford: don't lose it through error; accept only what is supported by the evidence.

Chapter 16: The Love of Truth

- James: don't lose it through a sceptical holding back or fear; be bold, accept a risk of error.

Both are concerned with the evidence:

- Clifford: the focus is on our duty to believe in-relation to the evidence.

- James: the focus is on our right to believe in-relation to the evidence.

Both are concerned with the love of truth:

- Clifford: do not violate love of truth and duty to truth by holding unjustified beliefs.

- James: do not violate love of truth and corresponding duty to truth by being overly cautious and thus losing out on the truth, not gaining the truth.

[5] CAN WE WILL TO BELIEVE?

Wonder: can we will to believe? Can we control our beliefs? On the one hand both Clifford and James seem to assume that we can do this; for both tell us what we should or should not do or what we may or may not do in regard to what we believe.

On the other hand, don't our beliefs come to us automatically and spontaneously, so that we are not in control of what we believe? I look out the window and see the rain. Immediately and without any effort I form the belief that it is raining. I do not will to believe this and I cannot will to believe otherwise. In general, belief flows from the available evidence, not the will.

But perhaps there are cases where the will does play a role, where somehow it is up to me whether to believe or not believe. My close friend is accused of a serious crime. He comes to me with the question: do you believe in me? Don't I have to choose here between a *yes* and a *no*? I weigh the evidence; I reflect on my friendship with him, on my duty of fidelity. Isn't this a matter of willing to believe, in the one way or the other?

What are my beliefs in the important areas of life, such as my opinions of other people, my political views and my religious beliefs? Doesn't the will play an important role here? Let me suggest several ways in which the will does play a role, ways in which we are in control. We can divide this into a positive and a negative set of guidelines.

Positively we can resolve:

1. To seek the truth and only the truth.
2. Especially, to choose truth over being right.
3. To be careful by paying close attention to all important aspects.
4. To be open to the evidence and examine it carefully.

On the negative side we can resolve to avoid:

5. Believing something merely out of habit.
6. Believing something merely because others believe it.
7. Determining what to believe merely out of political correctness.
8. Determining what to believe merely by what we want to believe.
9. Suppressing doubts.
10. Suppressing unwelcomed ideas, theories and view-points.
11. Selectivity: selecting what supports a cherished belief and ignoring what is contrary to it.
12. Having an agenda: trying to prove a preconceived idea rather than finding the truth.

[6] ARE PRAGMATIC REASONS FOR BELIEF JUSTIFIED?

Wonder: can we follow James and believe something because of its value for our life? Or, as he puts it, believe what is in the line of our needs? We may call these *pragmatic reasons* for believing; that is, *believing x because it pays to do so*.

Surely this is sometimes wrong. Suppose the belief is not true. Or it is not based on sufficient evidence. Or it is a wish fulfillment; we believe it because we want to believe it.

Believing something for pragmatic reasons seems to be wrong, a failure to live up to the love of truth and give the right response to truth. *Is it true?* Isn't that the crucial question? If I really love truth as it should be loved, shouldn't this be the criterion for deciding on all my belief responses? Do I have adequate evidence that it is true? If I don't have this evidence should I not withhold belief? Doesn't Clifford have it right? Shouldn't we follow him faithfully?

I can still take a position: I can hope and seek. Pascal provides an illustration. If you feel you don't have sufficient evidence to arrive at a reasonable position on whether or not God exists then you should seek the truth about God. As Pascal expresses it: *"My heart inclines wholly to know where the truth is in order to follow it; nothing would be too dear to me for eternity."*

But is believing something for pragmatic reasons always wrong? James says *no*. Recall the case he uses to make his point. "Suppose you are climbing a mountain, and have worked yourself into a position from which the only escape is by a terrible leap. Have faith that you can successfully make it, and your feet are nerved to its accomplishment." Believe the proposition *I can jump over this abyss* is true and doing so will make it true. Pragmatic reasons work!

Another example: believe in the love of your friend if he has shown himself worthy of this love by his behavior. Believe it now even if there is some reason to doubt it now. Give him the credit of love. Perhaps doing so will itself help to strengthen and secure this love and thus make it true that his love is real. Again, pragmatic reasons work!

Wonder: what does love of truth call for? On the one hand, we should follow Clifford: the only valid reason for believing something is having sufficient evidence for it; believing for pragmatic reasons is wrong. On the other hand, perhaps we will gain by following James: there is sometimes a valid place for pragmatic reasons in the absence of sufficient evidence. Believe you can make the jump! Believe in the love of your friend! Where else might this work?

[7] PASCAL ON THE GREATNESS OF THE HUMAN PERSON

Pascal's love of truth leads him to *wonder* about the nature of the human person:

1. Man is but a reed, the most feeble thing in nature; but he is a thinking reed. The entire universe need not arm itself to crush him. A vapor, a drop of water suffices to kill him (#347).
2. But if the universe were to crush him, man would still be more noble than that which killed him because he knows that he dies; and the advantage the universe has over him, the universe knows nothing of this (#347).
3. All our dignity, then, consists in thought. By it we must elevate ourselves, and not by space and time, which we cannot fill. Let us endeavor, then, to think well; this is the principle of morality (#347).
4. A thinking reed. It is not from space that I must seek my dignity, but from the government of my thought. I shall have no more dignity even if I possess worlds (#348).
5. By space the universe encompasses and swallows me up like an atom; by thought I comprehend the world (#348).
6. The immateriality of the soul. Philosophers who have mastered their passions. What matter could do that? (#349)
7. Man is obviously made to think. It is his whole dignity and his whole merit. And his whole duty is to think as he ought. Now, the order of thought is to begin with self, and with its Author and with its ultimate end (#146).
8. But of what does the world actually think? Never of this, but of dancing, playing the lute, singing, making verses, running at the ring, fighting, etc.; and of making oneself king, without thinking what it is to be a king and what it is to be a man (#146).
9. Thought. All the dignity of man consists in thought. Thought is therefore by its nature a wonderful and incomparable thing. It must have strange defects to be contemptible. How great thought is in its nature! How vile it is in its defects! But what is this thought? (#365)
10. The heart has its reasons which the reason doesn't know. We feel it in a thousand things. Is it by reason that you love yourself? (#277)
11. It is the heart which experiences God, and not the reason. This, then, is faith: God felt by the heart, not by the reason (# 278).
12. Faith is a gift of God, not a gift of reasoning (#279).

Chapter 16: The Love of Truth

[8] FAITH

Wonder: what is faith? Are there different types of faith? There is religious faith and the faith I have in another person. I have faith in the love of my mother and of my close friend. What joins religious faith and faith in another person into one thing which we call *faith*?

Wonder: what is the relation between faith and belief? I have faith in the love of my mother and I have the belief that she loves me? Are they the same thing or two different things?

There is blind faith and not-blind faith; surely blind faith is not a good thing. Someone comes to me with a fantastic offer; my friend warns me that it is too good to be true. Indeed, I don't have evidence sufficient to reasonably believe it is true; accepting would be blind faith.

Can we say: blind faith is false faith and not-blind faith is true faith? Can we define true faith as faith with sufficient evidence? My faith in my mother is based on my experience which provides me with sufficient evidence. It follows Clifford's Rule: believe only with sufficient evidence. In contrast, false faith is faith lacking in sufficient evidence; or when there is actually contrary evidence, as faith in far-out cults and con-artists.

True faith is therefore a faith that has seen and false faith is a faith that has not seen. This shows that the assumption *believing without sufficient evidence is a moral virtue* is really a false claim; and even a dangerous one as it opens the door to all sorts of outlandish false claims.

Faith and reason are often seen as opposed; the idea being that you have the one or the other but not both. For false faith this is surely true; but for true faith? Are they not joined together? Is it not reasonable to have true faith? Recall that true faith is a faith that has seen, so that faith and reason, faith and vision are not opposed but united in one.

True faith has a positive moral quality because it is a commitment of faithfulness based on sufficient evidence. My faith in my mother has this quality; it is based on sufficient evidence.

In his essay "On Obstinacy in Belief" C. S. Lewis considers a faith held obstinately "even in the teeth of seeming contrary evidence." Is this a moral virtue? Yes and no. Yes, when it is true faith; when I continue to have faith in my mother and a trusted friend. No, when it is false faith as the faith in the example Lewis gives of the Bearded Man who asked people to stay in the burning theater and then escaped unharmed while they all burned to death! One should not have faith in such a person!

Wonder: is open-mindedness a good thing? Yes and no. Open-mindedness is always a good thing when it is openness to truth for the sake of truth. This includes cases where I should say *I could be wrong*. But sometimes open-mindedness is not the right response and attitude. Faithfulness to a true friend means not being open-minded to bad reports about him.

[9] SCEPTICISM

Wonder: what is scepticism? How does it relate to love of truth? We can start out by making explicit that scepticism is not the same thing as ignorance. Ignorance means *I don't know* while scepticism means *I can't know*. But what is it that I can't know? This leads to:

1. *Two basic types of scepticism:*

    One is practical scepticism. Is this a scam? I'm sceptical of it. We turn to this in #8-10. Two is philosophical scepticism, which we examine in #2-7:

2. *Two forms of philosophical scepticism:*

    One: moderate, the denial of the possibility of knowledge; restriction to mere belief. Two: extreme, the denial of even the possibility of reasonable mere belief.

3. ***Both types and both forms are positions.***

   Scepticism is not the absence of a position; it is the position that something we generally assume and take for granted doesn't really exist; namely a certain possibility: of knowledge, in one case, of mere belief in another.

4. ***Areas of philosophical scepticism and occasions for wonder:***

   The external world: how do you know there is a world out there existing independently of your consciousness? Perhaps your whole life is one big dream? Can you prove this is not so, that the physical world really exists, whether you see it or not?

   Other minds: how do you know there is a consciousness like yours behind those eyes of another person that you see? You can't see or feel their consciousness; yet you are quite certain it is there. Maybe "other people" are just robots? Can you prove they are not?

   The past: maybe the world and all the records that it contains, and that seems to come from a past that really existed independently of you, actually just sprang into existence this past second. That surely seems absurd. Can you prove it's not so?

   Ethics: is murder really wrong, wrong in itself, objectively wrong? Or is it that we only consider it wrong, call it wrong in our culture and our laws? The sceptic here adopts a form of ethical relativism; we will be examining this theory in Chapter 17.

5. ***Two positions that should be carefully distinguished:***

   One: denial. This is the claim that the above items don't actually exist; they are illusions.

Two: scepticism. This is the claim for each item that it might exist or might not exist; we just don't know one way or the other. This is the actual claim above.

6. **Notice again that scepticism is a position, as noted in #3. Scepticism makes a claim and thereby takes a position. It is the claim that we can't know or reasonably believe.**

7. **Motivations for philosophical scepticism. What is it that motivates the sceptic? Here are two possibilities:**

One is love of truth and obeying Clifford's Rule: no belief without sufficient evidence. Can this be reasonably applied to each of the above? Don't we have sufficient evidence in each case? Or perhaps even more than sufficient, an overabundance of evidence? Two is hesitancy: a reluctance to take a stand and claim to know or reasonably believe. Is such a state logically warranted? Or is it an inability to distinguish sufficient and insufficient evidence? Is it perhaps a misplaced fear of being in error?

8. *Practical scepticism.* Some is reasonable and called for: this looks like a scam. Two further examples: One: an old bridge that I am encouraged to cross. Is it really safe? I should be sceptical. Two: the example of Lewis, the Bearded Man who asked people to stay in the burning theater and then escaped unharmed while they all burned to death. If only they had the proper practical scepticism called for in such a situation!
This is often called a healthy scepticism.

9. **Healthy scepticism shows that not all scepticism is bad or wrong or misplaced. Some scepticism is called for as the right response. In general:**

One: there is really much that we can't know at all.
Two: there is really much that we can't *know* in the strict sense, but merely believe.

Three: there is really much that we can't even reasonably *merely believe*, where we have no evidence or insufficient evidence.

Four: in general we should be careful in what we claim:

Do I really *know* this? Often, we know much less than what we think we know or claim to know. Do I really have sufficient evidence to reasonably *believe* this? All this flows logically from following Clifford's Rule.

10. Practical scepticism. Some is unreasonable and uncalled for; an unhealthy scepticism.

My friend has been faithful to me for many years; he has always come through for me; he has never let me down. Now he asks for my trust. Do I believe him? Do I trust him? If I don't, am I not guilty of the sin of mistrust? My scepticism: isn't it unreasonable and uncalled for, an unhealthy scepticism?

[10] LOVE OF TRUTH: SOME CORE POINTS

1. Reverence for reality, for the way things really are.
2. Giving the right response; being in line with reality.
3. Faithfulness; not losing sight of the value of truth.
4. Avoiding false pragmatic reasons for believing.
5. Avoiding intellectual vices like carelessness, selectivity, agenda dominance.
6. A deep longing for truth: "My *heart inclines wholly to know where the truth is; nothing would be too dear for me for attaining this.*"-Pascal.

CHAPTER 17
TRUTH, REALITY, AND RELATIVISM

[1] TRUTH AS CORRESPONDENCE WITH REALITY

What is truth? What is the nature of truth? What does truth mean? We sometimes speak of "the truth"; consider an example where this phrase might come up. Mother and daughter are having a conversation. "Where were you at 2:00AM last night?" The reply doesn't sound very convincing. The dialogue goes back and forth. Finally Mom says with lots of emotion and emphasis: "OK, just tell me the truth!" Doesn't this mean "Tell me what *really happened*"? "Tell me *how it really is*, or really was at that time." Isn't the urgent request for the truth the request to be able to come to an awareness of *reality,* how it really is? If so this seems to be an important clue as to the nature of truth: reality.

Consider another example. I have a friend, John, who is accused of a serious crime. I look into the matter, carefully consider all the evidence and conclude that it clearly shows that he is innocent. I form the belief "John is innocent." I claim that he really is innocent, that this is the truth of the matter. Now suppose I am correct: in fact he really is innocent. Then my belief is what it is because it is about *truth*; it is about the *reality* that he actually is innocent.

Can we then simply say that truth is reality? Isn't it rather so: the *reality* is that John is innocent, the fact is that he is innocent -- while *truth* pertains to "saying" that this is so? It pertains to the belief or statement or proposition that asserts that this is so, that expresses this fact. And isn't the belief-statement-proposition "John is innocent" true because it *corresponds* to the reality that John is innocent? If so we have our answer to the nature of truth:

Truth means correspondence with reality.

This means we cannot simply say that truth is reality. The reality that he is innocent, the fact that he is innocent, just is; it is not something that can be true (or false).

The idea that the nature of truth is correspondence with reality goes back to Aristotle. In his words "To say of what is that it is, or of what is not that it is not, is true."[1] Basically, it is the idea that to say that something is true is to say that it asserts what is really the case; that what it claims is the case corresponds to what is *really* the case.

What is truth? Is truth objective or subjective? Is there such a thing as an absolute truth? These questions concern the *meaning* of truth, of what it *means* to say that something is true. Let us pursue them in this chapter. They are distinct from the question whether we can we *know* the truth, which we will take up the chapter two. Our present question is: what does truth *mean*?

REALITY

Truth means correspondence with reality. But what is that reality? Take the proposition "John is innocent." Does it correspond to John as an individual person? Does it correspond to the idea of innocence as such? Doesn't it correspond to a very different kind of reality: *that* John is innocent, or the fact that John is innocent? This is generally called a state of affairs or a fact. The state of affairs that John is innocent is the same thing as the fact that John is innocent. Thus, the reality to which a true proposition corresponds is a state of affairs: *that* such and such is the case. We can also say that a state of affairs is the referent of a proposition.

Reality is what makes propositions true; the reality that John is innocent is what makes the proposition "John is innocent" true. In the other direction we can say that a true proposition is one that asserts what is the case; for example, that says "John is innocent" when in fact he is innocent. This is the relation of correspondence. That the *proposition* "John is innocent" is true means that what it asserts really is so, that it corresponds to the *reality* "that John is innocent."

[2] FALSEHOODS, ERRORS AND LIES

---

[1] *Metaphysics,* 1011b, 25-28.

A false proposition is one that asserts what is not really the case. Thus if John really is innocent, then "John is guilty" is a false proposition. Alternatively, a false proposition is one that does not correspond to any actual state of affairs. For example, that Santa Claus is coming is not an actual state of affairs so the proposition "Santa Claus is coming" is a false proposition. The contradictory of a true proposition is always a false proposition and the contradictory of a false proposition is always a true proposition.

The truth of true propositions is independent of our believing them; in the same way the falseness of false propositions is independent of our disbelieving them, or considering them or believing them. What is false is *already false* before we come upon it and consider it; it does not have to be *seen as* false in order to *be* false.

It is *propositions* that are true or false and *persons* who can be in error. To be in error means to be convinced of a proposition that is false; to think it is true while in fact it is false. A proposition by itself can only be false, not an error. And if I consider a proposition that is false, or use it as an example, or doubt it, I am not in error. It is when I *believe* a false proposition that I am in error. It is this further point, this relation of a proposition to *belief* that makes it an error.

A proposition by itself cannot be an error, nor can it be a lie. It is only persons who can be in error or lie. What then are the differences between the two, errors and lies? First, an error involves only *one* person, the one who errs. A lie involves *two* persons, the liar and the victim.

Second, the liar believes the false proposition that is the content of the lie to be *false*, while the person in error believes the false proposition that is the content of the error to be *true*.

Third, an error means that a certain person *in fact* believes a false proposition. A lie is an *attempt* to bring about that another person believes a false proposition, for not all lies cause false beliefs; not all lies are successful.

Fourth, a lie has a *moral* significance that an error as such doesn't have. Generally lies are morally wrong while errors are morally neutral. Closely related to this is that you *decide* to lie but you do not decide to be in error; you fall into error.

The stark contrast between errors and lies, even though both have an essential relation to falsehoods, can be brought out by defining a lie through an A-B-C-D analysis. In a lie a person:

(E) Asserts what he
(F) Believes to be false, so as to
(G) Cause a false belief in another person, in order to
(H) Deceive him.

The C and D parts bring out the crucial difference between lies and several other things that can also include the A and B parts; things such as jokes, lines in a play, stories and using a false proposition in a process of reasoning to see what would follow logically from it.

IS THERE AN ABSOLUTE TRUTH?

What is truth? What is the nature of truth? One basic answer we have considered is that truth is correspondence with reality. This is very closely related to some further questions. Is truth objective or subjective? Is there such a thing as absolute truth? Many people attempt to deny absolute truth. What do they mean? There are two main possibilities here:

- There is no absolute truth; all truth is relative. This is the thesis of relativism.
- No one can have absolute possession of the truth. This is more complicated.

The second is very different from the first. The first refers to *truth itself*, to the nature of truth; the second refers to us, to *our having* or not having the truth; to whether we can know or reasonably believe the truth. Here our topic is only the first, the nature of truth. I suggest:

The thesis that there is an absolute truth simply means that truth is objective. For if truth is correspondence with reality and reality is objective, then truth must be objective.

IS TRUTH OBJECTIVE?

Thus, *absolute* truth simply means *objective* truth. Let us pursue the idea of objectivity.

I suggest that objectivity means first of all *independence.* What is objective exists in itself, independently of a knowing subject. Thus, we say the external world and the things in it are objective. Chairs and tables, apples and oranges, trees and stones, all exist in themselves, independently of us, of our perceiving them and knowing about them. They exist objectively. And there are of course many other things that have such an objective existence; and many where it is an interesting question whether they have it or not. Is time independent of us? Does it exist in itself, objectively? Wonder!

I suggest there is a second and very significant meaning of objectivity. When we say that knowledge is objective, we don't mean that it is independent of us, for obviously it is not. What we mean is that it is valid and authentic, as opposed to being "subjective" in the way a prejudice is invalid and inauthentic. Knowledge is objective in the sense that it *corresponds to what exists objectively and independently* of the knowing subject. This is simply a reflection of the fact that knowledge means knowledge of the truth and truth means correspondence with reality.

We might also say that the correspondence of our knowledge to reality, which is what makes it valid and authentic, is something that exists objectively and not merely for us. The objective correspondence of our knowledge to reality means simply that to know something is to know it as it is; to know that something is the case means *to know that it really is*. I can know that John is innocent only if he really is innocent. His being innocent is an objective fact, which exists independently of what anyone thinks. My knowing this independently existing fact is objective and valid in that it accurately corresponds to it. I know what is really the case.

There is a third point here. A human person is a subject; that is, he is the subject who knows, wills, loves, admires, fears and hopes, who feels love and anger, happiness and misery. A subject in this sense stands in contrast to an object; the subject knows the object; the subject "stands before" the object and is related to it in various ways. The key point is that a *personal subject is a reality that is fully objective* in both senses mentioned above; his being is a reality valid in the fullest possible way. It is only the term *subject* that has a resemblance to the subjective. In itself, in its own being, it is totally objective.

SUBJECTIVITY

Subjectivity seems to mean primarily and basically *dependence*. What is subjective is always something dependent on a subject, a person or an animal. In this way it contrasts to objectivity in the first of the two meanings given above. It sometimes has a second meaning, namely invalidity; here it contrasts to objectivity in the second meaning. There are many ways in which the term *subjective* may be used; they differ significantly from each other, and it is crucial to keep them distinct. Let us list six of them; the first four all seem to be valid forms of subjectivity, the last two seem to be invalid forms:

1. Personal subjectivity. This refers to what pertains to a person, personal acts and attitudes and characteristics. Thus, knowing is "subjective" in the sense that it presupposes a knowing subject, a personal subject. This is something objectively valid.
2. Deeply meaningful personal values. A gift that a beloved person gave me a long time ago has a significant value for me. It is precious, but only to me; again valid.
3. Subjective tastes. I like a certain food; another person dislikes it. Can't we say that no one is correct here, in that the goodness or badness of the quality of the taste is subjective? That it is valid only for the person concerned, not in itself objectively.
4. Subjective experiences, such as aches and pains, feelings of tiredness and energy. These exist only for the person who experiences them; hence they are not objective but only subjective. Some are pleasant, some are painful, and some are neutral.

These three forms of subjectivity all seem valid; we turn now to two invalid forms:

5. Illusory subjective experiences. This refers to hallucinations, dreams, and perceptual illusions, such as the appearance of the stick that is really straight but looks bent when half immersed in clear water. These images and appearances are subjective in that they exist only for the person experiencing them. They are invalid in that they are all in some way false, pretending to be what they are really not. In this they stand in contrast to subjective tastes like the goodness of candy and subjective experiences like pains, which make no pretense to be something they are not.
6. Invalid attitudes. These refer to prejudice, falsely favoring someone or something and other wrong forms of bias. They include all types of intellectual dishonesty such as selectivity in considering evidence in order to arrive at a pre-established desired outcome, and various forms of self-deception. These are invalid in a much deeper sense than illusory experiences. The latter happen to us while these stem actively from us.

IS THERE A SUBJECTIVE TRUTH?

Is truth subjective in any of these senses? People sometimes use phrases such as "true for me" or "my truth"; they seem to suggest that truth is subjective. That is, according to this idea "what's true for me may not be true for you" and vice versa. But do these phrases even make any sense? Perhaps what is meant by "true for me" is simply that I believe this to be true while you may not. But wouldn't this simply mean that *my opinion* is different from yours? And perhaps my opinion could be called "subjective" in that it belongs to me and not to you. Even so, how would any of this show that truth is not objective? Isn't my opinion *about* something? Isn't it about something existing independently of me, namely the objective truth?

And if it is such a claim, can't my opinion be correct in that what I believe to be true *really is true*, that it is *the truth*? If so then opinions and beliefs do not contradict objective truth; on the contrary they appeal to it and really would not make any sense without it. All this seems to suggest the objectivity of truth.

Recall again our example of my friend John who is accused of a serious crime. I look into the matter, carefully consider all the evidence and conclude that it clearly shows that he is innocent. I form the opinion "John is innocent." I claim that he really is innocent, that this is the truth of the matter, the objective truth. Now suppose I am correct: in fact, he really is innocent. Then my opinion is what it is because it is about an objective truth, the objective truth that he really is innocent. And so opinions, far from suggesting that truth is subjective, show rather that it is objective.

But suppose I am mistaken: he is not innocent, but guilty. Then something else is the truth of the matter, his being guilty. This is equally an objective truth. So, the objectivity of truth remains. *Something* is the case; something is the truth of the matter, the objective truth.

THE OBJECTIVITY OF TRUTH

The core idea of the objectivity of truth can be expressed by saying that what is true is *already true*, before it comes into any relation with us, such as believing it, knowing it, or showing it to be true. And this objectivity of true propositions applies to false propositions as well. What is false is *already false* before we come upon it and consider it. And just as the truth of true propositions is independent of our believing them, so too the falseness of false propositions is independent of our disbelieving them (or considering them, or believing them). What is false is already false; it does not have to be seen as false in order to be false.

THE OBJECTIVITY OF TRUTH AS ROCK BOTTOM

Can't we say that the objectivity of truth is something which we can know with an absolute certainty? How else could it be? Couldn't we say that it forms part of the *rock bottom* of our whole intellectual life? Could anyone deny it without self-contradiction? Consider the claim: "Truth is not objective." Suppose someone says this; let us then ask: is *that* true? If the answer is no we can say: correct, it is not true, for truth is objective. If the answer given is yes, "truth is not objective," we can again ask: is *that* true? Presumably one will claim that it is true.

What else could one do? But what can this mean except the claim, "so it really is"? Is it supposedly *really true* that truth is not objective? Isn't this is the same as saying it is *objectively true* that *truth is not objective*. Isn't this a blatant contradiction?

Isn't it so that anyone who tries to claim that truth is not objective can only do so by claiming that truth isn't really objective, but is really something else? But doesn't this simply reintroduce the very objectivity of truth that one tried to deny? Doesn't the same apply if someone claims, "There is no objective truth."? Is *that* true? Is it really true? Suppose the reply is, "yes, that's true, really true"; doesn't this amounts to saying, "It's really true that there is no real truth." Wonder at this strange contradiction! Is the objectivity of truth part of *the rock bottom*? Does it not form the basis for all thinking, not only in that it is something absolutely certain, in that any attempt to deny it must necessarily appeal to it, and thus reintroduce it; but, also, in the sense that it is a basis for everything else in the domain of thinking?

SCEPTICISM

Is scepticism an exception to this? On the contrary, isn't it a typical example of this? If scepticism claims "we cannot know anything about x" isn't it appealing to truth, objective truth? And isn't it doing so in two ways?

- First, isn't it claiming we cannot know how x really is: *the truth* about x?
- Second, isn't it claiming that it is really *true:* we cannot know anything about x?

Isn't scepticism a theory that begins with and builds on the unmistakable fact that we cannot always reach truth? Isn't it a theory that then moves beyond this to the further thesis, "we can never reach truth"? That is: "we can never get at reality as it really is." So, isn't the very thesis of scepticism necessarily expressed in terms of objective truth, namely the claim that objective truth is always beyond our reach?

A DENIAL OF OBJECTIVITY: RELATIVISM ABOUT TRUTH

One way of trying to deny the objectivity of truth is by claiming that truth is *subjective*. Another, somewhat parallel way is to try to claim truth is *relative*. This is relativism as a theory of the meaning of truth: truth is relative to individuals, there is no absolute truth, no objective truth, no "how it really is." That is, according to the theory, there is no truth independent of persons. "If there were, who's to say what it is? No one can say what it is. Hence it makes no sense to say, "*P* is true independently of what you believe, or what anyone believes." Thus, some people will say "If you believe in God, then God's existence is true for you; if you don't then His existence is not true for you."

Try applying this theory to practical matters, such as whether pouring gasoline on a fire will extinguish the fire or not. Isn't there clearly an absolute, non-relative truth of the matter in such cases? Here the theory seems too absurd to be taken seriously. But perhaps it is false on a much deeper level than that; perhaps it is mistaken at its very core? Is it perhaps mistaken about the very nature of truth? Does its mistake apply to all truths, including the truth about God's existence and other matters that people disagree about, such as politics and ethics?

SOME CRITICAL QUESTIONS ABOUT THE RELATIVISTIC THEORY OF TRUTH

1. Doesn't it confuse *I don't know* with *there is nothing there to be known*? A denial of objective truth means a denial of the corresponding reality, and this is what relativism intends. But surely *something is the case* about God, about life after death, even if some people do not know what it is, or are mistaken in what they believe about it.
2. In a similar way doesn't it confuse *I can't prove this to be true* with *it isn't really true*? But can't something be true without my being able to prove this, or show it? Can't John really be innocent even if he can't prove it? We will return to this point in the next section.
3. Doesn't relativism fail by not having adequate room for being mistaken? We are mistaken when we hold a *false belief*. Consider a male chauvinist

who believes "women are inferior to men" or a sadist who believes "torturing people for fun is morally acceptable." Are these beliefs not clearly false? Are such people not clearly mistaken? Who could seriously say to them, "That's true – it's true for you." And suppose someone said, "Relativism regarding truth is a false theory." Wouldn't the relativist want to say he is mistaken? Yet he couldn't without contradicting his theory; for to be consistent, he would have to say, "If you believe that then it's true for you." If he says of someone that he is mistaken, that what he believes is false, he is abandoning his position that "if you believe it, it's true – it's true for you."

4. Is relativism *itself true*? Is the relativistic theory of truth supposed to be really true? Is it supposed to be objectively true, true whether we realize it or not? If the claim is made that it is, isn't the contradiction obvious? The denial that there is an objective truth is put forward as a claim to be itself an objective truth! If relativism acknowledges that its own theory is not really true, can we not simply say: yes, agreed, it is not true and reject it?

Isn't there an important lesson here? That is, *every theory rests on the notion of objective truth*. Every theory, to be meaningful, must be put forth as the claim *so it really is*; the claim to be objectively true. Lacking this claim, it cannot be a serious theory. But relativism, to be consistent, must lack this claim. Wonder at the problem that arises!

Take any theory put forth by one of the sciences: Newton's theory of gravity, Einstein's theory of gravity, evolution, theories about climate change, theories of personality type, and many others. Don't they all make claims that such-and-such is really the case? Some are more established, so that one might claim they are really facts; others are less established. But even here there is an essential reference to objective truth. Doesn't *established* mean likely to be true?

GENUINE RELATIVITY

Some things really are relative: what is on the right and what is on the left are relative to your point of view; up and down are relative to the center of the earth.

Rules about touching the ball are relative to specific games: in football touching is allowed but in soccer (except for the goalie) it is not allowed. None of these cases show that truth is relative; on the contrary they are further examples of truth as objective. In each of these cases, *that* such and such is relative to this framework and not to another, that it is relative in this way and not in another – all these are *really the case*, they are *objectively the case*. And so propositions stating such relativities are themselves absolutely true, objectively true; or false. They are true if the relativity they express is in fact the case; false if it is not. Thus, all relativity depends ultimately on an absolute, or objective, basis. *It is really so, it is objectively so, that such and such is relative.* The relativist theory of truth fails to capture this fundamental fact. The nature of truth as objective, as stating what is really the case underlies absolutely everything, including all theories. Relativism of truth is thus self-contradictory at the most fundamental level.

IS TRUTH INDEPENDENT OF PROOF?

Another way to deny the objectivity of truth is to say that truth depends on proof. "If it's not proved it's not true." Is that correct? Has *that* been proved? If so how? Isn't there at least some significant doubt about whether this claim has been proved? If it hasn't doesn't it fall by its own weight? That is, doesn't it refute itself? "It hasn't been proved; therefore, it's not true." Isn't this what a logically coherent view would have to be? But doesn't this also show that the claim is simply false, that truth does *not require or depend on* proof? "*If it's true it's true, whether it has been proved or not.*" Isn't *this* the correct approach?

Let us examine this more closely. Let *p* stand for any proposition, such as the one about John being innocent. Doesn't *proving p* mean *showing that p* is true? But I can show that *p* is true only if it is *already true*. It must already be true in order to be displayed as true, which is what proof means.

Proof does not "make" something true. It is *reality* that "makes" propositions true; or we can say that it is the correspondence between a proposition and reality that makes a proposition true. It is the *reality* that John really is innocent that "makes" the proposition "John is innocent" true. Whether it is proved or not may be very important to John; but proof does not affect reality, nor does it affect the truth that depends on it.

Proof is a form of evidence: to prove *p* means to give conclusive evidence that *p* is true. Proof is therefore relevant to the reasonableness or *justification* of *belief*; it is not necessary for the *truth* of a *proposition*.

I can prove to you that I know how to ride a bicycle by actually doing it. Now the proposition "I know how to ride a bicycle" has been proved. But it was true before the proof and it would be true even if it were not proved, even if I didn't have a bicycle to prove it true, to show you that it is true.

Consider the thesis: "A proposition must be proved, or provable, in order to be true." Is *that* true? It has not been proved, nor can it be proved. Therefore, by its own logic it cannot be true. Isn't this is enough reason to reject it? Those who advance this thesis cannot do so without falling into self-contradiction. The crucial point that proof is not necessary for truth may be summed up in these five points:

1. If p is true, it is true independently of whether anyone can prove it, or whether anyone has proved it. If John is in fact innocent, then the proposition "John is innocent" is true even though no one can prove it.
2. Truth depends -- not on proof -- but on correspondence with reality. Thus the proposition "John is innocent" is true if and only if it asserts what is really the case. It is correspondence with reality that makes propositions true, not proof.
3. Proof means showing that something is true. To prove that p is true is to show that it is true. But this is possible only if p is already true, true "before" any proof. The proposition must be true before it can be shown to be true.
4. What is proved must be true, for to prove something means to show that it is true. But what is true need not be proved. John may not be able to prove his innocence, even though he is in fact innocent.
5. Proof is a form of evidence. Evidence refers not to what makes p true but to our "grasp" of p: our knowing it, or having good reasons to believe it.

The proof fallacy means assuming that if a proposition or belief is not proved, or cannot be proved, then it cannot be true.

In contrast to this fallacy, the objectivity of truth means that truth is independent: independent of our beliefs, independent of our showing that something is true. What is true is true *before* we believe it (if we do), and *before* we show it to be true (if we do).

FURTHER THOUGHTS ON THE IDEA OF "TRUE FOR ME"

TWO ASPECTS OF THE IDEA OF TRUE FOR ME

The idea that truth exists "for" a person, expressed in the phrases *true for me* and *true for you* can be seen as having two aspects or two reference points:

- First a reference to the nature of truth itself. This is the claim that truth is not objective but only subjective; that truth doesn't exist objectively, independently of us but only subjectively or relatively to us, only "for us."
- Second a reference to our relation to truth, to "our end of it." This is the claim that we can have only opinions, where opinions are contrasted to truth instead of being seen as claims to truth; claims which are sometimes valid in being correct opinions. A correct opinion reaches the truth; that's what correct means.

It is important to be clear about these two very different concepts:

- Truth is relational.
- Truth is relative.

The first is part of the *objectivity* view of truth. Truth means correspondence with reality; correspondence is the relation between a true proposition and the reality it refers to. The second as it is usually meant is precisely the *denial of the objectivity* of truth, claiming instead that truth is somehow relative, perhaps to individuals as in "true for me" and "true for you."

Chapter 17: Truth, Reality, and Relativism

INDIVIDUAL ETHICAL RELATIVISM ABOUT TRUTH

Three concepts to understand:

Ethical Nihilism is the denial of any real morality binding on us. It includes both "good" things and "bad" things. So love, forgiveness, compassion are not really good in themselves, and child abuse, rape, and slavery are not really wrong and evil in them-selves. They are only good or evil because we label them that way. In themselves they are neither good nor evil, only neutral, like chewing gum. This means: *do anything you like, as long as you can get away with it.*

Ethical Scepticism. Is there a real morality binding on us? This is the view that we can ever know (a) whether or not it exists; and (b) what it is if it does. We can't know any truth about morality or even have any reasonable beliefs. We're totally in the dark. Scepticism is a claim about our ability to *reach* truth. Relativism is a claim about the *existence* of truth.

Individual Ethical Relativism. This view, often accepted only implicitly, holds that on ethical matters where people have different opinions, no opinion is correct; no opinion can express the real truth of the matter. The basic idea is captured in the phrase *that's just your opinion;* or *that's just an opinion.* What does this mean? Wonder at these comments that we hear all the time:

It's just an opinion, not the truth, not the real truth; there is no real truth about these matters because we can't know what it is. Who's to say what it is? No one can say, because no one is in any better position to see the real truth than anyone else. So, let's just forget about any supposed real truth. It's just a matter of how you feel about these things. You feel one way, I feel another, and that's it. There are just different feelings and opinions, and no opinions are any better than any others; no opinions are correct or incorrect, no opinions are closer to the truth than any others.

This means that all we can have are our own opinions, not the real truth. *That's just your opinion.* Opinion is set off against truth; we have opinions **instead of** truth:

What happens when your opinion is yours; it's true for you; not true in itself? This means that if it is your opinion that x is good (compassion, forgiveness; slavery, rape) then it is true that these things are "good to you"; that your opinion is "true for you." If I say the opposite, then these things are "evil to me" or "not true for me." We each have our own morality and it is true for us, but not true for anyone else. So, if I like compassion, then compassion is good and true to me. If you don't believe in compassion, then it's not good to you, not true for you. The same goes for rape. If Joe believes in rape and thinks it's OK, then that is what is true for Joe. If George doesn't think rape is OK, then that is what is true for George. There is nothing evil about things like rape, slavery and child abuse in and of themselves; and nothing good about love, compassion and forgiveness in and of them-selves. I would never beat my children or rape someone, but that applies only to me; I wouldn't impose my morality on anyone else. Wonder at this dilemma!

Reasons for adopting Individual Ethical Relativism:

(i) Who is to say what is really right or wrong, what the real truth is?
(ii) Reverence towards others and their opinions.
(iii) A desire to be humble, not to claim too much, to avoid arrogance.
(iv) A desire to be accepting and tolerant of others.

These are certainly noble motives. Why do they lead to such shifting sands about reality? Wonder at how much you value your own opinion and how relativism devalues it!

The Objective Morality—Objective Truth view of ethics. What it holds:

- There is an objective moral order that exist independently of our recognizing it, and independently of how well we adhere to it. *Gratitude is really good.*
- There is objective truth about this moral order: ethical truth.
- Ethical truth exists whether we know it or not, whether anyone can prove it or not.
- In fact we do know many ethical truths and can justifiably believe many others.

Let us turn now to a defense of the objective morality-truth view.

1. A basic criticism of ethical relativism: Rape is really wrong, in itself! We can know this to be true! Really true! It is not "just an opinion"! Is it just "true for me"?! Wonder!
2. The practical equivalence of Nihilism, Scepticism and Relativism. Are these three theories really different from each other? In all three we can't get at a real objective moral order binding on us. We can't say that rape is really evil and wrong, and compassion really good and right; that these things can be known to be true, true objectively, true in themselves – and are not "just opinions" which can have no validity beyond the person who holds them. This means that relativism reduces to nihilism or scepticism; it is not really different from them. Isn't this enough to reject relativism?
3. But people do have different opinions. Let us now see how the objective view deals with disagreements and controversies. This will actually strengthen the objective view by showing how it alone can really account for disagreements.
4. The Take Seriously Argument. I should take your opinion seriously. I can do this only by recognizing that what you intend to do in holding an opinion is to express what you believe to be really true; that your opinion a claim to state the truth, how it really is. I should not dismiss it as "just an opinion." Isn't it relativism that is arrogant?
5. The Meaningful Disagreement Argument. On relativism there is nothing to disagree about since what each side has is "just an opinion." On objec-

tive morality -- the view that there is an objective truth about ethical matters and that morality itself is objectively real -- disagreements are meaningful because each side claims to be correct, to express objective truth; which is possible only with objective morality, where opinions are claims to objective truth.
6. Partial Relativism will not work. Partial relativism looks like this:

> Slavery is really wrong! It is objectively wrong, wrong independently of us; and we can know with certainty that it is wrong. But is abortion right or is it wrong? That's very controversial. Who's to say what it really is? It's just a matter of opinion, not of truth.

For a refutation of this, apply the historical perspective:

- If slavery is really wrong, then it was wrong in 1860 when it was controversial.
- In 1860 those who saw that slavery is wrong saw the truth; they were correct.
- Therefore, somebody was correct in 1860 even though not everyone saw the truth.
- The same applies to controversies like abortion today: somebody is correct.
- Some people see the truth, and some do not.
- That x is controversial means not everyone sees the truth. Not that there is no truth.
- Controversy means we don't all agree on where the truth lies.
- Without truth, controversies or disagreements would make no sense.

Some Important Clarifications

1. **Opinions are claims to truth, claims that something is really the case.** "In my opinion, cruelty to animals is wrong" means "I claim cruelty to animals *really is* wrong, I hold this to be the truth of the matter." Consider an expert's opinion in a courtroom or getting a second opinion from another doctor. When the doctor says "You have cancer" he means *you*

Chapter 17: Truth, Reality, and Relativism

really have it, so it really is; it is not *just his opinion* but the truth of the matter; unless he is mistaken, in which case something else is the truth of the matter. Opinions make no sense apart from real truth.

2. **Ethical opinions are beliefs about moral reality.** They are claims to ethical truth. Some are correct and some are mistaken; some come closer to the truth than others. Hence some are clearly better than others. Consider the phrase, "I value your opinion." Why would we say this? It is because we value the truth which the opinion is about. And we value the opinion because we think the person holding it is in a good position to know the truth and tell us what it is.

3. The objective truth view holds that there is a truth about ethical matters, not that this or that ethical opinion is the truth: ***There is truth***; not *I have the truth*.

4. The claim here is that truth is ***objective***, not that it is ***absolute***. Objective truth is simply truth that exists whether anyone recognizes it or not.

5. Some ethical truths we can see immediately (wonder!) by insight (*gratitude is good*), others are complex; we should try to find good reasons and good arguments to support the positions we adopt. That is,

6. **Ethical opinions can be supported by reasons and arguments.** "Why do you hold this opinion?" "Here are my reasons, the reasons that I claim support my opinion and show that it is correct." Think of such issues as animal rights, capital punishment, legalized physician assisted suicide, and abortion. In a meaningful dispute, each side claims it is expressing the truth, and tries to present reasons and arguments aimed at showing that its side is the true one. We should use our reason to try to come to the best moral judgments possible.

7. Rather than a relativistic denial that truth exists, let us seek to find the truth; to do the best we can if it seems hard to find it. This means being open to the truth, eager to learn the truth, and having the humility to recognize one's mistakes.

Is relativism itself true? If not, we can forget about it. If the relativist claims it is true, he is saying that there is a truth here even though not everyone recognizes it.

But relativism is precisely the view that there can be no such truth. On relativism one can say of relativism only *that's just your opinion, not the real truth, there is no real truth*. So a good relativist has to deny that his own theory of relativism is true! Or if he tries to say it is really true, true whether you recognize it or not, he is contradicting himself. "It is true that there is no truth." It is impossible to defend relativism. To defend it means to lose it. Defending a position means claiming it is really true, which is impossible on relativism. This is a fascinating source of wonder!

[3] CULTURAL ETHICAL RELATIVISM

Ethics and culture. There is surely a close link between ethics and culture. (1) Ethics is *expressed* in the context of culture. Often different cultures have different ways of expressing the same ethical reality, such as respect for persons. But it is one and the same reality that is expressed in these culturally different ways. (2) We *learn* our ethics through our culture. But what we learn, I suggest, is not simply a cultural matter, but an ethical reality itself. We can see, for example, that gratitude is really good. We have an innate aptitude for understanding basic ethical realities, and that's why we can learn our ethics through our culture. Cats and dogs do not have this ability.

Multiculturalism. There are two essentially different ways of understanding the rich diversity of cultures in the world. One is characterized by reverence and openness to cultures other than our own, trying to understand them and to learn from them when they have something important and valuable to teach us, especially if we can correct our own failures and shortcomings by learning from them. This is a beautiful source of wonder! The other is an ethical relativism that basically says all cultures are equal, a form of cultural ethical relativism.

Cultural ethical relativism. This view has been proposed by certain thinkers such as Ruth Benedict, Edward Westermark, William Graham Sumner, Melville Herskovits, and Gilbert Harman. It has always been a decidedly minority view, with most thinkers adopting some form of objective morality. It may be summarized in this way:

- **A denial that morality is objective. This is the relativism-dependency thesis.** Nothing really *is* right or wrong, objectively, in itself. Certain things are called right, others wrong, in different ways in different cultures. Morality is dependent on certain factors in a culture. In other words, each culture has its own morality. Nothing is **really** right or **really** wrong in itself, only approved or disapproved in a culture. This means that slavery isn't **really** wrong; it's just that some cultures have disapproved of it. Morality is *dependent* on certain factors in a culture.
- **A denial that morality is universal. This is the relativism-diversity thesis**. There is no moral order of right and wrong that is universally valid for all people. Each culture has its own moral code, valid for it but not for others and irreducibly *diverse*.
- **Custom is king.** What we call moral right and wrong, or good and evil, are nothing but customs. Moral customs derive their authority from their acceptance by a culture. They are valid only within and for that culture. This combines the dependency thesis and the diversity thesis: moral customs *depend* for their validity on their culture, and they are *diverse* throughout the world.

The main arguments for this theory are the following:

1. **Who decides?** That is, who decides what is really right or wrong? Why should it be one person rather than another or one culture rather than another?
2. **Tolerance.** Accepting relativism insures tolerance of views other than one's own. Each culture has its own moral code, valid for it alone. To claim a single moral code universally valid for all people and for all cultures encourages intolerance, arrogance and bigotry. Relativism encourages humility and tolerance.

3. **Diversity.** The best explanation for the diversity of moral beliefs and practices throughout the world is relativism. Isn't arrogant to claim that one's own moral code is superior to all the others? Each cultures code is valid for it, not for others.

The alternative view is the objective morality view: There is an objective moral reality, universally valid, independent of cultures; and there is objective moral truth:

- First: **Reality.** There is an objective moral order that exists independently of our recognizing it, that overarches different cultures. Consider slavery: that it existed is a fact, a historical and social fact; that it is morally wrong is also a fact, a moral fact. The moral fact is just as real as the historical.
- Second: **Truth.** There is a truth about moral reality that exists in itself, independently of our recognizing it and that overarches different cultures. That is, moral statements such as *gratitude is good* are true (or false) in exactly the same sense in which statements about the world such as *ice is cold* are true (or false).

A basic criticism of cultural relativism. The theory of cultural relativism would imply that torture, slavery, child abuse, the subjugation of women, cruelty to animals and other horrors would be morally right as long as they were accepted by some culture. This criticism aims directly at the *dependency* thesis. Contrary to this thesis moral right and wrong do not depend on social approval or social structures. If anything, it is the other way around: social approval should depend on what is really right. But is also disposes of the *diversity* thesis, in that if torture and the other evils are really wrong (and not dependent on what a culture says), then they are wrong everywhere; that is, universally.

REPLIES TO CULTURAL ETHICAL RELATIVISM

1. **Who decides what is really right or wrong? This is a false question.** No one decides; it is not a matter of deciding. Rather it is a matter of discov-

ering what is really right or wrong. Wonder at this! Sometimes this is clear and obvious and sometimes it is difficult. If one answers this question by specifying a person or group, one actually destroys ethics. Pirates who kidnap you can "decide" what they will do to you and call it "right"; cruelty is still really painful and really wrong!

2. **Who decides what is really right or wrong? It rests on a false assumption.** This is the assumption that a judgment or a "decision" is necessary for truth. This is simply not the case. Gratitude is good and right, cruelty is evil and wrong, each one is so in itself, independently of anyone's judgment or decision. Truth does not depend on judgment; it is the other way around: valid judgments depend on truth, they are valid, or true, because they express what is really true.

3. **The Tolerance argument: this is an argument against relativism! Relativism makes genuine tolerance impossible.** Is the value of tolerance a good reason for accepting relativism? I want to suggest exactly the opposite: the relativist cannot consistently endorse tolerance. We can ask: is tolerance where appropriate really good? Is intolerance really bad? The relativist wants to say yes, and to use this to support his position, but he cannot do so consistently, since on relativism nothing is really good or bad. That is, the relativist is caught in a self-contradiction here: on the one hand, he says that *nothing* is really right or good [his position]; on the other hand, he says that *tolerance* is really right and good [one of his major arguments].

4. **Why is there diversity in moral beliefs and practices?** Diversity is consistent with objective morality. Some diversity is the result of *applying* moral rules differently in different situations. Some is the result of adopting *different ethical theories*, such as utilitarianism and deontological ethics. Some is the result of *moral blindness*. Some is the result of varying and conflicting *traditions*, such as the adoption of honor codes that call for killing.

5. **Diversity as such does not contradict objectivity and universal validity.** There is diversity among scientists but scientific truth is objective and universal.

6. **Does ethics change?** (A) Moral realities themselves do not change. Love, compassion, reverence, gratitude always were and always will be good; cruelty always was and always will be evil. (B) Applications of principles and rules change according to context and circumstances. (C) Our perceptions change. Wonder at these ideas!

CONSEQUENCES OF CULTURAL ETHICAL RELATIVISM

1. **Relativism makes moral progress impossible.** Do we not see now that slavery and burning witches are *really* wrong, that they are terrible moral evils? And do we not see the matter clearly and correctly now? But on relativism, we can only say that we now see it differently, since no view can be really correct. This means that on relativism there can be no moral progress, from failing to see a real wrong to recognizing it as really wrong. This applies both to a whole culture and to an individual person; both to intellectual vision and to conduct.
2. **Relativism makes it impossible for there to be genuine moral reformers.** A moral reformer calls our attention to our blindness and our failings. He or she goes against the stream of current cultural opinion. On relativism that is all there is, so the reformer is ruled out of court before he even starts. But aren't reformers like Martin Luther King among our greatest and most admired heroes? This is ruled out on relativism where nothing is really right or wrong.
3. **Relativism makes it impossible to say that a law is unjust.** On relativism it is impossible to distinguish between just and unjust laws. What is it that makes one law just and another unjust? The just law conforms to objective moral standards and the unjust law violates them.
4. **Relativism makes it impossible for there to be conflicts between cultures.** We criticize racial discrimination, the suppression of minorities, and the subjugation of women in another country. Is this not at least a meaningful disagreement? More than that, can we not confidently say that we are correct in such cases? Relativists like to criticize members of culture A who go to culture B to "impose" their religious or ethical beliefs. Is this not at least a meaningful criticism? But on relativism it be-

comes meaningless, as cultures A and B each have their own moral systems that cannot be compared. And do we not want to say that perhaps this criticism is sometimes warranted and sometimes not? That it is very much warranted, indeed called for, when the practices criticized represent the violation of basic human rights and cause terrible sufferings? In such cases the criticism is fully justified; it goes towards trying to really benefit other people.

ANALYSIS ONE: CLARIFICATION AND ALTERNATIVE

1. **Judge only *actions*, not *persons*.** We look at another culture where women are denied their basic human rights, where they are punished after being victims of rape. We are horrified but may be reluctant to make a moral judgment. We are horrified because we see the wrongness of the *actions*; we hesitate to judge the *persons* because we are not of his culture and cannot see how it looks to him.

2. **Utilitarianism.** In some cultures, it is accepted practice to kill the aged or some infants because of scarce resources. Is this justified or wrong? Instead of saying morality is relative to culture ("right for them but wrong for us"), let us rather say that they are acting according to a certain ethical theory, utilitarianism, and we are not. According to this theory killing innocent people is justified when it is for the greater good, when the good consequences are judged to outweigh the bad. It is a theory that is part of objective morality; that says some things are really right and others really wrong, independently of what a culture says.

ANALYSIS TWO: PERCEIVING MORAL REALITY

1. **A whole culture can be mistaken about a moral truth.** Just as an individual can be mistaken, so can a whole culture. We were once mistaken as a culture about slavery. Is there something that we as a culture are mistaken about today? Wonder!

2. **What varies is not ethical truth but rather how people perceive the truth.** Consider again the case of slavery. Why was it accepted? Basically, because people were blinded from seeing the truth. Some of the factors involved were: (1) passively going along with what was done by others. (2) Confusing legal right and wrong with moral right and wrong. (3) Letting one's own self-interest get in the way. (4) The moral failure of lacking empathy for others. (5) Traditions.
3. **Moral realities themselves do not vary across cultures or change with time.** Love, compassion, reverence, and gratitude are in themselves good and right; they are so always and everywhere. Cruelty is in itself evil and wrong; it is so always and everywhere. What varies and changes are applications of principles and rules according to context and circumstances; the adoption of different ethical theories, such as utilitarianism or deontological ethics; and our perceptions.
4. **The C. S. Lewis Vision.** An objective, universal moral order, an "eternal Moral Wisdom," exists above individual cultures. "A nation's moral outlook is just so much of its share in eternal Moral Wisdom as its history, economics, etc., let through. In the same way the voice of the Announcer is just so much of a human voice as the [radio] receiving set lets through."[2] This is a wonderful way to explain why there is both diversity *and* an objective, universally valid morality.

CONCLUSIONS CONSIDERED

1. **Morality is something overarching individuals and cultures.** Wonder at a shared morality, a universal morality, and ethical truths apply universally!
2. **Not all cultures are equal!** Are those that allow slavery and those that subjugate women equal to those that condemn these? In moral terms some cultures are clearly better than others. Of course, culture A may be morally superior to culture B in one respect while culture B is superior to

---

[2] C. S. Lewis, *Miracles* (San Francisco: Harper Collins, 2001), p. 62. First published, London, 1947.

A in another respect. A good measure here is how well a culture is faithful to Gert's rules, which we will examine in the next section. They include do not kill and do not cause pain.

3. **Relativism contradicts our experience.** Isn't it absolutely clear and evident that child abuse is wrong? That racial bigotry is wrong? That loving kindness is good? That a humble, open-minded seeking of truth is good? Yet all these and many more are destroyed by a relativism which says nothing is really right or wrong, good or evil. Besides, why would we make excuses for our immoral behavior if we didn't take it seriously as something important and real in itself? Also, when we get angry at others for the wrong they do to us, do we not clearly see that such a wrong is an important reality in itself? The very power that moral anger and indignation have is a clear testimony to the reality of moral evil.

4. **Relativism means the death of ethics and morality.** If nothing is really right or wrong, good or evil, what is left for ethics? Why bother trying to do right and avoid doing wrong? And if no ethical statements are true or false, or closer to the truth than others, what is there to think about, to discuss, to learn? Why be open-minded if there is no ethical truth to be open to? On relativism, all one can do is acknowledge how different people think, feel and react.

5. **Relativism is incompatible with the seriousness of ethics.** Plato expressed it beautifully. In speaking of ethics, he says, "For no light matter is at stake; the question concerns the very nature in which human life is to be lived."[3]

Wonder at the ways in which ethical relativism plays a role in your life, your culture, your world?!

Wonder: is there an essential difference between errors and incomplete truths? Is there a clear line separating the two? I suggest there are two essentially different points of view here:

---

[3] Plato, *Republic*, Book I, 352d.

First, there is the *reality* point of view; what is in fact really the case. Under this point of view there is an essential difference between errors and incomplete truths, a line separating them. An incomplete truth is still a truth; what it says is true even if it doesn't say all that is true. In fact all truths are incomplete in the sense that none can say all there is to be said, the whole of truth. There is always more that is true. This is so both in general and in specific cases. I tell you that I went to the library and I don't tell you that I also went to the bank. What I say to you is the truth without being the whole truth. In contrast, an error is by definition not a truth but a falsehood and thus a failure to say what is true. It is a falsehood which is believed to be true. If I believe John is guilty when he is in fact not guilty I am in error on this point. It is not an incomplete truth.

Second, there is the *awareness* point of view having to do with our knowledge and beliefs about reality. Under this point of view the difference between errors and incomplete truths is sometimes not so clear and evident. Here there may be a mixture of error and incomplete truth so that is difficult to discern which is which. I tell you that Rose took money which didn't belong to her. I don't tell you that her action was authorized as a loan. Here my omission distorts what I say. It creates a false impression; you may end up believing Rose is a thief. That would surely be an error; she is not a thief. Still, what I said was true even though it was not the whole truth. But what was left out was a crucial element and that makes a significant difference.

Wonder: perhaps in such cases we should not say there is mixture of error and incomplete truths but rather a mixture of a *truth* and *false impressions*. It is true that Rose took the money; the false impression is that she is a thief. There is no error here; only a false impression.

It is important to distinguish these two things:

- False impressions: a true statement that is misinterpreted; Rose took the money.
- Errors: a false statement; Rose stole the money.

THE PARTLY-TRUE AND OUR WHOLE INTELLECTUAL LIFE

Wonder: does the idea of partly true or perhaps a more general *partly* pervade our whole intellectual life? There are some indications that it does. Consider:

1. There is so much we know! And also so much we don't know! Try making a list of all the things you do know. It will be long, and you will want to stop long before you're finished. Then try making a list of all the things you don't know. It too will be long and you will want to stop long before you're finished. For know, use knowledge-loose.
2. How adequate is your knowledge? Some surely is adequate enough. But if you take a long-range view isn't much of it probably inadequate? If you tend to doubt that, can you reasonably rule out the possibility that much of your knowledge is inadequate?
3. Isn't the bottom line that we have a mixed bag here: partly adequate, partly inadequate? If so, how much is on each side of this ledger? If you find that it is difficult to answer this question or even to get started on an answer isn't this a further inadequacy? *We seem not to fully understand our inadequacy; more inadequacy!*
4. The Statement of Socrates: True wisdom is realizing how much we don't know. Or, true wisdom is realizing and acknowledging the limits of our wisdom. Or perhaps even, true wisdom is realizing and acknowledging that we don't have wisdom. A paradox! *The Statement of Socrates: does it lead to skepticism, or does it encourage a true intellectual humility? Wonder!*

CHAPTER 18
GOOD AND EVIL

[1] ORIGINAL WONDER ABOUT GOOD AND EVIL

GOOD AND MOTIVATION

Wonder: what does *good* mean? Here is a term we use all the time. Shouldn't it be clear and obvious what it means? One meaning of *good* defines it in relation to motivation; thus:

Good is what can motivate us to take an interest in something. Aren't we are always motivated by good in some sense? Never by what is neutral, never by evil as evil?

Often, we are motivated by what is really good, objectively good, and valuable in itself, such as a deed of genuine love or fulfilling a moral obligation; often by subjective but perfectly valid goods, such as the pleasure of a warm bath on a cold day or a thrilling ride or chocolate.

But now consider a radically different kind of case; radically different in its objective nature but subjectively still a case of being motivated. Consider the sadist: he takes pleasure in making others suffer. Surely this is not a good, but an evil, in fact a terrible evil. Is he motivated by this evil? In some sense he is. He is motivated by the pleasure he gets from this evil; he is motivated by an evil pleasure, something evil. Yet we saw that we are never motivated by evil but always by good in some sense. Good and evil: can we reconcile them logically?

Let us try to reconcile them by distinguishing two basic meanings of *good*. That is:

- *Good as what can motivate us; this can include evil in the form of evil pleasures [and]*
- *Good as what is really good; the real good which stands logically opposed to evil.*

329

What can motivate us isn't necessarily really good; the sadist is a perfect example. We are always motivated by *good* in some sense but not always by a real good. And what is really good doesn't always motivate us. I see a person in great need. Do I reach out and help him? Hopefully I do. I should be motivated by this good but sometimes I'm not.

Good as what can motivate us can be divided into different kinds of good:

- *Good-1: the real good of an objective moral value, as in self-giving love and honesty.*
- *Good-2: the real good of something objectively good for a person, as in being loved.*
- *Good-3: the real good of a subjective and legitimate pleasure, as in delicious chocolate.*
- *Good-4: the merely feel good, only subjective, really evil, as in the pleasure of revenge.*

There is clearly a sharp contrast between 1-3 and 4:

- *In 1-3 good and motivation go together: we are motivated by what is really good.*
- *In 4 they diverge sharply: we are motivated by what merely feels good but is really evil.*

The first three will be our topic in section [2]. Note that *real good* can apply to both the objective and the subjective. And *subjective* can apply to both the *real good* and the *really evil*.

Wonder: that one term good has such radically different meanings. It can refer to what is really good; it can also refer to what can motivate us. However, as noted, the real good doesn't always motivate us and what does motivate us isn't always really good, as in evil pleasures.

Wonder: that good as what can motivate us can also include objective evils.

WHY DO WE DO EVIL?

Wonder: why do we do evil? Surely there are many reasons for this; and many ways of doing evil. Some are various forms of selfishness, undue concern for my own interests. Some go in an opposite direction, as in helping a friend cheat out of love. Another is failing to take individual responsibility for my actions as in blindly going along with an authority figure or with immoral traditions in my culture. In each of these there is still some element of goodness even though it is overshadowed by the evil elements. My own interests, love, authority, and traditions are or at least can be goods. Are we sometimes motivated simply by pleasure from evil?

Wonder: is the appeal of evil pleasures a case of being motivated by evil? For example, deliberately hurting a person in order to see him suffer as a way of getting even? The expression *revenge is sweet* is telling here. Objectively, inflicting harm in order to see a person suffer out of revenge is an evil. Yet it appeals to some people because they enjoy it. What is objectively an evil can sometimes feel subjectively as a kind of good, a form of pleasure. How can this be?

Domestic violence: isn't it often motivated by a desire to control another person? Isn't the sensation of controlling another itself already an evil pleasure?

Shakespeare's play *Macbeth*: why does Macbeth murder Duncan? He has a passionate desire to be king himself. He sees the crown before him; it glitters in its appeal to him. But Duncan, the present king, stands in his way. Macbeth has a choice: the value response of respecting Duncan as a person -- and the appeal of an evil pleasure, his lust for power, having the crown himself. He murders Duncan so that this lust for power can be satisfied. The appeal of an evil pleasure triumphs over the appeal of the value response of respecting another person.

Can we be motivated by evil? Not simply doing evil but actually being motivated by evil as pleasure rather than by some real good? Isn't the answer *yes*? That sometimes evil can have the power to attract us to indulge in it? Evil pleasures can have a certain quality in them that we can relish; a merely *feel good* quality. And they can therefore somehow appeal to us but a in a way radically different from the appeal of what is really and objectively good.

Wonder: we often assume that pleasure as such is something good. But is it really? Perhaps we should say: pleasure is not as such objectively good. There are good pleasures and there are evil pleasures, as there is clean water and pleasant tasting toxic water. The concept in modern culture of *if it feels good, do it* might be in need of a careful examination.

Wonder: when we avoid evil and our motivation is something good, is it always the same kind of good? Or are there different kinds of good? Different ways of being motivated by good? To these questions we now turn.

[2] THREE DIFFERENT KINDS OF GOOD

THE FIRST KIND OF GOOD: INTRINSIC VALUE

My roof is leaking. The water is all over the floor and on my bed. It's not a nice situation, so I go and fix it. I am motivated by self-interest, by a good for me.

My neighbor's roof is leaking. He is an old man, not very good with tools, so he can't fix the roof himself, nor does he have enough money to hire someone else to fix it. He's not a close friend; I hardly know him. But I feel sorry for him. I empathize with him, and I can't stand the thought of his suffering in that mess. So I go over and I fix his roof for him.

We have two similar actions but with a significant difference. In the second case my aim and motivation are essentially different from the first case. I care about another person for his own sake. I transcend my own self-interest and enter into the realm of another person; and I do so for his sake.

I do so for his sake. This is crucial. If I care about him and help him out only because I expect something in return my aim and motivation would be self-interest. My caring for him would simply be a means towards attaining something good for me.

But in our second case here I care about another person *for his own sake*. He is important in my eyes for his own sake, in himself, intrinsically. He is not a good for me but a good in himself. I look up at him as important in himself. I transcend my own self-interest to someone for his own sake.

I respond to him as a value, as an *intrinsic value*, valuable in himself, and not simply as a good *for* someone or something. We can say, following the insight of Dietrich von Hildebrand and the terminology he introduced, that my response to him is a *value response*, where his being as a person is the intrinsic value to which I am responding. (See his *Ethics*, Chicago, 1972)

Caring about another person for his own sake is one example of a value response. Here's another. My friend is in academic trouble. He is in danger of failing his chemistry class. He's tried everything; tutors, even studying hard! But it is all to no avail. He comes to me: "I have devised a fool-proof method of cheating; no one will find out. You are an expert in chemistry. Can you help me?" My heart goes out to him. I want to help him. But I can't. I say "No, I'm sorry; I cannot be part of a dishonest scheme." Here my value response is different from the first example. Here it is the desire to do what is right because it is right, and to avoid what is wrong because it is wrong. It is a response to moral integrity as a value in itself, as good for its own sake, as something that should be, simply because it is intrinsically valuable that it is.

Go back to the first example of value response, fixing my neighbor's roof, this time from his point of view, the person who was helped. After I help him he comes to me to thank me. He is grateful to me, and he expresses this gratitude by thanking me. Gratitude is another example of value response. When I receive a favor from another person, I should respond in gratitude to him. It is the value response due, the fitting response, the appropriate response.

A value response is one motivated by the intrinsic value to which it is a response. Not every response that has an intrinsic value as its object is a value response. Consider the phrase *using another person as a means*. This indicates a response to a value, another person that is not only not a value response but even a response antithetical to a value response.

Wonder: what then is this first kind of good? Is it intrinsic value? Or value response? Perhaps it includes both? Let me suggest it is basically intrinsic value; but in order to understand this category of good we need to approach it through value response because such a response is the only adequate response to value and therefore the only path to a true understanding of it.

A LIST OF SOME MAJOR TYPES OF VALUE RESPONSE

To come to a deeper understanding of value consider some types of value response:

1. Love: caring about others and helping them by practicing loving kindness.
2. Compassion: an inner response to others in their suffering; a response of deeply caring; even when I cannot alleviate their sufferings but simply responds from my heart.
3. Gratitude: an inner appreciation for what another person has lovingly done for me; and conveying this inner appreciation by thanking him in an outer act. I receive something: a good for me. Then I go beyond myself in a value response: I thank you.
4. Forgiveness: if another person hurts me I feel the hurt inside me. If I then forgive that person I go out of myself, I go beyond myself and somehow enter that person's realm. I forgive him for his sake because I care about him, and because I want to do the right thing.
5. Respect for persons: reverence for each person as a person regardless of any features of that person. This is the basic antidote to all negative attitudes such as prejudices.
6. Respect for truth: we should seek to discover the truth; not what we want to believe, not what is convenient, not what we are used to believing. We should do so simply because truth and our knowledge of it are intrinsic values, realities valuable in their own right. This is what is captured in the popular and very telling phrase, truth for its own sake.
7. Moral integrity: the desire to do what is right because it is right and to avoid what is wrong because it is wrong. It includes my desire to be a morally good person, to have a good character; and my striving to attain

this. It is the value response in our example above where I say no to the request to help my friend cheat on his chemistry exam.

Moral integrity provides us with an answer to the question *why be moral?* Because it's right! For its own sake! Wonder! No external reason can be given; it can only be a value response. This is the basic value response of doing the right thing simply because it's right. It refers to honesty which includes not cheating, not lying and not defrauding others. It means many other things as well: being loving and compassionate, grateful and forgiving; and exemplifying the other moral virtues that characterize a morally good person. Complete moral integrity includes knowing the good (intellect), doing the good (will), and loving the good (heart).

THE SECOND KIND OF GOOD: THE OBJECTIVE GOOD FOR A PERSON

Some goods refer to what is good in itself, intrinsic value. Others are good *for* a person. We can think of this as a good being turned towards a person and shinning on that person. How does this kind of good enter our lives? How can we experience it in our daily lives? Three ways come to mind; three approaches to this kind of good:

First, true happiness. What is it? Where is it to be found? Here are some sources:

1. To be loved and affirmed by others: who does not long for this? Isn't a happy child one who is loved and affirmed by his parents? He must be disciplined, and sometimes corrected, but always on the background and basis of true love and affirmation. He must feel this love. Angry put-downs, being ignored, being shunned tend to destroy and undermine the basic feeling of being loved and affirmed. As we grow up doesn't the same basic need remain though it now takes different forms? Among family, friends and those close to us, what do we long for more deeply than really being loved? And isn't a happy marriage above all a relationship of deep love and affirmation?
2. Friendship in its many dimensions: isn't this a wonderful source of true happiness?

3. Intellectual development: isn't this enriching for us and a source of true happiness?
4. Challenging work and being creative: aren't these further sources of true happiness?
5. Beauty in nature, art and music: aren't these also further sources of true happiness?

There is another item to consider: physical and mental health and having the necessities of life such as food, water and shelter. Are these also sources of true happiness? Perhaps we should say they are necessary conditions for true happiness in that their absence results in misery rather than their presence being a positive source of happiness. Unfortunately, isn't it possible to have all the necessities of life and still be very unhappy?

Second, gratitude. Review all the things we just considered: being loved and affirmed, friendship, intellectual development, challenging work and being creative, beauty, health and the necessities of life. Is there something that unites them into one? I suggest there is: they are all things for which I can be grateful and should be grateful. *Thank you for your love.* How often do we say this? Should we say it more often? Gratitude is not only a response due to the one who gives me something that is a source of true happiness; it is also something which is a great good for me. Being grateful is itself a source of true happiness. Isn't it true that to a large extent we can say that a truly happy person is grateful, and a grateful person is truly happy? If this is so, is it possible for an ungrateful person to ever be truly happy?

Gratitude is specifically correlated to objective goods for a person. The very meaning of gratitude is that it is a response of acknowledgement and appreciation for something really good given to a person. I am or should be grateful because I have received an objective good for me.

Third, good character. To be an honest person, fair and just; to be a loving person, kind, compassionate and caring; a generous person; a grateful person; a forgiving person, one who is ready to ask for forgiveness and to grant it; a humble person, not conceited, not eager to control and dominate, ready to learn and ready to acknowledge *I was wrong* -- all these are first and foremost intrinsically valuable, valuable in themselves, for their own sake. They are therefore primarily examples of the first kind of good. But isn't each one also a great good *for* a person? Isn't it better *for me* that I am honest, loving, grateful, forgiving, and humble than that I am the opposite of these? Isn't it actually a great evil *for me* if I am the opposite of these?

Doesn't the importance of good character often play a role in our motivation and decision making? Suppose I am tempted to dishonesty, perhaps even strongly tempted. *I really need the money and I can get away with it and the other won't really miss it.* But then I say *no* to the idea of dishonesty and choose honesty. *No, I won't do it!* My basic motivation is value response: do the right thing because it's right. But a second element of motivation may also enter, one entirely consonant with the basic value response and even flowing from it and supplementing it: concern for my own good character. *No, I won't do it! I don't want to become that kind of person, one who cheats, cuts corners, and lies.* So, interest in my own good character, in having it and preserving it, plays a meaningful role here.

THE THIRD KIND OF GOOD: VALID PLEASURES

In contrast to evil pleasures there are also good and valid pleasures. They vary according to individual tastes but for many people they include things such as ice cream, chocolate, a swim in cool water on a hot day, the warmth of fire in a fireplace on a cold day, doing exciting things and a cozy bed when tired.

These things can also be seen as objective goods for a person; in fact shouldn't they be seen primarily in this way, as gifts calling for appreciation and gratitude? Isn't this especially so when they are gifts from another person given to me out of love and kindness?

Are there cases of conflict between objective goods for a person and pleasures? The cake I eat is delicious but has little nutritional value and lots of calories; so, it is not really an objective good for me; it may even be an objective evil for me if I am diabetic. In such cases doesn't the negative outweigh the positive? In general, shouldn't the question of what is objectively good or evil for a person have priority over pleasures? Shouldn't it include the moderation of pleasures?

VALID PLEASURES AND TRUE HAPPINESSS

Isn't the priority of objective goods for a person over pleasures connected to something else, namely that the true happiness that comes from objective goods is essentially different from pleasures? Valid pleasures contribute to happiness; but can a life consisting of only of pleasures really be a happy life? If not, doesn't this indicate that human beings are made for something more and greater? And it seems to be the point that J. S. Mill makes when he says, "It is better to be a human being dissatisfied than a pig satisfied; better to be Socrates dissatisfied than a fool satisfied."[1] The pig and the fool have a life of only pleasures; the human being and Socrates are dissatisfied because they are made for a life of true happiness coming from real objective goods.

Doesn't this suggest a key principle? *Pleasures do not constitute true happiness.* They are part of a truly happy life but not the whole of it. Aren't they a less important part than real objective goods such as love? True, a life without any pleasures is an impoverished life; but isn't a life without real objective goods even more impoverished? Think of hunger and homelessness, two prime examples. Doesn't such a life fall short of what human life really should be? Real objective goods include not only basic necessities but also true happiness and good character.

SUMMARY OF SOME KEY TERMS

1. Intrinsic value and value response: intrinsic values are objective goods, things valuable in themselves. Value response is a response to an intrinsic value for its own sake, motivated by its value importance. A value response is itself an intrinsic value.

---

[1] John Stuart Mill, *Utilitarianism*, first pub. 1861, chap. 2, (London: Everyman, 1910, 1993), 10.

2. The objective good for a person: it is the source of true happiness; it is the proper object of gratitude; good character is primarily an intrinsic value, but it is also a great good for a person.
3. Valid pleasures: they are not sufficient to give us true happiness; but isn't having at least some valid pleasures a necessary part of true happiness? Imagine a life totally devoid of any valid pleasures; could this ever be a truly happy life? Valid pleasures certainly seem to be an essential ingredient in true happiness.
4. Evil pleasures: they are not objective goods; though evil, they sometimes attract us.

Wonder: in terms of motivation are these four things the only ways we can be motivated? Or are there other ways? If so what are they?

How are we motivated by genuine goods (#1-3)? There is: enjoying them when we have them and hope for attaining them when we don't. Sometimes there is fear of losing them; or fear of corresponding evils.

TWO DISTINCTIONS WITHIN THE OBJECTIVE GOOD FOR A PERSON

One, we can have an interest in an objective good for a person in two ways:

- *I'm hungry, so I get something to eat: I am motivated by an objective good for myself.*
- *You're hungry, so I provide for you: I am motivated by an objective good for another.*

Isn't *you're hungry* most significant as an occasion for the moral value of loving concern and generosity? And isn't *I'm hungry* primarily significant as a reference to the morally neutral, natural-spontaneous concern we all have for our own well-being? We can say this while at the same time recognizing the moral obligation we have to take care of our own health.

Two, there are two ways objective goods for a person can come into our lives:

- **By motivation:** I can be motivated by concern for my own health to try to achieve it.
- **As gifts:** a small child whose parents take good care of him receives the objective good of health without being motivated to try to achieve it; it is just given to him. Happiness to a large extent comes to us as a gift when we give a value response; when our aim is to seek other goods, especially for other persons out of love, for their own sake. Good character dispositions that a person is born with, such as love and gratitude, are further important examples of things that come to us as gifts.

[3] THREE DIFFERENT KINDS OF EVIL

Wonder: we have examined three kinds of good; are there also three kinds of evil, each one corresponding to one of the kinds of good? If we say justice is an intrinsic good, we can also say that injustice is an *intrinsic evil*. The rich sometimes defraud the poor; this should not be. It is an injustice, an intrinsic evil.

Of course, being defrauded is also an *objective evil for the persons* who are its victims. The two go logically together. And there are also other evils for a person that do not result from moral evil as when a person catches a disease and falls sick.

What would be the evil corresponding to valid pleasures? Would it be invalid pleasures as in relishing the idea of another person suffering, such as a rival? But isn't this a perverted good on the level of experience rather than something evil on the level of pleasure? Perhaps we should turn to the pleasure aspect to find the corresponding evil. If so, what would it be? Some people will point to pain as in the familiar pleasure-pain opposition. But isn't pain primarily an objective evil for a person rather than the absence or opposite of a pleasure?

All pleasures are agreeable so the opposite of a pleasure would be what is disagreeable. Thus, wouldn't the evil corresponding to valid pleasures be what is *disagreeable*?

[4] OBJECTIVE EVILS FOR A PERSON

THE STATEMENT OF SOCRATES

Wonder: what different kinds of objective evils for a person are there? And, how do such evils come upon us? One way surely is through suffering, such as physical pain, emotional pain, being betrayed by a loved one and losing something of value. Are there other ways? Does the experience of suffering cover the whole territory here? Is there perhaps something else of great significance that we should consider? As a way of entry into this topic consider this question:

Which is worse: to suffer from an injustice or to commit an injustice? If you had to choose between these two, which would you choose? When we ask *which is worse,* we should be looking to see which is worse *for a person*, not which is intrinsically worse because suffering an injustice is not intrinsically evil at all. So, which is worse *for a person?* Is it suffering from an injustice or committing an injustice? Socrates is noted for his answer to this question. His claim is that committing an injustice is worse for a person than suffering from it. This may surprise some people who might spontaneously choose doing over suffering; and then go on to claim that doing is better than suffering. His claim is noteworthy and so we may call it:

- The Statement of Socrates: "It is better to suffer from injustice than to commit it."
  Or:
- It is a worse evil for a person to be the doer of injustice than the victim of injustice.

Socrates speaks of injustice, but we can understand him to be referring to moral evil in general; hence to be referring to all moral evil.

It is important to distinguish clearly what the Statement of Socrates specifically says and what it is based on. It is based on the intrinsic nature of moral evil; that moral evil is evil in itself. But what it specifically says is that moral evil has *an effect on the person* who commits it. Its focus, its message and its warning points to *what happens to persons*. Because moral evil is evil in itself, it is *also* a great evil *for* the person who commits it. The specific point of the Statement of Socrates concerns this *for* relation to a person. That is:

> **Because injustice is in itself a moral evil, it is also an objective evil for the person.**

HOW CAN DOING MORAL EVIL HURT A PERSON?

The Statement of Socrates means that moral evil does something to the person who commits it; it hurts the person in a profound way.

Wonder: how can doing evil hurt a person?

1. **Conscience**. Have you ever done something wrong and then felt really bad about it? That is, experienced feelings of guilt and pangs of conscience? Is this a proof that the Statement of Socrates is correct? We will return to the topic of conscience shortly.
2. **Harmful effect on character**. Can we say that, just as doing good makes us healthy in character, doing evil makes us unhealthy? That persons with a healthy character have moral vision and strength of will? And that persons with an unhealthy or sick character lack moral vision and strength of will? Don't they often become weak and fail to see evil for what it is and then succumb to excuses and rationalizations? Is this more proof that Socrates is correct?
3. **Doing good becomes harder**. To the extent that the harmful effect on character from doing evil takes place, doesn't it also mean that even if we want to do what is right and good it becomes more difficult? That it's no

longer part of our nature? For example, wasn't telling the first lie a major decision because basically we wanted to do only what is right and good? But suppose we did tell that first lie. Isn't it then likely and even quite understandable that a pattern of lying would set in? That lying would become easy, even second nature and taken for granted? And correspondingly, that truthfulness would become more and more difficult? Have we seen instances of this pattern in other persons in our experience? More proof for Socrates?

4. **Destroying good relations with others**. Who wants to trust a liar? Who wants to deal with a dishonest person? Who wants to have an unloving person as a friend? More proof?
5. **Punishment**. **Wonder**: does moral evil call for a just punishment as a proper response? If a moral evil goes unpunished is something significant missing? Is a just punishment a way of making it true that doing evil will hurt the person who does the evil? Some people object to punishment, claiming it merely adds more evil to the evil that already exists. **Wonder**: do they have a point? Are they correct? Or are they missing something important? To get a handle on this imagine a world where the greatest saint and the worst sinner come out exactly even. Would this be a good world, one you would want to live in?

Wonder: we should not confuse just punishment and revenge. Isn't revenge something wrong? How do the two differ? Try this: just punishment is a matter of justice; it is the right response called for by evil. Revenge is contrary to justice; it is a wrong response, a form of evil pleasure in the sense described earlier.

[5] CONSCIENCE

Wonder: what is conscience? It seems to be two things: a guide and a warning. It is a guide when we speak of consulting our conscience in trying to decide what is morally called for in a given situation. I don't know what I should do; and so I consult my conscience to try to answer the question: what should I do in this situation that I now find myself in?

It is a warning when I do know what to do or not to do. I know what I should do; will I actually do it? Will I do the right thing, what is morally called for? Here conscience functions as an inner voice, a warning that urges me to do what is right and avoid what is wrong.

It is conscience in the sense of an inner warning that is closely related to moral good and evil *for each person*. My conscience warns me not to do a moral evil, first because it is evil in itself; but then also because it is an evil *for me*. Doesn't its persuasive power over us rest largely on our realizing that moral evil is also an evil *for us*? Consider what John Henry Newman says about the deep reality of conscience and the intimate link between moral evil and evil *for us*:

> Man has within his breast a certain commanding dictate, not a mere sentiment, not a mere opinion or impression or view of things, but a law, an authoritative voice, bidding him to do certain things and avoid others. I do not say that its particular injunctions are always clear, or that they are always consistent with each other; but what I am insisting on here is this, that it *commands*; that it praises, it blames, it threatens, it implies a future, and it witnesses of the unseen. It is more than a man's own self. The man himself has no power over it, or only with extreme difficulty; he did not make it, he cannot destroy it. He may silence it in particular cases or directions; he may distort its enunciation's but he cannot, or it is quite the exception if he can, he cannot emancipate himself from it. He can disobey it; he may refuse to use it; but it remains.[2]

Wonder: how can conscience be both of these two things? Namely:

One: it is *something deep within us*, deep within our breast, at the core of our being, at the center of our heart; an inner voice.

---

[2] Adrian J. Boekraad and Henry Tristan, *The Argument from Conscience to the Existence of God according to J.H. Newman* (Louvain: Editions Nauwelaerts, 1961) p. 114. The text quoted here is Newman's own words.

Two: it is *something beyond us*, an authoritative voice; it threatens us before acting and it torments us afterwards. It is more than a man's own self. The man himself has no power over it; he did not make it, he cannot destroy it; he cannot emancipate himself from it.

How can conscience be so close, almost identical with our own being; and yet speak to us with an authority and a stature that are essentially beyond us?

Wonder: how can one reality be both these things: deep within us and beyond us?

It is important to understand that the conscience is not a magical organ that in and of itself completely knows right from wrong. The conscience must be informed by the intellect as well as by that *deep voice* within us that perhaps knows basic rights and wrongs. We are responsible for the proper formation of our conscience, lest it remain un-formed or become de-formed.

CHAPTER 19
ACTIONS

[1] BASIC WONDER ABOUT MORAL RIGHT AND WRONG

PRELIMINARY POINTS ABOUT MORAL RIGHT AND WRONG

Wonder: we often talk about actions as morally right or wrong. But what do these terms really mean? Do they always mean the same thing? We can start off by noting:

> First, that they stand in logical opposition to each other: *right* stands in contrast to *wrong*. What is right is not wrong and what is wrong is not right.

> Second, that *wrong* refers to prohibitions: things that we have a duty to not do because of their moral wrongness; for example, murder, assault, theft and lying. Those are the easy parts.

> Now to the harder parts; also, the more interesting. In regard to *right* we can distinguish:

- ***What the term morally right means.***
- ***What the term morally right includes.***

WHAT DOES MORALLY RIGHT MEAN?

What it includes is the broader category, covering what it means and other things beyond what it means. Let us start with the question: what does right *mean*? How do we use this term? There seem to be two meanings of *right*:

1. **He did the right thing when he returned the stolen goods, for he had a duty to do so.**
2. **He was morally justified in killing the man who attacked him, so what he did was right.**

Thus in #1 *right* means morally *required*, what we ought to do, our duty or obligation. If goods were stolen there is a duty to return them. But in #2 *right* has a very different meaning. Here it means morally *justified*, something we are allowed to do under the circumstances.

But note that *allowed* has other applications as well. For example, everything that is morally neutral such as taking a walk is of course also allowed. Are there other examples?

Wonder: do we notice that *right* has these two very different meanings? Why should one word, *right*, refer in its meaning to two such very different things, the morally required and the morally justified-allowed? They don't seem to be connected closely enough to each other to be joined together logically under the heading of a single term. So much for what *right* means; let us turn now to what it includes.

WHAT DOES MORALLY RIGHT INCLUDE?

What does right *include*? It includes all that is not wrong. And what is that? Consider:

1. *Morally required, right in the sense of obligatory or duty;(#1 above)*
2. *Morally justified, right in the sense of allowed by the situation; (#2 above.)*
3. *Morally neutral, right in the sense of allowed because not morally relevant.*
4. *Supererogatory, right in the sense of morally good heroism, beyond call of duty.*

Further reflections on these four categories of what *right* includes, as opposed to wrong:

1. ***Right: morally required as obligatory; what we have a duty to do.*** This divides into:

    (A) <u>Positive Duties:</u> to do what is right: respect others, keep promises, tell the truth, etc.
    (B) <u>Negative Duties:</u> to avoid doing what is wrong: avoid disrespect, lying, etc.

These two, (A) and (B), are of course closely linked; and a positive duty often implies a negative counterpart duty. Thus, we have the positive duty to tell the truth, which implies the negative duty to not tell a lie. Fulfilling the positive duty to respect another person implies the negative duty to not assault him.

2. ***Right: morally justified as allowed or permissible by the moral situation.***

To say that a particular action is justified is also to say that it is not wrong; and to say that it is wrong is also to say that it is not justified. Other things that stand in opposition to what is morally wrong include the morally right as required, the morally right and good as beyond the morally required (supererogatory) and the morally neutral.

A typical example of the claim that something is morally justified is the thesis that we have a right to use force to defend ourselves. This is generally taken as including the claim that there is a right to kill an attacker in defense, of oneself or another, when the threat is grave and there is no reasonable alternative form of defense. Killing another person is as such and usually seriously morally wrong. But in this case the claim is that it is morally justified; that there is another factor – the right to defense against an unjust aggressor – that outweighs or overrides the usual prohibition against killing; that supersedes the usual requirement to refrain from killing.

There are other examples of claims that appeal to the morally justified; that something ordinarily wrong is not wrong under existing conditions. Some are clear and command virtually unanimous agreement that they are morally right as justified; others are controversial.

Here are some examples of this mix: breaking a promise, telling a lie, deceiving a person by omitting something important, stealing, causing bodily injury and causing death.

3. **Right: morally neutral as allowed or permissible because not morally relevant.**

This is the sense of *right* conveyed by the expression *all right* as in "It's all right to take this home with you." Some examples: reading a newspaper, going for a walk, taking a nap and drinking a soda. There is neither a prohibition against these things nor a requirement to do them.

4. **Right: supererogatory actions, super-moral goodness, and heroism beyond the call of duty; what we are often encouraged to do but where there is no requirement to do it.**

This includes acts of kindness and going out of our way to help a person which costs us a great deal, which involves a significant sacrifice on our part. Some are small deeds, some are larger, and some are very large. Some are extraordinary, such as the deed of Maximilian Kolbe.

Maximilian Kolbe was a prisoner in a Nazi concentration-death camp, Auschwitz. Ten men were sentenced to die a horrible death of starvation and dehydration; they were to be simply left in a cellar to die. One of the ten men expressed his agony, especially that his wife and child would be left without him. Whereupon Kolbe went up to the Camp Commander and said: "Let me take that man's place." The commander agreed. Kolbe stepped in to take his place, the man was saved, and Kolbe died from the horrible treatment two weeks later.

THE ESSENTIAL DIFFERENCE BETWEEN THE JUSTIFIED (2) AND THE NEUTRAL (3)

These two categories may seem similar as both are opposed to the wrong and they can be described as *right* or *all right*, as allowed or permissible; but they are in fact essentially different. They are neither prohibitions nor obligations but fall in between them. They are both *allowed*, but for very different reasons. The neutral is allowed because it is not relevant to morality. The justified is allowed because one morally relevant concern outweighs another, as when killing a person who is an unjust attacker is justified as a defense. It is thus very relevant to morality.

The neutral is not morally relevant while the justified is highly morally relevant because it is part of morality. The neutral is *outside* morally, not affected by it and thus need not be considered here. This is not true of the justified, which is very much *inside* morality, in that it concerns highly important moral questions, topics that are often difficult and hotly debated. In fact, don't most of the controversies about right and wrong actions concern questions of what is morally justified or not? Killing human beings is ordinarily wrong, not justified and therefore not right. But is mercy killing right? Abortion killing? Killing in war? Killing as capital punishment? These are all questions of moral justification. Other questions of moral justification include controversies about such things as lying, confidentiality and withholding what is needed for life.

[2] ACTIONS AND OMISSIONS

Conduct is about actions; but isn't it also about omissions, about what we don't do? Like actions, omissions can also be wrong, obligatory, justified, neutral or supererogatory. As in the case of actions the basic distinction for omissions is between morally right and wrong:

When are omissions wrong? It is wrong to omit what is obligatory, required as a duty such as neglecting one's responsibilities. Are there other ways that omissions can be wrong?

When are omissions right? The four general categories noted for actions apply also to omissions. Thus, omissions are right when they are one or more of the following:

1. <u>Morally required-obligatory:</u> omitting all actions that are morally wrong.
2. <u>Morally justified:</u> omitting an action that is not obligatory. If I have no duty to give up my life to save another person's life, then omitting a life-saving action is morally justified. If I can save only one of two persons in danger, then if I save the first, I cannot also save the second. Since I cannot have a duty to do the impossible, omitting the saving of the second person is morally justified.
3. <u>Morally neutral:</u> omitting an action that is not morally relevant.
4. <u>Supererogatory:</u> omitting an action that is not obligatory because it is beyond the call of duty, as in the example above in #2 about not giving up my life. Thus, the supererogatory covers one part of the broader category of the morally justified.

Wonder about omissions: when is an omission morally significant? That is, when is it of such a nature that we need to pay attention to it, to see if it is right-justified-allowed or right-obligatory or morally wrong, rather than morally neutral? After all, in every situation there are always an infinite number of omissions, of things that we don't do. If I'm washing my hands at my sink, I'm not climbing a mountain or singing in the choir or anything else that is incompatible with washing my hands, an endless list.

Wonder about actions: what is an action? What counts as an action? Rescuing a person in danger of death is surely an action; so tragically, is murdering a person. If I'm brushing my teeth does that count as an action? If I'm lying on my bed day-dreaming does that count as an action? Some people would deny that the latter two things are actions because they are too insignificant. But suppose a child is brushing his teeth in obedience to his parents; would that make it worthy of being called an action? Perhaps deserving some praise? Does the possibility of being praise-worthy make something worthy of being called an action?

What lies behind these questions is the sense we seem to have that not every activity is worthy of being called an action. Actions seem to have a certain rank or dignity that raises them above mere activities such as day-dreaming. What is it that gives them this rank or dignity? Is it that an action is not just any activity but only one that accomplishes something? And not just anything but only something significant? Especially something morally significant? Should we also include under actions attempts at accomplishing something where this attempt fails?

[3] FOUR TYPES OF CONSEQUENCES OF ACTIONS

Wonder: why are actions significant for morality? One reason is their consequences. But we need to go further. It is not just *that* certain consequences occur but *how* they are brought about that is morally significant. They can be brought about in different ways. Can these different ways then be seen as different types of consequences of actions which are essentially different in their moral significance? I suggest they can; and to bring this out here is a list to consider. The consequences of an action may be:

I. INTENDED
II. NOT INTENDED BUT FORESEEN
III. NOT FORESEEN BUT FORESEEABLE
IV. NOT FORESEEABLE

I. INTENDED. A man wants to kill his rival. He aims his gun, he fires, and the victim falls dead. The death of the person is the intended result of the shooting. The man shoots him *in order to* kill him, an action. Or, seeing that he is already dying, he simply lets him die, an omission; his intention in refraining from saving him being the same as pulling the trigger. On the positive side, a man rushes into a burning building in order to rescue a person trapped inside. The man does so with the intention of saving him; his being saved is the intended result of his action. He acts *in order to* save the life of this person.

II. NOT INTENDED BUT FORESEEN. The pain a doctor causes you in the process of life-saving surgery is foreseen (he knows it will result), but it is not intended (he does not want it to happen; he does not act in order to cause you pain). In a very different type of case, a person drives recklessly. He foresees that he may cause a serious accident, but he doesn't care. Tragically, the accident occurs. He didn't intend it, he didn't drive recklessly in order to cause it; but still he caused it, and he is of course responsible.

III. NOT FORESEEN BUT FORESEEABLE. Suppose the reckless driver doesn't foresee the possibility of a serious accident. "I never thought of that!" Still, isn't he responsible because he *could have* foreseen it, and he *should have* foreseen it? Another example is that of a person who says something which gravely offends another person. He didn't mean to hurt that person; he didn't intend it, he didn't foresee it, and he now deeply regrets it. But if he could reasonably have foreseen this effect, isn't he responsible for causing it?

Isn't this type of consequence commonly called negligence? Aren't we responsible for what we bring about through our negligence? "I didn't mean to" and "I didn't foresee it": aren't these invalid as excuses in this context of what is reasonably foreseeable? Rather: you *should have* foreseen it, at least as a possibility?

IV. NOT FORESEEABLE. Suppose you drive carefully and still an accident occurs. As you drive slowly and very cautiously, a small child darts out in front of your car. Tragically he is struck and dies! It is a horrible accident; and it is surely the result or consequence of your action of driving. You are in shock, overwhelmed with grief. But, are you morally responsible? Clearly you neither intended this result (I) nor did you foresee it (II). Nor is it something which you *could have* foreseen (III). Doesn't it follow that you are not morally responsible for the death of this child? His death, though a consequence of your action was not foreseeable; hence not something that you *could have* taken into account; hence not something that you *should have* taken into account; hence not something for which you can be held morally responsible.

Isn't it true that one is not morally responsible for the consequences of one's actions that could not have been foreseen, except in those cases where the action itself is one that should not have been performed? For example, a child of the age of reason disobeys his parents, drives a tractor, and runs over another child, killing him. True, he could not have foreseen this tragic result; but still, doesn't he bear a grave responsibility for this death because of his disobedience, since this is what led to it?

Wonder: we have examined the consequences of *actions*; do our findings apply also to *omissions*?

[4] GERT'S SYSTEM OF COMMON MORALITY

WHAT MAKES ACTIONS AND OMISSIONS RIGHT OR WRONG?

Wonder: what is it that makes actions and omissions morally right or wrong? In many cases, especially those that do not involve complicated moral questions or controversial issues we can usually tell *that* something is morally right or wrong; but can we specify *why* it is right or wrong? Can we explain what it is that makes it right or wrong? We may know this implicitly; but can we make this knowledge explicit? Let us see if a philosophical analysis can help to make this explicit. Let us examine a moral system that can be seen as a way of answering our question above, what is it that makes actions and omissions morally right or wrong?

WHAT IS COMMON MORALITY?

Bernard Gert offers us a moral system that he calls Common Morality.[1] He proposes it as the moral system that thoughtful people use, usually implicitly, when they make moral decisions and judgments. It has two key elements: a set of moral rules and ideals closely associated with these rules. He claims it provides a

---

[1] Bernard Gert, *Common Morality: Deciding What to Do* (New York: Oxford University Press, 2004).

general moral framework that can be accepted by all rational persons. They can agree on the basic framework, while disagreeing on many of the details. And the basic framework provides a context in which disagreements can be rationally discussed and often resolved. Common morality thus seems to provide an excellent answer to the relativist's challenge. It can also be seen as a foundation for philosophical theories of morality such as those of Kant and Mill. Each theory incorporates some valid features of common morality such as the need for impartiality and the importance of consequences. Finally, common morality is the moral system that it would be rational for all persons to use themselves, to want everyone else to be taught and trained to follow, and to want everyone else to actually follow in their conduct.

THE MORAL RULES

Gert claims that the ten general moral rules listed here account for all actions that are either wrong-prohibited or obligatory-required for all people in all cultures and at all times. Without these rules a society cannot even begin to exist and certainly cannot continue to exist and function. The rules are what allow individuals to come together on a level of trust and safety that is necessary for cohesion.

All violations of these rules are immoral, unless there is an adequate justification for the violation.

Wonder: do these ten rules account for *all* actions that are either prohibited or obligatory

THE FIRST SET OF FIVE RULES	THE SECOND SET OF FIVE RULES
1. Do not kill.	6. Do not deceive.
2. Do not cause pain.	7. Keep your promises.
3. Do not disable.	8. Do not cheat.
4. Do not deprive of freedom.	9. Obey the law.
5. Do not deprive of pleasure.	10. Do your duty.

Chapter 19: Actions 357

- Rule #1 forbids killing. It forbids not only intentionally killing a person by an action but also intentional letting die: omitting something so that a person dies. Does it also forbid killing animals? Does killing an animal need some justification? Any animal?
- Rule #2 forbids intentionally causing pain. It refers not only to physical pain but also mental and emotional pain, such as insults and offensive language. It forbids deliberate cruelty to animals.
- Rule #3 forbids disabling. This includes depriving others of special abilities such as the ability to play the piano.
- Rule #4 forbids depriving others of their freedom. This can be done by various forms of coercion; or by locking them up, or by depriving them of opportunities; all these are serious moral wrongs unless there is an adequate justification for them. It also includes discrimination in its common forms and trying to control and manipulate other persons.
- Rule #6 forbids deceiving. This applies especially to lying, which is making a statement known or believed to be false with the intention of causing another person to believe it to be true. It also forbids other forms of deception, such as withholding information a person has a right to have.
- Deceiving always needs some justification in order not to be morally wrong.
- Rule # 7 tells us to keep our promises. By saying I promise I put myself under a moral obligation to actually do what I have said I promise to do.
- Rule #9 refers to obeying the laws of society when these are just laws, for such laws are necessary for society to function successfully. It does not include obeying unjust laws and immoral traditions such as honor killings, which violate justice and human rights.
- Rule #10 requires us to fulfill our duties which arise from our roles in life, such as parent, child in his family, doctor, lawyer, public official and jobholder in the workplace. It also requires us to fulfill the duties which arise from the circumstances we find ourselves in, such as rescuing a drowning person or helping someone who is being attacked.
- In Gert's system, these rules are not absolute; they all allow for exceptions where they may be violated. But violations always require some morally adequate justification. This rule, that all exceptions require an adequate justification, is not one that has exceptions; it is absolute, allowing for no exceptions.

To whom do the moral rules apply? Who is bound by the moral rules? Gert's answer is that all and only moral agents are bound by the moral rules. A moral agent is someone who understands the moral rules and can guide his conduct accordingly; and who therefore ought to guide his conduct accordingly. Human beings are the only moral agents known to us; but not all human beings are moral agents. Infants and persons who are so severely handicapped mentally that they cannot understand the rules are not bound by them and so they are not moral agents and not subject to moral judgment.

Whom do the moral rules protect? Gert's answer is that all moral agents are protected by all ten rules. Animals are protected only by the first set of five rules; any violation of these rules towards animals needs an adequate justification. Animals are not protected by the second set of five rules. This is made clear by two significant observations about our treatment of animals:

1. It is not wrong to deceive an animal. Animal training sometimes involves deceptions.
2. It is impossible to break a promise to an animal. Isn't this because it is impossible to make a promise to an animal? Animals cannot receive promises as we can.

On the last point, when we "promise" our dog that we will take him for a walk this afternoon that "promise" is really a resolution for ourselves. A true promise requires a certain degree of mutual understanding that does not exist between human persons and animals.

THE MORAL IDEALS

What are the moral ideals? Acting on a moral ideal is intentionally acting so as to avoid, prevent, or relieve the suffering of harm by a person or an animal. It refers to those actions that are not covered by the moral rules and therefore obligatory. And so people are encouraged, even strongly encouraged, but not required, to follow the moral ideals. The moral ideals encourage people to prevent or relieve the harms that the moral rules prohibit them from causing. Deeds of love are typical moral ideals. Several key points about them should be noted:

1. **Wonder**: doesn't a moral rule seem to have a greater weight and urgency than an ideal? And yet, isn't it sometimes justified to break a moral rule in order to act on a moral ideal? Consider: I break a promise to meet you for dinner tonight in order to visit a friend who is very sick in the hospital. Isn't that a justified breaking of a rule for a significant ideal?
2. Impartiality basically means fairness, not unduly favoring myself or my friends or my associates. It does not rule out the special duties I have to my own family and others close to me, those for whom I am responsible, and those to whom I have made promises.
3. Impartiality is required in following moral rules; moral ideals allow for some flexibility. I can legitimately favor my own family and friends over strangers in doing deeds of love that are not required as duties by the moral rules.
4. **Wonder**: consider a person who never violates a moral rule; is that enough to make him a morally good person? Suppose he never follows any moral ideals. Gert says he cannot be a morally good person if he never follows any moral ideals. Is Gert correct in this? Imagine a person who simply stays at home and takes care of himself, never reaching out in love and kindness to anyone else. He never does anything wrong, never hurts anyone; but he never does anything good either. How morally good can such a person be?
5. A society needs general obedience to the moral rules simply in order to exist.
6. Gert says it cannot flourish unless a significant number of its members follow the moral ideals. Is he correct in this?
7. Doesn't the existence and importance of moral ideals make it clear that morality is more than a set of rules that prohibit certain things and require others?

WHAT JUSTIFIES A VIOLATION OF THE MORAL RULES

Whenever possible all the rules are to be followed. But this is not always possible for there are situations where two or more of the rules conflict. One must then determine which rule has the greatest weight and urgency. Clearly the rules are not all of equal force, weight, strength and urgency. For example, *do not kill* has a much greater force and urgency than *do not deprive of pleasure* or even *do not deprive of freedom*. Thus, to imprison a criminal (*deprive of freedom*) is justified to save others from harm; especially to prevent the criminal from violating the rules against killing, causing pain, disabling and depriving of freedom; and not obeying the law.

Wonder: how do we choose which rule to violate in cases of conflict? Consider:

1. Are there reasonable alternatives to violating any of the rules involved in the conflict?
2. The priority of avoiding harm. Other things being equal, isn't my duty to not harm you stronger and of greater force, urgency, and weight than my duty to benefit you? I may not steal your food; but I don't always have a duty to provide you with food, especially if I'm short of food myself. I may not harm Peter to benefit Paul, at least in most cases.
3. Does causing harm include setting a bad precedent?
4. Can I sometimes cause a smaller harm in order to prevent a much greater harm?
5. Are special relationships between persons morally relevant (your child-another's child)?

CHAPTER 20
FORGIVENESS

[1] ASKING AND GRANTING FORGIVENESS

Wonder: what is forgiveness? Let us start with a basic distinction:

- <u>*Asking for forgiveness*</u> *when I have done wrong to another person.*
- <u>*Granting forgiveness*</u> *to another person when he has done wrong to me.*

Isn't asking for forgiveness when I have done wrong clearly morally obligatory?

Wonder: is granting forgiveness to another who has wronged me and asks for forgiveness also obligatory? If it is obligatory in small matters, is it also obligatory in very grave matters? If a murderer asks a mother to forgive him for the murder of her child, is she under an obligation to grant it? Suppose she says *I cannot forgive you; the wrong you did, the hurt you inflicted on me is too great; I can never be reconciled to you.* Is she now wrong in her not granting forgiveness?

Wonder: can we apply the Golden Rule here? If I do something wrong and then deeply repent it and long to be forgiven, do I not want the other person to forgive me? If so, then when the shoe is on the other foot should I not grant forgiveness to a person who is truly sorry and who now comes to me to ask me for forgiveness?

Wonder: is granting forgiveness a process? Perhaps there is a third way between simply granting forgiveness and simply refusing to do so. *I'm deeply hurt, and I cannot simply forgive you but I realize that I should forgive you. I should do so both for your sake and for my sake. I can't just do it but I'm working on it.* Granting forgiveness as a process means working one's way from being unforgiving to being forgiving.

This applies especially where there is a relation of love between the persons. *Because I love you, I take the wrong you have done to me very seriously. And so, I cannot just forgive you, I cannot immediately forgive you. But deep down I want to forgive you; and so, I'll work on it.*

[2] TWO FORMS OF GRANTING FORGIVENESS

Wonder: can I forgive another person if he or she does not ask me for forgiveness? In one way the answer is *no*. Granting forgiveness is the granting of a request and I cannot grant a request that was not made. To grant forgive is to respond to the other's request to be forgiven and thereby to re-establish the bond that was broken by his offense.

But isn't there also another form of granting forgiveness which does not require that the other person has asked me for forgiveness? In this type of case, it is I, the person offended by the other, who initiates the forgiveness. It can be expressed as *I forgive you in my heart; I hold no grudge against you, no resentment and no anger. I continue to love you and I am ready to grant you your request for forgiveness. I am eager to do so and will do so when you ask me for it.*

We may then distinguish two forms of granting forgiveness:

- One is <u>*responding forgiveness*</u>: **the person offended forgives at the request to be forgiven.**
- Two is <u>*initiating forgiveness*</u>: **the person offended forgives by taking the initiative.**

[3] INITIATING FORGIVENESS

THE IMPORTANCE OF INITIATING FORGIVENESSS

Jesus prays for the people who are crucifying him: *Father, forgive them for they know not what they are doing* (Luke 23: 34). He takes the initiative as his executioners did not ask him for forgiveness.

It is said that we should forgive because being unforgiving hurts us, scars our soul, makes us bitter and unhappy, and damages our relation to the other person. To be unforgiving tends toward vindictiveness, revenge, violence, and an escalation of the strained relation. The opposite of being unforgiving is to be forgiving: in one's heart with initiating forgiveness. It means to have this basic attitude even though the other person has not asked for forgiveness.

Martin Luther King, in his essay "Loving Your Enemies"[1] speaks mainly of forgiveness in this sense, *initiating forgiveness,* forgiving the other in one's heart. *It is necessary to realize that the forgiving act must always be initiated by the person who has been wronged.* He connects this with his theme by remarking that *it is impossible even to begin the act of loving one's enemies without the prior acceptance of the necessity, over and over again, of forgiving those who inflict evil and injury upon us.*

Initiating forgiveness is an antidote to hate. He who forgives in his heart has repudiated hatred; he who has not forgiven in his heart has not repudiated hatred and has opened his heart to the influx of hatred, in some form and to some degree. Hatred is evil in itself, and its effects are evil. *Returning hate for hate multiplies hate, adding deeper darkness to a night already devoid of stars. Darkness cannot drive out darkness; only light can do that. Hate cannot drive out hate; only love can do that.*[2]

Hate is also evil in its effects on the person who hates, that is, who remains unforgiving, refusing to forgive in his heart. *Hate scars the soul and distorts the personality* [of the one who hates].[3] Hate of course hurts the person who is its object, the "other person"; but there is more: *Hate is just as injurious to the person who hates. Like an unchecked cancer, hate corrodes the personality and eats away its vital unity. Hate destroys a man's sense of values and his objectivity.*[4]

---

[1] Martin Luther King, *Strength to Love,* chapter 5, (New York: Pocket Books, 1968), 42-49.

[2] *Ibid.,* 45.

[3] *Ibid.*

[4] *Ibid.*

OCCASIONS FOR INITIATING FORGIVENESSS

When is initiating forgiveness called for? It is when the other person doesn't reach out in asking for forgiveness. There are many reasons why this might be the case. Consider:

1. *The person is happy that they hurt you.*
2. *The person doesn't care one way or the other that they hurt you.*
3. *The person is unaware that they hurt you.*
4. *The person thinks (rightly or wrongly) that the entire matter was your fault, not theirs.*
5. *The person has forgotten that they hurt you.*
6. *The person hopes or assumes that you have forgotten the matter.*
7. *The person is embarrassed that they hurt you or too shy to come to you.*
8. *The person is afraid to bring up the bad matter and renew the wound.*
9. *The person would like to ask forgiveness but has lost touch with you.*
10. *The person has died.*

Wonder: how is the character of initiating forgiveness affected by these different factors? One way is the degree of difficulty in forgiving. It is obviously much easier to forgive a person who is embarrassed or afraid than the person who doesn't care whether they hurt you, let alone the extreme case of the one who is happy they hurt you. What other ways are there?

[4] TWO EXAMPLES OF GRANTING FORGIVENESS

INITIATING FORGIVENESSS: JANE EYRE FORGIVES MRS. REED

A beautiful and deeply moving example of *initiating forgiveness* is that of Jane Eyre towards her cold-hearted, spiteful, and vindictive aunt, Mrs. Reed, in the novel *Jane Eyre*. Out of hatred for Jane, and as revenge for some unkind things Jane said to her when she was but a child, Mrs. Reed commits two serious wrongs against Jane. She breaks a promise made to her husband to bring Jane up as her own child, and she sees to it that Jane is denied an inheritance that is rightfully hers. Referring to these, she says to Jane, *Well, I have twice done you a wrong which I regret now.*[5] She regrets doing these things, but she does not repent them, and she does not ask Jane for forgiveness; in fact, she remains totally unforgiving towards Jane. *I could not forget your conduct to me, Jane.*[6] And again, a bit later, *I tell you I could not forget it; and I took my revenge.*[7] The sentiment "I could not forget" means in this context "I could not forgive you." And, "I took my revenge" is the total antithesis, the absolute contrary to being forgiving. Because she remains unforgiving towards Jane, to the point of being vindictive and hateful in her hard-heartedness, she cannot bring herself to ask Jane for forgiveness for the two wrongs she did against her, and which she clearly recognizes. Nevertheless, even though Mrs. Reed does not ask for forgiveness and even though her attitude remains a hardened, bitter attitude of anti-forgiveness, Jane lovingly forgives her: *You have my full and free forgiveness; ask now for God's and be at peace.*[8] Thus Jane forgives Mrs. Reed in her heart, a beautiful example of *initiating forgiveness*, one that takes place without the wrongdoer asking for forgiveness; in this case, a forgiveness even in the face of a totally contrary, hateful attitude on the part of the wrongdoer.

RESPONDING FORGIVENESS: AFANASY FORGIVES ZOSSIMA

For an example of *responding forgiveness*, we turn to the case of Zossima and his servant Afanasy in Dostoevsky's novel *The Brothers Karamazov*. Zossima is an officer in the Russian army and Afanasy is his personal servant. One day Zossima comes home, and, being in a foul mood, angrily and violently strikes his servant, Afanasy, who dares not resist him. Here is the scene, as described by Zossima:

---

[5] Charlotte Bronte, *Jane Eyre*, first pub. 1847 (New York: Doubleday, 1997, Vol. II, chap. 6), 281.

[6] *Ibid.*, 282.

[7] *Ibid.*

[8] *Ibid.*, 283. Emphasis added.

In the evening, returning home in a savage and brutal humor, I flew into a rage with my orderly Afanasy, and gave him two blows in the face with all my might, so that it was covered with blood. He had not long been in my service, and I had struck him before, but never with such ferocious cruelty. And, believe me, though it's forty years ago, I recall it now with shame and pain. I went to bed and slept for about three hours; when I woke up the day was breaking. I got up -- I did not want to sleep any more -- I went to the window -- opened it, it looked out upon the garden; I saw the sun rising; it was warm and beautiful, the birds were singing.

What's the meaning of it, I thought, I feel in my heart as it were something vile and shameful? Is it because I am going to shed blood? No, I thought, I feel it's not that. Can it be that I am afraid of death, afraid of being killed? No, that's not it, that's not it at all. And all at once I knew what it was: it was because I had beaten Afanasy the evening before! It all rose before my mind, it all was as it were repeated over again; he stood before me and I was beating him straight on the face and he was holding his arms stiffly down, his head erect, his eyes fixed on me as though on parade. He staggered at every blow and did not even dare to raise his hands to protect himself. That is what a man has been brought to, and that was a man beating a fellow creature! What a crime! It was as though a sharp dagger had pierced me right through. I stood as if I were struck dumb, while the sun was shining, the leaves were rejoicing, and the birds were trilling the praises of God. I hid my face in my hands, fell on my bed and broke into a storm of tears.

A bit later I ran back alone, straight to Afanasy's little room. *Afanasy*, I said, *I gave you two blows on the face yesterday, forgive me*, I said.

He started as though he were frightened and looked at me; and I saw that it was not enough, and on the spot, in my full officer's uniform, I dropped at his feet and bowed my head to the ground.

Forgive me, I said.

Then he was completely aghast. *Your honor! Sir, what are you doing? Am I worth It?* And he burst out crying as I had done before, hid his face in his hands, turned to the window and shook all over with his sobs.[9]

COMPARING AFANASY AND JANE EYRE

Both Mrs. Reed and Zossima have committed terrible wrongs. In sharp contrast to Mrs. Reed, Zossima fully acknowledges his evil -- he does not merely regret it as Mrs. Reed regrets hers. He deeply repents of it in the depth of his heart; he is shaken to the core of his soul by the incredible evil that he did to a poor, helpless, suffering fellow human being. And he fully asks for forgiveness; he kneels before his servant in a total gesture of humility and begs him for forgiveness. Poor Afanasy is so taken aback by this extra-ordinary behavior on the part of Zossima; he is so perplexed, even stunned by it that he doesn't know what to say or what to do at the moment. But isn't likely that after he collected himself, he forgave Zossima? The forgiving of Afanasy would be *responding forgiveness*, a response to the request to be forgiven; in contrast to the forgiving of Jane Eyre, which was *initiating forgiveness*, an initiative directed to a person who did not ask for forgiveness.

[5] BEING A FORGIVING PERSON

The importance of *initiating forgiveness*, especially as a forgiving in one's heart, cannot be stressed enough. It is important not only for the specific occasions when it is called for; but, also, as a disposition, a basic attitude of the person, a moral virtue as a lasting characteristic of a person, which exists in the soul all

---

[9] Fyodor Dostoyevsky, *The Brothers Karamazov*. Tr. Constance Garnett (London: William Heineman, Ltd., 1912), Part II, Book VI, chap. 2, 307-308.

the time, and not merely when it is actualized. In this way, it refers to *being a forgiving person*, parallel to being a loving person, a generous person, a humble person and a grateful person. Such a person will of course also act with *responding forgiveness*.

Being forgiving in one's heart by *being a forgiving person* is important for the person himself. It is the only way to be liberated from the poison of holding a grudge, which, though intended towards the other person and directed at him, is something which "comes back to" the one who holds the grudge, and "scars his soul," as Martin Luther King points out. We cannot be at peace unless we are forgiving in our hearts.

Being forgiving in one's heart by *being a forgiving person* is also essential for healthy and loving relations to others, for peace in families and small communities, such as a group of persons who are together in one place of work. Holding grudges separates people, makes true union impossible and robs the family and community of peace. Being forgiving dissolves grudges and brings people together and thereby bringing peace.

[6] FORGIVENESS: INNER ACT, OUTER ACT AND COMPLETION

IS FORGIVENESS AN INNER ACT OR AN OUTER ACT?

Wonder: is forgiveness an inner act or an outer act? Forgiving in one's heart is basically an inner act and sometimes only an inner act. But does it reach its full reality in this way?

Isn't there something incomplete in a forgiveness hidden away inside a person's heart? Doesn't forgiveness attain its full reality only when it is spoken to the other person in the social act of forgiving, thereby "reaching" the other and creating the new bond that results from the act of actually forgiving the other? If so, actual forgiveness must be conveyed by an outer act. An inner act of forgiving is essential here in the sense that every outer act presupposes an inner act of which it is the expression. I must first forgive the other inwardly, bring into being an inner act of forgiveness; then I can convey this inner act of forgiveness to him by saying, "I forgive you," the outer act, the action of forgiving.

The inner act which is then expressed in responding forgiveness is not the same as the "forgiving in my heart" of initiating forgiveness. The former *is part of* responding forgiveness, the social act of granting forgiveness in response to the person asking for it; the latter *occurs in contrast to* responding forgiveness, when that is not possible because the other person has not asked for forgiveness.

THE COMPLETION OF FORGIVENESS

We may speak of the completion of forgiveness in two different senses. One, the other person asks me for forgiveness, and I grant him forgiveness, thereby completing what the other person had initiated. Two, there is the completion when the outer act of forgiving reaches the person being forgiven.

[7] WHAT FORGIVING IS NOT

1. *Forgiving is not the same thing as granting pardon*, as the remission of punishment. If I am in a position of authority to punish someone who has wronged me, I may say "I forgive you, but I must still punish you." A parent, for example, may say this to his child. Conversely, I may let a person off and not punish him, but not forgive him. I still resent the evil he has done against me, I do not forgive him, but I do not punish him either.

2. *Forgiving is not condoning.* To condone means to acquiesce, to give in. To confuse forgiving and condoning can lead to serious misunderstandings. For example, it might be objected: "Forgiveness is not always right and good. A wife who forgives her battering husband, over and over again, is not doing right. It only encourages him to continue. He sees her forgiveness as weakness, and he goes on battering her. She will be more and more hurt. She may even die!"

Clearly, what the wife is doing is not right. But it is not forgiveness. It is condoning, a false giving in. We must distinguish between: (A) *genuine forgiveness*, which means taking the evil seriously, and (B) *a false giving in,* out of weakness, which is then mislabeled "forgiveness." The wife in this case should defend herself with a proper use of force. She must take the evil seriously and say an emphatic *no* to the abuse; and clearly convey this to him. This is perfectly compatible with initiating forgiveness, forgiving him in her heart, being ready to fully forgive him if and when he asks her for it, which includes, of course, the firm resolve to not repeat this terrible evil against her.

3. Forgiving is not simply ceasing to resent. It means more than ceasing to resent, although it also includes this. I may cease to resent a wrong done to me because I no longer care about it. This is obviously very different from forgiving. Ceasing to resent is a mere absence, referring to something I don't do. But forgiving is an eminently positive thing, a real act; one that takes humility, courage, and a generous heart.

4. "Forgiving does not mean ignoring what has been done or putting a false label on an evil act."[10] This is similar to the two previous points.

Rather, "It means that *the evil act no longer remains as a barrier* to the relationship. Forgiveness is a catalyst creating the atmosphere necessary for a fresh start and a new beginning."[11] Where forgiveness takes place in the context of a friendship, *it restores the bond* that existed before; it restores the relationship to its true status. "Forgiveness means reconciliation, a coming together again."[12] When forgiveness takes place after a situation of danger or abuse, it may not and need not lead to a restoration of the original relationship, but a new one of safety that still includes forgiveness.

---

[10] Martin Luther King, *Ibid.,* 42. Emphasis added.

[11] *Ibid.*

[12] *Ibid.,* 43.

[8] SOME QUESTIONS

1. Does forgiving imply forgetting? Yes and no, depending on how the term *forgetting* is understood.

> (A) No, we cannot forget in the usual, literal sense of erasing the event from our memory. This is not in our power; we cannot will to do it, though it may happen of its own accord.

> (B) Yes, forgiving does mean a kind of forgetting, in the sense that the evil is put away; it is no longer part of the relationship between the persons; it is no longer a barrier between them, and it no longer colors the attitude of the victim to the wrongdoer. All this is included in that central feature of forgiveness, namely the overcoming of resentment.
>
> That is, if *not forgetting* means that the victim continues to hold a grudge against the offender, if he holds the offense "over him" by continually reminding him of it, then of course he has not forgiven him. His resentment is alive and well, and this means that forgiveness has not taken place. On the other hand:

> (C) No, forgiving does not mean forgetting in the sense of letting your guard down. The wife in the example of the battering husband, though she forgives him, has to remain on guard. She must do so to protect herself from possible future recurrences of his violence. With all his good intentions not to repeat the offense, he may relapse into it. Just as he must remain on guard to prevent this, she must also remain on guard in case his efforts are unsuccessful. Resentment, *no*; being realistic and being careful and being on guard, *yes*.

2. Does forgiveness imply restitution? In many cases the answer to this seems to be *no*. If I have hurt another person by something I said to him, or about him to another; if I have been unloving towards him, or neglectful, there is really nothing I can do concretely to "make it up." The only restitution, or "restoration" is

the restoration of love, of the bond of friendship, and this is accomplished by my act of full and sincere asking for forgiveness.

But where the wrong I have done is or includes damage to the other's property, or something similar, then of course my asking for forgiveness includes and necessarily implies my willingness to make the appropriate restitution. I should offer to do this of my own accord, and then do it; the other should not have to ask me to do it.

3. Is there a moral obligation to *grant forgiveness* when asked to do so? There is certainly a moral obligation to *ask* for forgiveness if one has done wrong. This is clear and self-evident. In the other direction, is there also an obligation to *grant* forgiveness when the wrongdoer asks me? This is a more complicated, and a more controversial, matter. Let me suggest the following.

In relatively small matters, isn't it clearly wrong to refuse to forgive someone who has wronged me and now asks me for forgiveness? Isn't it a lack of love and of humility and even of common decency and courtesy? Doesn't it display pettiness, a "small" mind? In serious and grave matters, the phrase *I can never forgive you* is certainly understandable. We can empathize with such a person. Still, we must ask, is the refusal to forgive morally justified? I think not. I think there is an obligation to grant forgiveness.

The obligation to forgive is certainly part of the Christian way of life. *If you forgive others their offenses [against you] your heavenly Father will also forgive you your offenses. But if you do not forgive others neither will your Father forgive you your offenses.*[13] I want to suggest that the obligation to forgive applies universally, to all people, not just to Christians, as it is a part of morality itself.

Isn't this clear from an application of the Golden Rule? *Do unto others as you would have them do unto you.* If I were in the position of a wrongdoer, if I had done a wrong against you, a serious wrong, and if I subsequently acknowledged my wrong, fully repented it, and begged you to forgive me, I would want to receive forgiveness from you; I would expect it from you and would be deeply saddened and distressed not to receive it. I would look upon your forgiving me as the

---

[13] Matthew 6:14-15.

natural and fitting resolution of the process initiated by my asking you for forgiveness. I would not claim that I have a strict right to be forgiven, only that your forgiveness is the called-for response.

Doesn't the refusal to forgive when asked to do so show a lack of concern for others, a lack of love and a lack of humility? Isn't it in a way a relapse into the same kind of interpersonal hostility that existed between the parties as a result of the wrongdoing before the wrongdoer asked for forgiveness?

4. Is there also a moral obligation to *initiate forgiveness,* to forgive another in one's heart before the other asks for forgiveness or in cases where he never does? I think so. It is part of the Christian way, and I think it is also part of morality as such. It is a thesis eloquently defended by Martin Luther King in "Loving Your Enemies," as we have seen. In small matters, it seems fairly easy to see that a forgiving attitude should be preferred to a vindictive, "resentful" attitude. In large matters, it is more difficult to have a forgiving attitude. Still, it is usually the case that if we are not forgiving in our hearts, we will be vindictive, even hateful towards the wrongdoer. Neutrality does not seem to be a viable option. And vindictiveness, hatefulness, a desire for revenge, and above all revenge itself, are intrinsically evil and wrong. To keep them out we need to be forgiving. Let us also remember what Martin Luther King stresses, that hate, including being unforgiving, scars the soul of the one who hates. Thus, because it is right and good in itself, and because it is also a great good for us, we *should be* forgiving towards all people.

5. Is forgiveness a momentary event or is it a process? For simple offences the act of forgiveness may take place in the will and in the heart rather quickly as a momentary event, however for very serious offences that deeply wound an individual or an entire family or societal group, forgiveness may well be a process that takes a great deal of time and effort, sometimes even over a period of years. The important thing to note is that one is either moving towards forgiveness or one is not. Forgiveness, it seems, is a dynamic process that moves forward towards its fulfillment. Wonder at the effect time to help heal us.

6. How does one begin to forgive huge horrible serious offences like child abuse or murder? One thing to consider is that a lack of forgiveness allows the perpetrator of the offence to continue to hurt your soul as you live in hatred. Second, a lack of forgiveness does not un-do the offence. The offence remains as an offence, forever not undoable in the past. Therefore, especially in these cases, it is perhaps best to consider forgiveness as person-directed rather than event-directed. Here we consider the wonder of the power to forgive a person, when the event itself, in the past, cannot be undone.

CHAPTER 21
LOVE

[1] WHAT IS LOVE? SOME CORE ELEMENTS OF LOVE

Wonder: what is love? What do we do when we love? What are the qualities of love?

One: Affirmation. If I go out to you in love, I affirm you as the unique "you" that you are. If the opposite of love is indifference, then love as affirmation stands out as a key feature of love. And isn't affirmation a major part of what we long for from other persons when we long for love? Shouldn't it be a key element in our love for others? Can it be expressed in such a way that the other person feels this affirmation?

Two: Empathy. How do I view another human being? I can take an external view that leaves him outside me as a kind of object. This is typical of indifference. For example, do I sometimes go about my own busy and self-concerned ways with only an external awareness of the presence of others? Do I sometimes treat others almost as if they were merely things? Do I act without an adequate realization of their inner and unique worlds of personal experience?

Or do I try to enter into the inner being of another person and imagine myself in his place making his concerns my concerns. This entering into another is *loving empathy*. It means vividly realizing in my imagination and with my feeling the inner life of another person, his interests, his joys and his sufferings. It means being aware of others as persons, as important to themselves as we are to ourselves.

Three: Benevolence. Love as benevolence means a direct concern for the well-being of other persons for their own sake. For example, rescuers who stop by to give a ride to a stranded motorist in a snowstorm are typically motivated by benevolence. Their sympathy is aroused by the sight of the stranded motorist suffering from the severely cold weather and by a fear that he might freeze to death if left alone in the storm. Rescuers motivated by benevolence care about the well-being of the stranded motorists for his own sake; they are reacting to the plight of another person by being concerned to do something to alleviate it.

Benevolence also includes a cognitive dimension. Persons who are benevolent tend to notice someone who needs help, to think of ways to give it or to remember (for example) that today is the day when a friend needs a ride to get to a doctor's appointment.

Four: Reverence. Love goes beyond reverence but also includes reverence as a vital and indispensable element. Reverence means respect for another person, letting him be his own person, not trying to control him. It means really listening, seeking first to understand. It means resisting the urge to criticize, and above all any urge to "get back" at the other.

Five: Faithfulness. If I really love you, I will stay with you in good times and in hard times. Isn't love essentially a commitment and faithfulness the living out of this commitment? This means more than just faithfulness as we ordinarily understand it in romantic relationships. Here, in its fullness, we refer to holding fast to our original view of the person, the view that we fell in love with, when a less desirable view comes into the relationship, within reason and safety.

Six: Forgiveness. In all human relationships things sometimes go wrong. Did I cause the wrong? Shouldn't I ask myself this question? And then say: *if I've done anything wrong, please forgive me*. And have the readiness to forgive the other if he asks me.

Seven: Gratitude. The love that we receive from another person, and the deeds of love that this love expresses: do we always appreciate these adequately? Or do we often take them for granted? The antidote to taking them for granted is very simple: appreciation and showing this appreciation in gratitude to the other.

Eight: The Golden Rule as a Guide to Love. How do I put love into practice? What do I do? What do I avoid doing? As a guide to answering these questions try the Golden Rule. *How do I want to be loved by others*? That's how I should love them.

[2] WHY DO WE LOVE? TWO TYPES OF LOVE

Wonder: why do we love? What is the motive for love? Perhaps there is more than one answer to this. Perhaps there are two answers corresponding to two basic kinds of love:

One type of love arises when we see the beauty and lovableness of another person. Why did he fall in love with her? He saw and was moved by the beauty of her being, and his love to her is a response to this, a desire for union with her motivated by his vision. Or you see a sweet, small child and your love for that child immediately springs up. It is a different kind of love, but in both cases, it is awakened and motivated by the beauty and lovableness of another person.

For the second type of love consider this case. You love another person, not because you see the beauty of that person but because you want to see him happy. Take an extreme case, that of a person no one loves, no one likes because of the way this person comes across to others. You find yourself with a deep, perhaps surprising love for that person. Why do you love him? What is it that constitutes this love? It is not just feeling sorry for the person, although that is surely part of it. But your response goes significantly beyond feeling sorry: you really *love* this person. You want the good for him and you want to be part of bringing this good to him.

It will be helpful to have names for these two types of love:

Delight love is the first type: the love that delights in the beauty and lovableness of the other person; and where delight characterizes this love in its nature and how we experience it.

Donation love is the second type: where the focus of the love is on giving to the other; on his happiness and his fulfillment as a person and on my bringing him what leads to these.

[3] DELIGHT LOVE AND DONATION LOVE COMPARED

Delight and donation may be seen in terms of several contrasts and comparisons:

1. ***Heart and will: is love from the heart or from the will?*** Perhaps it is both: from the heart as delight love and from the will as donation love? More on this shortly.
2. ***Unconditional love: is all love unconditional***? Or should we say that being unconditional is characteristic of donation but not delight love? Isn't delight love somehow conditioned on the delight I find in the other person? If I don't find any, can I still have delight love? Must my love not be donation in such a type of case? More on this shortly.
3. ***Loving all persons:*** some moral and religious codes call on us to love all persons. Some say that if we fail to love all persons even our enemies, we cannot truly love those who are close to us, for whom we would have delight love. Is this true? In any case if we have a love for all persons including our enemies must this not be donation love? Aren't there people we know whom we cannot love with a delight love?
4. ***Feeling guilty***: some people believe they are called on to love all persons but feel there are some persons they cannot love; and they then feel guilty at their lack of love. Perhaps the delight-donation distinction can be of help here. We can try to cultivate a donation love for all persons while realizing that delight love is not realistic towards all persons.
5. ***Loving and liking:*** how are these related? Sometimes they go in the same direction, in delight love; that kind of love includes liking but goes further and deeper. If you love in this way you also like; but if you only like you do not yet love.

6. *Sometimes loving and liking go in opposite directions,* where you love but do not like, as in love of enemies, which can only be a donation love, never a delight love.

7. *Can delight love exist all by itself?* Can it exist without donation love? Try to imagine a love that is only delight without any element of donation. Would that really be love? Could it last? It seems then that delight must include donation in order to be truly love. Once the person we delight-love disappoints us, doesn't donation love have to tide the relationship over until the delight returns?

8. *There can be donation without delight but not delight without donation.* Does this mean that donation is more important and more basic to the nature of love? Does donation characterize love in its essence more than delight?

9. *And yet a donation without delight is somehow lacking in the fullness of love; something is missing that should be there.* There can be something heroic, even touching in a love that is only donation, as when a parent deeply loves a rebellious and hostile child. Still, doesn't one always hope for the completion of such a love by a mutual giving and the delight love that this provides?

10. *Wonder: both seem to be true; namely that there is something noble and beautiful and calling for admiration in a heroic love that is only donation; and also that such a love is not the fullness of love that should be there since delight is missing.*

[4] IS LOVE FROM THE HEART OR IS IT FROM THE WILL?

Wonder: could it be that love is from both the heart and the will? Isn't the heart the seat of love, the center in our soul which gives and receives love? Consider a love which is not felt: is this a true love? Isn't here a world of difference between *I will to love you* and *I love you*?

Isn't the joy of love is felt in the heart? And when there is the bitter sadness of losing love and the disappointments that sometimes come with love, aren't these too felt in the heart?

But isn't the will also of crucial importance for love? Isn't it from the will that we find the strength to love? Love is faithfulness in good times and in hard times, and it is through the strength of the will that love continues faithfully. Love as a response to the other entirely for his sake should come from the heart but it also needs the will.

It might seem that delight love is from the heart and donation love is from the will? But is this really so? Doesn't the fullness of love necessarily include the heart? If so, this would of course include donation love as coming from the heart. And doesn't delight love also need the will to direct it, to keep it strong and to preserve it when necessary?

Wonder: the fullness of love that includes the heart and is experienced in the heart: is this delight love? I want to suggest it is not. Donation love is still donation love even when deeply felt in the heart; it does not thereby become delight love. A deeply felt donation love to another person is a total focus on *giving* happiness to the other person and is thereby distinguished from the delight love where part of the focus is on the *receiving* of happiness. Each love, delight, and donation has its own theme, and so the two loves are essentially distinct. What we can say is that in many cases is they may co-exist side-by-side.

[5] IS LOVE UNCONDITIONAL?

Wonder: is love essentially unconditional, so that a conditional love is not really love? Many people would say *yes*, that love must be unconditional to count as love. There certainly seems to be much truth in this; but let me suggest there is also another side, that there are two sides here or two aspects.

How is love not unconditional but conditional? Consider the different types of love. For example, there is friendship love (*philia*) and romantic love (*eros*). These types of love come about between some people and not others because of the conditions that are present and absent. Doesn't this mean that these types of love are conditional in regard to their coming into being? More generally delight love is conditional in that it is dependent on certain conditions for its coming into existence and its continuing in existence. Delight love will arise in my heart only if I perceive the other person in his beauty and lovableness.

How is love unconditional? First, the continuation of friendship love and romantic love requires that this love is unconditional in the sense that it continues in good times and hard times. A love that is vulnerable to the ups and downs of human relationships is not true love; and this is because it lacks the faithfulness and strength of love that is unconditional love. True love is unconditional: I will be there for you, and I will continue to love you even when I'm hurt; even when certain things threaten to come between us that might lessen or destroy our love. Note that what we have been describing here is delight love: friendship love and romantic love.

Second, there is donation love, love as a response to another person entirely for his sake (*agape*). This is essentially an unconditional love, motivated by benevolence as a deep concern for the good of other and directed to him by empathy.

Third, there is the credit of love. So much of human behavior can be interpreted in more than one way and often dividing into two basic parts, a good and a bad. The credit of love means that I interpret the other person's behavior in a positive light as something good and that his motivation is from love or at least in the direction of love. It is the application to love of the idea of giving the other the benefit of the doubt. Doesn't love call on us to do that? Or at least to go in this direction and keep going as long as possible?

[6] IS SELF-LOVE A FORM OF LOVE?

Wonder: is self-love a form of love? Some people think so. They say love can be turned to oneself just as readily as to another. They point to affirmation: in love I affirm a person, either another person as in friendship love and love of neighbor; or my own person. Some go even further and say that self-love is a necessary condition for love of others; a basis from which to go out to others. If I do not first have love for myself I cannot have it for another.

But there is another side that says love is in its very nature something directed to another person. Take the matter of concern. If I tell you that Joe has a strong concern for his own well-being, that he makes sure he is well-fed and well-rested, have I indicted that Joe is a loving person? Couldn't he be a scoundrel, hateful and close to being devoid of all love? But if I tell you that Joe has this concern for *another* person, motivated by the good for that person for *his* sake, then I have told you that Joe is a loving person, for this is an essential part of what it means to be a loving person. What can we conclude from this? Let me suggest this:

Love in its proper meaning is essentially love for *another* person, a response to another for his own sake. It is a going beyond myself in concern for another. Given this meaning of love isn't it impossible to have love for oneself? This would mean that self-love is not really love.

Further, consider delight love. Isn't it absurd to think that I could have this kind of love for myself? Isn't the delight of delight love precisely the delight I receive from another person? And doesn't donation love reveal a similar pattern? Isn't the beauty, indeed the very essence of donation love that I leave my own being in order to go out to another for his own sake?

It is of course true that in love I affirm a person. But affirmation is not yet love. If I love I also affirm; but, if I affirm, I do not necessarily love. Love is a going out to another from one's heart, a giving of one's heart that is not necessarily present in affirmation; that goes beyond it.

Isn't the valid point in self-love simply self-affirmation? Could we then say that self-affirmation is a necessary condition for affirming others? But couldn't even this be questioned? Imagine a person who feels very low about himself; he lacks self-affirmation. Then he finds that another person loves him loves him very deeply and has a profound understanding of his person which he totally affirms. Couldn't it be that through this being lifted up by the love he receives from another person he finds the strength to affirm his own being?

If this is so the process can be reversed. Instead of my self-affirmation leading to my affirming another person, it is the affirmation of another person for me that I feel which allows me to go out of myself in affirming another person.

[7] CAN WE LOVE OUR ENEMIES?

Wonder: can we love our enemies? Let us start with a first small step: not hating them. Why not hate them? The question is worth reflecting on. To begin with, how can this possibly do any good? Where does it lead? Doesn't returning hate for hate actually multiply hate, adding deeper darkness to a night already very dark? Darkness cannot drive out darkness; only light can do that. Hate cannot drive out hate; only love can do that.

Meeting hate with hate never works; we can never get rid of an enemy that way. The only way we can get rid of an enemy is by getting rid of enmity. Hate by its very nature destroys and tears down; love creates and build up. Only love has the power of transforming an enemy into a friend.

But this raises the question: how do we love our enemies?

First, we must develop and maintain the capacity to forgive. If we cannot forgive, we cannot love. It is impossible to love our enemies without realizing and accepting the necessity, over and over again, of forgiving those who inflict evil and injury upon us.

Forgiveness does not mean ignoring what has been done or putting a false label on an evil act. Rather, it means that the evil act no longer remains a barrier to the relationship. Forgiveness is a catalyst creating the atmosphere necessary for a fresh start and a new beginning. It is the lifting of a burden; it is the canceling of a debt

Second, we must recognize that the evil deed of the enemy-neighbor, the thing that hurts never completely expresses all that he is. An element of goodness may be found even in our worst enemy. Each of us is something of a schizophrenic personality; we are tragically divided within ourselves and against ourselves. A kind of civil war rages within all of our lives.

Doesn't this mean there is some good in the worst of us and some evil in the best of us? When we discover this, we are less prone to hate our enemies. We look beneath the surface, beneath the impulsive evil deed; we see within our enemy-neighbor a measure of goodness and know that the viciousness and evilness of his acts are not really representative of what he is. We see him in a new light. We recognize that his hate grows out of fear, pride, ignorance, prejudice, and misunderstanding. Then we love our enemies by realizing that they are not totally bad.

Third, we must not seek to defeat or humiliate the enemy but to win his friendship and understanding. At times we may be able to humiliate our enemy if his weak moments come and we can thrust in his side the spear of defeat. But this we must not do. Our every word and deed must contribute to an understanding with our enemy and release the reservoir of good will which has been blocked by impenetrable walls of hate.

[8] HOW CAN WE LOVE OUR ENEMIES?

I

Let us be practical and ask the question, *How do we love our enemies?*[1]

First, we must develop and maintain the capacity to forgive. He who is devoid of the power to forgive is devoid of the power to love. It is impossible even to begin the act of loving one's enemies without the prior acceptance of the necessity, repeatedly, of forgiving those who inflict evil and injury upon us. It is also necessary to realize that the forgiving act must always be initiated by the person who has been wronged, the victim of some great hurt, the recipient of some tortuous injustice, the absorber of some terrible act of oppression. The wrongdoer may request forgiveness. He may come to himself, and, like the prodigal son, move up some dusty road, his heart palpitating with the desire for forgiveness.

---

[1] From Martin Luther King, *Strength to Love*, chap. 5. "Loving your Enemies." (New York: Pocket Books, 1968), pp. 42-49. Reprinted with permission.

But only the injured neighbor, the loving father back home, can really pour out the warm waters of forgiveness.

Forgiveness does not mean ignoring what has been done or putting a false label on an evil act. It means, rather, that the evil act no longer remains as a barrier to the relationship. Forgiveness is a catalyst creating the atmosphere necessary for a fresh start and a new beginning. It is the lifting of a burden or the canceling of a debt. The words "I will forgive you, but I'll never forget what you've done" never explain the real nature of forgiveness. Certainly, one can never forget, if that means erasing it totally from his mind. But when we forgive, we forget in the sense that the evil deed is no longer a mental block impeding a new relationship. Likewise, we can never say, "I will forgive you, but I won't have anything further to do with you." Forgiveness means reconciliation, a coming together again. Without this, no man can love his enemies. The degree to which we are able to forgive determines the degree to which we are able to love our enemies.

Second, we must recognize that the evil deed of the enemy-neighbor, the thing that hurts, never quite expresses all that he is. An element of goodness may be found even in our worst enemy. Each of us is something of a schizophrenic personality, tragically divided against ourselves. A persistent civil war rages within all of our lives. Something within us causes us to lament with Ovid, the Latin poet, "I see and approve the better things, but follow worse," or to agree with Plato that human personality is like a charioteer having two headstrong horses, each wanting to go in a different direction, or to repeat with the Apostle Paul, "The good that I would I do not: but the evil which I would not, that I do."

This simply means that there is some good in the worst of us and some evil in the best of us. When we discover this, we are less prone to hate our enemies. We look beneath the surface, beneath the impulsive evil deed, we see within our enemy-neighbor a measure of goodness and know that the viciousness and evilness of his acts are not quite representative of all that he is. We see him in a new light. We recognize that his hate grows out of fear, pride, ignorance, prejudice, and misunderstanding, but in spite of this, we know God's image is ineffably etched in his being. Then we love our enemies by realizing that they are not totally bad and that they are not beyond the reach of God's redemptive love.

Third, we must not seek to defeat or humiliate the enemy but to win his friendship and understanding. At times, we are able to humiliate our worst enemy. Inevitably, his weak moments come, and we are able to thrust in his side the spear of defeat. But this we must not do. Every word and deed must contribute to an understanding with the enemy and release those vast reservoirs of good will which have been blocked by impenetrable walls of hate.

The meaning of love is not to be confused with some sentimental outpouring. Love is something much deeper than emotional bosh. Perhaps the Greek language can clear our confusion at this point. In the Greek New Testament are three words for love. The word *eros* is a sort of aesthetic or romantic love. In the Platonic dialogue *eros* is a yearning of the soul for the realm of the divine. The second word is *philia,* a reciprocal love and the intimate affection and friendship between friends. We love those whom we like, and we love because we are loved. The third word is *agape,* understanding and creative, redemptive goodwill for all men. An overflowing love which seeks nothing in return, *agape* is the love of God operating in the human heart. At this level, we love men not because we like them, nor because their ways appeal to us, nor even because they possess some type of divine spark; we love every man because God loves him. At this level, we love the person who does an evil deed, although we hate the deed that he does.

Now we can see what Jesus meant when he said, "Love your enemies." We should be happy that he did not say, "Like your enemies." It is almost impossible to like some people. "Like" is a sentimental and affectionate word. How can we be affectionate toward a person whose avowed aim is to crush our very being and place innumerable stumbling blocks in our path? How can we like a person who is threatening our children and bombing our homes? This is impossible. But Jesus recognized that *love* is greater than *like.* When Jesus bids us to love our enemies, he is speaking neither of *eros* nor *philia;* he is speaking of *agape,* understanding and creative, redemptive goodwill for all men. Only by following this way and responding with this type of love are we able to be children of our Father who is in heaven.

II

Let us move now from the practical *how* to the theoretical *why:* **Why should we love our enemies?** The first reason is fairly obvious. **Returning hate for hate multiplies hate, adding deeper darkness to a night already devoid of stars.** Darkness cannot drive out darkness; only light can do that. Hate cannot drive out hate; only love can do that. Hate multiplies hate, violence multiplies violence, and toughness multiplies toughness in a descending spiral of destruction. So, when Jesus says, "Love your enemies," he is setting forth a profound and ultimately inescapable admonition. Have we not come to such an impasse in the modern world that we must love our enemies -- or else? The chain reaction of evil -- hate begetting hate, wars producing more wars -- must be broken, or we shall be plunged into the dark abyss of annihilation.

Another reason why we must love our enemies is that hate scars the soul and distorts the personality. Mindful that hate is an evil and dangerous force, we too often think of what it does to the person hated. This is understandable, for hate brings irreparable damage to its victims. We have seen its ugly consequences in the ignominious deaths brought to six million Jews by a hate-obsessed madman named Hitler, in the unspeakable violence inflicted upon Negroes by bloodthirsty mobs, in the dark horrors of war, and in the terrible indignities and injustices perpetrated against millions of God's children by unconscionable oppressors.

But there is another side which we must never overlook. Hate is just as injurious to the person who hates. Like an unchecked cancer, hate corrodes the personality and eats away its vital unity. Hate destroys a man's sense of values and his objectivity. It causes him to describe the beautiful as ugly and the ugly as beautiful, and to confuse the true with the false and the false with the true.

Dr. E. Franklin Frazier, in an interesting essay entitled "The Pathology of Race Prejudice," included several examples of white persons who were normal, amiable, and congenial in their day-to-day relationships with other white persons, but when they were challenged to think of Negroes as equals or even to discuss the question of racial injustice, they reacted with unbelievable irrationality and an abnormal unbalance. This happens when hate lingers in our minds. Psychiatrists report that many of the strange things that happen in the subconscious, many of our inner conflicts, are rooted in hate. They say, "Love or perish." Modern psychology recognizes what Jesus taught centuries ago: hate divides the personality and love in an amazing and inexorable way unites it.

A third reason why we should love our enemies is that love is the only force capable of transforming an enemy into a friend. We never get rid of an enemy by meeting hate with hate; we get rid of an enemy by getting rid of enmity. By its very nature, hate destroys and tears down; by its very nature, love creates and builds up. Love transforms with redemptive power.

Lincoln tried love and left for all history a magnificent drama of reconciliation. When he was campaigning for the presidency one of his archenemies was a man named Stanton. For some reason Stanton hated Lincoln. He used every ounce of his energy to degrade him in the eyes of the public. So deep rooted was Stanton's hate for Lincoln that he uttered unkind words about his physical appearance and sought to embarrass him at every point with the bitterest diatribes. But in spite of this Lincoln was elected President of the United States. Then came the period when he had to select his cabinet which would consist of the persons who would be his most intimate associates in implementing his program. He started choosing men here and there for the various secretaryships. The day finally came for Lincoln to select a man to fill the all-important post of Secretary of War. Can you imagine whom Lincoln chose to fill this post? None other than the man named Stanton. There was an immediate uproar in the inner circle when the news began to spread. Adviser after adviser was heard saying, "Mr. President, you are making a mistake. Do you know this man Stanton? Are you familiar with all of the ugly things he said about you? He is your enemy. He will seek to sabotage your program. Have you thought this through, Mr. President?" Mr. Lincoln's answer was terse and to the point: "Yes, I know Mr. Stanton. I am aware of all the terrible things he has said about me. But after looking over the nation, I find that he is the best man for the job." So, Stanton became Abraham Lincoln's Secretary of War and rendered an invaluable service to his nation and his President. Not many years later Lincoln was assassinated. Many laudable things were said about him. Even today millions of people still adore him as the greatest of all Americans. H. G. Wells selected him as one of the six great men of history. But of all the great statements made about Abraham Lincoln, the words of Stanton remain among the greatest. Standing near the dead body of the man he once hated, Stanton referred to him as one of the greatest men that ever lived and said, "He now belongs to the ages." If Lincoln had hated Stanton both men would have gone to their graves as bitter enemies. But through the power of love Lincoln transformed an enemy into a friend. It was this same attitude that made it possible for Lincoln to speak a kind word about the South during the Civil War when feeling was most bitter. Asked by a shocked bystander how he could do this, Lincoln said, "Madam, do I not destroy my enemies when I make them my friends?" This is the power of redemptive love.

We must hasten to say that these are not the ultimate reasons why we should love our enemies. An even more basic reason why we are commanded to love is expressed explicitly in Jesus' words, "Love your enemies . . . *that ye may be children of your Father which is in heaven.*" We are called to this difficult task in order to realize a unique relationship with God. We are potential sons of God. Through love that potentiality becomes actuality. We must love our enemies, because only by loving them can we know God and experience the beauty of his holiness.

The relevance of what I have said to the crisis in race relations should be readily apparent. There will be no permanent solution to the race problem until oppressed men develop the capacity to love their enemies. The darkness of racial injustice will be dispelled only by the light of forgiving love. For more than three centuries American Negroes have been battered by the iron rod of oppression, frustrated by day and bewildered by night by unbearable injustice, and burdened with the ugly weight of discrimination. Forced to live with these shameful conditions, we are tempted to become bitter and to retaliate with a corresponding hate. But if this happens, the new order we seek will be little more than a duplicate of the old order. We must in strength and humility meet hate with love.

Of course, this is not *practical.* Life is a matter of getting even, of hitting back, of dog eat dog. Am I saying that Jesus commands us to love those who hurt and oppress us? Do I sound like most preachers -- idealistic and impractical? Maybe in some distant Utopia, you say, that idea will work, but not in the hard, cold world in which we live.

My friends, we have followed the so-called practical way for too long a time now, and it has led inexorably to deeper confusion and chaos. Time is cluttered with the wreckage of communities which surrendered to hatred and violence. For the salvation of our nation and the salvation of mankind, we must follow another way. This does not mean that we abandon our righteous efforts. With every ounce of our energy we must continue to rid this nation of the incubus of segregation. But we shall not in the process relinquish our privilege and our obligation to love. While abhorring segregation, we shall love the segregationist. This is the only way to create the beloved community.

To our most bitter opponents we say: "We shall match your capacity to inflict suffering by our capacity to endure suffering. We shall meet your physical force with soul force. Do to us what you will, and we shall continue to love you. We cannot in all good conscience obey your unjust laws, because non-co-operation with evil is as much a moral obligation as is co-operation with good. Throw us in jail, and we shall still love you. Bomb our homes and threaten our children, and we shall still love you. Send your hooded perpetrators of violence into our community at the midnight hour and beat us and leave us half dead, and we shall still love you. But be ye assured that we will wear you down by our capacity to suffer. One day we shall win freedom, but not only for ourselves. We shall so appeal to your heart and conscience that we shall win *you* in the process, and our victory will be a double victory."

Love is the most durable power in the world. Wonder!

CHAPTER 22
GRATITUDE

[1] WHAT IS GRATITUDE?

THREE EXAMPLES OF GRATITUDE

Wonder: what is gratitude? How does it arise? Let us consider three examples:

First, the case of the scarf. I have a scarf which is very precious to me because it is a gift from a person I love deeply. I put it on and go about my day assuming it stays on but in fact it falls off without my realizing it; then someone hands it back to me. Not only am I happy to have it back, I am also grateful to the person who returns it to me. If I had noticed myself that I had dropped it the element of being happy would also be there but the element of being grateful would not. That comes in when I recognize the role of another person. That is:

> I am grateful and I respond in gratitude when I recognize that another person has favored me by providing me with something which is beneficial for me, a "good for me."

The inner response of gratitude is distinct from and additional to that of the happiness of having my scarf back, although it seems to be somehow intertwined with it.

Second, my life is saved. I am in enemy-occupied territory; if I am discovered I will be killed. A stranger grasps the situation and at great risk to his own life saves my life. I turn to him in deep gratitude, hardly able to express it sufficiently. He has given me the greatest "good for me," my very own being.

Third, gratitude for love. I turn to a person I love deeply and who loves me deeply, and I say *thank you for your love*. I recognize what a gift it is, I do not take it for granted; and then I express this inner response of gratitude to the other by an outer act of thanking.

The first and second reveal gratitude for a specific act at a specific time; in contrast, the third reveals gratitude for an ongoing, spiritual reality at a deeper level of existence. The first is gratitude for a relatively small matter; the second and third, each in its own way is gratitude for realities that are far more significant for the person favored.

THREE DOMAINS OF GRATITUDE

Wonder: how does gratitude exist? What different forms can it take? Here are three:

One, gratitude can exist as an *inner response*. That is the initial and the basic reality. I get my scarf back and I am grateful: the inner response of gratitude.

Two, gratitude can exist an *outer act*. I convey this inner response to the person who has favored me by of an outer act of thanking.

Three, gratitude can exist as a *moral virtue*. It is the basic attitude of being appreciative for the good things in one's life, not taking them for granted. Only a grateful person can be truly blessed with gifts because only a grateful person can really appreciate them.

Thus, to have the virtue of gratitude is to have the character trait that disposes us to appreciate the good things of life, rather than taking them for granted or claiming them as our rights, to be inwardly grateful to others when they favor us with kindness, and to express this gratitude by acts of thanking.

[2] GRATITUDE AS INNER RESPONSE

THE COGNITIVE ELEMENT IN GRATITUDE

1. The Cognitive Element: Recognizing the Presence of Another Person. Isn't it typical of gratitude as an inner response that it wells up in us spontaneously, that we find ourselves filled with this feeling? Yet it is not identical with our spontaneous joy when something good happens to us. We do not feel it, for example, when the good is entirely of our own doing. When do we feel it? Isn't it only when we find ourselves in a situation in which we believe *another person* has *freely favored* us? When we realize that another person has done something for us as a favor the feeling immediately appears. This realization is the cognitive element in gratitude. Thus: I can respond in gratitude only when I recognize that another person has favored me, has bestowed on me what I experience as a good for me, a beneficial good. The inner response of gratitude is distinct from and additional to that of joy, although it is intertwined with the joy.

2. The Cognitive Element: Its Place in the Experience of Gratitude. Between my joy as a recognition that the scarf is still mine, and the specific warm emotional feeling of gratitude as an inner response, some sort of cognitive process has taken place. In a process quicker than thought I have asked myself some questions and answered them: "Has this just happened to me or has *someone* done it to me? And, if the latter, has he done so *out of kindness*?" Only then, as a meaningful inner response to the other person based on this recognition, does gratitude as a feeling spontaneously arise. I acknowledge what the other has done for me and turn to him as he had turned to me. For a short moment we enter into an "interpersonal space" together.

GRATITUDE: A RESPONSE TO ANOTHER PERSON

3. Gratitude is an I-Thou Response to Another person. Gratitude as an inner response belongs to those responses which are possible only towards *persons*, and only towards persons *other than myself*. We cannot say I ought not to have gratitude towards myself, for I simply cannot have it. I may be highly satisfied with myself, or I may pity myself, and in this way two layers in myself are related. Gratitude, however, presupposes a real "I-Thou" relationship; and it is only a true Thou, that is, another person, to whom I can turn in gratitude. It cannot be an impersonal reality such as Nature, the Cosmos, or Life. Where such seems to be the case, it is just that these entities are treated like persons.

4. Why Gratitude can be given only to *Another* Person. Gratitude as an inner response occurs when I recognize that another person has made something which is in itself important to me his concern. He has taken a concern that is originally *mine* and made it *his own*; a concern such as my safety or my property as in the scarf example, and ultimately my happiness. In this there is an affirmation of my person by another person. Gratitude is my response to this affirmation of my person by another person. It is "aimed at" it and "corresponds" to it. From this it should be clear why I cannot be grateful to myself. My own concern is already my concern; there is no room here for that *making* of the concern of one person, the concern of another. There is no affirmation of my person by another to which I could respond, hence no occasion for gratitude.

WHAT GRATITUDE REQUIRES

5. Gratitude Requires a Trusting Assumption. Gratitude as an inner response depends on a trusting assumption, based on evidence such as words and gestures that the other wanted to do something good for me because it is good for me; that he acted out of genuine kindness. I interpret his deed as to its motivation, that it was done out of kindness, and with my positive, trusting assumption, the emotional response of gratitude takes place. This response is ingrained in human nature as such. In order not to experience such a feeling I would have to explicitly counteract that feeling which can be done only by removing the object, that is, by the attempt to convince myself that, notwithstanding apparent evidence, the other had not acted from genuine kindness.

6. Gratitude Requires Humility. Such an attempt will always have some motive of its own. For example, a person may wish not to have the feeling of gratitude arise in him because it is a somewhat humbling feeling. In it his human condition of dependence is brought home to him. He will "unconsciously" seek reasons not to be grateful. By some sort of general decision, he may tend to deny the reality in principle of non-egoistic acts. He will develop the habit of deep-rooted suspicion and, in this way, he may succeed in making the sources of gratitude dry up in himself. As Thompson remarks, "Suspicion creates its own cause: distrust begets reason for distrust."

7. Gratitude as the willingness to recognize a good I have received. In some cases we *feel* grateful; it "wells up" in us as noted earlier. In other cases, we may not feel any gratitude, but still should *be* grateful. "Thus, school children may not *feel* grateful at a given moment to their teachers, but we urge them to acknowledge at least with a "Thank You!" services rendered them. Not to acknowledge an unearned good because one does not feel grateful is a *moral weakness*."[1]

8. Summary: Four Essential Features of Gratitude as an Inner Act. Gratitude is a response to [1] a person, [2] other than myself, who has [3] favored me [4] out of kindness. The cognitive element refers to all of these. It is the recognition that the beneficial good that has come to me is a favor from another person, who has acted out of kindness. The trusting assumption makes this recognition possible.

Interpersonal Human Solidarity and Love

9. The World of Interpersonal Universal Human Solidarity. If I see someone in need of help, and such help is easy for me to give -- for instance, I see a person drop her scarf, and all I have to do is pick it up and give it back to her -- I *ought* to give that help. I do not have to produce any example of my ever having done something of the kind before, to establish beyond any doubt that the human situation *calls for* acts which are to be characterized as genuinely caring and friendly. Thus, gratitude appears in the context of a world of interpersonal universal human solidarity.

10. The Negative Test. Although the act of returning the scarf, and the response of gratitude to it, are only small actualizations of the sphere of interpersonal hu-

---

[1] Peter A. Bertocci and Richard M. Millard, *Personality and the Good: Psychological and Ethical Perspectives* (New York: David McKay, 1962), p.389.

man solidarity, the strength of its reality becomes visible in the negative. The refusal to care, to provide help -- and the refusal to acknowledge help when I receive it, by an act of thanking -- usually tend to stir up astonished indignation in an onlooker. This is because they bespeak a foolhardy readiness to ignore the human condition of interpersonal solidarity, and instead try to "go it alone."

11. Gratitude: A Response to an Affirmation of My Being. As we have seen, gratitude arises when another person makes something important to me, *his* concern; when he takes a concern that is mine and makes it *his own*. In this there is an affirmation of my person. Gratitude is the response to this affirmation of my person. But to really give the response of gratitude, I must allow the gift and the caring intention of the other to reach a point in my being where the affirmation of my person becomes real and is actually experienced as such. The caring affirmation by the other person also represents a call addressed to me to be a more caring, affirming person myself.

[3] GRATITUDE AS AN OUTER ACT

1. Gratitude as an Outer Act: The Social Act of Thanking. In the normal course of events this feeling of gratitude to another person as an inner act will tend to become expressed in an outer act of thanking. That is, it will tend to find its embodiment in a social act. I experience an obligation to convey my gratitude to the person who has favored me by thanking him. Thanking is a *social act* in the strict sense of the word. It is, as we have seen, an act which is not only the expression of a feeling but has a specific interpersonal character: it is in need of being perceived and understood by the other person in order to be accomplished. If the other has vanished from the scene before I have realized what has happened and before I can turn to him and say "thank you," my gratitude will still be there as an inner act, as something which springs up in me. But the social act of thanking cannot become real; for it can be given only to the person who did the deed. In thanking and in the subsequent acceptance of the thanking, the sequence finds its natural completion.

2. Gratitude and Thanking as Looking Up for a Moment. In our spontaneous reactive feelings, our implicit awareness of existential matters usually comes out with much greater precision and vividness than in reasoning alone. Thanking as an outer act-social act, and the underlying feeling of gratitude as an inner act, occur in the context of human interpersonal solidarity. Thanking means that I look up for a moment, so to speak, and recognize the other as a *person*, as something other than a complicated means for the attainment of my own good. He certainly has been instrumental in this. But my gratitude assumes, and thereby recognizes and testifies, that he has done what he did out of genuine kindness, and as an actualization of his acknowledgment of the interpersonal solidarity among human beings. He has thereby transcended the realm of seeing things only as a means to his own end. He has emerged for a moment from being absorbed in his own affairs; he has paid a tribute to me as a person. He has recognized me as living under the same human condition as he does, leading a life of labor and danger, a being in need of help. He has counteracted the tendency to "thingification" which that very labor and danger make more acute.

3. Gratitude and Thanking as Antidotes to Dehumanization. Thanking -- like other small acts of genuine kindness and politeness -- has a redeeming quality. In a social world, genuine acts of thanking are an antidote to dehumanization by a minimal, yet explicit, affirmation of what is truly human. Of course, there can be thanking which does not arise from real gratefulness. But even this, as a form of politeness, may have a value as a kind of lubricant for social relations. But where thanking appears as simply a means in the pursuit of my own concerns, where there is no quality of "looking up for a moment," no real turning to the other as person, it loses its character as an actualization of interpersonal solidarity. If thanking contains no element of recognition, however slight, of our human solidarity and of our being in need, it will probably assume an almost offensive character. Often, it is just a dread of this counterfeit which blocks the way to a belief in the genuine. But this very dread contains an indirect testimony that solidarity must be a part of the human world understood at its deeper level.

GRATITUDE AS GRATEFULNESS

[1] Receptivity. Appreciation. Antidote to Taking-For-Granted

Only a grateful person can be truly blessed with gifts because only a grateful person can really appreciate them.[2] Emmons and Hill tell us:

> The more grateful we are, the more reasons we have to be grateful. This knowledge can create a shift from gratitude as a response to gratitude as an attitude, as a receptive state that allows blessings to flow in.[3]

Gratefulness, or "gratitude as an attitude," counteracts the general human tend-envy to take things for granted, to make the goods of our life a mere matter of course. We often realize this tendency with a sharp, deep pain when we lose what we had taken for granted, for in our grief the regret that we have been ungrateful plays a great role. If we become blind, we feel that we have not sufficiently appreciated what a gift our eyesight was; or, if a beloved person dies, what a gift his presence was, although we may often have been annoyed with him. Grief and sorrow over the loss of great goods tend at least to show us the level of depth to which we should have gone to receive them adequately when they were given, that is, in gratitude. The ungrateful matter-of-fact attitude to the significant gifts we receive in our life has a stifling general effect. Gratefulness, in its capacity as an antidote to the tendency to take things for granted, proves its deep significance in enriching human life.

Gratefulness Opens Our Eyes. Just as we can stand in the middle of a world full of bright colors with our eyes closed so, too, we can stand in the middle of a

---

[2] See Balduin Schwarz, "The Healing Power of Gratitude" in Stephen Schwarz and Fritz Wenisch (eds.), *Values and Human Experience: Essays in Honor of the Memory of Balduin Schwarz* (New York: Peter Lang, 1999) pp. 15-23. See also "Transcendent Gratitude," pp. 25-26.

[3] Emmons and Hill, p.19.

world full of beautiful gifts offered to us that can make us deeply happy and yet not notice them because we are spiritually blind. Gratefulness frees us from such blindness.

Gratefulness reveals itself as most important through its fruitful contact with reality. Its opening-up power can be seen when we consider its negative counterparts. The ungrateful, envious, complaining person shuts himself off from what he receives. He cripples himself. He is focused on what he has not, particularly on what someone else has or seems to have, and by that he tends to poison his world, and thereby poisons himself. In gratefulness, I come to *appreciate* what I have received. In envy, I have my eyes on what another has received and blind myself to what I have received.

Gratefulness Awakens the Heart. We must distinguish between a quick "thank you," not ungenuine but not fully thought out, not invalid but lacking the full measure of real gratitude -- and the gratitude that really comes from the heart, that is "thought through," that is affirmed from the depth of one's being, that is fully conscious and articulate. This fullness of gratitude awakens our heart in manifold ways: humility, reverence, love, and many other responses of the heart. The word "heart" is taken here in its classic sense, as the core of the person. Gratitude is the voice of the heart, in which a person actualizes his ultimate status as a person, namely that his being transcends itself, that the meaning of his life lies beyond the confines of his individual self; and that his life falls into meaninglessness if he tries to find its meaning in itself.

Gratefulness places me at the point where I am able to receive fully. It is the fertile ground in which the reverent recognition, the real "receiving" with its aspects of humility, becomes actualized. Gratitude as a *response* follows the receiving; gratefulness as a *disposition* precedes and intermingles with the receiving. Gratefulness, together with reverence, are anticipatory attitudes preparing the way for a fruitful contact with the beneficial goods I receive and become elements in the joy of receiving. Thus, gratefulness is the underlying attitude which alone places me in a position to receive a gift. It is a basic orientation of the person, actualized and carried out by the will, a commitment of the whole person. It includes being awake and ready for obstacles that may come in the way of responding in gratitude (such as complaining). Gratefulness as a disposition, the readiness to respond in gratitude, belongs to the sphere of virtues as lasting characteristics of the person, the dimension of *being*.

The Upright Cup. "Our soul is like a cup: if it stands upright, it can be filled; but if it lies on its side, our soul will receive nothing even if it is pouring rain!" That is, only the soul that is opened through gratefulness can be enriched by gifts. Through gratefulness, I hold onto the gifts I have received. I remain awake to them. Gratefulness is a form of remembering. *Gratitude is the way the heart remembers.*

[2] Antidote to Sadness

If sadness comes over me because I have lost, or are about to lose, a precious gift, I can turn to gratefulness for that gift as an antidote to the sadness. That is, instead of the negative response of sadness at what I don't have, I can focus in *positive gratefulness* on the gift I *did* have. For example, a beautiful time with a beloved person is about to end. My first reaction is sadness at what I am about to lose. But I can go to a deeper level and be grateful that I *had* this beautiful time, grateful that I *had* and *still have*, this beloved person in my life. If death separates us, I will of course be saddened, I will grieve the loss. But I can redeem the sadness and grief through gratefulness. I can accentuate the positive: gratefulness that I *had* this person in my life, gratefulness for his love, gratefulness for the many beautiful times we had together.

[3] Antidote to Wrong Attitudes. A Protection against Vices

Gratefulness is something simple and unpretentious, and a person who is truly grateful will himself become true and genuine, simple, and unpretentious. He will leave behind him for a moment everything which is distorted or repressed in him. One cannot, at one and the same time, be both cynical and grateful; or sly, crafty, cunning and grateful; or deceitful, fraudulent and grateful. These vices may return, they may even come to dominate a person; but in the moment of true gratitude, they cannot be present. In such a moment a person becomes truly genuine, simple, and unpretentious like a child.

Gratefulness cannot be combined with envy, which resents what another person possesses. Gratefulness is diametrically opposed to envy since it leads me to rejoice with the other person because of what he has received. Such an attitude is also an inner liberation. In fact, there are a number of attitudes that are incompatible with gratefulness, that cannot coexist with it in the soul at the same time. They are: envy, greed, mistrust, complaining and murmuring, resentment, hateful anger, self-centeredness as manifested in pride, conceit and vanity. Emmons and Hill say the same thing:

> Focusing on the gifts one has been given is an antidote to envy, resentment, regret, and other negative states that undermine long-term happiness.[4]

The Power of Conversion in Gratefulness. Gratefulness has a power of conversion, for it dissolves our self-centeredness, it leads us out of selfishness, greed, and the pursuit of immediate pleasure. Gratefulness is also a fruit and sign of conversion.

[4] A Healing Power that gives us Peace

Gratefulness as the opposite of pride is experienced as peace. Pride means being inwardly torn in self-alienation, since it means a denial of a basic truth about ourselves: that we are receptive beings, called to be grateful for what we are and for what we have. Pride is a loss of peace; gratefulness is the key to peace.

When assailed by envy or self-pity, we may turn inwardly to a recognition of the good things we have received, the many gifts in life, and find again the "place of peace." In this power of gratefulness to bring us back to ourselves, to liberate us when destructive forces are at work in us, the deep spiritual power of gratefulness becomes apparent.

---

[4] *Ibid.*, p.69.

[5] A Healing Power that Gives us Humility

In being grateful, we recognize that our essence includes not only acting but also receiving. *The human person is essentially a being who receives, who is and lives by what he receives.* Gratefulness is an awakened, deep acknowledgment of our essence as beings who receive. It includes a "lived" readiness to believe in love. And by being grateful, this belief in love proves itself, since gratefulness makes us capable of seeing a gift as what it really is and seeing the love that is manifested in it. Gratefulness is also vital for each of us if we are to understand ourselves; for gratefulness sees, and fully affirms, our basic dependency, our need to receive all that which we cannot provide for ourselves. Gratefulness is to life what the keel is to the ship: it provides a steady course. It acknowledges the ultimate importance of the world of interpersonal relations, the world in which we exist essentially as persons.

[6] Overcoming our Notion of Entitlement

Many people assume they have "a right" to all sorts of different things that would make life easier and more enjoyable; that these things are somehow "owed" to them, that they are "entitled" to them. A better attitude is gratefulness, seeing everything good as a gift which calls for appreciation. Brother David Steindl-Rast calls our attention to this:

> The most harmful form of pride is our contemporary notion of entitlement. By considering every gift as ours by right, we set no limits to our wants, impoverishing our lives in the midst of abundance. Nothing causes content but gratitude.[5]

[7] Gratefulness and Wonder

Two attitudes stand in sharp contrast to taking things for granted in an habitual, routine way: *wonder* and *gratefulness*, and these are intimately bound to-

---

[5] Brother David Steindl-Rast, "Introduction" in Emmons and Hill, p. 9.

gether. Wonder is an essential element in our being grateful for the gifts received in our lives. The world, all of reality, is something so incredibly marvelous, and worthy of wonder, that if we do not wonder at it, we have not really seen it as it is. Wonder opens up our dialogue with reality; or rather takes it up and continues it, since reality has already spoken the first word in addressing us as persons. To have this dialogue, we must open ourselves inwardly to what is given to us, cooperate with it, bring it to completion in ourselves, and work together with it; we must even become co-creative with it, "recreating" it in ourselves, as when we become "co-poetic" in order to really appreciate a work of poetry. This dialogue sets into motion an *active receptivity*. So it is with all things that, in themselves, have the capacity to move us, to touch us, to affect us deeply: they cannot do so unless there is this active receptivity, in which we become co-creative with the object.

[8] The Social Benefits of Gratitude

There is in all forms of gratitude -- in the inner response of gratitude, in the outer act of conveying it to others and in the basic attitude of gratefulness -- a power to change us, not only as individuals but also in our being together as persons joined by the bonds of friendship and family. A home in which grateful appreciation reigns, and replaces complaining and arguing, will be a happy home, a peaceful home. Emmons and Hill:

> The experience of gratitude, and the actions stimulated by it, also build and strengthen social bonds and friendships. Encouraging people to focus on the benefits they have received from others leads them to feel loved and cared for, and perceived social support is vital to physical and psychological health.[6]

---

[6] Emmons and Hill, p. 69.

[9] The Psychological Benefits of Gratefulness

Psychologist Robert Emmons has done extensive research in this area. He and Joanna Hill report that people whom they studied who practiced gratefulness

> felt better about their lives as a whole, they felt more alive and energetic and they were more optimistic concerning the upcoming week. They reported fewer physical complaints and spent more time exercising...[They] reported higher levels of alertness and energy compared to those focusing on hassles...[They] were also more likely to report helping someone with a personal problem or offering emotional support to another, suggesting that positive social behavior is a consequence of being grateful. Not only did they feel good, they also did good.[7]

[4] TRANSCENDENT GRATITUDE

Gratitude where there is no Human Person to turn to. We have seen that there is a correspondence between the loving intention of another human being towards me and the spontaneous feeling of gratitude in me. But then, how are we to interpret the feeling of tremendous gratitude -- not only gratefulness -- that arises spontaneously in me, in situations where a great good is given to me but no human being has given it to me? A soldier returns to his wife who had given up all hope of ever seeing him again. Here a great evil has been averted, the life of a beloved person has been saved. The response of deep joy is like a light leaping up. There is a deep correspondence between the joy and the event. But there is another quality intermingled with the joy. The person who receives this great good feels an impulse to do something: to have gratitude, to give thanks. There is no human being to whom he can turn. Even where there is someone who has played some role in bringing about this great good, the person will still feel that his obligation to be grateful has not been fulfilled when he has thanked this person.

---

[7] *Ibid.*, p. 65.

Gratitude to God. People who believe in God can turn to Him at such a time and thank Him. But even people who usually do not think of God may nevertheless, in such moments, turn to God to thank Him. Chesterton writes: *Rossetti makes the remark somewhere, bitterly but with great truth, that the worst moment for an atheist is when he is really thankful but has nobody to thank.*[8] Is gratitude to God meaningful? Can such gratitude be a way of seeking God? Of finding God? Wonder!

---

[8] G. K. Chesterton, *St. Francis of Assisi* (London: Tavistock, 1957), p. 88.

CHAPTER 23
LOYALTY

IS LOYALTY ALWAYS A GOOD?

Wonder: is loyalty always a positive, a good, a moral virtue? We often praise loyalty and assume it is a good thing. Isn't part of this that disloyalty is something we shun as ugly and evil? But does it follow that all loyalty is good? Consider:

The Nazis demanded loyalty from their followers. Surely such a loyalty was not a good thing but an evil. So perhaps we need to ask: *loyalty to whom and loyalty to what?*

I am loyal to my mother and take care of her needs as she gets older. I am loyal to her because I love her and she loves me and took care of me when I was young. Loyalty here is good because it is the right response to another person. Thus isn't loyalty relational: good or bad depending on its relation to its object? *What are you loyal to?* Isn't that the all-important question?

Gratitude is intrinsically good, good in its very nature, by its very essence. The example of the Nazis shows that this does not apply to loyalty. Loyalty as such or loyalty alone does not yet contain the moral goodness we tend to attribute to it. We must look beyond it to its object. *What is loyalty directed to?*

WHERE LOYALTY IS GOOD AND NECESSARY

The ability to be loyal is surely a good thing. But it is only preparatory. To be really good it must be applied in the proper way, where it is the right response, the deserved response.

Consider cases where loyalty is surely a good. Loyalty to friends and family is basically a great good, necessary for friendships and community and sometimes even for survival.

"For the survivors of the Bataan Death March [in World War II Pacific Theater] loyalties made the difference between living and dying."[1]

"A loyal pair of buddies acted as a unit. The men in these partnerships provided each other something even more important than protection from the predations of fellow prisoners. They gave emotional support essential in an environment where going into a funk was lethal."[2]

"Loyalty is more than just a matter of working together. Loyalty is about being reliable. Sometimes that helps a group effort, but it can also empower individuals. Sure, we can do more when working together. But I can also accomplish more by myself if I know I've got someone watching my back." Loyalty is a bit like walking the tightrope. "Loyalty is what makes us hold the net taut for our friends. Even if they never need us to catch them, our friends are empowered by the knowledge that we're there."[3] Isn't that a large part of what loyalty is all about?

Wonder: why do we see loyalty as basically a good, a vital good? Perhaps because it is part of the very fabric of human relations: *we need to stick together.* The loyal person does that, the disloyal person walks away and thereby betrays his friends; he becomes a traitor and there is hardly anyone we loathe more than a traitor. A traitor is one who stabs you in the back.

WHERE LOYALTY IS NOT A GOOD THING

But is loyalty always a good thing? Hitler demanded loyalty from his supporters; surely such loyalty was not a good thing. Wasn't such loyalty really a vice? Once again, we see that loyalty is relational: good or bad all depending on its relation to its object. *What are you loyal to?* That is the all-important question.

---

[1] Eric Felten, *Loyalty: the Vexing Virtue*, (New York: Simon and Schuster, 2011), 17.

[2] Ibid., 19.

[3] Ibid., 22-23.

Chapter 23: Loyalty

Wonder: we praise loyalty as a good; then realize it is not always a good. Doesn't this mean that loyalty is not as such a good because we must always ask *loyalty to what?* It is only the right kind of loyalty that is good, that is a good in itself and good as such.

Wonder: loyalty is not always a good. And yet its opposite, betrayal, is also not a good. Isn't betrayal universally condemned as an evil? Isn't even the criminal who betrays his friends seen as evil? Or does it depend on why he betrays them? If he turns them in so that the evil they have been doing stops, isn't that a good thing? But then we wouldn't call that betrayal. We would call it loyalty to a higher calling: doing the right thing.

Does this mean that betrayal is not the only opposite of loyalty? And that being disloyal is not the only way of not being loyal? Refusing loyalty to evil is not disloyalty or betrayal.

WHERE LOYALTY IS A MIXED BAG

Mixed bag: on the one hand loyalty has a basically positive quality. We admire it and we loathe disloyalty. On the other hand, we don't admire loyalty to the Nazis. So, it isn't just loyalty that we admire; it must be loyalty properly directed, to something that deserves it.

Mixed bag: we don't always admire loyalty; yet we never seem to admire disloyalty or betrayal. A person starts out being loyal to the Nazis. Then he sees the light and quits. The Nazis call it being disloyalty and a betrayal; perhaps from their evil point of view it is. But in a deeper and truer sense it is not at all betrayal but rather true loyalty: to truth and goodness. Perhaps pulling away from evil is not disloyalty or betrayal but rather honorable and called for.

Mixed bag: consider loyalty in the military. On the one hand it is a great good, one of crucial importance. Eric Felton, author of *Loyalty: the Vexing Virtue*, notes that group loyalty is far more important than leadership:

> A unit with a fine officer but in which the men had no commitment to one another was a bust. A platoon made up of pals from

some small town could fight effectively even if burdened with a lousy commander.[4]

Above all there is the loyalty of never leaving a fallen comrade behind.

On the other hand, loyalty in the military is not always a good thing. Consider: "soldiers' loyalty to one another can lead them to cover up for a comrade who commits war crimes."[5]

WHERE LOYALTY MEANS CONFLICTS

Conflicts: loyalty sometimes leads to conflicts. Consider some examples:

I have two friends and they have a falling out; they won't talk to each other. By being loyal to one friend I become disloyal to the other. It is so painful to have to choose sides.

Then there is the conflict between friendship and principle. My friend is about to walk away from one of his commitments. He asks for my support. To say *yes* to my friend is to say *no* to a moral principle; to say *yes* to the moral principle is to say *no* to my friend.

My country asks loyalty of me. In normal times I gladly give it. But now it is embarked on an unjust war. I cannot support this war and I cannot join those who support my country in fighting this war. Am I disloyal? Perhaps I am. But am I a traitor? Don't we want to say *no* because being a traitor is a bad thing and refusing to fight in an unjust war is a good thing?

Wonder: we seem to identify being disloyal and being a traitor. And yet in this case being disloyal is a good thing. If being a traitor remains a bad thing while disloyalty here is a good thing then being disloyal is not identical to being a traitor. A traitor is one who is disloyal when loyalty is called for. Evil attaches to being a traitor in way that it doesn't to disloyalty.

---

[4] Ibid., 24.

[5] Ibid., 10.

LOYALTY AND MORALITY

Wonder: is loyalty when it is good always a moral good? I'm in the military and I stay loyal to my buddies. Mainly this is because loyalty is the right response; I owe them my loyalty. But it is also a great benefit to me; without my buddies I would not survive. A lack of loyalty is both a moral failure and foolishness. Loyalty then has both a moral value and a non-moral value.

An important distinction: loyalty as a *moral* value and as a *practical* value. As a moral value loyalty is the response called for. You are my friend: I owe you my loyalty; I promise it to you and you can expect it of me. As a practical value loyalty is seen in the example of soldiers who must stick together to survive. Failure in loyalty as a moral value is a moral vice; failure in loyalty as a practical value is foolishness.

Wonder: is not being loyal the same as betrayal? All betrayal is not being loyal but is all not being loyal a betrayal? If I'm not loyal to a stranger that hardly counts as betrayal. Betrayal requires that I *owe* the person my loyalty. I can betray a friend or my spouse because loyalty is what I owe them. I shop at a small food store for many years; they know me as a loyal customer. Then I switch to another store. Have I become disloyal to the first store? Is not being loyal the same as being disloyal?

What we seem to have: not being loyal, being disloyal and betrayal; how are they related? If I betray, I am not being loyal but if I'm not loyal I don't necessarily betray, as in switching to another store. But disloyalty and betrayal do seem to go together. If I'm disloyal I betray, and if I betray I'm being disloyal. But they are not the same. Betrayal is a personal act at a particular time while being disloyal is a state that a person is in and stays in for a certain time. They are related in that betrayal leads to disloyalty. Are there also other things that lead to disloyalty?

Not being loyal is not the same thing as being disloyal. If I am disloyal, I am not being loyal but not being loyal does not mean I am disloyal. I am not loyal to a person I'm not married to but that is not a case of being disloyal. Being disloyal only applies where loyalty is called for.

LOYALTY: SOME MAIN POINTS

Where does this leave us? We can't simply say that loyalty is always good; as we saw loyalty to the Nazis it is not good. Let us bring together some main points:

1. Loyalty has a flavor of goodness about it. This comes out especially when we contrast it to its antithesis, disloyalty as betrayal of a friend or one's country.
2. Loyalty to friends and country is generally and basically a good.
3. Loyalty to friends in their doing evil is not a good. Loyalty is sometimes invoked as an excuse to stay with friends to cover their bad behavior. This is not a genuine loyalty.
4. Extricating yourself from an evil that you have been loyal to is not disloyalty. Thus:
5. Pulling away from friends in their doing evil is not disloyalty but good and necessary (though it may be painful). Isn't it actually loyalty to a higher calling?

What about the inner ability to be loyal? Some people do not seem to have this inner ability regardless of what it is directed to, good or evil. Is the inner ability to be loyal a good before one looks at what it is directed to? Wonder!

Let us look at someone who does not seem to be capable of loyalty to anything, neither good nor evil? This person simply lacks the entire virtue of loyalty to anything. Is that good?

Now let us look at the person who is capable of being loyal, has the inner capacity, but does not have the ability to discern what he should be loyal to. He is easily swayed, due to lack of intelligence or lack of prudence, to be loyal to whatever comes his way. Is this bad? What exactly is bad? Is it the inner ability to be loyal or the lack of clarity of what is deserving of that inner ability?

Surely, we do not want to be, or be friends with, or rely upon, a person who is internally incapable of loyalty. But we also do not want to be capable of misdirected loyalty.

Chapter 23: Loyalty 413

Which is worse? No capacity for loyalty or a strong capacity for misdirected loyalty? Of course, we all want the capacity of properly directed loyalty in ourselves and others.

If so, wonder at how we can safeguard the direction of our loyalty to the good rather than to evil?

CHAPTER 24
HONESTY & HUMILITY

ONE: BASIC HONESTY

Bertocci and Millard hold that "there is one virtue that nourishes all the other virtues and all values of life. It is the will to become honest."[1] It is summarized in the familiar phrases "Face Reality" and "Know Thyself." To have the virtue of honesty is to have the willingness, the deep and intense desire, to know the truth as fully and as accurately as possible about all that is relevant to oneself and to one's situation. Honesty is deeply and meaningfully related to reverence; the truly reverent person will be honest, and the honest person manifests an important aspect of reverence. If this is the case, then honesty is a cause for wonder. Why do we care so deeply about honesty? Both in ourselves and in others? One might say that honesty as understood here is the truth dimension of reverence. It means to be reverent before truth, in one's relation to truth. Why does this matter?

TWO: HONESTY IN THE POPULAR SENSE

Here honesty refers to not lying, not cheating and closely related notions, a vast topic that we unfortunately cannot pursue fully here. But one thing might be mentioned, as it is both instructive and revealing of the core idea of honesty in this sense. If, in buying something or in some other business exchange, a mistake is made that goes against me, I will naturally call it to the attention of the other person. But suppose the mistake is in my favor. Do I have the same desire to see that the mistake is rectified as I do when it goes against me? If I have the virtue of honesty the answer will be yes. Is this in fact a mark, a test of honesty? Does honesty have to go both ways, be a two-way street in our lives? Or not?

---

[1] Bertocci and Millard, *Ibid.,* p.382

THREE: HONESTY AS THE ANTITHESIS TO SELF-DECEPTION

There is a third dimension of honesty to which we now turn, namely honesty as the virtue of being free of the vice of self-deception. David Jones offers an analysis of this vice in the context of persons in Nazi Germany who evaded their responsibility for helping victims of Nazi atrocities, those who did so through the practice of self-deception. But might his analysis apply universally to all of us, in whatever situation we might be in? Is self-deception a pervasive human danger? Do we encounter it in ourselves? Can it be seen by ourselves? Or is its imperceptibility part of its very essence? This is a source of wonder, that we can perhaps not see things as the one who sees!

"How could it have happened?" we ask as we contemplate the horror of the Nazi Holocaust, the murder of six million Jews and many, many, others, the horrific conditions at camps, and much, much more. How could it have happened? The answers are complex, many-sided, and not easy to dig out. But one aspect is that ordinary people often did apparently nothing to stop it, or too little. Why? In large part because of fear, but also an aspect of self-deception. They "looked the other way," and so they didn't see. They were "ignorant," but it was the willful ignorance of self-deception. How can normally good and honest people choose self-deception? Is it willfully chosen? Is it something we slide into unawares?

How did this self-deception possibly work? Let us examine Jones' analysis. He explains it in terms of the Nazi program of exterminating Jews. As we read it, let us put a blank where their program is mentioned and fill it in with the kinds of things that apply to us, in our lives, where we might be inclined to fall into self-deception. To think, "I would not have practiced *this* kind of self-deception," as Jones describes it, is not enough. Even if true, there may be other kinds of self-deception or applications of it that I might practice, or actually have practiced. What can we learn from Jones' analysis for our own lives? For our own life is an immediate source of wonder!

Self-deception is basically a kind of evasion. It means evading, or trying to evade, the realization or acknowledgement of some truth which would be painful, unpleasant, or burdensome. The truth, or its possibility, is dimly perceived but

Chapter 24: Honesty & Humility

not fully acknowledged. People who engage in self-deception employ a variety of tactics. Jones explains:

> People whose goal is to *evade the full acknowledgment* of...the belief that the Jews are being exterminated, engage in one or more of a variety of tactics of self-deception. They may (1) avoid thinking explicitly about Jews facing death or being killed; (2) distract themselves with rationalizations, such as thoughts that the Jews are safe and working somewhere in the "East"; (3) evade belief...[that the Jews are being exterminated] by systematically failing to make any inquiries, distracting their attention from and ignoring available evidence (such as the trainloads of used clothing); (4) block appropriate emotional responses such as horror, sorrow, and indignation and assume an attitude of indifference....
>
> A sustained project of evasion of this kind results in a state of self-deception that is best characterized as *willful ignorance*. It is "willful" because the state of ignorance is not an accident but is a goal that is purposefully and intentionally sought; once it is achieved, it is assiduously maintained and protected. The person is motivated by a desire not to know or find out the truth of the matter.[2]

Can self-deception be tied to a lack of courage? To fear? Lack of courage may be a major factor leading to self-deception as Jones explains that some people (probably many),

> engaged in self-deception because they anticipated that even if they knew that the Jews are being exterminated, they would not have the courage to help. Since they had a strong desire to keep their self-respect and avoid feeling guilty and ashamed of themselves, they

---

[2] David H. Jones, *Ibid.*, p. 82. In this and in the next passage, I have made a small editorial change: where Jones uses "J" to designate the proposition "the Jews are being exterminated" I have used the full text.

were likely to find it very easy to avoid reaching the conclusion that the Jews are being exterminated.[3]

Do people explicitly decide to practice self-deception? Jones thinks not exactly:

"There is...very little (if any) premeditation in, for example, the choice not to pay attention to some piece of evidence pointing to the ongoing extermination of a group of people. Nonetheless, one is aware at the moment of shifting attention from the disturbing facts to someone else.[4]

Do you agree with this assessment, that a person who engages in a project of self-deception is somehow aware of it, sometimes more, sometimes less? This idea is brought out in a striking way in the testimony of Albert Speer, a high official in Nazi Germany.

He describes his response to a warning from a close friend to never visit a certain concentration camp in lower Silesia (he was alluding to Auschwitz) because he had seen something there that was to be kept secret and was indescribable:[5]

I did not query him, I did not query Himmler, I did not query Hitler, I did not speak with personal friends. I did not investigate--for I did not want to know what was happening there...From that moment on, I was inescapably contaminated morally; from fear of discovering something which might have made me turn from my course, I had closed my eyes. This deliberate blindness outweighs whatever good I may have done or tried to do in the last period of the war.[6]

---

[3] *Ibid.*, p. 83.

[4] *Ibid.*, p. 84.

[5] *Ibid.*, pp. 92-93.

[6] Albert Speer, *Inside the Third Reich* (New York: Macmillan, 1970), p. 447. Quoted in Jones, p. 93.

Does to be truly conscientious and honest include asking oneself: *Is there an area in my life where I have practiced self-deception? Or where I might have practiced it?* Are we required to try to answer these questions with a view towards truth? Can we ever rightly choose "how it really is," or "how can I protect myself?" These matters are a cause for deep consideration and wonder.

Honesty appears to be a multicultural and universal value throughout human time and place, and generally considered to be a virtue. One might wonder if honesty is a necessary factor in the rise of culture? Can human community exist without some accepted degree of honesty? Take time to wonder at the importance of honesty both in the world in general and in your own life specifically!

HUMILITY, The Misunderstood Virtue

The virtue of humility is often confused with other concepts which it is not, therefore let us begin with a clear definition and then look at the misunderstandings with which it is associated. To have the virtue of humility is to have the character trait that disposes a person to be receptive to other persons, to new things, to be ready to acknowledge one's mistakes and faults, and to be modest. It is the virtue that stands in opposition to pride as self-glorification, vanity, the relishing of power, and haughtiness. In contrast to forgiveness and gratitude which are outward directed, humility refers to a proper relation to one's own person.

THREE ASPECTS OF HUMILITY

One: Receptivity. The humble person is ready to receive, to appreciate what he receives, to receive gratefully. He thereby acknowledges that he is not self-sufficient, that he is receptive in his being. A humble person is receptive in that he is open to being told something by another, even if it is unpleasant. He is open to learning something new, he is open to change. All of this is opposed to the "I know it all" attitude of pride. Wonder at how difficult this can be at times!

Two: Readiness to Acknowledge one's mistakes/faults, and to Ask for Forgiveness. Our natural tendency is self-defense, to defend the correctness of our ideas and the moral rightness of our actions. Humility means a readiness to drop this self-defense mechanism when necessary, a readiness to acknowledge "I was wrong"; both in the sense of mistaken and in the moral sense, I did something wrong. Humility is only a readiness; it allows us to see clearly but does not in itself determine whether we are actually right or wrong (correct/incorrect; morally right/wrong). To have humility is to have the same objectivity in our own case that we would naturally have towards another person. Wonder again at why this is so difficult for most of us!

Humility means not only a readiness to acknowledge what is the case, in mind and in heart but also a readiness to act: to ask for forgiveness. Recall the beautiful example of Zossima kneeling before his servant Afanasi to ask him for forgiveness. Few things testify as vividly to the character and to the beauty of humility as an act of genuine asking for forgiveness. Once again, wonder at how painfully difficult this can be. Why is humility difficult?

Three: Modesty, being unassuming. Humility also means recognizing my limitations, not boasting about myself, not wanting to be "center stage"; it includes the readiness to step aside in favor of someone else where appropriate. (This is not to be confused with false modesty, stepping aside when you ought not, when not appropriate.) Wonder at the difficulty of seeing one's self clearly!

Humility is Truth. It is often said that *humility is truth*. It is of course not the whole of truth, but it is an important part of it. If I have really made a mistake or I'm mistaken in my judgment, to recognize this is to recognize the truth, as it really is. If humility is what frees me to do this, is humility an aspect of true freedom? Wonder! It seems that I need humility to recognize the truth when it pertains to *my* mistakes; but I don't need it to recognize the truth about the mistakes of others. Why is that?! How does humility free me to recognize the truth about my own moral faults and failings and to respond to them adequately? Humility as truth is evident also when I recognize my gifts *as gifts*, that I have received through nature and nurture certain abilities and can take no credit for them, only for cooperating with them perhaps. Wonder!

Humility is Strength. It is most important to emphasize that humility is strength. Many people see it as weakness; it is in fact the very opposite of weakness. It is the inner strength to face reality and acknowledge that I made a mistake, that I did something wrong. It is weak and easy to evade these things, to blame others, to make excuses, to be in denial. It is these evasions which are weakness. It takes an inner strength to overcome them, the strength of humility. In a similar way, it takes strength, the inner strength of humility to acknowledge my dependence on others, that I am essentially a receiving being, not self-sufficient, as I like to think of myself.

What Humility is not. The virtue of humility should be carefully distinguished from false self-relations. Humility emphatically does not mean the weakness of servility, "letting people walk all over you," being overly submissive, having no "backbone." On the contrary, as was already stressed, ***humility is strength***! It is the strength to be "big enough" to acknowledge one's mistakes and faults. Pride is very pervasive in human nature; it takes strength to stand up to it and resist it. Humility is fully compatible with genuine self-respect, self-esteem, self-confidence, happiness at being praised, happiness in success, and with a recognition of one's gifts. Humility recognizes one's own gifts: it recognizes them *as* gifts and manifests itself especially in gratitude for them.

PRIDE AS OPPOSITE HUMILITY

The Core of Pride: Self-glorification. Let us turn to an examination of pride as the opposite of humility. At the core of pride is self-glorification, especially in comparison with others. Humility tries to avoid self-glorification and focuses instead on the value of objects outside of us; it avoids comparisons with others intended to glorify the self. I suggest there are at least three main forms of pride:

One: Vanity-Competitive pride. A vain person wants to be praised and admired by others. He wants to stand high above others. He wants to receive the admiring glances of others in order to be lifted up in their eyes. Their praise produces its effect in him: self-glorification. Vanity is a relation of a person to himself with reference to others. It is a relation to oneself as seen and admired, perhaps envied, by others. Why do we dislike pride in others but often hang on to it in ourselves? This discrepancy is a cause for wonder at the complexity of the human person.

Vanity goes in two directions, *being* and *having*. In both, we see the competitive dimension of pride as vanity. If I am vain, I want to be seen <u>in the eyes of others</u> as intelligent, skilled, morally good, witty, industrious, etc. I want to glory in being something excellent to others, not just within myself as such. Furthermore, my self-glory is not simply in being as such to others, but in *being better and having more than others*. And when it comes to having, my self-glory is not simply in having, but in *having more*, in having more than others. Again, we see the reference to others. The vanity of being and of having is a form of competition. Why is this the case?

Not all competition of course is vain. There is the legitimate competition of games, sports and the marketplace. But there is also this vanity of competitive pride. C. S. Lewis describes it well:

> The point is that each person's pride is in competition with every one else's pride. It is because I wanted to be the big noise at the party that I am so annoyed at someone else being the big noise....Pride is *essentially* competitive -- it is competitive by its very nature....Pride gets no pleasure out of having something, only out of having more of it than the next man. We say that people are proud of being rich, or clever, or good-looking, but they are not. They are proud of being richer, or cleverer, or better-looking than others. If every one else became equally rich, or clever, or good looking there would be nothing to be proud about. It is the comparison that makes you proud: the pleasure of being above the rest. Once the element of competition has gone, pride has gone.[7]

C. S. Lewis compares pride to greed.

> Greed may drive men into competition if there is not enough to go round; but the proud man, even when he has got more than he can possibly want, will try to get still more just to assert his

---

[7] *Mere Christianity* (New York: Macmillan, 1960), pp. 109-110.

power. Nearly all those evils in the world which people put down to greed or selfishness are really far more the result of Pride. Take it with money. Greed will certainly make a man want money, for the sake of a better house, better holidays, better things to eat and drink. But only up to a point. What is it that makes a man with 10,000 pounds a year anxious to get 20,000 pounds a year? It is not the greed for more pleasure. 10,000 pounds will give all the luxuries that any man can really enjoy. It is Pride -- the wish to be richer than some other rich man.[8]

Two: Power. There is a morally valid form of power, namely in the proper exercise of legitimate authority. In human affairs, it is often the case that someone is required to have authority. Adopting the role of authority, of parent, teacher, political leader, can and should be done however in a spirit of humility. The office and its responsibility can and should be seen as something entrusted, for which one is accountable. It can be seen as an occasion for promoting good, especially in matters of justice.

But obviously power appeals to us also as something subjectively satisfying; it feels good. Does it then constitute pride as power? Again, in inappropriate power there is the focus on self, the self-centeredness, the self-glorification, this time in the form of exercising control. "*I am in control.*" Again, we find the reference to another person, or several other persons: "I am in control over you." Pride as power stands over the other person, not in being something great or in having great things in large quantities, but in controlling others, in having power over them. "I am over you because I control you." This inappropriate power may be physical, it may be psychological, it may involve both. It may be obvious, it may be subtle, hardly noticed. It can occur in the political arena, in businesses, in schools, in the home, between friends and family members. It finds its ultimate expression in violent crimes such as rape and murder. Wonder at when appropriate power slips over into inappropriate power! What is the tipping point? Can we know it in others? In ourselves?

C. S. Lewis, continuing the previously quoted passage, observes:

---

[8] *Ibid.*, p.110.

> It is Pride -- the wish to be richer than some other rich man, and (still more) the wish for power. For, of course, power is what pride really enjoys: there is nothing that makes a man feel so superior to others as being able to move them about like toy soldiers…What is it that makes a political leader…go on and on, demanding more and more? Pride again.[9]

Three: Haughtiness. Haughtiness resists admitting one's mistakes and faults, and even more, it resists asking for forgiveness. It also resists being grateful. Haughtiness is a way of "standing up high before others," and thus refusing "to come down," never admitting "I was wrong," in regard to mistakes, errors in judgment and moral failings, never admitting "I was dependent on others" and should now be grateful. Like all pride it is a self-glorification: "I'm too good to be wrong, or mistaken, or dependent on others." Like the other form of pride, it functions in reference to other people; there is an unwillingness to "bend down" because that would place me below the level of others.

There is much more to pride than these three main forms. Pride, or the tendency to it, is something usually deep-seated in all of us, mostly in ways that we do not realize, or even suspect. It manifests itself constantly in human relations, much to their detriment; heated arguments between people are only one, rather obvious, manifestation of it. Two other forms of pride should be mentioned: **conceit** and **arrogance**.

Our Mixed Character. All of us are partly proud and partly humble, in very complex mixtures and on different levels. Even a basically humble person has some elements of pride. Pride creeps into many of our responses. Usually we do not notice it; we are unaware of our own pride, mainly because of that very pride! We notice pride much more readily in others than in ourselves. C. S. Lewis says of pride: "There is no fault which makes a man more unpopular, and no fault which we are more unconscious of in ourselves. And the more we have it ourselves, the more we dislike it in others"[10]

---

[9] *Ibid.*

[10] *Ibid.*, p. 109.

What Pride is not. Pride should be carefully distinguished from the many valid, positive relations a person can and should have to himself. Let us consider five of them. The first three have to do directly with oneself:

(1) *Self-respect* is not pride. It is the proper response to your own intrinsic value and dignity as a person.

(2) *Self-esteem* is not pride. Liking yourself, being at peace within yourself is a proper response to yourself.

(3) *Self-confidence* is not pride. Proper self-confidence is good and necessary for all of us.

The other two have to do with high achievements in life:

(4) **Pleasure in being praised** is not pride. C. S. Lewis explains:

> The child who is patted on the back for doing a lesson well, the woman whose beauty is praised by her lover,...are pleased and ought to be. For here the pleasure lies not in what you are but in the fact that you have pleased someone you wanted (and rightly wanted) to please. The trouble begins when you pass from thinking, "I have pleased him; all is well," to thinking, "What a fine person I must be to have done it." The more you delight in yourself and the less you delight in the praise, the worse you are becoming.[11]

(5) **Happiness in being successful** is not pride. For example, to be happy at winning a game or a contest is not pride. It is a valid, legitimate response to a genuine accomplishment. It does not in itself imply or include self-glorification, though of course it may lead to it. But many things which are in themselves not vices may lead to vices. If I am successful at my work, if I write a book, or complete some important research, and I am

---

[11] *Ibid.*, p. 112. Italics added.

happy at such an accomplishment, I am not as such proud, though these things easily lead to pride. If I have a gift for something, artistic, literary, scientific, and then realize it, I am not as such proud. The recognition of gifts, and the accomplishments that stem from them, may easily be combined with the humble acknowledgment that these gifts are exactly that -- *gifts*. That is, I recognize that I have received something, I do not take credit for it, and I respond in gratitude for the gift. Pride results when I forget that the gift is a gift and take all credit for it myself, and glory in my having it and others not having it.

All five of these valid, positive relations a person has with himself differ radically from pride with its self-glorification and its odious comparison with others, wanting to stand above them. All of them fit perfectly with humility, with receiving, with being grateful, with acknowledging one's mistakes and faults and with asking for forgiveness.

Finally, in addition to the six points just considered, to say that I am proud of my son or daughter, or my school, or my team is not at all pride in the sense of a vice. It is in a way opposite to pride, for it is essentially a *positive response to another person*, or to something outside me. Pride means glorifying myself, while these are cases of "glorying" in someone else, or something else.

Both Honesty and Humility are sources of wonder within the human person! We see them as vitally important for myriad reasons in ourselves and in others, yet at the same time we find them difficult to maintain in ourselves while easily expecting them in others. These matters are all cause for both concern and wonder!

CHAPTER 25
WHY IS THERE SOMETHING AND NOT NOTHING?

[1] THE BASIC QUESTION AND THREE KEY POINTS

Why is there something and not nothing? Is this perhaps the deepest wonder question? We take the existence of the world, the things in it, other persons and ourselves for granted. But if we step back and wonder to ask ourselves this question, we will see that it is a truly remarkable thing that anything exists at all. To begin with, three key points should be noted:

First, there is the intended meaning of *nothing* in our question. By nothing is meant here something truly drastic: *nothing at all, absolutely nothing.* It is not easy to appreciate this in its full impact. We often say things like "there's nothing here" meaning there is nothing in this box. Or "there's nothing wrong with you" meaning you are in good health. But our question goes far beyond this, and so to speak asks us to imagine a state of affairs where *absolutely everything* is wiped off the map that is reality. We need to stop to contemplate this in order to try to get some intellectual grasp of it. Can we grasp it in our imagination?

When we think of *absolute nothingness,* we are likely to imagine empty space. But space, whether empty or filled, is *something*: it has physical characteristics, such as being curved. We probably can't really imagine absolute nothingness, but only try to grasp it by our intellect.

Second, the question *why is there something and not nothing* has two distinct dimensions, two essentially different parts, which are not usually distinguished:

1. **Why is there the vast physical universe?** Why are there the billions and billions of galaxies of stars and planets and other cosmic things; and not just nothing, nothing at all?

2. ***Why is there the world of human persons?*** That is, why is there the world of human literature, science, philosophy, other disciplines, art, music, all the things humans have made, history, political systems, friendships, marriages, schools, religious institutions and so much more? Why do these things exist rather than not exist? After all, there might have been just the physical universe; or absolutely nothing at all.

Third, when we ask our big *why* questions regarding the physical and the world of human persons, we may mean either:

1. Why is there something: what brought it into existence, what is its cause?
2. Why is there something: what is its reason for existing, or its purpose, or its meaning?
3. We will take up question #1 in this chapter and #2 in the remaining chapters.

[2] A SIMPLE AND COMMON EXAMPLE

To get a handle on the first of these points, that our question is why there is something in contrast to *absolutely nothing*, let us consider a simple and common example. That there should be nothing in the cupboard of my kitchen is not a remarkable thing; no one put anything there. But now imagine that there are a dozen plates, cups and saucers there. Why are they there? Simple: someone put them there. That is, there is some cause for them being there. Now let us branch out from the small, humble cupboard to bigger and bigger places and things. Why are there houses making up a little village on the vast plains, surrounded by areas with no houses? Again simple: some people built them there. Keep going in this way. Why are there things on planet earth? Here there is no simple and easy answer; but there is an answer, or rather a huge set of answers, all adding up to the causes for there being things on planet earth and why it is just those things. Next: why is there a planet earth at all, with the life-sustaining features it has?

Chapter 25: Why is There Something and Not Nothing?

Why are there any planets in our solar system? Why is there such a thing as our solar system? Why is there our galaxy, Milky Way? Why is there the huge number of galaxies out there? These questions should be understood as referring to our two distinct dimensions:

1. Why is there the vast physical universe?
2. Why is there the world of human persons?

[3] SCIENCE AND PHILOSOPHY

The first of these questions, about the physical universe, seems to call for an answer from natural science. But can natural science really answer this question? Why is there a physical universe at all? Can science answer that? Is it even a scientific question? Doesn't science have to start with the universe as a given? But here we are going beyond this given and questioning it. Must we not make a leap here to a different kind of question, one that goes beyond what science is equipped to deal with? Are we not dealing here with a *philosophical* question, perhaps the ultimate philosophical question and the ultimate wonder question?

[4] THE ROLE OF THE BIG BANG

To see how science and philosophy are related in these basic questions let us ask some more questions, wonder questions. Surely one important item here is the Big Bang. Where does the universe come from? The standard answer is the Big Bang, an original creative event that set the universe on its way, that is the Big Start for everything that exists today. Now, about the Big Bang we can ask two essentially different kinds of questions:

First, we can ask the kind of questions that science can answer, either providing an actual answer in terms of scientific theories and data, or an answer in principle, with actual answers perhaps coming in the future. For example, it can answer questions about what happened immediately after the Big Bang, how long it took for stars and planets to form, and so on.

Second, there are a very different set of questions. Science can take over so to speak *at* and *after* the Big Bang. But what about *before* the Big Bang? What was happening just before? Perhaps that question makes no sense: time came into being with the Big Bang; before that there was nothing, no physical matter, no space and no time. But are we not strongly inclined to ask what was the case before the Big Bang? For every other event, big and small, we feel the need and the meaningfulness of asking what came before it. In part this is in order to understand the event; what came before is generally part of the cause or reason why the event occurred at all.

The second kinds of questions are our questions, the *philosophical* as distinct from the *scientific* questions. The philosophical questions are by no means limited to asking what came before the Big Bang. In fact, since this question is problematic as we have seen, let us pursue a different set of philosophical wonder questions.

[5] PHILOSOPHICAL WONDER QUESTIONS ABOUT THE BIG BANG

One, just *how did the Big Bang lead to the world in its present state*? To appreciate the force of this question, contemplate the total amount of what exists here now and has existed for much of human history. This total reality is mind-boggling in its vastness. Just consider a small part of this: all of human literature, science, philosophy, all the other disciplines, art, music, all the things that have been made (pottery, houses, boats, cars, bicycles, beds, computers, books, cans of food), human history, political systems, friendships, marriages, contracts, schools, religious institutions – we are just scratching the surface, but hopefully we need not continue. The point is this: how does all of this vast reality relate to the Big Bang? Was it all contained in the material of the Big Bang in potency, on a vast scale, but essentially in the way an oak tree with its trunk, branches and leaves is contained in potency in the acorn? Somehow that seems hard to imagine, so much squeezed into so little. Were all the works of Shakespeare and Bach already in that tiny speck? But what is the alternative, that it was not contained in the material of the Big Bang in potency? But then where did it all come from? If it wasn't from *within* the universe it must have come in from the *outside*. What outside factor could that be?

Here it is important to recall that our question *why is there something and not nothing* has two distinct dimensions or two essentially different parts:

1. Why is there the vast physical universe, and not just nothing, nothing at all?
2. Why is there the world of human persons, the world of literature, science, philosophy, art, music, the things humans have made, rather than just the physical universe, or absolutely nothing at all?

The Big Bang seems to speak only to #1 and leaves #2 untouched. Mozart, a wonderful example in #2, is reported to have said that the music just flowed to him from somewhere beyond him, above him; and his task was simply to write it down, to try to keep up with the torrential flow of inspired beauty. If so what was that higher something, that source of musical beauty? And if it was somehow already within him, what explains that? On any account, the treasure that is the music of Mozart: why does it exist rather than not exist?

Two, why was there a Big Bang at all, *any Big Bang*? Why wasn't there rather just nothing, absolutely nothing that stayed at nothing? Are we now back to our original question? Have we made any progress at all by invoking the Big Bang? In one important way we have: we can now realize that appealing to the Big Bang does not end wonder; it does not "settle matters" by providing "answers" that end our quest for understanding. On the contrary it increases our sense of wonder by making it clearer to us how mysterious and "wonderful" reality actually is.

Three, why was there *the particular Big Bang* that actually occurred and not some other one? The actual Big Bang had the results that followed, a few of which we know, most of which we don't. But couldn't there have been a different Big Bang with very different results? Aren't there a vast number of possible Big Bangs that could have occurred instead of the one that actually did occur? Again, appeal to Big Bang does not stop the questions and the occasion for wonder; it amplifies them.

[6] THE APPEAL TO GOD

Where did it all come from, the vast *physical universe* and the vast reality that now exists as our world, the *world of human persons*? For both of these, if the sufficient reason cannot come from *within* the universe, it must have come from the *outside*. What outside factor could that be? Many people have an answer: God. Here too it remains to show that appeal to God, like appeal to the Big Bang, does not end the occasions for wonder but rather enhances them.

First, assuming God exists and is the answer we are looking for here we can ask: why did God create just this world and not another one? This question becomes perplexing when we conceive of God as all-good and all-powerful and then look at the enormous amount of evil and suffering in the world, human and animal. Why this world and not another with no suffering or significantly less?

Second, still assuming that God exists and provides the factor missing when appeal only to the Big Bang falls short, how exactly is this factor operative? Was it provided entirely at the Big Bang beginning? Or is it continuous, what is called Divine Providence, that God somehow rules over the world? If so, how is this rule related to natural causes? How is it related to human actions? This becomes a pressing problem when we consider evil and human freedom.

Third, not everyone accepts the "God answer" to this problem. It is sometimes asked: who created God? If the world needs a creative force beyond itself what accounts for that force? Doesn't appeal to God just push the problem one step further back without in any way solving it? The usual answer to this objection is that while the universe needs a sufficient reason for its existence beyond itself, since it might have not existed, this is not true of God: if He exists, He exists necessarily; it is not true that He might have not existed. It is part of His essence that He must exist. He "contains" within himself His own sufficient reason for existing.

If this answer is accepted, it calls for wonder. How amazing that a certain being doesn't simply exist, like this tree or that dog, but exists necessarily, so that He couldn't "not exist"! But some people will not accept this answer, or a "God answer" in any form; and this leads to some further points.

[7] THE DENIAL OF THE APPEAL TO GOD

If there is no God to supplement the Big Bang account then we are back to our original question: why does the universe exist at all, rather than not exist? What can those who deny God say at this point? Here are some suggestions that have been made:

1. The universe has no creator; there is nothing beyond the Big Bang. The universe has always existed. But isn't it hard to conceive a reality like the universe as always existing? If the universe has always existed, then time must have always existed. But isn't it hard to think of past time as infinite? But then isn't it also hard to think of past time as finite, as having a beginning? What came before that? We're not supposed to ask that, but somehow we always do. But let us waive these points. The most serious objection to the "always existed" answer for the universe is that it is an answer to the wrong question. It is not a matter of how long the universe has existed; let it be infinite time if you want. The question is why it exists, what is the sufficient reason for its existence, the cause of its existence. What factor explains why it exists rather than not existing? Adding time, no matter how much of it, does nothing to solve the why question, the need for a sufficient reason for the universe existing.
2. The universe has no creator; there is nothing beyond the Big Bang. It just popped into existence by itself, out of nowhere. But does anyone really take this answer seriously? If such an answer were proposed in any other context everyone with any degree of common sense would immediately reject it. Where did you get this money, what reason accounts for why you have it? Answer: it just popped into existence in my hand; it just came to me out of nowhere. Isn't this absolutely impossible? Why is the case of the universe any different?
3. The universe has no creator; there is nothing beyond the Big Bang to account for the universe. One way of trying to salvage a "no cause" or "no sufficient reason" answer is to claim that these terms apply only within the universe but not to the universe as such, to the universe as a whole. But apart from getting out of a jam to explain the reality of the universe, and to do so without an appeal to God, what is there to speak for such an answer? Isn't it just a way of evading the question instead of facing it squarely? A planet, a galaxy and what they contain: these all require a suf-

ficient reason; why do they exist rather than not existing? "The Universe" is simply all of these seen together. How could the shift from considering some of these to considering all of them change the need for a sufficient reason why they exist: some need it but all of them together don't need it?

If we do not accept the existence of God to account for why there is something rather than nothing; and if we reject the three proposals considered above, what can we say? What can an honest atheist say about the reason why there is a universe rather than nothing? Must there not be *something*, even if we don't know what it is? That is, something that accounts for the strange fact that we are here, that this magnificent and also terrible universe actually exists?

[8] GOD OR NO GOD: WONDER IN ANY CASE

No matter which way we turn, whether we accept God or reject God as the ultimate sufficient reason for why there is something and not nothing, we have occasions for wonder. In what follows the term *universe* should be understood as including both the *physical universe* and the total reality of what now exists as our world, the *world of human persons*:

- A universe without God? How can this be? Why then does it exist rather than not exist?
- A universe without God? How can this be? Could there be a sufficient reason other than God to account for why the universe exists? But perhaps part of the very meaning of the term God is "sufficient reason for the existence of the universe."
- A universe with God, created by God? How can this be? Why did God create just this universe and not another one?
- A universe with God, created by God? How can this be? Is His role only at the beginning or throughout the whole time that the universe has existed? Or is there perhaps some other alternative?
- A universe with God, created by God? How could God create something out of nothing? And yet, how else could the universe have come into being?

- A universe with God, created by God? What can we know about God other than that He is the one who created the universe, that He is the sufficient reason for its existing?
- A universe with God, created by God? Must God be a personal being in order to be the sufficient reason for the existence of human persons? It seems He cannot be less than a person, an impersonal being like a tree or a machine, if He is to be the creator of persons. But can we conceive God as personal without falling into the trap of making Him into our own image? We have no conception of a personal being other than human persons. God cannot be merely like a human person; yet He must somehow be a person. How?

[9] CONTINGENCY

Why is there something and not nothing? Why is there the vast physical universe? Why is there the vast world of human persons? Wonder about these questions arises because these realities are contingent realities: they exist but they might have not existed. The house you live in exists, but it might easily have not existed. It would not have existed if the builder had not built it. Something very noteworthy seems to follow from this. If there is to be a sufficient reason why there is something and not rather nothing, that sufficient reason cannot itself also be contingent. For if it is, the problem is just pushed one level further back: why does it exist rather than not exist? At some point must we not reach a necessary being, who doesn't simply happen to exist but must exist? A being who exists necessarily? Who has being and reality as part of its essence and nature? It is hard to imagine such a being, but if one denies that such a being exists, isn't the whole of reality -- the physical universe and the world of human persons – left hanging in the air? And isn't this a philosophically impossible situation? Whether this necessary being is "God" in any traditional sense is a further question. The point here is simply that the very question why there is something and not nothing assumes the contingency of this something and thereby points beyond itself to something radically new and different. It points to a being who exists necessarily, who exists of its own accord; and who is thereby the sufficient reason for the universe and the world of persons.

And why does this necessary being exist rather than not exist? Some of us may want to ask this question, to keep probing further and further into why realities exist rather than not exist. But is this question really meaningful? It seems to be asking for the sufficient reason why the necessary being exists, a sufficient reason outside itself. But it cannot have a sufficient reason for existing that is outside itself for if it did it would be dependent on that sufficient reason and thereby a dependent being. And dependent beings cannot be necessary beings; dependent beings must be contingent beings in that they might have not existed and would in fact not have existed if their sufficient reason didn't exist. Doesn't it then follow that the necessary being must have its sufficient reason for existing in itself? Hard as it is to imagine this, isn't it a major part of what we mean by necessary being? We have an occasion to wonder:

- Reality with a necessary being: is this hard to imagine? Wonder!
- Reality with no necessary being: is this even harder to imagine, perhaps impossible? Wonder!

[10] SIX FINAL WONDER QUESTIONS

One, why is there evil in the world? Why is there the immense suffering of animals and humans? Why is there moral evil, the evil of hatred and the words and actions that flow from it? Imagine a world with just being and goodness. Why isn't that our actual world? That is already a very deep question. Now add to it all the vast suffering and the vast moral evil in the world and it becomes immensely deeper and more problematic. We can bring these things together:

1. Why is there something and not rather nothing, absolutely nothing? Why is there being?
2. Why is there goodness: love, moral virtue, moral heroism, beauty in nature and music?
3. Why is there evil: suffering, hatred, injustice, betrayal?
4. Why is there both good and evil in one world? This calls for some further reflection:

Chapter 25: Why is There Something and Not Nothing?

Good and evil are absolute contraries, utterly opposed to each other. How then can they both exist in the same world? Is there a single sufficient reason that accounts for both of them, why each exists and why they both exist together in the same world? Or are there two ultimate sufficient reasons, one that accounts for the good and the other that accounts for the evil? Is there something that accounts for their joint existence in the world?

Two, why is there *just this world and not another*? Think of all the many ways in which this world could be different from what it actually is. Try to imagine all the possible worlds that could exist but don't. Try to imagine a world without Mozart; what a loss that would be! Now try to imagine a world with Mozart plus Mozart having a twin brother or sister with comparable musical genius. If this is possible, we would have one of an infinite number of worlds different from the one we actually have. Why don't we have such a different world? Out of an infinite number of possible worlds we have just this one and not another. Why?

Three, if there were really nothing at all, absolutely nothing, *would it be true that there is nothing*? No, because truth is something and not nothing; and we have stipulated that there is nothing, meaning nothing at all. So this would include any and all truth, including the supposed truth that there is nothing. On the other hand, if we go this route and deny truth to this statement aren't we in effect denying what we originally set out to assert? "There is absolutely nothing and it is not true that there is absolutely nothing." But isn't this a flat-out contradiction? "There are no cookies in this jar and it is not true that there are no cookies in this jar." That's absurd. But isn't the one about there being nothing in the same logical form? If so it too is absurd. So then it seems that we can't deny truth to the statement that there is nothing if it is to be meaningful.

It seems to follow that truth cannot be part of the *something* in the question *why there is something and not rather nothing*. Truth seems to be a necessary being, one which exists in any case even if there is nothing else, no contingent beings. If so, are there other necessary beings, such as the laws of logic, numbers, mathematical relations and triangles? On the other hand isn't it hard, and perhaps impossible to imagine a state of affairs where there is no physical universe and no world of persons but only a set of necessary beings like truth and numbers?

Wherever we turn we have occasions to wonder:

- Why is there a physical universe and a world of persons, all contingent beings?
- Could there be no universe and no person-world but only necessary beings like truth?

Four, let's say you're travelling through space, for miles and miles, for years and years. You see nothing and you are overwhelmed by the sense of a seeming absolute nothingness. True, you exist, and your spaceship exists and the space you're traveling through is something and not nothing. But let us disregard these things and try to see this journey as an experience of nothingness. You look and look but there is nothing. Then after twenty years of nothingness you see a rock. Wow, there's something there after all! What is this wow experience? It is the realization that there is something out there, and not just nothing. This is really the original wonder experience underlying our question why there is something and not nothing. The wow experience is of the rock just as a "something"; it is not a particularly pretty rock, and it is not special in any significant sense. It's just something, and not nothing.

This wow experience points to something that even precedes our two questions:

1. Why is there something: what brought it into existence, what is its cause?
2. Why is there something: what is its reason for existing, or its purpose, or its meaning?

The wow experience highlights the ultimate wonder about anything: that it exists at all!

Why don't we usually have this kind of wow experience? It is because we are constantly surrounded by a multitude of things. We take them for granted and don't wonder at the amazing fact that they exist. They actually exist rather than not existing! To appreciate this, the thought experiment of the journey through empty space, surrounded by a seeming absolute nothingness may be helpful. The point is that the universe and the world of persons surrounding us is just as amazing in that it actually exists as the rock up in empty space. It takes the contrast between the being of the rock and the seeming nothingness of the space around it for us to see this. But the same point applies to our actual situation.

<u>The gap between the rock as an actually existing reality and absolute nothingness is huge, perhaps infinite.</u> The gap between a simple rock and a rock sculptured into the most beautiful statue is in some way very significant; but it pales in comparison with just the rock and nothing.

Five, are there necessary beings like truth, numbers and the laws of logic? If there were nothing else, wouldn't it still be true that there is nothing else? Truth seems to be something that exists in any case, and this seems to make truth a necessary being. Could it have been the case that only necessary beings like truth and numbers exist, and nothing else? It is hard to imagine them "floating" in an otherwise empty "space" with there being no physical universe and no world of persons. On the other hand, if they are truly necessary beings wouldn't they exist in any case? If they exist only in minds or are somehow dependent on minds, they are not really necessary. Yet, must they not be necessary beings in order to be what they really are? Wonder!

Six, there are then several ultimate wonder questions:

1. That there is this amazing physical universe!
2. How did this amazing physical universe come to be? What is its cause?
3. That there is this amazing world of persons!
4. How did this amazing world of persons come to be? What is its cause?
5. Necessary beings like truth and numbers: they must exist. But how can they exist?
6. Wow, that there is anything at all, no matter what it is, even if it's only a simple rock!

CHAPTER 26
WHAT GIVES HUMAN LIFE MEANING?

[1] WHAT ARE THE INGREDIENTS OF MEANING?

Is my life worth living? If it is, what makes it worth living? There seems to be a single basic answer to this: my life is worth living if it is meaningful. It will have its ups and downs, its times of joy and its times of suffering, but if it is meaningful, it will be worthwhile.

What makes life meaningful? I think the answer to this goes in two directions. The first is *experienced* meaning, sketched in the 12-point list below. The second is the meaning that is rooted in the very being of a person as person, the *ontological value* of the person, sections 4-6.

Let us turn then to *experienced* meaning. Life is meaningful if it contains things that are meaningful. What are these things? What are the ingredients of experienced meaning?

1. One is having a sense of accomplishment. "I actually did something!" But that brings us to the further question: what did you do? Was it worthwhile? Was it meaningful?
2. I worked for justice, for example that poor people are given a decent wage, that wealth and prosperity are more justly and equitably shared. These surely are worthwhile.
3. Happiness seems to be the basic ingredient here. The justice accomplished in the above means basically that people are happier than before. But can we simply equate meaning with happiness?
4. A mother toils for her children, to ensure that they have a good life. It is hard work, and it includes much suffering. She will tell you it is absolutely worthwhile, fully meaningful. She is looking beyond her own experience to something valuable in itself. In some sense she was not happy because she was suffering; but her suffering did not render her life devoid of meaning.

5. Still, much meaning does seem to correspond to happiness. I feel I am recognized and accepted by others, both for what I have accomplished and for who I am. This gives me a sense of meaning and with it of happiness.
6. Receiving love is a great source of meaning, and of happiness.
7. Giving love is a great source of meaning, and of happiness.
8. Friendships are great sources of meaning, and of happiness.
9. Beauty is a great source of meaning, and of happiness.
10. Gratitude, forgiveness, integrity, and the whole realm of moral virtues is a huge area of meaningfulness. Imagine a person who is truly grateful, who expresses his gratitude to others, even for small things; whose very being emanates gratitude; who is grateful where others are complaining. Isn't this a picture of meaningfulness?
11. Knowledge is another source of meaning, and of happiness. I come to an understanding of the vast physical universe, of the nature of the human person, of time, and so many other things. I am enriched by these experiences because of their meaningfulness.
12. Pleasure should also be mentioned as a source of meaning, and of happiness. Most people would agree that it cannot be the only source of meaning or even the main source; still, a life with no pleasures at all would be lacking in something important. A delicious chocolate, a swim in a cool lake on a hot day; do these not add meaning to life?

[2] IS VALUE A NECESSARY FEATURE OF MEANING?

Consider the things we've just looked at in the previous section, the things that constitute meaning as the ingredients of experienced meaning. Is value a key feature of each of them? By value is meant here both what is valuable in itself or intrinsically valuable and what is valuable for a person, such as recognition and receiving love. Does pleasure come under this heading in that it has a value for the person who is enjoying it? Some pleasures but not others? For those that count, how do they compare in importance as values to, say, moral integrity and love?

In saying that life is worth living if it is meaningful, doesn't the *worth* in "worth living" refer to value? Don't our lives get their meaning from values? And isn't part of the importance of values their contribution to meaningfulness?

Can you imagine finding meaning in something that you also see as completely worthless because it has no value? Doesn't at least the claim to meaning include the claim to value?

[3] IS TRUTH A NECESSARY FEATURE OF MEANING?

A person is praying, reaching out to God. Is this something meaningful? Consider two possible views. The first view says this is meaningful only if his prayer actually "reaches" a God who is really there and who hears it. His prayer is based on the belief that God actually exists and hears his prayer and is therefore meaningful only if this belief is a true belief, if it actually corresponds to what is the really the case. Were he to discover that there is no God, he would of course immediately cease his praying. What would be the point? Wouldn't it be like writing a letter to a deceased person or talking into a telephone with no one on the other end to "take up" the words I speak? The meaningfulness of all intentional communication – whether it is talking on the phone, writing a letter or praying to God – depends on the person "at the other end" really being there, hearing what I want to communicate and "taking it in." In short, it depends on truth, the truth of the belief which forms the basis of the communication: God is really there.

The second view says that the actual reality of God receiving our prayer is not essential. If you find prayer meaningful, if it gives you a sense of peace, that's enough for it to actually be meaningful. Call it a subjective meaning, a meaning "for" a person. But is this a real meaning? That is, doesn't prayer in a world without God fail in a fundamental way? It fails to do what it is intended to do, what it is "meant" to do: reach a God who is really there. If so, then doesn't the real meaningfulness or lack thereof of prayer hinge on whether or not it "reaches" God? This would mean that real meaningfulness in such cases depends on truth: is the belief at the basis of the prayer, that God actually exists and hears the prayer, a true belief or not?

One might suggest that there is a distinction between two kinds of meaning:

1. Objective meaning: one that corresponds to reality and thus meets the truth requirement.
2. Subjective meaning: whatever is meaningful for a particular person. Prayer in a world without God might have subjective meaning but no objective meaning.

When people seek meaning in their lives isn't it always objective meaning? What good is a mere subjective meaning? Let us then focus on objective meaning as the real meaning.

[4] MEANING THROUGH THE ONTOLOGICAL VALUE OF THE HUMAN PERSON

We have looked at some aspects of *experienced* meaning. Let us turn now to the other direction of meaning in a meaningful life. This is the meaning and value of *the person simply as such* and of human life simply as such; of this person and this life regardless of whether it has experienced meaning. Notice that value is still part of the picture for it is the *value* of human life, of the person simply as such. We can say in general that meaning and value go essentially together: where there is meaning there is value and where there is value there is meaning. Is it that meaning gives value? Or that value gives meaning? Is it both, each in different ways?

To designate this value let us use the term introduced by Dietrich von Hildebrand: the *ontological value* of the human person. "When we speak of the value of the human person, of the dignity of a human being, endowed with reason and free will, when we face the preciousness of personal being, of an immortal soul, then we are undoubtedly confronted with something important in itself." The *important in itself* refers to value, intrinsic value, to what is important for its own sake, in contrast to all that has "value" in terms of its importance for something else, such as food for a person or water for a garden. Von Hildebrand describes the *ontological value* of the human person as "the value which a human person possesses as such"; and as the "preciousness of a human being, which calls for respect and love."[1] It is the value that underlies and accounts for the *dignity* of the human person. "Furthermore, we can say that the ontological value of a person is proper to this being as such. Once this being exists, it has this ontological value, and there is no possibility of its losing it."[2] The *ontological value* of the human person can be seen through the lenses of three essential metaphysical features of the human person:

1. Personal identity. I am always me, the same person.
2. Personal uniqueness. There is only one me, even if there is someone else like me.
3. Being a person in distinction to functioning as a person, as in thinking and deciding.

First, there is *personal identity*. I am always *me*, the *same person* through all sorts of changes including radical changes such as from new-born baby to adult or in cases of profound, soul-shaking moral conversions. Personal identity applies to me as a person and not as someone in a particular situation or having certain talents. It belongs to my ontological value as a person that I have the metaphysical permanence of *always being me*, the same person. I cannot lose my ontological value as I cannot lose my personal identity, and these two are deeply connected. We turn now to the other two features.

[5] PERSONAL UNIQUENESS: THERE IS ONLY ONE ME

Second, another essential metaphysical feature of being a person is *uniqueness*. Consider other persons. Each person is different from me in a multitude of ways: personality, beliefs, attitudes, mannerisms, etc. Many differ in age, gender, physical make-up and degree of health. Every other person is different from me

---

[1] Dietrich von Hildebrand, *Ethics* (Chicago: Franciscan Herald Press, 1972), 130-31.

[2] Ibid., 135.

in their personal features, psychological and physical. But everyone else is different from me also in another, deeper way:

There is only one me. That is, there cannot be another *me* even if there is someone else who is exactly *like me*. In one way this seems simple and easy and superficially obvious; but it is actually a very profound idea, one that takes us deep into the core essence of what it means to be a person. It requires us to think carefully as its significance may not be immediately apparent.

To see what personal uniqueness means imagine another person who is exactly like you; a person whose personal features duplicate yours, like a photocopy or a clone. You and your double appear among your friends, and they are baffled since they can't tell the two of you apart. You give a lecture; the next day another lecture is given to the same audience. Was it *you again* or was it *your double*? You know; your double knows. The audience doesn't, for every feature noticeable in one person is present also in the other person.

This is surely a bizarre situation. But notice one important thing. You know perfectly well who you are, and this includes your knowing that that other person, your double, is not you. He or she is just as much "not you" as a person who is very different from you in their personal features such as personality, age and physical make-up. Imagine a parallel universe, where everything in ours is exactly duplicated. There is another person in that universe who is feature for feature exactly like you: face, body structure, personality, beliefs, skills and everything else. Notice: exactly like you. But, of course, he or she isn't you! *Only you are you!* In this is contained personal uniqueness. There cannot be another you, regardless of persons like you.

This means that other people are different from me in two different ways: (i) in their *different personal features*; (ii) in being *somebody else*. It is the second that is crucial here.

Only I know what it's like to be me. A consequence of the uniqueness of my *being* as a person is a corresponding *knowledge* of this reality. Have you ever wondered what it's like to be so-and-so? Think of a person you know well, a specific person in your life. You know him or her well; but you know him or her only from the outside. Perhaps it is not entirely from the outside since you empathize with him and feel at one with him. But still, you cannot "get inside" that person and feel as he feels and see the world as he sees it. You are inside only in your own consciousness. For each person: *only I know what it's like to be me.*

This is not just a matter of what you know or don't know. So-and-so has a secret; you don't know it. Then she tells you her secret and now you do know it, a significant change. But the inner "what it feels like" reality is still entirely her own and can never be conveyed to you. You can look inside another person's body, like a doctor with sophisticated diagnostic machines. But you can never "look inside" another person's consciousness, his or her conscious inner life. You can never see it and really know it; you can never feel it, you can never experience it.

The uniqueness of my being as a person, that there is only one me, that there can be only one me, this surely is something of great value; and is experienced as a great value. It belongs to my *ontological value* as a person and is independent of any accomplishments I may have.

[6] *BEING A PERSON IN DISTINCTION TO FUNCTIONING AS A PERSON*

Third, there is the *being* of a person in distinction to *functioning* as a person. Being refers to what you are as a person. Functioning refers to your consciousness and to what you can do as a conscious person, to your experiences. It includes thinking, feeling happy or sad, making a decision, talking, making a promise, appreciating beauty and much more. The abilities that make it possible for us to do these things are the abilities we have to *function* as persons. But in their nature these abilities are rooted in and made possible by our essence as *being* persons.

Functioning as a person makes possible experienced meaning, a life meaningful in that it contains the ingredients of meaning, the 12-point list above in section 1. Again, this functioning is rooted in and made possible by our *being* persons.

Functioning as the term is used here does not refer to bodily functions such as a heartbeat, but to personal functions such as saying "I," reasoning, deliberating and experiencing love and beauty; they all center on our consciousness and inner life. Someone under total anesthesia lacks the experiences of consciousness and inner life, but he or she still *is* a person. He or she still has the *being* of a person without having the present ability to *function* as a person. Wonder!

Functioning as a person is a matter of degree; a baby has some ability to function as a person but less than an older child. Accidents and illness may impair the ability to function in various degrees. But even in extreme cases some ability to function remains as long as the person retains consciousness. In contrast, isn't *being* absolute? Something either is a person or is not a person? Some animals are very much like persons; do they have the being of a person?

Being refers to what you are; *functioning* to what you can do or experience. Though they are distinct the two notions are essentially related: functioning is rooted in being. The reason you can function as a person is that you have the being of a person. And you have that being essentially; it is your nature as a person. You therefore have that being even when for some reason you cannot function as a person, or your ability to do so is severely diminished. Thus, all who can function as persons must also have the being of a person; but not all who have the being of a person can also function as persons or do so fully. *Being without functioning* can be divided into three types of cases:

1. Not yet functioning or not doing so fully: as in a new-born baby.
2. Temporarily not functioning: as in a deep sleep, a coma or when under total anesthesia.
3. No longer functioning or not doing so fully: as in dementia in various degrees.

Being a person is the basis of your *ontological value*. You have your ontological value because you *are* a person, because you have the *being* of a person; not because you can now *function* as a person. And being a person means that you have identity and uniqueness; they are both essential features of being a person. We always have our being as persons even when we cannot function as persons or that ability is diminished. And our abilities to function as persons are rooted in our being persons, which they presuppose.

[7] ENJOYMENT AND EXPERIENCED MEANING

Let us return now to experienced meaning. How is enjoyment related to meaning? If I enjoy an activity, does this endow it with meaning? Suppose a person enjoys hurting others. Surely this is not meaningful. It may have a subjective meaning for that person but no objective real meaning. Thus, enjoyment is not sufficient for objective meaning. More is needed. What is that "more"? Is it a combination of truth and value? Must it not either be endowed with genuine value as in deeds of love or at least not go against the call of value as in hurting others? And so, we see again that objective meaning and subjective meaning stand in opposition to each other; and that objective meaning is the only real meaning, as in the prayer case above (section 3).

But if enjoyment is not sufficient for objective meaning, isn't it still of some importance? Doesn't it play some role in meaning? Enjoyable work is more meaningful than tedious work, even if both accomplish the same worthwhile goals.

[8] EXPERIENCED OBJECTIVE MEANING THROUGH RECEIVING AND GIVING

Perhaps we can say that experienced objective meaning has two basic dimensions:

1. Enjoyment, what I receive from the experience.
2. The right response, what I give to the objective reality in question.

If we look at the 12-point list in section 1 we will see instances of both of these. In some cases, they are distinct: receiving love as #6 and giving love as #7. In other cases, they are combined: #1, a sense of accomplishment means that I receive this, that I experience it; but I do so because accomplishing something means getting it done, "giving" it to the world. So too #9, in the experience of beauty I receive the delight of beauty because I recognize the beauty in the object, and this recognition is a form of response to the object, hence of "giving." And doesn't the fullness of love always require both dimensions, receiving and giving?

[9] EXPERIENCED OBJECTIVE MEANING THROUGH VIRTUE ETHICS

What is the most important form of meaning through giving? One candidate for this is virtue ethics, our theme in chapters 9 and 10. Here is a brief general sample of virtue ethics:

1. Deeds of love. I am in great danger, and you save my life.
2. Gratitude. In response I am grateful to you. I am also grateful for small deeds of love, little acts of kindness. And I share this gratitude with you by thanking you.
3. Forgiveness: Asking. If I have hurt you, I should come to you to ask for your forgiveness.
4. Forgiveness: Granting. If you ask me for forgiveness, should I not grant it? Forgiveness in these two dimensions restores the good order that existed before the harm was done.
5. Humility. Not claiming more for myself than is justified. Being ready to acknowledge my mistake. Being ready to acknowledge that I was the one who did wrong.
6. Justice. Working to create a more just social order. Working to alleviate poverty.
7. Respect for persons. Treating others as persons; avoiding prejudice and stereotyping.
8. The Golden Rule. Do unto others as you would want them to do unto you.
9. Seeking Truth. Seeking to believe "how it really is" regarding all matters.

[10] THE SOURCES OF EXPERIENCED OBJECTIVE MEANING

What are the sources of experienced meaning, of genuinely and objectively meaningful experiences and activities in life? What does the presence or absence of experienced meaning in life depend on? There seem to be two aspects or levels:

1. What is given to me, as my heredity and environment, as my situation in life.
2. What I do, what I create, what I accomplish, what I bring about.

I am given good physical health, good mental health, intelligence, the capacity to acquire skills; I am deeply loved by my parents and other family members and friends. I live in a free country with a reasonably high standard of living. Given all this I have the opportunity for much that is meaningful in life. Compare this with a person whose situation in life is at the opposite end of the spectrum. He is unwanted, rejected by his parents and sent off to a foster home. Later, in desperation, he turns to a life of crime; he is caught, imprisoned and spends the rest of his days in prison, doing nothing, wasting the time away. What a tragedy! And isn't the reason for this that his life was devoid of meaning? In such cases isn't it hard to say that life is worth living? Isn't the honest appraisal that it isn't worth living because it is so utterly lacking in any real meaning? And it lacks meaning because it lacks the necessary sources of meaning.

But the given is only half the story. What I do with it is the other half. The given is an opportunity; do I make good use of it? The given is a necessary condition; it is not sufficient. I must make good use of it in order to bring about meaning in life. Two persons may be given the same combination of good sources in terms of heredity and family environment. One uses them meaningfully, the other squanders these resources. The key point here is that meaning is largely up to me. This is probably the valid point in the common saying that we "create" meanings. We surely do not somehow create meanings whole and entire out of nothing. Rather we "create" in the sense that we cooperate with the given in our experience. We are offered a friendship by another person. We gladly accept, and respond accordingly; we cooperate with what is given to us. Beautiful music comes to us; we take it in, respond accordingly and thereby do our part.

[11] OPPOSITES OF EXPERIENCED OBJECTIVE MEANING

We can come to a better and deeper understanding of objective meaning in human life if we see what such meaning stands opposed to. There seem to be four main areas of anti-meaning, things not just lacking in objective meaning but consisting of what is contrary to meaning, as evil is contrary to good. Cruelty is the contrary of respect, kindness and love; daydreaming is merely an absence of moral good, something morally neutral. These four areas apply to both individual persons in their life-experiences and to interpersonal relations, the world of human persons.

1. **Emptiness.** Imagine being stuck in an empty room; no one else is there, there is nothing to read, nothing to do. You are desperate for something, almost anything to fill the time. This seems to be the ultimate boredom. Note that it is not the mere emptiness as such, or by itself that causes anti-meaning but the fact that we humans are hardwired for meaning, that we are "meant" for meaning, so that such an absence is keenly felt as a deprivation of something that should be there and is therefore experienced as an anti-meaning.

2. **Pointless repetition.** The classic example of this is the Myth of Sisyphus, the poor man who was condemned by the gods of ancient Greece to roll a stone up to the top of a hill, the stone then falling back down, whereupon he had to roll it back up again, and so on without end. This is not the emptiness of the first area; indeed, he does something. It is that what he does is absolutely pointless; it has no meaning, it just is. Again, we see that it is not the thing as such or by itself that is devoid of meaning but that thing in the human context, persons hardwired for meaning, meant for meaning. If we imagine a human-like robot doing the work of Sisyphus, we are not appalled by anti-meaning; we can easily see it as just another event in nature, like water running down stream, an endless repetition.

3. **Sheer incongruity.** Recalling a previous example, imagine a person talking eagerly on the phone, full of enthusiasm, wanting to share his ideas with the person at the other end. But there is no one there! Here too there is something that is pointless but in a way very different from Sisyphus. It is in some ways a deeper pointlessness, as it somehow attacks the very meaningfulness that is supposed to attach to human activities such as talking, communicating with another person. A love that is not returned may be another example of this. John deeply loves Mary, but she does not love

him in return. His love for her is essentially experienced as something that should be returned; and when it isn't the incongruity is a deep wound in his soul.

4. **Heavy incongruity.** This refers to things that are primarily evils, and whose seriousness is primarily their moral evil, but which also display a significant opposition to meaning. We honor a famous person who is in fact a scoundrel, guilty of terrible crimes. We should not do this; it is morally wrong. What is noteworthy is that this is also a failure against meaning, an incongruity; a heavy incongruity because if its seriousness, its heavy moral weight. Consider the state of affairs that millions of people around the world are living on the edge of starvation, many actually starving to death while some people have yearly incomes of 20 or 30 or 40 million dollars, sometimes even more. What can one do with that much money? They sit on it while others could be saved by a mere fraction of this wealth! Heavy incongruity! In the USA an 18-year old can't buy beer; he's under age. But if he wants to buy an assault weapon that he can use to kill 17 children in a school, that's permitted. Heavy incongruity! Take the killing of the 17 children. We say it is "senseless." It is of course so much more, a horrific evil beyond description. But it is also senseless, utterly opposed to meaning. Heavy incongruity! Finally, we sometimes protect rare plants from becoming extinct and fail to protect our own innocent and very vulnerable little children because they are seen as "in the way." Heavy incongruity!

[12] THE PRIMACY OF MEANING: VIKTOR FRANKL

What keeps us going through our lives? What motivates us to do what we do? Surely there are many types of motives in our lives. But is there perhaps a primary motivational force, a single basic answer to these questions: meaning? This is the thesis of Viktor Frankl; he discusses three candidates for what could be the primary motivational forces in human life[3]:

---

[3] *Man's Search for Meaning: an Introduction to Logotherapy* (New York: Washington Square Press, 1963), 151-59.

1. The will to power.
2. The will to pleasure.
3. The will to meaning.

How are these related? When we want to be in control of a situation, and perhaps of another person, isn't it the will to power that is dominant? And why do we want to seek power? Isn't it because having power, being in control gives us pleasure? And why seek pleasure? That seems too obvious, but if we look carefully isn't it because pleasure is something meaningful? What follows from this? Isn't it that the will to meaning is the primary motivational force in human life? That as noted above is indeed Frankl's conclusion and main thesis.

But perhaps meaning comes into play as the primary motivational force in human life in another way as well. Consider the other two candidates: pleasure and power. Is a life consisting only of these really worthwhile? Aren't we hardwired for more? Aren't we meant for more? And doesn't that "more" consist largely of things in the 12-point list of ingredients of meaning in section 1? Indeed, aren't pleasure and power worthwhile only to the extent that they are part of a broader life that is objectively meaningful through these ingredients of meaning?

In pleasure and power, we are somehow turned in on ourselves. In love we reach out to others, we transcend ourselves, we go beyond ourselves. Isn't the deepest kind of meaning the one that displays this transcendent character? I see a person in terrible suffering. I am moved to the depth of my being; my heart reaches out to him. This is the transcendence of meaning. And doesn't the "more" we spoke about consist precisely in meaning as self-transcendence?

[13] THREE WAYS EXPERIENCED MEANING CAN FILL OUR LIVES

Three other points in Frankl can be helpful for us. *First*, Frankl speaks of an existential vacuum (167-71), by which he means the emptiness that some people feel when they have lots of leisure time but don't know how to fill it. There is a ready answer to this problem: fill it with meaning! There are so many ways of doing this! Again the 12-point list comes into play; it provides a good start for how to fill our lives with authentic and objective meaning.

Second, and in a somewhat parallel way some people feel that their lives are like that of Sisyphus, a mere endless repetition of daily routine tasks: get up, go to work, get back home, go to bed, get up and repeat it all over again. Stripped to these bare bones, life is indeed empty and hardly worth living. But it need not be so! Fill it with meaning! Work for justice. Reach out to others in kindness and love, kind and loving deeds. Read about the marvels of this world.

Third, suffering can be meaningful. In itself suffering is surely not meaningful. It is terrible! It should not be! Much that is morally evil is so because it is the causing of suffering in others. Think cruelty, assault and torture. But Frankl suggests that suffering can be redeemed, and thereby made meaningful, by being instrumental for a good beyond itself (178-83). If my suffering spares you a similar suffering doesn't my suffering acquire meaning through this? If so there can be meaning despite suffering. Frankl quotes Nietzsche: "He who has a *why* to live can bear almost any *how*" (164). The *why* comes from meaning and the *how* refers to suffering.

We have here another instance of the importance of value in meaning (section 2), that our lives get meaning from values. Suffering acquires meaning when it has a value for someone. Wonder!

[14] MEANING AND PURPOSE

Often these two terms are used interchangeably. In asking *why did he do it?* we may be looking for his purpose: what did he set out to accomplish? And in doing so we are wondering what the meaning of his action was, or indeed if it even had any. And we feel that when we are given a purpose, we are also given the meaning; the meaning just seems to be the purpose. We seem to get some initial sense of knowing the meaning of something when we know its purpose.

And yet a little further reflection reveals that the two terms are not the same. Purpose points beyond itself: purpose for what? If that is not something meaningful, a purpose hardly answers the request for meaning. Suppose the further thing is also a purpose. Again: a purpose for what? If we just have an infinite series of purpose for purpose for purpose, we will have made no progress in finding meaning. Purpose by itself does not insure meaning; it must lead in the end to something worthwhile in itself, meaningful for its own sake. Consider a single push of the rock by Sisyphus as he trudges up the mountain. Surely it has a purpose: to get the rock up a little higher. But does it have a meaning? If the whole project is devoid of meaning, then a single push can hardly be said to have a meaning. It shares in the meaninglessness of the whole.

I make a journey to the top of a mountain. It is not very pleasant, but it is meaningful by virtue of its purpose. It gets me to the top where I have a breathtaking view of the Swiss Alps. The beauty overwhelms me! That is meaningful! It is meaningful in itself, for its own sake; not for something beyond it. Here meaning and purpose diverge. The experience is full of meaning, but not because it is purposeful; in fact it isn't.

[15] *MEANING* IN *LIFE AND THE MEANING* OF *LIFE*

A common distinction in discussions of meaning is the following:

1. Meaning in life: what must be in my life for it to be worthwhile and meaningful?
2. Meaning of life: is my life as a whole worthwhile; is it ultimately meaningful?

In this chapter we examined #1. In the next chapter we turn to #2: what is necessary for life to have a meaning as a whole; to be ultimately meaningful? Is it enough if it is filled with meaning in life? As I look back on my life near its end, I might ask myself: was it meaningful and worthwhile? Did I make a difference? Did I accomplish something lasting and worthwhile in itself and for others? What could that be? A young person is unjustly accused of a crime he didn't commit. Nonetheless a court declares him guilty and sentences him to life imprisonment. He goes to prison at age 20 and after 60 years in prison with nothing to do his life ends. It was empty of experienced meaning as there was nothing *in* his life to give it meaning. Are we also forced to say that there was no meaning *of* life for him? If not, if there was some meaning what could it be? Where could it come from? After the 60 years in prison, he dies. But we must all die. Our lives are different with an abundance of meaning *in* them. But does that guarantee also a meaning *of* our lives, an ultimate meaning? Or does death destroy such meaning? What is the impact of death on the meaning of life? To these themes we turn in the next chapter.

Meaning *in* life and meaning *of* life is generally seen as *experienced* meaning. How does the value and meaning of *being* a person, the *ontological value* of a person fit in here?

[16] IS LIFE ULTIMATELY MEANINGFUL?

[a] THREE BASIC FACTORS AND THREE VIEWS

THREE BASIC FACTORS

What determines whether my life as a whole is worthwhile and meaningful; whether it is ultimately meaningful; whether there is a meaning of my life? I suggest there are three factors:

First, there is the matter of <u>meaning *in* life.</u> Recall the person unjustly accused of a crime he didn't commit who is sentenced to life imprisonment. Since there was virtually nothing *in* his life to give it meaning does it follow that there was also no meaning *of* life for him? In general:

- Can there be a meaning of life where there is no experienced meaning in life? Is my ontological value sufficient for giving me a meaning of life where I have no or very little experienced meaning in my life? More briefly:
- Is experienced meaning in life a necessary condition for the meaning of life?
- Is experienced meaning in life a sufficient condition for the meaning of life?

Second, and following up on the last point, whether having meaning *in* life is a sufficient condition for the meaning *of* life, we face the question of the impact of death on the meaning *of* life. One view is that meaning *in* is *not* sufficient for meaning *of*; that if death is our total annihilation our life is ultimately absurd. We will examine this below as view one. A second view is that meaning *in* life is indeed a sufficient condition for the meaning *of* life; that even if death is our total annihilation our life can still be meaningful; meaning *in is* sufficient. We will examine this below as view two. A big part of all this is the huge question whether death is in fact our total annihilation, whether there is a life after death. We will turn to this in chapters 4-7.

Third, there is the question of God. Is the existence of God a necessary condition for the meaning *of* life? Again, two basic views are possible: yes and no. But much more is at stake here, including the nature of God: what kind of God is even relevant to the question of meaning? These will be among our topics in chapters 7 and 8.

THREE VIEWS:

Let us turn now to the *second* of these factors, the question of the impact of death on the meaning *of* life. That is, if my death is the total annihilation of my being, can my life still be meaningful? Here are three views that can be offered in answer to this question:

1. No: death as annihilation robs my life of its meaning. Meaning in is not sufficient.
2. Yes: even if death is annihilation life can still be meaningful. Meaning in is sufficient.
3. Yes and no: Yes, there can be meaning in my life even if death is its total end. And, in some sense, there can also be a meaning of my life in the face of annihilation. But no, there is another sense in which annihilation does rob life of its meaning; it destroys the ultimate meaning of my life, the ultimate meaning of my life.

[b] VIEW ONE: DEATH AS ANNIHILATION ROBS LIFE OF ITS MEANING

Sartre: A meaning can come only from subjectivity. Since death does not appear on the foundation of our subjectivity, it can only remove all meaning from life. If we must die, then our life has no meaning because its problems receive no solution. It is absurd that we are born, it is absurd that we die.[4]

[Suppose a man expecting to be executed in a very short time is given a reprieve. How will he react?] Several hours or several years of waiting is all the same when you have lost the illusion of being eternal [of having immortality, an eternal life after death].[5]

Unamuno: Why do I wish to know whence I come and whither I go, whence comes and whither goes everything that environs me, and what is the meaning of it all? For I do not wish to die utterly, and I wish to know whether I am to die or not definitely. If I do not die, what is my destiny? And if I die, then nothing has any meaning for me.

If at the death of the body which sustains me, and which I call mine to distinguish it from the self that is I, my consciousness returns to the absolute unconsciousness from which it sprang, and if a like fate befalls all my brothers in humanity, then is our toil-worn human race nothing but a fatidic procession of phantoms, going from nothingness to nothingness.

If we die utterly, wherefore does everything exist?

Descriptions of the tortures of hell however terrible never made me tremble, for I always felt that nothingness was much more terrifying. He who suffers lives. It is better to live in pain than to cease to be in peace.

---

[4] Jean-Paul Sartre, *Being and Nothingness*, tr. Hazel E. Barnes (New York: Citadel Press, 1965), 515-16 and 523.

[5] "The Wall" in Walter Kaufman, *Existentialism from Dostoevsky to Sartre* (New York: Meridian Books, 1956), 235.

I want to live forever and ever and ever. Therefore, the problem of the duration of my soul, of my own soul, tortures me.[6]

Tolstoy: Why do I live? Why do I wish for anything, or do anything?

What will come of what I do today or tomorrow? What will come of my entire life?

Is there any meaning in my life that will not be annihilated by the inevitability of death which awaits me?

What is the meaning of my life? It has none. Or: what will come of my life? Nothing. Or: why does everything there is exist, and why do I exist? Because it does.[7]

[c] VIEW TWO: DEATH AS ANNIHILATION DOES NOT ROB LIFE OF ITS MEANING

Kurt Baier: It is now clear that death is simply irrelevant. If life can be worthwhile at all, then it can be so even if it is short. And if it is not worthwhile at all, then an eternity of it is simply a nightmare. It may be sad that we have to leave this beautiful world, but it is so only because it is beautiful. And it is no less beautiful for coming to an end. I rather suspect that an eternity of it might make us less appreciative, and in the end it would be tedious.

Acceptance of the scientific world provides no reason for saying that life is meaningless, but on the contrary every reason for saying that there are many lives which are meaningful and significant.[8]

E. D. Klemke: If I am to find any meaning in life, I must attempt to find it without the aid of crutches, illusory hopes, and incredulous beliefs and aspirations. I

---

[6] Miguel De Unamuno, *Tragic Sense of Life*, tr. J. E. Crawford Flitch (New York: Dover Publications, 1954), 33 and 42-45.

[7] Leo Tolstoy, *A Confession and Other Religious Writings*, tr. Jane Kentish (London: Penguin Books, 1987), 34-39.

[8] Kurt Baier, "The Meaning of Life" in Steven Sanders and David R. Cheney, eds. *The Meaning of Life: Questions, Answers and Analysis* (Englewood Cliffs, NJ: Prentice Hall, 1980), 61 and 63.

am perfectly willing to admit that *I may not find any meaning at all* (although I think I can, even if it is not of the noble variety of which the transcendentalist speaks). But at least *I must try* to find it on my own. And this much I know: I can strive for meaning only if it is one which is within the range of my comprehension as an inquiring, rational *man*.

It is true that life has no objective meaning. Let us face it once and for all. But from this it does not follow that life is not *worthwhile*, for it can still be subjectively meaningful. And, really, the latter is the only kind of meaning worth shouting about. An objective meaning – that is, one which is inherent within the universe or dependent upon external agencies – would, frankly, leave me cold. It would not be *mine*. It would be an outer, neutral thing, rather than an inner, dynamic achievement. I, for one, am *glad* the universe has no meaning, for thereby is *man all the more glorious*.[9]

Kai Nielsen: I shall argue that, even if death is, as I believe it to be, utter annihilation, we can still find significance in our lives, and that, if we will think carefully and indeed humanly – from the emotions or existentially if you will – we need not, and indeed should not, feel death to be such a stark terror.

Even though Tolstoy, Dostoevsky and Pascal have deeply touched my life, I do not feel terror when I dwell on death. Yet I know full well it must come, and I firmly believe – believe without a shadow of doubt – that it will mean my utter annihilation.

I certainly do not want to die. I should very much like, in such a state [possession of my normal powers, pleasures and people I care for], to go on living forever. Yet plainly I cannot. In the face of this, it seems to me both a sane response and a human response to that inevitability to rather wistfully regret that fact about our common human lot and to want to make the most of the life one has.[10]

---

[9] E. D. Klemke, "Living Without Appeal: An Affirmative Philosophy of Life" in E. D. Klemke, ed., *The Meaning of Life* (New York and Oxford: Oxford University Press, 1981), 170 and 172.

[10] Kai Nielsen, *Ethics without God*, revised edition, (Amherst NY: Prometheus Books, 1990), 185 and 186.

[d] VIEW THREE: ANOTHER PERSPECTIVE ON DEATH AND MEANING

The third view has much in common with the first view; and it also shares a common element with the second view. In common with the first view, it recognizes that if death means our complete destruction, our utter annihilation, this would be a horror beyond words, beyond imagining. *We shrink from death!* We want to *be*, as Unamuno forcefully expresses it. Most unhappy people do not commit suicide. They still want to *be*, even if it is a miserable existence. Those who do commit suicide want to escape their current existence, not their existence as such. Perhaps they hope that death will bring them into a new and better existence.

The horror of death as utter annihilation comes out also when we consider meaning *in* life. Imagine a spectrum of human lives. At one end is a life full of meaning; at the other is one devoid of meaning. If we have a life full of wonderful, meaningful experiences don't we want to hold on to them and not lose them? Don't we want more? We are enriched by love, knowledge, and beauty. We want more, in quantity and in quality. We want to understand more deeply. We want more beautiful music, and we want to probe into it more deeply. The beautiful things we have are like a foretaste of a greater and deeper whole beyond them; one which we will never be able to attain in this life but may hope for in a life beyond this one. If death is utter annihilation this hope is forever dashed. And *in this sense,* such a death robs life of its deepest meaning.

Now consider the other end of the spectrum of human lives, a life devoid of meaning. Recall the person spending almost his whole life in prison for a crime he didn't commit (chapter 2, section 15). His life is virtually empty of meaning since there is nothing *in* his life to give it meaning. Now death ends everything! Doesn't it follow that here is now also no meaning *of* his life? If so, there is no meaning at all for his life! Is this not an unspeakable tragedy?

The third view has a basic element in common with the first view: death as annihilation would be absolutely horrible! It would rob life of meaning, the *ultimate* meaning *of* life. But it would not rob life of all meaning; and with this we come to the common element it shares with the second view. The third view agrees with the second view that there can be meaning *in* life even if death ends everything; and that in such a case even life as a whole can be worthwhile and meaningful in a non-ultimate sense, a meaning *of* life. This is the point made by Kurt Baier when he says there is "every reason for saying that there are many lives which are meaningful and significant." They are meaningful by virtue of there being meaning *in* life.

The third view holds four key points:

1. Death as annihilation robs life of its ultimate meaning.
2. This refers to the ultimate meaning of life.
3. Death as annihilation does not rob life of the possibility of experienced meaning in life.
4. And it does not rule out a meaning of life in a second, non-ultimate sense. If a life has been filled with experienced meaning in life, this gives life as a whole some meaning.

Items #1 and #2 represent agreement with the first view; items #3 and #4 with the second.

[e] REFLECTIONS ON SOME OF THESE VIEWS

There are significant differences among the three thinkers in View One. Sartre is an atheist, Unamuno a theist and Tolstoy hard to classify. He is neither a theist in the traditional sense nor an atheist. He seems to change his position and to struggle with the God-question.

When Unamuno says he would rather suffer the torments of hell than to cease to be, is he speaking literally? Or is this his way of emphasizing and highlighting the basic point that above all he wants to *be*, to *exist*, to *live*, and to do so forever. I strongly suspect it is the latter. It is plainly obvious to me that non-existence is infinitely preferable to existence in a hell.

The writers in View One all seem to consider only the *ultimate* meaning *of* life. They seem to ignore the question of meaning *in* life; and the question of the meaning *of* life in a *non-ultimate* sense, the meaning of life taken as a whole. This seems especially evident in Tolstoy.

Turning to View Two, how can Baier say that death is irrelevant? Has he never faced the prospect of his non-existence? Aren't the three View One writers far more in touch with actual human experience? Of course, an eternity of meaningless life would be a nightmare but that is surely not what those who long for an eternity of life after death believe in and hope for. Baier seems to be missing the point here, that eternity is to be *another kind of* existence, one that gives us the fullness of meaning and happiness that we often do not find in this life.

Surely Klemke is correct to reject crutches, illusory hopes, and incredulous beliefs and aspirations. But can he be sure that belief in a life after death really falls into these categories? Perhaps such a belief rests on solid logical grounds. And the meaning we are pursuing here is a meaning which *is* within the range of our comprehension as inquiring, rational persons. And it is "objective" only in the sense that is genuine and real, not in the sense that it is alien to us, as Klemke supposes.

Does one get the impression that Baier and Klemke have simply closed off their minds and hearts to *any* meaningful conception of life after death? Are they open to any evidence that might show them that their position is mistaken? Wonder!

Compare Baier and Nielsen on the question of death. Baier claims it is irrelevant while Nielsen says "I certainly do not want to die. I should very much like to go on living forever." In this respect Nielsen is more like the View One writers, Sartre, Unamuno and Tolstoy, than his fellow atheists in View Two, Baier and Klemke.

Nielsen claims to *know* death is the absolute end. Regarding his death, "I know full well it must come, and I firmly believe – believe without a shadow of doubt – that it will mean my utter annihilation." How can he be so sure? Isn't this at least a question we should keep open?

Unamuno stands out in a class by himself. All the others have shut the door on life after death, claiming to know it does not exist. Unamuno keeps it open and passionately wants it to exist, hopes that it exists and that it will be his. "I want to live forever and ever and ever. Therefore, the problem of the duration of my soul, of my own soul, tortures me."

[f] THOUGHTS FROM PASCAL

*When I consider the short duration of my life, swallowed up in the eternity before and after, the little space which I fill and even can see, engulfed in the infinite immensity of spaces of which I am ignorant and which know me not, I am frightened and am astonished at being here rather than there; for there is no reason why here rather than there, why now rather than then. (#205)[11]

*Who has put me here? By whose order and direction have this place and time been allotted to me? (#205)

*Nothing is so important to a person as his own state; nothing is so formidable to him as eternity. And thus it is not natural that there should be persons who are indifferent to the loss of their existence and the possibility of eternal suffering. (#194)

*They are quite different with regard to all other things. They are afraid of mere trifles; they foresee them and feel them. And this same person who spends days and nights in rage and despair for the loss of an office, or for some imaginary insult to his honor, is the very one who knows without anxiety and without emotion that he will lose all at death. (#194)

*It is a monstrous thing to see in the same heart and at the same time this sensibility to trifles and this strange insensibility to the greatest things. (#194)

*For it is not to be doubted that the duration of this life is but a moment and that the state of death is eternal, whatever may be its nature. (#195)

*The immortality of the soul is a matter which is of so great consequence to us, and which touches us so profoundly, that we must have lost all feeling to be indifferent as to knowing what it is. (#194)

---

[11] Pascal, *Pensées* (*Thoughts*), tr. W. F. Trotter, with minor editorial changes.

*All our actions and thoughts must take such different courses, according to whether there are or are not eternal joys to hope for, that it is impossible to take one step with sense and judgment, unless we regulate our course in life by our view of this point, which ought to be our ultimate end. (#194)

*Atheists. What reason have they for saying that we cannot rise from the dead? What is more difficult, to be born or to rise again; that what has never been should be, or that what has been should be again? Is it more difficult to come into existence than to return to it? Habit makes the one appear easy to us; want of habit makes the other impossible. A popular way of thinking! (#222)

[g] REFLECTIONS ON THOUGHTS FROM PASCAL

Passages 1-2 express Pascal's own deep wonder at ultimate questions and his passionate concern about these matters. Unamuno represents the same spirit of mind and heart.

Passages 3-8 express Pascal's deep concern that many other people do not have this same passionate interest in what most deeply concerns their own life, happiness and meaning. How can anyone be indifferent to such questions? Imagine Pascal reading Baier and Klemke!

Passage 9 is a challenge to Sartre, Baier, Klemke, and Nielsen who claim to know that we cannot rise from the dead; that is, continue our existence in a life after death.

When we search for the meaning *of* life, whether life is worth living, whether it has a meaning as a whole, an ultimate meaning, two dimensions appear:

1. What must be the case for there to be meaning, the meaning of life?
2. What must we do to achieve such meaning? What is our part?

The first refers to the question of the impact of death on meaning, the question of whether death ends everything or there is a life after death; and to the question of God. The second, what is our part, is Pascal's passionate concern in passages 3-8. It will be our theme in chapter 10.

[h] RUSSELL: A DENIAL OF ULTIMATE MEANINGFULNESS

That man is the product of causes which had no prevision of the end they were achieving; that his origin, his growth, his hopes and fears, his loves and his beliefs, are but the outcome of accidental collocations of atoms; that no fire, no heroism, no intensity of thought and feeling, can preserve an individual life beyond the grave; that all the labors of the ages, all the devotion, all the inspiration, all the noonday brightness of human genius, are destined to extinction in the vast death of the solar system, and that the whole temple of man's achievement must inevitably be buried beneath the debris of a universe in ruins – all these things, if not quite beyond dispute, are yet so nearly certain that no philosophy which rejects them can hope to stand. Only within the scaffolding of these truths, only on the firm foundation of unyielding despair, can the soul's habitation henceforth be safely built.

How, in such an alien and inhuman world, can so powerless a creature as man preserve his aspirations untarnished? A strange mystery it is that nature, omnipotent but blind, in the revolutions of her secular hurryings through the abysses of space, has brought forth at last a child, subject still to her power, but gifted with sight, with knowledge of good and evil, with the capacity of judging all the works of his unthinking mother. In spite of death, the mark and seal of the parental control, man is yet free, during his brief years, to examine, to criticize, to know, and in imagination to create. To him alone, in the world with which he is acquainted, this freedom belongs; and in this lies his superiority to the resistless forces that control his outward life.[12]

[i] JAMES: AN AFFIRMATION OF ULTIMATE MEANINGFULNESS

Religions differ so much in their accidents that in discussing the religious question we must make it very generic and broad. What then do we now mean by the religious hypothesis? Science says things are; morality says some things are

---

[12] Bertrand Russell, "A Free Man's Worship" in *Why I am not a Christian* (New York: Simon and Schuster, 1957), 107.

better than other things; and religion says essentially two things. [Religion means here affirmation of a higher being and a life after death.]

First, she says the best things are the more eternal things, the overlapping things, the things in the universe that throw the last stone, so to speak, and say the final word. "Perfection is eternal" – this phrase of Charles Secrétan seems a good way of putting this first affirmation of religion, an affirmation which obviously cannot yet be verified scientifically at all. The second affirmation of religion is that we are better off even now if we believe her first affirmation to be true.

Religion has meant many things in human history; but when from now onward I use the word I mean to use it in the supernaturalist sense, as declaring that the so-called order of nature, which constitutes this world's experience, is only one portion of the total universe, and that there stretches beyond this visible world an unseen world of which we now know nothing positive, but in its relation to which the true significance of our present mundane life consists. A man's religious faith means for me essentially his faith in the existence of an unseen order of some kind in which the riddles of the natural order may be found explained.

Now, I wish to make you feel that we have a right to believe the physical order to be only a partial order; that we have a right to supplement it by an unseen spiritual order which we assume on trust, if only thereby life may seem to us better worth living again. But as such a trust will seem to some of you sadly mystical and execrably unscientific, I must first say a word or two to weaken the veto which you may consider that science opposes to our act.

Science has made such glorious leaps in the last three hundred years and extended our knowledge of nature so enormously both in general and in detail; men of science, moreover, have as a class displayed such admirable virtues – that it is no wonder if the worshippers of science lose their head. Think how many absolutely new scientific conceptions have arisen in our own generation, how many new problems have been formulated that were never thought of before, and then cast an eye on the brevity of science's career. Is it credible that such a mushroom knowledge, such a growth overnight as this, *can* represent more than the minutest glimpse of what the universe will really prove to be when adequately understood? No! Our science is a drop, our ignorance a sea. Whatever else be certain, this at least is certain – that the world of our present knowledge *is* enveloped in a larger world of *some* sort of whose residual properties we can at present frame no positive idea.

These, then, are my last words to you: Be not afraid of life. Believe that life *is* worth living, and your belief will help create the fact. The "scientific proof" that you are right may not be clear before the day of judgment (or some stage of being which that expression may serve to symbolize) is reached.[13]

---

[13] William James, "The Will to Believe" (paragraphs 1-2) and "Is Life Worth Living?" (rest of paragraphs).

CHAPTER 27
LIFE AFTER DEATH: IS IT POSSIBLE?

[1] WONDER AT DEATH

We can wonder at the death of *another person*. A person we loved dies; we are grief-stricken! We go to the calling hours and look into the casket. The person we loved is not there! Yet what we see, his or her body, is what we saw when we were in his presence. How can this be? How can the person not be in the body? We don't wonder at this because we are all too familiar with the answer: that's what death means, the separation of person and body. But does the person I loved still exist? That is the question of life after death.

I can wonder at *my own* death. Will I cease to exist? Is death my utter annihilation? Or will I continue to exist in some other way? Is death the gateway to a new existence? Again, that is the question of life after death. Let us begin by asking whether life after death is possible.

IS LIFE AFTER DEATH POSSIBLE? THE NO ANSWER

[2] BASIC MATERIALISM: A PERSON IS HIS BODY, NOTHING MORE

Perhaps the most important reason given for saying that life after death is not possible is the view that a person simply *is* his body, or his brain, *nothing more*. A person's consciousness is not a reality "over and above" the physical; it *is* the physical, even though it does not appear the way physical things usually do. This view is materialism, that there is no such thing as a soul distinct from the body, a soul that might continue to live on after the death of the body. There is no such thing as a mind distinct from the body, especially from the brain. Mind is the way the brain functions. Mental events are physical events; consciousness is a brain function.

If materialism is correct, isn't it clear that there can be no life after death? A tree is a living thing but when it is cut down and dies it ceases to exist. Would anyone ever dream of suggesting that there could be a life after death for trees? Materialism says the same thing is basically true of animals and human persons. Just like the tree a dog simply *is* his body so that when the dog dies, he ceases to exist. And the same applies to us: when we die, we also cease to exist. If there is nothing more to our being than our bodies as materialism claims and as is surely true of trees, then our death, the end of the life of our bodies is our absolute end as well.

Even if materialism is not correct some people say that life after death is not possible. The reason is that they hold that the conscious person, while distinct from the brain and the rest of the body, is still so dependent on the body and especially the brain, that the death of the body necessarily means the end of the person, his utter annihilation, no life after death. Still, the main reason for the denial of the possibility of life after death is materialism; let us now return to it.

There are many varieties of materialism. A good representative of all of them, typical of them in its core thesis is the Mind-Brain Identity Theory. Its central claim is that mental states simply *are* physical states of the brain. Every mental state or process is numerically identical with some physical state or process of the brain. The mental state is one and the very same thing as the brain state. Matter can think.

But don't we use different terms to refer to mind and matter? I have a thought. I have a brain process. True enough, but they still refer to the same thing. Think of the morning star and the evening star. Here we have two terms and for some time it was thought that there were two stars. Now we know that there is only one, and it is not really a star but the planet Venus. So, the fact that there are two terms doesn't mean that there are two realities; the two terms may turn out to refer to one and the same thing. This is what materialism claims for thoughts and brain processes, and more generally for a person and his body.

The only kind of causation allowed in materialism is the kind that stems from physical reality. Mental events such as beliefs, fears and desires can never function as causes. All my conscious thoughts are effects of brain processes as their causes; conscious thoughts can never be causes themselves. The same applies to me as a person, to my personal self. If I am the cause of something it is actually my body and especially my brain that is really the cause of that thing.

Why adopt materialism? Among the reasons four may be mentioned. *First*, materialism is *simple* compared to its rival theory, dualism. Whenever possible we should adopt a simple theory rather than a complex one. Materialism claims to be able to account for the reality of the human person by postulating just one thing, the body, rather than two, body and something else over and above the body, a soul of some kind.

Second, there is *evolution*. At the beginning we have simple organisms, no spiritual soul. As they evolve, they grow in complexity but no spiritual soul needs to be postulated. When we come to human beings we have maximum complexity, amazing abilities, but again no spiritual soul is needed. Evolution paints a picture of smooth developments and transitions; to hold that a soul enters the scene at some point is to introduce a radical break and a loss of this smoothness.

Third, many people assume that *the real is the physical*. Persons are real; their bodies are real; therefore, persons are simply their bodies. Materialism follows naturally.

Fourth, the *unity* of person and body is easily explained by materialism. I am my body. If my body is 6 feet tall this means that I am 6 feet tall. The same applies to other physical characteristics, such as weight and skin color. When I walk or swim or jump up and down, it's my body that's doing these things. When my body is sick, I'm sick. When you see my body, you see me. When I hug your body, I hug you.

Think of all the activities that constitute your day. You get up in the morning, brush your teeth, have a cup of coffee and go off to work. All these are bodily activities. You type a letter, you pick up the phone; again it's your body. You talk, using your voice, a part of your body. You use your body: that's you in action. Others see your body; they see you. The picture seems pretty clear: I as a person and my body seem to be *one and the same thing*.

IS LIFE AFTER DEATH POSSIBLE?

THE YES ANSWER

[3] CRITICAL REFLECTIONS ON BASIC MATERIALISM

But are they really *one and the same thing*? As an introduction to the yes answer, let us take another look at these four reasons for adopting materialism. *One* (corresponding to first above), a theory may be simple, but is it true? Isn't that the crucial question? Simplicity doesn't guarantee truth. *Two*, perhaps evolution isn't only a matter of smooth developments. Think of the emergence of consciousness; isn't that a radical break? Couldn't a soul be a similar break? Do we fully understand evolution? As we dig deeper, we will perhaps discover new dimensions of reality here. And evolution deals with physical development; whether or not there is a non-physical dimension of a human person is surely a new question, one outside the range of physical scientific evolution.

Three, there is the assumption that the real is the physical. But an assumption is not an argument, and it is surely not a good logical reason for adopting a position. Philosophy is in the business of questioning assumptions, not simply continuing them. This is true especially for wonder. *Four*, while the unity of person and body may be explained by materialism it hardly follows that only materialism can do this. What does it really mean to say that I am united to my body? Don't I have to be something other than my body in order to be united to it? The body is not united to the body; only a reality essentially distinct from the body can then also be united to it. That means basic dualism and a denial of materialism. Let us now examine this view.

[4] BASIC DUALISM: A PERSON IS NOT SIMPLY HIS BODY, HE IS MORE

Basic dualism is the view that a person is *not* simply his body or his brain. He *has* a body and that includes his brain, but his being a person is a reality *distinct* from these, irreducible to these. A person as person and the features that make him a person, his consciousness, thinking and feeling, are realities that exist "over and above" the physical. They are not reducible to the body and to the physical and chemical processes that make up bodily life, as materialism claims. The mind is distinct from the body, especially the brain. Mental events are essentially distinct from physical events.

Basic dualism means the *distinction* between person and body, not a *separation* between them. How they are related is a question that goes beyond the simple assertion of basic dualism. This theory holds that there is a *real distinction* between person and body, not just a difference of terms that might refer to one and the same thing, such as "Joe" and "the boss" who are really one and the same person.

Let us reflect on the *unity* of person and body and the relation of unity to the materialist claim of *identity* between person and body. I am so united to my body that we like to say that I *am* my body. But what does it really mean to say that I am my body? It cannot mean that I am reducible to my body, that I am nothing but my body as materialism claims, for then there would be no real, concrete "I" that is united to my body. As noted, I have to be a reality other than my body in order to be united to it. The body is not united to the body; only a reality that is essentially distinct from the body can then also be united to it. To say that I am my body really means that I *identify with my body* as a dimension of my being, as something that is in some sense a part of me but is not simply me or the whole of me. *Thus, basic dualism is essential for true unity.* It is a strange paradox that those who denounce all forms of "dualism" in the name of unity actually lose the unity they want to stress because they lose the "I" that must be distinct from the body (basic dualism) in order that it may be intimately united to this body. It is one thing to deny a separatist dualism which makes unity difficult or impossible; it is quite another to deny all forms of dualism or what we have called basic dualism.

The wonder of unity is precisely that a being, the conscious "I" can be so deeply and intimately united to a thing that is not itself but that nonetheless partakes of its being, as we can see when we say that you touched *me* when you touch my arm or kiss me. Or that *I* walk and *I* swim when it is my body that goes through these motions. Let us now explore some of the main reasons for holding that there is real distinction between person and body; that *I am not my body*, meaning that I am not only my body; and that the truth in the phrase *I am my body* consists in its expression of the unity of me and my body, a *me* that is not basically my body.

[5] BASIC DUALISM: A PERSON IS NOT AS SUCH HIS BODY

Why is it that I am not my body? The basic reason is that I am a *person* and persons are not as such bodies even though they are deeply united to their bodies. What then is a person?

1. Only a person is a being capable of saying "I."
2. Only a person is a being that I can address as "you."
3. Only a person is a being capable of understanding.
4. Only a person can be morally good or evil.
5. Only a person can laugh and appreciate humor.
6. Only a person can make a promise or receive one.
7. Only a person can appreciate beauty.
8. Only persons have a history.

These items reveal the essence of *being* person by noting some ways of *functioning* as a person. Thus, to say "I" means that I can reflect back perfectly on myself and know that I am and what I am. It means I possess myself in a way no other being could ever possess me. What material being could ever do these things? I can understand at least basically what it means to be a person, again something beyond the reach of mere matter. Think about what it means to make a promise and try to imagine a dog making a promise and receiving a promise we make to him. If this could happen wouldn't the dog be a person? And finally, contemplate what it means to have a history. This applies to persons not as individuals but as the totality of all persons. Have you ever realized that animals have no history? There is one generation after another, say of beavers, but no ancient history or medieval history or modern history of beavers. This is related to the fact that beavers continue to build their dams in the same way, one generation after the next.

Humans invent new and better ways; humans make inventions. Is it that only persons can make inventions? And only persons have cultures? And only cultures develop historically? Culturally, modern human persons are significantly different from the ancient Greek persons of the days of Socrates and Plato. To continue this reflection on what it means to be a person let us now consider eight reasons why a person is distinct from his body.

[6] ARGUMENTS FOR PERSON-BODY DISTINCTION

#1. I am not my body: consciousness

I am conscious. Is my body as a physical organism conscious? Is any physical organism, just as a biological organism, conscious? Parts of my body as organisms such as my heart and my lungs are not conscious. How could all of them together as a larger organism be conscious? Recall the eight items just examined; isn't it clear that none of them apply to my body as such? My body cannot say "I," it cannot understand, and it cannot be morally good or evil. Doesn't this show that I am not my body, that I am something distinct from my body?

#2. I can oppose my body

I can oppose my body. My body is tired, but I resolve to keep going. I thereby take a distance from my body; it is in this respect not me. I control my body; for example, I move my hand. Or I fail to control it, as a paralysis comes over me. I the one who controls or who fails to control cannot be this body that *I* control or that *I* don't control.

#3. Loss of body parts does not diminish me as a person

If I lose an arm or a leg to amputation, my body is diminished. But I as a conscious person am not diminished. We can think of "half my body," say my left half. But does it make any sense to speak of "half a person"? Bodies are spatial and can be divided, at least in imagination; persons are very different in this respect. And doesn't this show the radical difference between person and body? If "I" were simply my body, if I and my body were one and the same thing, then a diminishing of my body would be a diminishing of "me" as a person. Clearly it is not. Therefore, I am not my body.

#4. The argument from death

What happens at the death of a person? The body is radically changed; it is no longer a living body with blood circulation and other active bodily functions. But are these the only changes, or even the most important ones? Isn't the main thing that the person is gone? The body is still there while we mourn the *loss of a person*! I see and talk to my friend. He is there in front of me, *alive*. Then death strikes. The body is still there, but he is gone! *The person is gone!* Death is the radical separation of a person and his body. In view of my ultimate death, I am not my body. As I get older my body gets weaker and eventually it wears out and I die. My body dies; but far more important, *I* die. I die: my death is not just the death of a physical organism, a human body; it is above all the death of a person, of *me the person*, the being who can say "I." At my death my body leaves me; it can no longer support me. I am no longer united to that body, which has died. Where does that leave *me*, the person?

#5. The radically different characteristics argument

My thoughts as a person and the physical processes in my body such as those in my brain cannot be the same thing because they have radically different characteristics. My thoughts about another person can be loving thoughts; could this apply to a brain process? My thoughts can be rational or irrational; could this ever apply to a brain process? Brain processes can be measured by scientific instruments; could my desire to know the truth be detected by scientific instruments? My thoughts are my own in a way that brain processes could never be. Since thoughts and physical processes have these radically different characteristics, they cannot be one and the same. My thoughts are mine as a person; physical processes belong to my body. I am a being that can think; my body is not. I am not my body.

I know my thoughts and feelings from the inside in a way that no one else can. No brain process could ever be known in this way. A scientist can examine my brain and its electro-chemical processes; these are part of the public domain, accessible to anyone. But my thoughts are mine, absolutely and exclusively mine. They are part of my inner life as a conscious person, and thus stand in radical contrast to anything public such as a brain and its processes.

Physical things including human bodies are spatially extended but consciousness and all the features of a person rooted in it, such as reasoning, deciding, being grateful and being loving are not. Therefore, they cannot be the same thing. My body may be six feet tall but surely my consciousness is not. For any physical thing, it makes sense to imagine half of it. Thus, my brain has two halves, two hemispheres. But it makes no sense to speak of half a person, half an "I." An "I" is absolutely one. A person has many powers, many mental states; and he may be torn within himself. But these are not literally parts that can be "taken apart," as when a physical object like a machine is taken apart. A physical object is divisible. A person as a center of consciousness is absolutely indivisible. Therefore, a person, an "I" cannot be a physical object such as his brain or his whole body. I am not my body.

#6. The interiority argument

"I am I" as perfect interiority in my inner being. This can never be true of a physical object. Take a log for example. It has an "outside." Cut it open, and you get more of the same, smaller pieces of wood each with their "outside." Keep this up as long as you like; there will always be only "outsides," never the interiority that I experience when I say "I am I." The same thing is of course true of my body. As a physical body it has only externality; to have interiority one must bring in the person as distinct from the body. I as a person can then know myself as a bodily being, a person intimately united to my body. The body alone, the body as such – the way it exists for materialism – has only externality; not the interiority proper to persons. Interiority thus shows once again: I am not my body. I have interiority, my body does not.

I know myself as myself. I know my own being, the center of consciousness that is me. The remarkable thing here is the *perfect coinciding* of knower and object known. In all other cases the subject that knows and the object that is known are two separate and distinct things. I see a tree, I know my friend, and I know a historical fact. In all these cases there is a duality of knower and known. But a person is radically different. I know myself in a perfect oneness of the being who knows and the being who is known. *Only I know what it's like to be me.*

No physical thing could ever be known by its own being as itself. If it is known it is known by another, as an object distinct from the knower. Even my own body can be seen as an example of this. I look at my hand. I can examine it as an object, just as I examine the hand of another person or as a doctor would examine his patient's hand. As an object *out there,* it is not my own being as *I* am my own being; it is known to me only as an object.

This applies with special force to my brain. I am not my brain because I know myself and know myself as a center of consciousness; I generally do not know my brain. And if I do know it, I know it as an object out there and not as myself, and not as a center of consciousness.

Even in my experience of my own body as being me, intimate though it is, we do not find this absolute convergence of knower and known into one. First, I know myself as a center of consciousness, an "I" who thinks and understands and wills and feels, all of which do not refer to any of my body experiences. Second, I know my body as a multiplicity; my right arm, my left arm, my right leg, my left leg, my head, my body as a whole. This multiplicity stands in sharp contrast to the absolute simplicity of "I am I"; I know myself as myself. I am subject and object in one. In this way I know myself from within and thereby I have true interiority. Only I know myself from the inside. *Again, only I know what it's like to be me.*

#7: My body is a world of its own

I eat my dinner and turn my attention to other things. While I do so my stomach digests my food. How does this happen? Apart from learning about it from science I have no idea. Yet it is happening inside me and in some way very close to me. And yet it is so far from me in my total ignorance of it in terms of my immediate experience. It is in a world of its own. I bruise my hand, and this causes a wound. What does my skin do to heal this wound? It is happening right here in my body; yet I have no idea how this is happening. My body: a world of its own.

How did my body grow and develop from a tiny cell into the developed body I now have, that enables me to reflect on these things, and wonder about them? For the first few years of my life my body grew in height; then it stopped growing. How did that happen? How did it "know" when it was time to stop growing? How did it bring this about? It happened in me. Yet I have no idea how it happened. My body is a world of its own, removed from my awareness.

#8. I am not my brain

Think of your brain. Here surely, you might say, is a case of "I am my body." Your brain is the central organ essential for all bodily life and functioning. It is essential for rational thought, for saying "I," for seeing and hearing, for all the five senses. Surely this is me.

But is it really? Think about it again. What do you know about your brain? How do you even know you have a brain? Isn't everything you know here only what others have told you? In terms of what you know and feel directly as a matter of immediate experience, in particular what you know and feel to be your very self, isn't your brain as far removed from being you, even from being united to you, as an object out there in front of you?

How strange that the same body that I know so well, so intimately as *my body* and even as *me* should be so removed from me when it is viewed as a physical organ! But we must look a bit deeper into the role of the brain for being a person and functioning as a person.

[7] ARGUMENTS CONCERNING LIFE AFTER DEATH AND THE BRAIN

[a] THE BRAIN AS NECESSARY CONDITION

It is clear that the brain is immensely important. For example, without my brain I would not be able to think and act. If my brain functioning is impaired, my abilities to think and act are correspondingly impaired. The ravages of Alzheimer's disease provide a tragic example.

I move my hand; it is not my brain that does so. But, of course, my brain is a necessary condition for this. So too my brain is a necessary condition for thinking, but it is not that which thinks; it is not the agent of thinking. *I* think; not "my brain thinks." Think of reading a book. To do this you need light; you cannot read in total darkness. Thus, light is a necessary condition for reading, but it is not the agent of reading; you are. You are the one who does the reading. And the light does not actually cause the content of what you read; it only makes possible your access to this content as it is contained in the book.

Again, the brain is immensely important; I depend on my brain. This means I depend on something else to function as a person. To say "I depend on my brain" is not only not equivalent to "I am my brain," but is even incompatible with it. My seeing depends on my eyes, but it is *I* who see, not my eyes. I see *with* my eyes, *by means of* my eyes. So too, in an analogous though very different way my thinking depends on my brain. I think with my brain, by means of my brain, but it is *I* who thinks, not my brain.

Again, my brain is a necessary condition for thinking, but it is not that which thinks; it is not the agent of thinking. *I* think; and I do so *with* my brain. How this "with" relation actually works is a deep mystery, though brain science can tell us some things. What we should notice, and make an object of our wonder, is that the relation of thinking and brain processes is at the same time so close, so intimate in terms of actual dependence—and yet so distant, so utterly removed in terms of my conscious experience. I am conscious of a person I love deeply; I am conscious of that love. I understand the importance of truth, that what I believe should not be what I find convenient, but what is really true, what corresponds to reality, what expresses "how it really is." Compare this clear, lucid conscious experience, a part of my life as a person, a conscious center, an "*I*," with a gray soft piece of matter, and electrical and chemical impulses sent with amazing frequency along nerves. What two things could be more different?

Wonder: *two things so radically different, I as a conscious person and my brain*; and yet my brain is so intimately tied in with the "I," my consciousness and its activities. I need my brain to think; but it is *I* who is doing the thinking, not my brain. The role of the brain here, as a necessary condition for thinking but not the agent of thinking, can be seen under four headings:

First, there is the basic and general necessary condition: no brain, no thought; no brain process, no thinking. Second, there is the more specific necessary condition: no proper functioning brain, no proper thinking. What this means is that damage to the brain or significant alterations to brain chemistry can radically alter a person's consciousness and his ability to think rationally. Think of a drug overdose or brain damage that causes dementia. Other alterations to brain chemistry are not radical but still significant. Thus, even a normal case of tiredness can slow down our thinking and make it less effective. We can say that the necessary condition for proper thinking is a properly functioning brain.

Put another way, the brain sometimes exerts *negative causal influences* on thinking, in that damage to the brain may prevent thought, or rational thought. But from the possibility of negative causal influences nothing follows for *positive causal agency*. A bomb which can destroy a building cannot bring it into existence. An electric malfunction can impede, distort or prevent a telephone conversation between two people. But the electric equipment that either makes possible a normal conversation or prevents it does not positively cause this conversation. The people do. There is a similar relation between brain process and thinking. The causal relation runs only in one direction: brain processes may prevent normal thinking or make it possible; they cannot positively bring it into existence.

Third, there may also be positive causal influences from brain to thinking, in that certain ways of enhancing brain functioning thereby enhance thinking.

Fourth, if a person's behavior is actually caused by his brain or brain processes, then it is not really his behavior. He is not acting as a person. A deranged person may kill another person. If it is determined that his action was caused by a brain tumor and not by him as a person, we do not hold him responsible. Thus we can say that *in so far as* a person's behavior is actually caused by his brain or brain processes, it is not really his behavior and he is not responsible for it.

Another comparison to the brain as necessary condition for thinking is the tongue for speaking. *I* speak, not my tongue. I need my tongue; I use my tongue and I would not be able to speak without my tongue. We can use both these comparisons – light for reading and the tongue for speaking – to highlight the four points just made. First, without light there can be no reading and without a tongue there can be no speaking. Second, poor light or damage to the tongue will impair reading or speaking. Third, better light allows for more efficient reading and certain medications may enable a speaking-impaired person to improve his speech, perhaps overcome stuttering. Fourth, in the hard-to-imagine case where the agent of speaking is the tongue instead of the person, we would obviously say that the person is not the one who is speaking. The comparison to eyes needed for seeing but not the agent of seeing fits here as well. Thus, for example poor eyesight interferes with a person's ability to see while good eyesight enhances it.

[b] THE BRAIN AS COMPUTER

Perhaps one way we can understand the relation between a person and his brain is on the analogy of agent and computer. Not *I am my brain*, but I *have a brain*. I have a brain as a kind of automatic computer. Of course, I do not operate it consciously and deliberately; it works for me automatically. I need only will something and my inner computer works automatically for me to bring it about. Wilder Penfield remarks that "Inasmuch as the brain is a place for newly acquired automatic mechanisms, it is a computer."[1] Mathematical calculations and information processing are operations performed both by human persons and by computers, though of course in essentially different ways; for persons do these consciously and deliberately while computers do not. Persons consciously follow

---

[1] Wilder Penfield, *The Mystery of the Mind: A Critical Study of Consciousness and the Human Brain* (Princeton, 1975), 60.

[c] THE BRAIN AS TRANSMITTER

William James in his book *Human Immortality* offers a striking defense of the person-body distinction. He argues for the possibility of human immortality or life-after-death and thereby for the reality of the conscious person distinct from the brain. His starting point is the doctrine that "thought is a function of the brain." He then asks: "Does this doctrine logically compel us to disbelieve in immortality"[2] and to deny the person-body distinction? His answer is an emphatic *no*. He suggests that there are several different kinds of functions.

One kind of function is *productive*, that is causal. A trumpet produces a sound, the motor of a car produces its motion, and a generator produces electricity. But there are other kinds of functions, and these do not imply that the brain produces thinking in the sense that it causes it, or that thinking just is a brain process. Specifically, there is also a *transmissive* function. That is, when a materialist uses the phrase "thought is a function of the brain" to express his theory, he is using it in only one of its senses. In James' words,

> But in the world of physical nature productive function of this sort is not the only kind of function with which we are familiar. We have also…transmissive function….
>
> In the case of a colored glass, a prism, or a refracting lens, we have transmissive function. The energy of light, no matter how produced, is by the glass sifted and limited in color, and by the lens or prism determined to a certain path and shape. Similarly, the keys of an organ have only a transmissive function. They open successively the various pipes and let the wind in the air-chest escape in various ways. The voices of

---

[2] William James, *Human Immortality*, 2nd ed., in *The Will to Believe and Human Immortality* (Dover, 1956), 10.

the various pipes are constituted by the columns of air trembling as they emerge. But the air is not engendered in the organ. The organ proper, as distinguished from its air-chest, is only an apparatus for letting portions of it loose upon the world in these peculiarly limited shapes.

My thesis now is this: that, when we think of the law that thought is a function of the brain, we are not required to think of productive function only; *we are entitled also to consider…transmissive function*. And this the ordinary psycho-physiologist leaves out of his account.[3]

[d] THE SCHILLER VISION: THE ROLE OF THE BRAIN AS LIMITED

Clearly there is a close relationship between brain processes and consciousness. When brain processes are affected, consciousness is likewise affected. Brain damage can cause damage to consciousness, especially reasoning ability and memory. But how are they really related? On materialism (the denial of the person-body distinction) the brain and its processes have primacy. Given the brain consciousness follows as a causal effect. Consciousness is caused by the brain; thinking is a brain process.

But suppose we reverse this picture and think of consciousness as having the primacy. Consciousness, and specifically the conscious subject, the "I" exists in its own right, though intimately united with the body and closely dependent on the body. The conscious subject acts *through* the body as a medium of expression. Think of the body, in particular the brain, as a screen or window, and consciousness as a light. The screen or window lets more light or less light shine through, but the light is there in any case. The light exists in its own right. On this view, the brain acts as a *limit* to consciousness. This is the Schiller vision. Doesn't it provide an interesting and challenging, even an illuminating answer to the materialist thesis that the brain causes consciousness? In Schiller's own words:

---

[3] Ibid., 13-15. Italics in original.

Matter is an admirably calculated machinery for regulating, limiting, and restraining consciousness which it encases. If the material encasement be coarse and simple, as in the lower organisms, it permits only a little intelligence to permeate through it; if it is delicate and complex, it leaves more pores and exits, as it were, for the manifestations of consciousness.

On this analogy, then, we may say that the lower animals are still entranced in the lower stage of brute *lethargy*, while we have passed into the higher phase of *somnambulism*, which already permits us strange glimpses of a lucidity that divines the realities of a transcendent world.

And this gives the final answer to Materialism: it consists in showing in detail that Materialism is a hysteron proteron, a putting of the cart before the horse, which may be rectified by just inverting the connection between Matter and Consciousness. Matter is not that which *produces* Consciousness, but that which *limits* it, and confines its intensity within certain limits: material organization does not construct consciousness out of arrangements of atoms, but contracts its manifestation within the sphere which it permits.

This explanation admits the connection of Matter and Consciousness, but contends that the course of interpretation must proceed in the contrary direction. Thus, it will fit the facts alleged in favor of Materialism equally well, besides enabling us to understand facts which Materialism rejected as 'supernatural.' It explains the lower by the higher, Matter by Spirit, instead of *vice versa*, and thereby attains to an explanation which is ultimately tenable, instead of one which is ultimately absurd.

And it is an explanation the possibility of which no evidence in favor of Materialism can possibly affect. For if, *e.g.*, a man loses consciousness as soon as his brain is injured, it is clearly as good an explanation to say the injury to the brain destroyed the mechanism by which the manifestation of the consciousness was rendered possible [as in the Schiller Vision], as to say that it destroyed the seat of consciousness [as in materialism, where the seat of consciousness is the brain].

On the other hand, there are facts which the former theory [the Schiller Vision] suits far better. If, *e.g.*, as sometimes happens, the man, after a time, more or less, recovers the faculties of which the injury to his brain had deprived him, and that not in consequence of a renewal of the injured part, but in consequence of the inhibited functions being performed by the vicarious action of other parts, the easiest explanation certainly is that, after a time, consciousness constitutes the remaining parts into a mechanism capable of acting as a substitute for the lost parts.[4]

Let us note some of Schiller's key points:

- Materialism puts the cart before the horse; this can be rectified by just inverting the connection between matter and consciousness.
- Matter is not that which *produces* consciousness, but that which *limits* it, and confines its intensity within certain limits.
- Material organization does not construct consciousness out of arrangements of atoms, but contracts its manifestation within the sphere which it permits.

The analogy to my eyes. None of this is meant in any way to deny that I depend on my brain, as was noted above. Precisely, I depend on something else to function as a person. Recall the comparison: my seeing depends on my eyes, but it is *I* who see, not my eyes. I see with my eyes, *by means* of my eyes. So too my thinking depends on my brain: I think with my brain, by means of my brain, but it is *I* who thinks, not my brain. As in Schiller's vision, the better my eyes function, the more clearly I can see. My eyes are "windows" through which I reach reality.

---

[4] F. C. S. Schiller, *Riddles of the Sphinx* (London: Swan Sonnenschein, 1891), 293 ff. Quoted by William James in his *Human Immortality*, 66-68. Ellipses in James' text have been deleted; division into short paragraphs added.

[e] THE BRAIN IS NOT THE SOURCE OF CAUSAL INITIATIVE

Another way to see the limiting role of the brain is to ask: does the brain have a causal role? Surely it does; think of its activity in regulating the heart, the lungs, body temperature and so much else. But suppose my brain caused my hand to move.

I didn't do that. You did. Wilder Penfield conducted experiments in which we can see the radical contrast between the normal cases where *I* move my hand, and cases where it is really a brain event that causes my hand to move. He tells us:

> When I have caused a conscious patient to move his hand by applying an electrode to the motor cortex of one hemisphere [of the brain], I have often asked him about it. Invariably his response was: "I didn't do that. You did." When I caused him to vocalize, he said: "I didn't make that sound. You pulled it out of me."[5]

What a brain state causes is not my action; it is something that happens to me. If my physical actions were always caused by my brain, the effects of the brain states, my daily life would be just like that of Penfield's patients. Clearly it is not. This means that *I* as a conscious being self-initiate and cause my physical actions, not my brain. Therefore, I am not my brain, and more generally I am not my body.

[f] THE MANY ASPECTS OF THE BRAIN

The brain: so important and so central; and yet also a limiting force on consciousness. It is central and important as a necessary condition for our being and functioning as persons; it is our inner computer and transmitter. Yet as the Schiller vision shows it also limits us. It is so close to us in making our consciousness possible; yet so far removed from our consciousness itself in that we don't know

---

[5] Penfield, 76.

it directly and hardly think of it as it does its job. We depend on it to control our lives as we move about and do things. And yet it also controls us: it determines our body temperature, blood pressure, digestion and so much more. The brain: a source of wonder!

[g] TWO VIEWS OF THE HUMAN PERSON

There are basically two views one can take of human beings:

1. *Human beings are fundamentally biological organisms.*
2. *Human beings are fundamentally persons.*

View #1 starts with *the body* as its primary datum. It goes on to add that it is a highly complex body, one capable of highly complex behavior. It stresses that humans are products of evolution. While not strictly equivalent to materialism, it is a view congenial to materialism and has the same flavor. All materialists adopt this view; perhaps the converse is also true.

View #2 starts with human beings as *persons* as its primary datum. This was the view adopted in the previous chapter and in the present one. We are primarily persons; that is by far the most important and significant fact about us. It is the basis of our dignity as human persons and our human rights. We also have bodies, and we are intimately united to these bodies and dependent on them. We act as bodily persons. The role of the body can hardly be overstated. And yet in the core of our being we are not pieces of matter and biological organisms. We are *persons*, beings capable of saying "I," of understanding philosophical and scientific ideas, of loving other persons, of being morally responsible, of longing to continue to exist in a life after death and so much more.

View #1 is obviously friendly to science and congenial to its spirit; view #2 is equally so. Someone filled with the love of science and seeing the world and his experience in a spirit of scientific objectivity will recognize that the fundamental truth about us is that we are persons.

View #1 is not congenial to life after death while view #2 is very congenial to it. We are now bodily persons. If we continue to exist in a life after death what kind of persons will we be?

On view #2 we now rely on our brain to function as persons. In a life after death we will rely on something else; *the brain will no longer be needed.* Who can imagine what that is? On the Schiller Vision, the brain is now a limiting factor that holds us back to some extent. In a life after death this will no longer be the case; *the brain will no longer hold us back.*

[h] ARGUMENTS CONCERNING LIFE AFTER DEATH AND PERSONAL IDENTITY

[1] HOW IS PERSONAL IDENTITY RELEVANT FOR LIFE AFTER DEATH?

Personal identity is the idea that you always remain *the same person* over time. How is it relevant to our topic, life after death? There are three ways. *First*, it refers to what we *mean* by life after death. If there is a life after death my personal identity continues in a new life after this one. *Second*, if personal identity applies only to persons and not to impersonal things it provides an additional argument for the essential distinction between a person and his body. It thus gives us another reason for the *yes* answer to the question whether life after death is possible. *Third*, there are several theories that claim to account for personal identity, to explain what it is. Some of these theories would rule out the possibility of life after death and thus support the *no* answer. We will return to these three things in section 5 below.

[2] PERSONAL IDENTITY AND THE IDENTITY OF THINGS

Are you the same person now as the day when you were born? Of course, you are, else it would not be the case that it was you who were born that day. But haven't you changed? In fact, haven't you changed considerably, even radically? Your body then and your body now are radically different. You were an infant then; you are a mature grown-up now. All the things you know now you didn't know then. The same is true for so much else, such as the skills you now have but didn't have then. If you've changed so much, how can you still be the same person? Think of physical objects; when they change radically, don't they lose their identity? You eat a tomato; you chew it and swallow it; it gets digested and is so completely changed that it loses its original identity. Why doesn't the same apply to you and to human persons generally? It seems we don't ever lose our identity as persons the way a tomato loses its identity as a tomato. But why not? What is it that makes us different?

DIFFERENT KINDS OF IDENTITY

Is the answer perhaps in this direction: persons and things like tomatoes are very different in terms of their identity; they have *different kinds of identity*? In what ways are they different?

First, can the identity of a person ever be lost? What could it mean to lose your identity? Isn't it so that no matter how much you change you are always *you,* the same person? Consider an example. Karl is a guard in a Nazi camp, a very cruel and sadistic guard. But then, much later in his life he has a dramatic, soul-shaking moral and religious conversion. He sees the evil of what he used to do, deeply repents it and now strives to be the exact opposite of what he used to be; he tries very hard to be a very loving person. Isn't he in a very real sense "a new person" in that his character has changed so dramatically? But in another, even deeper sense, isn't he still *the same person*? Didn't the radical change occur in the life of one and the same person? After the conversion can he not truthfully say "I was once a cruel Nazi guard"? And when he says this, doesn't he mean that I now and the former Nazi guard am one and the same person?

If this is so we can say that personal identity means: *I am always the same person.* When I change, I do not change into another person, I do not become another person. I always remain the same person. The deep metaphysical fact that personal identity can never be lost is captured by the simple phrase: *I am always me.* As long as I exist at all I am always me, the same person.

What follows from this is the huge difference between these two phrases:

Chapter 27: Life after Death: Is it Possible?

- "I am always *the same*." This is clearly false: I change.
- "I am always *the same person*." This is true, this is personal identity.

Second, there seems to be another point, closely related to the first. Isn't the identity of persons *absolute* as opposed to being a matter of degree? Consider another example, a wooden ship. If you change a few of its planks, can it not still be considered the same ship, with no loss of its identity? Change a few more: isn't it still the same ship? But if you keep changing the planks until you have finally changed all of them, will it not then be the case that you no longer have the same original ship? That the original ship will have lost its identity? But at what point in this set of changes has the original identity been lost? It seems impossible to say. Doesn't this mean that the identity of a ship is not something definite and clear-cut, but merely something that attaches loosely to the ship? Isn't it something that is mainly of practical use, as in identifying it (and not another ship) as the one legally owned by a certain person? Can we say that the ship's identity as "the same ship" over a period of time is merely a matter of degree, perhaps even only a matter of practical convenience? Doesn't the identity of a person, his being "the same person" over a period of time stand in radical contrast to this because it is absolute? A ship can be more or less the same ship as before; but a person: isn't he either absolutely the same person or not at all the same person? Isn't it true that there can be no in-between?

Our experience bears this out. You see someone who looks like your old friend Jim. Is it Jim? You're not sure; you approach him and see if he recognizes you, and if you recognize him. But isn't one thing quite certain: it's either that particular person or it's someone else, there's no in-between? Isn't it clear that there can't be a relative, matter-of-degree identity with a person as there is with a ship? And doesn't it follow from this that identity for persons means something radically different from what it means for ships?

Third, isn't there also this difference? Radical changes not only do not destroy personal identity in that personal identity can never be lost (first point); they are *meaningful only because of personal identity*. What is striking about the Nazi guard who converts? Isn't it precisely that it is one and *the same person* who is first extremely evil, and is then very good? Suppose there were two persons, one evil and the other good; wouldn't this point be lost? Here then we have a striking difference between the two kinds of identities: radical changes wipe out the thin identity that mere things have; but radical changes play a significant role in the identity of persons in that radical changes become highly significant only on the basis of personal identity.

A BRIEF SUMMARY

A brief summary may be helpful. Personal identity means I am always *the same person*; I am always *me*. This holds even through radical changes:

1. Radical changes do not destroy or take away personal identity; it can never be lost.
2. Personal identity is absolute: totally present or totally absent, never in degrees.
3. Radical changes are meaningful only because of personal identity.

Personal identity can never be lost: as long as I exist at all *I am always me*. But do we not sometimes say that a person acquires a new identity? He changes so much that we say he has a new identity. We might say of Karl, the former Nazi guard, that he is now a different person. Yes, we say this, but what do we mean? Do we mean that he is literally a new, different person, no longer the same "I" or the same "me"? Do we not rather mean that he, *the very same person*, has changed so dramatically that we now view him very differently? Isn't it simply that the term *identity* as used here in "new identity" is meant to convey two related ideas: his dramatic change in character and our now viewing him very differently? Identity in this second sense then refers to "what a person is known as." That of course often changes. Thus, we have:

- PI *primary sense*: who you *really are*, the same person; it *never changes*.
- PI *secondary sense*: what you *are known as*, not the same person; it *can change*.

Chapter 27: Life after Death: Is it Possible?

AN IMPORTANT CLARIFICATION

Personal identity means that I am always the same person. But we must be very careful in how we understand the key term *the same*. Very often this means unchanging as when we say that the temperature has not changed; it is still the same as before. We should not think of personal identity as some strange, unchanging, ghostly core element deep in our being, one that cannot be seen or touched but must be postulated to account for personal identity. That would be a very wrong picture and one that would lead many of us to deny personal identity.

Personal identity is not something that is somehow "added" to our being as persons, either our mind or soul or our body. Rather it is an essential and necessary feature of our very being as persons. It's part of what we *are*, not something we *have* like our memory and our right hand. To say that we have personal identity can only mean that this is part of the description of what our being as persons consists in. The key to understanding this is to realize that personal identity is something of its own, something that must be seen and understood directly. It cannot be subsumed under some other category, as if it were an instance of some more general thing, as when we understand that a tiger is an instance of the more general category animal.

PERSONAL IDENTITY AND OUR EXPERIENCE

Isn't personal identity fundamental to our experience? Isn't it foundational for memory? Isn't our memory possible only on the basis of our continuity through our personal identity? I now remember an experience I had in the past, such as (say) a summer in Vermont. Isn't this possible only if the "I now" who remembers the experience is *the same person* as the "I then" who had the experience that took place in the past and is now remembered?

Doesn't the same structure apply also to intending? I now intend to go to the library later today. Doesn't this mean that the "I now" who intends to go there and the "I later" who will carry out this intention must be *the same person*? Isn't deliberating similar? "I now" who deliberate and "I later" who do what was decided in the deliberation must be *the same person.*

Aren't there also cases of dual identities? Think of gratitude. You save my life. I am immensely grateful to you! First there's *my identity*: I-now am grateful for what was done for me-then; must it not be the same I-me in both cases? Second, isn't there also *your identity* as the doer of the deed and the receiver of my gratitude? I-now am grateful to you-now for what you-then did for me in the past; must it not be the same you in both cases?

Are there other cases of dual identity? Think of promising, asking for forgiveness and granting forgiveness. In each case there seems to be *my identity* and *your identity*:

My identity: I-later who will keep the promise must be the same person as I-now who makes the promise. *Your identity*: you-later to whom I will keep my promise must be the same person as you-now to whom I make the promise.

My identity: I-now who ask for forgiveness must be the same person as I-then who did the wrong for which forgiveness is now sought. *Your identity*: you-now of whom I ask forgiveness and you-then who was wronged must be the same person.

My identity: I-now who grant forgiveness: the same person as the one who was wronged. *Your identity*: you-now being granted forgiveness: the same person who inflicted the wrong.

Here is a little story that brings out dramatically the significance of personal identity and its role in our experience. A woman is robbed as she attends her store. The robber flees. Later she is called to the police station and asked to identify a suspect. "Is he the man who robbed your store?" She says he is. "Are you sure?" "Yes, I'm absolutely sure." "Is there any doubt in your mind?" "No, there is absolutely no doubt; he's the one!" As she walks out of the police station, she sees a second suspect just being brought in. He looks exactly like the first suspect whom she swore is the man who robbed her. She is horrified! In an instance she realizes that the actual robber could just as easily be the second man as the first one. The first one could be innocent! Yet she identified him as the robber with absolute confidence. "What if I was mistaken?" What underlies this drama is the question of personal identity: which of the two suspects is really *the same person* as the real robber?

[3] THREE THEORIES ABOUT PERSONAL IDENTITY

What accounts for personal identity? How is it to be explained, especially its being so different from the identity of things like ships? Several theories have been proposed:

The Memory Theory. The classic expression of this theory is John Locke who refers to memory as consciousness. The idea is that my memory of myself in the past is what makes me the same person as that person in the past. He says:

> For, since consciousness always accompanies thinking, and it is that which makes everyone to be what he calls self, and thereby distinguishes himself from all other thinking things: in this alone consists personal identity, i.e., the sameness of a rational being; and as far as this consciousness can be extended backwards to any past action or thought, so far reaches the identity of that person; it is the same self now it was then; and it is by the same self with the present one that now reflects on it, that the action was done.[6]

Memory is certainly a *sufficient* condition for personal identity. As we have already seen memory is possible only on the basis of the continuity of personal identity. The "I now" who remembers a past experience must be *the same person* as the "I then" who had the experience. Thus, it is clear that if there is memory there must be personal identity; memory suffices to insure that there is personal identity.

But is memory a *necessary* condition for personal identity? Is it true that if there is no memory there cannot be personal identity? Is it true that "If there is personal identity there must be memory"? Isn't it rather so: memory is *not* a necessary condition for personal identity; and this for the following reasons?

---

[6] John Locke, *Essay Concerning Human Understanding*, 2nd ed., 1694, from chapter 27.

(1) Didn't I exist *before my earliest memories*? I cannot remember being born and the many moments following soon after my birth; but wasn't it *me*, the same person I am now, who was born then and had those early moments of existence? And, of course, I cannot remember the time before my birth in my mother's womb; but again, if I existed at all at that time, wasn't it *me* who existed then? If not, how could it be that I exist now?

(2) Suppose I suffer *amnesia*, so that there is a period in my past life of which I have no memories. Was it not I, the same person I am now, who suffered this amnesia? If not, what does it mean to say that *I* suffered amnesia? My consciousness cannot be extended backwards to this past time in my life; yet doesn't my identity reach that far back and indeed before that time? Doesn't the same hold for being unconscious during total anesthesia? My consciousness does not reach to that time; but wasn't it *me*, the same person I am now, who existed during that time?

(3) The memory theory cannot account for *the future*; it is entirely past-looking. But isn't my personal identity important also for the future? We plan to do certain things in the future, we anticipate the future; we deliberate what to do, we hope for good things, we fear evil things; and all these of course refer to the future, to *my* future as *the same person* I am now. And isn't this especially true for life after death? We will return to this point shortly.

(4) Doesn't the memory theory also fail in regard to the meaning of personal identity as it applies to *other persons*? Recall the story about the store robbery and the two suspects. Which of them is the same person as the actual robber? Isn't this is a matter of correctly identifying another person, his memory or lack thereof having nothing to do with this? If he in fact did the deed, isn't he the guilty person even if he were to forget his doing it?

(5) The most fundamental criticism of the memory theory is that it has it backwards. It is not that memory is a necessary condition for personal identity; but that *personal identity is a necessary condition for memory*. Personal identity is basic; memory comes later. This point, parallel to memory being a *sufficient* condition for personal identity, was made by Joseph Butler:

> And one should really think it self-evident, that consciousness of personal identity presupposes, and therefore cannot constitute, personal identity, any more than knowledge, in any other case, can constitute truth, which it presupposes.[7]

The Whole Body Continuity Theory. This is the idea that you are the same person as long as you exist continuously in the same body. Initially this may seem to work well, as we do remain in our bodies for our whole life. And we identify other persons in this way: you are the same person if I recognize your body, especially your face, as the same. But several problems arise; perhaps the most interesting is the logical possibility of bodily transfer. Locke considers this; he asks us to imagine a prince and a cobbler changing bodies and what it would be like for each to be considered the other. A more recent example of this is the movie, "Freaky Friday"[8] in which a mother and her teen daughter switch bodies. Each has to adapt to the other's usual life for one freaky Friday.

If person A goes into the body of person B (and vice versa), doesn't the identity of person A go along into the new body? And doesn't this mean a separation of personal identity from the previous body, that is, a break in bodily continuity? And doesn't this show that *bodily continuity is not the essence of personal identity*? It seems to be neither necessary nor sufficient, as bodily transfer shows. Of course, bodily transfer cannot in fact be carried out as in these fanciful cases. But consider their logical possibility: they do not seem to involve any logical contradiction. Isn't this enough to show that personal identity does not mean whole body continuity?

The Brain Continuity Theory. Given this objection to the whole body continuity theory those who want to find the meaning of personal identity in bodily continuity turn to the brain. The idea is that you are the same person if you have the same brain. But suppose my brain is gradually modified, one part removed and replaced by another that has the same function as the other part but is numerical-

---

[7] Joseph Butler, *The Analogy of Religion*, 1736, First Appendix.

[8] Based on a novel by Mary Rodgers; screenplay by Heather Hatch; released August 6, 2003.

ly distinct. Think of the ship being rebuilt plank by plank as in our example above on page 38. During the brain modification procedure my life goes on as before; I hardly notice any difference. But at the end of the procedure don't I have a *different brain*? Still, if it is I who now have a different brain must this I not be *the same person* as before?

[4] THE SOUL AS THE BASIS OF PERSONAL IDENTITY

Both the memory theory and the two bodily theories seem not to account for the reality of personal identity; that as long as I exist, I always exist as *me*, the *same person*. Let us look at one more theory. If my identity is not a capacity I have as a person (my memory), nor my body, then it must lie in *me*; it must lie in *me as a person*; it must be part of the essence of what I am as a person. The traditional term for this is *the soul*.

This theory goes back to Plato, particularly his *Phaedo*. Plato held a particular version of the soul theory, one that emphasized the radical distinction, even separation, of soul and body. What is being suggested here is a broader theory that reflects later developments emphasizing soul-body unity, holding that a human person is a single being, soul and body as two dimensions of one person. Today the term *mind* is generally used in place of *soul,* as in "the mind-body problem." The term *soul* should be understood as referring to the non-physical dimension of the person and is meant in a purely philosophic sense, not in a religious one.

In one way we can say that the soul is the real you. In the movie "Freaky Friday" when the mother and her daughter switched bodies it was the soul of each that went into the body of the other. But in another way the real you is the whole person, body-soul, as in "you are now standing up"; not just your body and surely not just your soul, but you, the whole person.

Can we then say that I have personal identity, that I am always *the same person* because of my soul? Can we also say that it is not the body that confers identity on the person but quite the opposite, that it is the person as soul that confers identity on the body? I experience my body over time as always *my body*, hence as *the same body*? Isn't the experienced identity over time that my body has something given to it through my soul, through my being as a person?

It should be noted that the reality and supreme importance of life after death is actually the main concern of Plato in his *Phaedo*. And many of us, maybe all of us, wonder: is death the absolute end of our existence? Or will we continue to exist after the death of our bodies?

[5] THE RELEVANCE OF PERSONAL IDENTITY FOR LIFE AFTER DEATH

How is personal identity relevant for life after death? That was the theme of section 1. *First*, the *meaning* of life after death is essentially that of personal identity: will I continue to exist in a life after death, the same "I" who exists now, *the same person* I am now?

Second, personal identity provides an argument for the essential distinction between a person and his body. Do I have the same body now that I had as a five year old child? The cells in my body have replaced themselves every seven years, so I no longer have the same body. Hasn't my body therefore lost its identity as a physical reality? But I am still *the same person* now as the person who existed as a small child and had that child-body. That is, persons have personal identity while physical things like the human body do not, and so they cannot be the same thing. I have personal identity; my body does not and therefore I am not my body. This in turn provides solid evidence for a *yes* answer: life after death is possible.

Third, the three theories in section 3 would rule out the possibility of life after death and thus they support the *no* answer to the question whether life after death is possible. As noted, the memory theory cannot account for the future; it is entirely past-looking. But we anticipate the future, and we hope for good things in the future; and these refer to *my* future as *the same person* I am now. This is especially true for life after death and so the memory theory falls short here. The two other theories also fall short as they are both bodily continuity theories. But death is the end of the life of the body, and thus the end of bodily continuity. If personal identity is defined by the body and bodily continuity, then clearly the end of the body must also be the end of the person, thus ruling out the possibility of life after death.

[6] PERSON-BODY UNITY AND LIFE AFTER DEATH

Wonder at the human person: *I am not my body,* and *I am my body.* As they stand, they cannot both be true as they contradict each other. But taken in different ways they are both true.

I am not my body means I am distinct from my body; I as a person am not simply my body; and a person cannot be reduced to his body. The other phrase *I am my body* means that I am intimately united to my body. I feel my body to be *me.* When my body moves or stands or lies down it is *I* who move or stand or lie down. When my body is sick or tired it is *I* who am sick or tired. When I drive my car or do some physical work like putting the dishes away, it is both *I* and my body that do these things; they manifest the intimate unity of person and body as one being, one reality, one bodily person. If you see my body, you see *me.* Isn't this one of the factors in the importance of wearing clothes? And if you touch my body, you touch *me.* Is this something good or something bad? Doesn't it all depend on the context, on who the other person is?

Given this intimate unity of *me* and *my body,* how could I exist in a life after death? That body that is now somehow me will no longer exist as my body. I will no longer exist as that bodily being in that mode of existence; I will have a different mode of existence, one which we cannot imagine now. I will not have the body I now have. How then will I exist? Let me suggest a formula:

- I now exist *in a bodily way.*
- I then will exist *in some other way.*

The mode of existence changes, from the present bodily mode to some other mode. But the being who exists in these two modes is the same being: I *the same person* exist now in one way and then in another way.

[7] SOME WONDER THOUGHTS ABOUT PERSONAL IDENTITY

All the things around me lose their identity when they change radically – except other persons. Think of a person you know and love, someone who has been a part of your life a very long time. It is of course the *same person* now as when he or she first came into your life; isn't that part of the very meaning of the relationship? Yet that person now has a different body. So it is not the body that has this continuity of identity; it is the person. Yet when you look at him isn't it the body you see? Yes, but in seeing the body you see the person. How is that possible?

All the things around me lose their identity when they change radically – but I don't lose my identity; I remain always the *same person*. How can this be? Am I not a bodily being like the things around me? Yes, but I am more than that; I am a person, and part of that is that I remain always the same person. If not, I could not have a memory of my experiences in the past; I could not be held accountable for what I did in the past; and much else.

The wonder of personal identity leads to many questions and points of reflection:

- What is personal identity? It is in some ways like other identities (such as a ship) and yet also very different. Is it perhaps more different from the identity of a ship than similar to it? Doesn't it have a permanence entirely lacking in the being of "the same ship"? Isn't it identity in a radically different sense?
- Where does this identity come from? Why do we have it while other things don't?
- Can we say that personal identity comes from the soul, not the body? But where does the soul come from? How does the soul bring with it personal identity? That is probably not the correct way to formulate it. How would the soul account for personal identity?
- Think of the unity you have with your body. As noted, if your body is sick, you are sick. If your body is seen or touched by another you are seen or touched. If you stretch your body you are stretching. And yet your body loses its identity while you don't? You no longer have the body of a five year old child. And yet you – the same person you are now – were once a five year old child. How can this be?
- You are intimately one with your body and yet your body doesn't have the continuing identity that you have. In one way you are your body: the intimate unity. In another way you are not your body: you are always the same person while your body is not always the same body. How can this be?

- It is not memory or the whole body or the brain that confers or accounts for personal identity. Whatever connects these to personal identity does so by presupposing it as its basis. Because we have identity, we can also have memory and a person-based bodily continuity. So, what confers personal identity must be something other than these things.
- One theory is that the soul accounts for personal identity. What is the soul? How is it related to the body? Is it that I am my soul or that I have a soul? My soul accounts for my consciousness; yet I remain the same person even through loss of consciousness.
- Think again of the tomato, the thing that loses its identity when it is eaten and digested. We aren't like the tomato, for we don't lose our identity as persons when we change radically, like the prison guard who converts. But why not? What is it about our inner being as persons that makes us the same person through our whole life? The same person even through radical changes such as the prison guard's dramatic conversion?

[8] SUMMARY OF KEY POINTS: PERSONAL IDENTITY AND LIFE AFTER DEATH

1. I may wonder about life after death, I may hope for it, or take another position towards it. In all these cases what is the object of my thoughts? It is that I the same person I am now will continue to exist in a life beyond this one. When I make plans for a future trip to a nice place and look forward to it, it is I the same person I am now who is the subject of these plans. I-now plan for next week when I-then will be in Hawaii. What this means is that the I-now and the I-then are one and the same person; else it would make no sense. I cannot look forward to your vacation, except in so far as it also involves me. I cannot look forward to experiencing your vacation in the way I can look forward to experiencing my own. It is in this way that personal identity is essentially involved in life after death.
2. If there is no personal identity as defined here, then there can also be no life after death.
3. If personal identity somehow exists but not in the way defined here; especially if it is tied to the continuity of our bodily existence, then there can also be no life after death.

4. Persons and human persons. Personal identity, consciousness, rationality, saying "I" and other such features apply to all persons, not just human persons. There may be persons on other planets, beings having these features, who are not human persons. All human persons are persons; but not all persons are necessarily human persons.

[9] ARGUMENTS CONCERNING IF LIFE AFTER DEATH IS ACTUAL

[a] SOME PRELIMINARIES

We asked whether life after death is possible. Now we turn to the question whether it is actual. I suggest there are three basic requirements for its actuality:

1. The reality of the person as a being distinct from his body, who may continue to exist after the death of the body.
2. The reality of personal identity as a unique form of identity essentially different from the identity of things such as ships. My life after death means that the same "I" who exists now will continue to exist in a life after death.
3. The existence of God as giver of life after death, one of our main themes in this chapter.

What is the life after death that we are pursuing here? What form is really worthwhile? There are several popular conceptions of it; are any of them meaningful? Consider:

1. "I will live on in my descendants." That's nice, but it is not "life" in any real and literal sense. If that's all it is, it amounts to annihilation.
2. "I will live on in the memory of those who follow me." Again, that's nice, but not "life" in any real and literal sense but actually annihilation.
3. "I will merge with the universe." What is this but annihilation? If I don't exist as myself, as a unique and individual person, then I don't exist at all. Think of a drop of water. It has a little bit of individuality as this drop of

water, set off from other waters. But then it falls into the sea and is merged with the sea. It ceases to exist. So too, if we fall into the vast sea of the universe and merge with it, we cease to exist.

The shortcomings of all three of these may be easily summed up and made evident by a simple question. For each of them, we may ask: If that is what life after death amounts to what good does it do me? I will not be around to appreciate any of this, assuming it happens.

There is another candidate here: reincarnation. I die and then I am reborn into a new life on this earth; one that is significantly changed but still basically more of the same because it is a form of life on this earth. Then what? More cycles of birth and death and birth and death? Then eventually I die "for good"; this is something not so different from the view that there is a life followed by death. Or does this birth-death cycle continue forever without end? If so, would this be something meaningful in any sense? There is much here for philosophic wonder.

But let us turn now to life after death in the usual and traditional sense: immortality. This is the life after death that Unamuno longs for, that Sartre and Tolstoy despair of. It is not life as more of the same but a new existence beyond this world; a fulfillment of our deepest longings, our deepest questions, and our desires to know and understand. Are there good reasons to believe that immortality is our destiny? Are there pointers in this direction? Let me offer six reasons or pointers for a yes answer. The first five are based on John Haynes Holmes.[9]

[b] SIX POINTERS TO IMMORTALITY

First, man's over-endowment as a creature of this earth, his surplus equipment for the adventure of his present life. Think of beauty, the beauty of nature, of the sublime music of Bach, Mozart and Beethoven. Why do we have these things? We don't need them to survive as creatures of this world. Or think of the

---

[9] John Haynes Holmes, "Ten Reasons for Believing in Immortality" in Paul Edwards and Arthur Pap (eds.), *A Modern Introduction to Philosophy*, 3d ed. (New York: The Free Press, 1973), 254-58. Italics added.

insights of great minds from Plato to Einstein and far beyond. Again, they are not part of the equipment for this world. Are they not pointers to a world beyond, to the world James calls "the unseen world"? In a word, are they not pointers to our life beyond this world, our immortality?

Second, the lack of coordination or proportion between a man's body and a man's mind. As we grow older body and mind pull apart: the body gets weaker, the mind expands and grows stronger. The mind, the core of the person wants to keep going, not held back by the ailments of old age and above all not by death. We want to continue living and thinking and receiving love and beauty. We want to continue to be in the life of immortality.

Third, the lack of coordination between our personalities and the physical world. Mozart died at age 35 and Schubert even earlier at age 31; Shelley at 30 and Pascal at 39. Each had so much more to give the world! Can death really be the final end of such a person? And what is true of such persons on a large scale is true of most of the rest of us: doesn't human life point to something more, something beyond this world and beyond the reach of death as an end? Again, we see the basic point: we are not only creatures of this world but of immortality.

Fourth, the logic of evolution. Evolution is a process of increasing development. Darwin proclaimed that "it is an intolerable thought that man and all other sentient beings are doomed to complete annihilation after such long-continued slow progress." Unless the universe is crazy, something must remain. And for us what is that something? What can it be but our continued existence as the same person we are now in an immortal life after death?

Fifth, the principle of persistence or conservation. That is, the idea that nothing in the universe is ever lost. All energy is conserved. Given the intimate unity between matter and mind if material energy is by nature always preserved doesn't it stand to reason that mental or spiritual energy is likewise always preserved? And this means human immortality. The soul of man is just as much a force in the world as magnetism or steam or electricity. It is madness to conceive that the heat of an engine must be preserved, while the love of a heart may be thrown away.

Sixth, where is the truth: with Russell in his claim that existence is ultimately absurd? Or with James in his claim that existence is ultimately meaningful?

(Chapter 3, sections 8 and 9). For Russell death is annihilation; for James death is the door to immortality. Russell's "truth" would be something horrible and ugly. Can that really be the actual truth? Must the real truth not be something noble and beautiful? Doesn't the nobility and beauty of truth speak in favor of immortality and thus provide a pointer to it? Truth must be on the side of good, and therefore of ultimate meaningfulness and immortality. Further, that I recognize the truth is something good and noble. Doesn't it follow that it cannot be the real truth that all will be destroyed in the end as Russell claims, meaning that absurdity has the last word? Good must have the last word, which must mean that our being is not destroyed by death but continues in a life of immortality.

[c] ANOTHER POINTER: NEAR DEATH EXPERIENCES

A man is dying and, as he reaches the point of greatest physical distress, he hears himself pronounced dead by his doctor. He begins to hear an uncomfortable noise, a loud ringing or buzzing, and at the same time he feels himself moving very rapidly through a long dark tunnel.

After this, he suddenly finds himself outside of his own physical body, but still in the immediate physical environment, and he sees his own body from a distance, as though he is a spectator. He watches the resuscitation attempt from this unusual vantage point and is in a state of emotional upheaval.

After a while, he collects himself and becomes more accustomed to his odd condition. He notices that he still has a "body," but one of a very different nature and with very different powers from the physical body he has left behind. Soon other things begin to happen. Others come to meet and to help him.

He glimpses the spirits of relatives and friends who have already died. And a loving, warm spirit of a kind he has never encountered before – a being of light – appears before him. This being asks him a question, nonverbally, to make him evaluate his life and helps him along by showing him a panoramic, instantaneous playback of the major events of his life.

At some point he finds himself approaching some sort of barrier or border, apparently representing the limit between earthly life and the next life. Yet, he finds that he must go back to the earth, that the time for his death has not yet come. At this point he resists, for by now he is taken up with his experiences in the afterlife and does not want to return. He is overwhelmed by intense feelings of joy, love and peace. Despite his attitude, though, he somehow reunites with his physical body and lives.

Later he tries to tell others, but he has trouble doing so. In the first place, he can find no human words adequate to describe these unearthly episodes. He also finds that others scoff, so he stops telling other people. Still, the experience affects his life profoundly, especially his view about death and its relationship to life.[10]

The author points out that this is not the account of any one person but "a composite of common elements found in very many stories," with each element appearing in many stories.[11]

Soon after Moody's book appeared the International Association for Near Death Studies was founded. It publishes the Journal of Near Death Studies.

[d] *THE EVIDENTIAL VALUE OF NEAR DEATH EXPERIENCES*

What is the significance of near death experiences (NDE's) for our investigation into the question whether immortality is an actual reality? I suggest four positive things:

---

[10] Raymond A. Moody, Jr., *Life after Life: The Investigation of a Phenomenon – Survival of Bodily Death* (Bantam Books, 1975), 21-23. Some paragraph divisions have been added. The original is all in italics.

[11] Ibid., 23-24.

First, NDE's confirm the real *distinction* between person and body. "He finds himself outside of his own physical body, and he sees his own body from a distance, as though he is a spectator." I experience myself as not being my body and literally take a distance form it as I look down on it and see it as I would see any other object that is not me, like a table.

Second, NDE's confirm the essential role of *personal identity* for life after death. The whole drama described here makes sense only on the basis of it being *the same person* who first lives, then dies, then has the near death experience and then comes back to this life.

Third, NDE's are *glimpses* into the world beyond, the life of immortality. You get to enter a new and vastly different land, briefly see it and get some feel for it, and then go back to your previous existence. This tells you something important: this land is real, it actually exists!

And there is a further dimension to this last point. "He glimpses the spirits of relatives and friends who have already died." Great news: my loved ones exist! I will see them again! We will be reunited! This is not only good news personally for me but also further confirmation that life after death is real. It must be real if they exist in it.

Fourth, NDE's show us that the world beyond is a *wonderful place to be*, one of intense joy and happiness. "He is taken up with his experiences in the afterlife and does not want to return. He is overwhelmed by intense feelings of joy, love and peace."

In all these ways NDE's are a source of wonder. We take our living for granted but what does it really mean for us to "live"? And then a person dies and undergoes an NDE. He is not really dead. But is he alive? Not in the usual sense, whatever that is, but some other sense? One that is *less real* because the person is officially "dead"; but *more real* because it is the foretaste, the beginning of our real life, life after death, immortality?

[e] PASCAL ON LIFE AFTER DEATH

"What reason have they for saying that we cannot rise from the dead? What is more difficult, to be born or to rise again; that what has never been should be, or that what has been should be again? Is it more difficult to come into existence than to return to it? Habit makes the one appear easy to us; want of habit makes the other impossible." (*Pensées,* Chapter 3, Section 6, on Atheists)

[f] THE ROLE OF GOD

The question of life after death naturally leads to the question of God. If life after death is real must there not be a God to provide it? And isn't the meaning and relevance of the God-question largely tied to the question of life after death? Thus, the topic of life after death leads naturally to that of God, to which we now turn.

CHAPTER 28
IS GOD REAL?

PART ONE
THE CONCEPT OF GOD

[1] WONDER ABOUT THE CONCEPT OF GOD

Is there a God? Many of us grow up believing there is a God, or even believing *in* God and praying to Him. Others don't believe there is a God. Who is correct? Both can't be correct; somebody is mistaken on this question. Isn't it a very important question? It invites our wonder, looking at the question anew and trying to go more deeply into it.

People say they believe in God, or don't believe in God, or wonder whether God exists. But what do they mean by the term *God*? How many have asked themselves this question and seriously considered it? How many realize what a difficult question it is? Why is it difficult?

Historically and culturally, there are many conceptions of God. Are they equally valid? Are some valid while others are not? If there is one God must there not be just one concept of God that is correct? If so which one, is it? If you claim yours is the correct one, how do you know it is correct? Can you prove it? Can you reasonably rule out all rival candidates?

[2] FOUR POSSIBLE CONCEPTS OF GOD

We can also ask the question: what counts as God? To get a start on this question let us consider four possible candidates for what might count as God, four possible concepts of God:

1. The *Judeo-Christian God*: the absolute being containing all perfections, infinitely good and powerful and knowing; the sufficient reason for the world by being its creator.
2. The God of *Pantheism*: God as the Grand Totality of all reality; the idea that God and the universe are one and the same.
3. The God of *Deism*: a God who is the sufficient reason for the world, an answer to the question why there is something and not nothing, but who is not involved in the world.
4. *Einstein's God*: there is Something Higher, a mysterious order, the sufficient reason for the world, an answer to the question why there is something and not nothing.

Let us note some comparisons and contrasts among these:

- #1 is transcendent, beyond the world and also immanent (involved) in the world; #2 is the opposite of transcendent, a being only immanent in the world in actually being the world.
- #1 is a being I can pray to, be grateful to and ask for forgiveness, in contrast to #2.
- #3 is a kind of thinned-out version of #1: only the idea of being the sufficient reason for the world is retained.
- #4 is a kind of pull-back from #1: a higher reality is retained that might function in some of the ways attributed to #1.
- #2 and #3 seem to be outside the realm God for the question of ultimate meaningfulness. Is there a God who is the source and reason for the meaningfulness of existence, of each human life in particular, including being the provider of immortality? These seem to apply only to #1 and #4; we will therefore focus only on these two concepts of God.

[3] THE JUDEO-CHRISTIAN CONCEPTION OF GOD

The Judeo-Christian God is a personal being, all-good, all-powerful, all-knowing; a being before whom we exist, especially in our moral life, a being who addresses

us in our conscience, whom we offend by our moral evil, whom we may ask for forgiveness, to whom we may be grateful, who will judge us after our death; and much else. This is God as creator of the world; a being who both transcends the world as "totally other" than the world and everything we know in our experience, and also somehow "immanent" in the world, as involved in the world.
This God is our beginning and our end: we come from God who made each of us and we go back to God after our death. And we exist before God at every moment in our lifetime.

What lies behind this conception of God? Why would one want to adopt it? The idea is that God is by definition the Highest Being, the Absolute Being in every positive way; the being greater than which nothing can even be conceived or thought of, as it is sometimes expressed. Anything less than this wouldn't be God.

Some people want to draw a line in the sand between "God" and "organized religion." They say *yes* to the former but *no* to the latter. How does the Judeo-Christian God fit in here? Let me suggest the following. People who reject "organized religion" may certainly still believe in and pray to the Judeo-Christian God. In the other direction, accepting "organized religion" usually includes accepting either the Judeo-Christian God or some other concept of God.

Therefore, rejecting "organized religion" emphatically does not mean rejecting "God." The question of "God" -- what that means, whether God exists, what my relation to God is – is a question of fundamental importance for everyone, one that calls for reflective wonder.

[4] ALBERT EINSTEIN'S CONCEPTION OF GOD

> We are in the position of a little child entering a huge library filled with books in many languages. The child knows that someone must have written those books. It does not know how. It does not understand the languages in which they are written. The child dimly suspects a mysterious order in the arrangement of

the books but doesn't know what it is. That, it seems to me, is the attitude of even the most intelligent human beings towards G-d.

What lies behind this conception of God? Why would one want to adopt it? The idea is here perhaps two-fold. First it is realized that the reality of the world calls for something beyond it to account for it. "There must be *Something* Higher!" And this Higher Reality one then calls "God." Second it is also realized or perhaps claimed that we don't really know what that Higher Reality is. We can't see it and we can't infer it from what we do see and know; it is beyond our comprehension.

[5] THE ROLE OF GOD IN WONDER ABOUT EXISTENCE

Why is the God-question important? What is the role of God in wonder about existence? Let us list some of the things that might come under this heading:

- God as the answer to our question: why is there something and not nothing?
- More specifically, God as the *sufficient reason* for the physical world and the world of persons. Why is there this world with all the many things in it, and not another world?
- God as the sufficient reason for our being as persons. God as the creator of each person.
- God as the source for the *ultimate meaningfulness* of existence.
- God as the source for the ultimate meaningfulness of each human life in particular.
- God as the *provider of immortality*. Death as annihilation would rob life of its ultimate meaning; but death as the gateway to immortality gives life its ultimate meaningfulness.
- God as the absolute person *before whom I exist* at every moment of my life.
- God as a being to whom I can pray.
- God to whom I can be grateful for my existence and for the good things in my life.

- God as basis of the *moral order*.
- God as the voice of conscience warning me to avoid doing wrong.
- God to whom I can turn and ask for forgiveness and mercy if I have done wrong.
- God as absolute judge to whom I am accountable, who will judge me after I die.
- God as being *worthy of worship*; only God is the being worthy of worship.
- A *God of Love* who looks at me in love and invites my response of love.

The list could easily be continued. Some items overlap with others. Some imply others; some do not imply others, though they play a role in many conceptions of God. For example, does the sufficient reason for the world need to be the absolute being? A God of Love? The absolute judge? A being worthy of worship? Does the absolute judge need to be a God of Love?

There is more. We have assumed one God. Is this correct? But if there were many gods would each really deserve the title of "God"? Doesn't what we mean by "God" include the idea of "supreme being"? If so, there can only be one such being.

Which of the items on our list apply to the Judeo-Christian conception of God? It seems they all do. In fact they provide a further amplification of this conception of God. Which of them apply to Einstein's conception of God? The first few do; then the question seems to remain open. In fact the very point of this conception is to leave this open, both in the sense of claiming that we don't have an answer and in the sense of opening the door to individual personal beliefs.

[6] FOUR WONDER QUESTIONS

1. Why is there *anything* at all? Why is there something and not nothing?
2. Why is there all the *good* in the world?
3. Why is there all the *evil* in the world?
4. Why is there *both* such immense good and also such immense evil in the *same* world?

Is the sufficient reason for the good also the sufficient reason for the evil?

How is the answer to one question related to that of each of the others?

[7] IS GOD A PERSONAL BEING?

The Judeo-Christian God is clearly a personal being; it is part of God's essence. What about Einstein's God? On the one hand, Einstein himself said he did not believe in a "personal God"; on the other hand, his conception is meant to be wide open, allowing for different ways of seeing God. Should this then not include God as in some sense a personal being?

What does wonder about God reveal to us? Must God not be a personal being in some sense? If "God" is seen merely as an impersonal force or energy, then God cannot fulfill the roles suggested here. I am a "person," a being capable of saying "I," of understanding, of making commitments, of love and joy and much more. If I am that kind of being God cannot be less than that. God *must be at least* a person; a Thou and not an It. God would be of course much more; being a person is a bare minimum, an initial start.

Of course, this God is not a human person with all the limitations and shortcomings we have. A human person is one kind of person, one way of being a person; there could be others.

If God is the absolute being, the highest possible being, then God must be at least what we are, a personal being. God must be *at least a person*; God *cannot be less than a person.*

If God is a *God of Love,* then God must be a person; an impersonal being cannot love.

This view of God is suggested by Martin Buber who remarks that "it is both permitted and necessary to say that God is *also* a Person"; and speaking of "the attribute of personal being" he says that "from this attribute would stem my and all men's being as persons."[1] God seems to be described here as the creator of

---

[1] Martin Buber, *I and Thou*, 2nd ed., translated by Ronald Gregor Smith (New York: Charles Scribner's Sons, 1958), 135. Italics in original.

persons. Do we each come from the hand of God individually created by God? What does this imply for us, for an adequate response from us?

We can speak of God as person and understand the reasons for this and the role it plays by stressing these four things:

1. God must be at least a person to account for *our being* as persons; God cannot be less than what we are as persons, an impersonal being, an "it."
2. God must be at least a person to account for why there is *something* and not nothing.
3. God must be at least a person to be a *God of Love*, a God who gives us *immortality* and thus provides the *ultimate meaningfulness* of existence and of each person's life.
4. God must be *at least a person* as we know ourselves to be persons; but God is of course infinitely more. God is beyond our comprehension. But we should point to God in the right direction, and that must be to say of God that God is at least a person.

But does God as a personal being exist? This is the question to which we now turn. Let us pursue the question in terms of a God who is all-good and all-powerful, as this is the conception of God most commonly adopted in reflections on the existence of God.

PART TWO
IS GOD REAL?

[1] GOOD AND EVIL AND GOD

Is there an all-good and all-powerful God? Some would say yes, of course. How else could the world have come into being? In particular how could I as a person and all other human persons have come into being? We can say that evolution is a good explanation of how our bodies came to be what they are now. But does it explain why there was an *original material* that evolved the way evolution claims? Even more, can evolution explain how and why *consciousness* came into existence? Can it explain how and why we as conscious *persons* came into existence? Think of the marvel of sperm and egg: how two tiny biological organisms merge and a short time later there is a little baby, a small person, a conscious being; a being who will soon be able to say "I," to think thoughts, to understand things, to wonder where it all came from, to wonder whether life is ultimately meaningful, whether there is a God; a being who can be morally good or evil, who can love or hate; a being who can read books, listen to music, talk to other persons, make plans for his future and so much else.

But there is another side: the enormous amount of evil and suffering in the world, all over the world and through all of history. It is the sufferings of humans and animals, vast sufferings in both cases. Some of it is brought about by humans: war, torture, death camps, persecutions, slavery, child abuse, elderly abuse, neglect of the poor and so much else. The Nazi Holocaust and Stalin's Gulag are some of the absolute worst evils in what is really a very long list of horrors.

Some of the suffering is caused by natural forces: killer storms, earthquakes, volcanoes, droughts, floods, extreme cold, extreme heat, babies born with severe birth defects, plagues such as the Black Death that wiped out millions in Medieval Europe, mudslides such as a recent one in Columbia that drowned several thousand people including small children.

In the face of these terrible evils can one still reasonably believe that an all-powerful and all-good God created the world and is governing it in wisdom? If God is all-good, a God of love, then God cares about his people. And if God is all-powerful that care will be totally effective, and God's people will not be suffering as they do. Yet they do suffer. Where is God? We look at the world with all its suffering and misery: *do we really* see the hand of God? Some would say no.

However, when we look elsewhere isn't it so that *we really do* see the hand of God? We see it in the wonder that there is anything at all and God as sufficient reason for this; the wonder of the human person, the wonder of the vast physical universe, beauty in nature, the beauty of sublime music and so much else. In these it is easier to say yes.

If the case *against* God based on all the terrible evil seems strong, perhaps an opposing case can be made *for* God, a case based on several things that seem to point to the reality of God.

[2] IS GOD REAL? SIX POINTERS TO GOD

1. Why is there something and not nothing? Why is there a physical universe? A world of persons? These realities call for a sufficient reason. What can that be but God?

2. Why do I exist rather than not exist? It can be said that my body comes from my parents. But where do *I* come from, I this conscious being, who is unique, who has personal identity, who can love, who can be morally responsible, who can say "I"? Again: God?

3. We have strong evidence for the reality of life after death, as we saw above. Life after death requires God to provide it, to sustain us in it. If life after death is real, God must be real.

4. What is the source of deeply moving human experiences? Doesn't a deep human love give us a glimpse of a beyond? Something eternal and ultimately God? Doesn't the birth of a child take us beyond our usual level of being to something higher, ultimately to God? Doesn't beauty, the beauty of nature such as lofty mountains, and especially the beauty of sublime music also point beyond itself, to the eternal, to God? Isn't there something beyond the merely human in the music of the great composers, Bach, Beethoven and Mozart? "There is the music of Johann Sebastian Bach; therefore, there must be a God."[2] Deep beauty points to the reality of God

5. Moral experience can point to God. We will examine this below, in section 3.

6. The experience of gratitude can point to God. We will examine this below, in section 4.

---

[2] Peter Kreeft and Ronald K. Tacelli, *Handbook of Christian Apologetics* (Downers Grove, IL: InterVarsity Press, 1994), 81.

[3] MORAL EXPERIENCE AS A POINTER TO GOD

John Henry Newman, in his argument from conscience, shows how moral experience can point to God, how it can lead our minds and hearts up to God:

> Man has within his breast a certain commanding dictate, not a mere sentiment, not a mere opinion or impression or view of things, but a law, an authoritative voice, bidding him to do certain things and avoid others. I do not say that its particular injunctions are always clear, or that they are always consistent with each other; but what I am insisting on here is this, that it *commands*; that it praises, it blames, it threatens, it implies a future, and it witnesses of the unseen. It is more than a man's own self. The man himself has no power over it, or only with extreme difficulty; he did not make it, he cannot destroy it. He may silence it in particular cases or directions; he may distort its enunciations, but he cannot, or it is quite the exception if he can, he cannot emancipate himself from it. He can disobey it; he may refuse to use it; but it remains.
>
> This is Conscience, and, from the nature of the case, its very existence carries on our minds to a Being exterior to ourselves; for else, whence did it come? And to a being superior to ourselves; else whence its strange, troublesome peremptoriness?[1]

In a further passage, quoting from his novel, *Callista*, he rejects the idea that the dictate of conscience "is a mere law of my nature":

> No, it is the echo of a person speaking to me. Nothing shall persuade me that it does not ultimately proceed from a person ex-

---

[1] Adrian J. Boekraad and Henry Tristan, *The Argument from Conscience to the Existence of God according to J.H. Newman* (Louvain: Editions Nauwelaerts, 1961) 114. The text consists of Newman's own words. Italics in original.

ternal to us. It carries with it its proof of its divine origin. My nature feels towards it as towards a person.[2]

[4] GRATITUDE AS A POINTER TO GOD

Can there be gratitude where there is no human person to turn to? Gratitude arises when I recognize that another person has favored me, has done a good deed for me; and has done so out of love and genuine concern for me and for my well-being. Thus there is a correspondence between the loving intention of another human being towards me and the spontaneous feeling of gratitude in me. But then how are we to interpret the feeling of tremendous gratitude that arises spontaneously in me in situations where a great good is given to me, but no human being has given it to me? Consider an example. A soldier returns to his wife who had given up all hope of ever seeing him again. Here a great evil has been averted; the life of a beloved person has been saved. The response of deep joy is like a light leaping up. There is a deep correspondence between the joy and the event. But there is also another quality intermingled with the joy. The person who receives this great good feels an impulse to do something: to have gratitude, to give thanks. There is no human being to whom he can turn. Even where there is someone who has played some role in bringing about this great good, the person will still feel that his obligation to be grateful has not been fulfilled when he has thanked this person.

Certainly, people who believe in God can turn to Him at such a time and give thanks. But even people who usually do not think of God may nevertheless, in such moments, turn to God in thanksgiving.[3] Could this perhaps include even atheists?

---

[2] *Ibid.*, p. 116. Newman's analysis of conscience as pointing to God is also developed in his book, *An Essay in Aid of a Grammar of Assent* (New York: Longmans, Green and Co., 1947; first pub., 1870), 295-301.

[3] Balduin Schwarz, "Transcendent Gratitude" in Stephen Schwarz and Fritz Wenisch, eds., *Values and Human Experience: Essays in Honor of the Memory of Balduin Schwarz* (New York: Peter Lang, 1999), 25.

Heather MacDonald is an atheist. Yet she says:

The one compelling reason for religion that I can see is the need to give thanks. I have had everything given to me. I have nobody to thank for that aside from my parents. When you realize how fortunate you are, there is a desire to give thanks in a broader way.[4]

Chesterton writes: "*Rossetti makes the remark somewhere, bitterly but with great truth, that the worst moment for an atheist is when he is really thankful but has nobody to thank.*"[5]

But perhaps such gratitude can be a pointer to the existence of God. Can it perhaps be a way of finding God? Balduin Schwarz suggests that indeed it can:

Gratitude can be a way of finding God. If I see my own existence and all the things in my life that are the sources of true and deep happiness as gifts for which I want to be grateful, for which I realize I should be grateful, what can I do? There are really only two alternatives. Either the experience of being grateful for my life and for the good things in my life is meaningful – in which case these things really are gifts, and there is a Giver behind these gifts, God, and my gratitude "reaches" God as the Loving Giver of these gifts. Or such a gratitude is absurd and meaningless – because these things are not really gifts and there is no Giver; they just fall into my life accidentally, and my deep feelings of gratitude are utterly misplaced and absurd. If I believe that existence is ultimately meaningful, then this second alternative is ruled out. I can then really be grateful for my own existence and for the good things of

---

[4] Heather MacDonald, quoted in Michael Novak, *No One Sees God: the Dark Night of Atheists and Believers* (New York: Doubleday, 2008), 129.

[5] G. K. Chesterton, *St. Francis of Assisi* (London: Tavistock, 1957), 88. Quoted by Balduin Schwarz, 25.

my life, a gratitude that reaches God, that brings me to God; a gratitude that enriches my life by opening my eyes and my heart to seeing all good things as gifts of God and to living my whole life as a continuous prayer of gratitude to God.[6]

[5] SIX POINTERS TO GOD AND THE TWO CONCEPTIONS OF GOD

We have examined six pointers to God. But to which God do they point? Do they point to the Judeo-Christian God? Or to Einstein's God? Or to both? Perhaps it is a mixed bag?

1. God as the reason why there is something and not nothing.
2. God as the reason why I exist rather than not exist.
3. God as the provider of life after death.
4. God as the source of deeply moving human experiences.
5. God as the source of our moral experiences.
6. God as the object of our gratitude.

Don't all these point to the Judeo-Christian God? It seems they do, as that conception of God has traditionally been understood to include all these. The interesting question, the real wonder question is whether they also point to Einstein's God. That conception is intentionally wide open: there is *something* beyond this world that the things of this world point to. Given that as a kind of premise, why couldn't all of them also point to Einstein's God?

If the Judeo-Christian God is real then Einstein's God is real as well, for the latter is a wide conception that includes the former among others. But the converse is not true. If it is Einstein's God who is real, the question remains whether the Judeo-Christian God is real. For Einstein there is *some* God, not necessarily the Judeo-Christian God.

Is the gap between these two conceptions of God perhaps especially significant when we consider the terrible evils in the world? Do they point to the non-

---

[6] Balduin Schwarz, 26.

existence of God? If God is both all good and all powerful why is there so much evil? Is the Judeo-Christian God affected by this objection? Is Einstein's God affected? How does this relate to how we think about God?

PART THREE
WHAT IF WE DON'T KNOW?

[1] GOD: TO BELIEVE OR NOT TO BELIEVE?

At the beginning of the previous chapter, we raised the question: is there an all-good and all-powerful God? Many people say that the good in the world points to a *yes* answer while the evil points to a *no* answer. Which is it? It seems we have two options:

1. *Believe* that God exists; believe that the good in the world points to God.
2. *Not believe* that God exists; believe that the evil in the world points away from God.

These paths, believing God exists and not believing God exists, seem to be in a kind of balance, each focusing on one part of the picture and running with it, while not coming to grips with the other part. But perhaps it is not so: there is really an imbalance, even *a non-parallelism* between believing and not believing. Why might this be so?

Perhaps God does not exist. But perhaps God does exist. There is a story told by Martin Buber in which "an adherent of the Enlightenment," an unbeliever pays a visit to a Rabbi to argue with him about the existence of God. The unbeliever lays down a challenge to the Rabbi "to lay God and His Kingdom on the table before you"; that is, to prove the existence of God. The Rabbi admits his inability "to lay God and His Kingdom on the table before you." But then he adds these words:

"But think, my son, perhaps it is true."

The story ends as the adherent of the Enlightenment opposed the Rabbi with all his strength, but to no avail. For this terrible *perhaps* haunted him and echoed back at him time after time and broke his resistance. What if it is true after all that God exists?[7]

Doesn't the non-believer sometimes wonder: perhaps there is a God? Shouldn't he wonder whether there is a God? *Perhaps* God does exist! If God does exist, is he not taking a huge chance? We can imagine the Rabbi asking him: if God does exist and you meet God after you die, what will you say to God if God asks you why you rejected God? Why you did not at least seek God if you were not sufficiently aware of God's existence, as Pascal forcefully urges?

Suppose we follow the route recommended by the Rabbi and by Pascal. Here are the thoughts of an imaginary person contemplating God and the ultimate meaning of his life.

I want to know the truth about God; specifically, the truth about a *God of Love*, a God who makes my life ultimately meaningful, who is the giver of immortality. This is the most important part of the idea of God held by those who believe in God and seek God. Important as is the conception of God as sufficient reason for all that is, the conception of God as God of Love is still more central and more significant. This is God who turns to me in love and to whom I can turn in loving response. If God is seen as the Highest Good, the Absolute and Infinite Good then such a conception of God as a God of Love seems eminently reasonable. For love is traditionally seen as the highest good. Of course, nothing here rules out the idea that the God of Love is also the Sufficient Reason for the universe and the world of persons. Recall the argument given above. "There is the music of Johann Sebastian Bach -- therefore there must be a God" which seems to fit in well with both God as God of Love and God as Sufficient Reason.

I want to know the truth about God. I want to give the right response to truth. I want to believe what is true. Where does the truth lie? Is it that God exists? Or is it that God does not exist? I don't have a direct and certain answer. But now I compare these two possible truths. If a God of love exists my life has an ultimate meaning; and I can live my life in response to God and receive this meaning. *This is a truth of enormous significance!* It makes all the difference in the

---

[7] Based on Martin Buber, *Works*, Volume III (Munich-Heidelberg, 1963), 348. Quoted in Joseph Ratzinger, *Introduction to Christianity*, translated by J. R. Foster (New York: Seabury Press, 1968), 20-21.

world. But if God does not exist then my life doesn't have an ultimate meaning and is threatened with ultimate absurdity and annihilation at my death. Thus if God does not exist there is only this one truth in regard to ultimate meaning: that God doesn't exist. There is nothing else is of real significance in regard to ultimate meaning. If God does exist there is not only the truth that God exists but so much more under the heading that my life has an ultimate meaning. This means that the two possible or potential truths about God are not at all parallel. And the two possible ways of going wrong in what one believes are also correspondingly not parallel. This brings us to Pascal's Wager.

[2] PASCAL'S WAGER

Basically, Pascal's Wager is a way of comparing two possible ways of going wrong regarding God. We can go wrong by believing God exists when God does not exist. But we can also go wrong in the opposite way, by failing to believe in God when God does in fact exist. The core point of Pascal's Wager is the claim that these two ways of going wrong are radically different, separated by an abyss. Let me first diagram the idea of Pascal's Wager and then pursue the question of why the two ways of going wrong are so radically different, why there is a basic non-parallelism between the two.

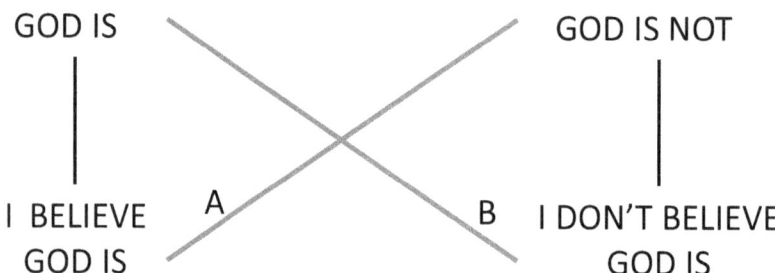

The vertical lines are clear [bottom to top on each side]. If God exists, I should believe in God; if God does not exist, I should not believe in God. It is the diagonal lines, A and B, that are crucial; both are ways of going wrong. Which is worse?

Chapter 28: Is God Real?

(A) I *believe* God exists when in reality God *does not exist*. Or:

(B) I *don't believe* God exists when in reality God *does exist*.

The core point of Pascal's Wager is that Diagonal B is infinitely worse than Diagonal A.

[3] PASCAL'S WAGER ELABORATED

Why is it that in Pascal's Wager Diagonal B is infinitely worse than Diagonal A? Why is there this imbalance, this non-parallelism?

One, the basic imbalance. If the atheist-non-believer is correct, what does he gain? He will die and cease to exist. He will never find out that he was correct in asserting that there is no God and no immortality. He will have this life and nothing more. But the believer also has his present life and so there is no real difference here. On the other hand, if the believer is correct, he gains enormously. God exists and is part of his life, his life is ultimately meaningful, and he has immortality. This is the basic imbalance, but there are also some further factors:

Two, giving the right response to Love. If there is a God of Love who is turning to me in love, I must respond to God; I must give God the right response or at least try to do so. Failure to do this if God exists is infinitely worse than believing this and responding accordingly when it is an intellectual illusion. Such an illusion is unfortunate but any evil it represents pales in comparison to the terrible evil of not responding to Infinite Love. We see again the non-parallelism of the two diagonals.

Three, avoiding the worst deception. Consider the words of Kierkegaard, the great 19th century Danish philosopher and religious personality who speaks to the non-parallelism of the diagonals in Pascal's Wager when he points out: "If it were true that one should believe nothing which one cannot see by means of his physical eyes, then first and foremost one ought to give up believing in love. If one did this and did it out of fear of being deceived, would one not then be deceived?" What applies to seeing by one's eyes applies equally to seeing by one's heart and mind in turning to God as Supreme Love. Kierkegaard concludes: "To cheat oneself out of love is the most terrible deception; it is an eternal loss for which there is no reparation, either in time or in eternity."[8] Diagonal B represents this terrible deception. The deception in diagonal A pales in comparison: again, we have the non-parallelism of the two diagonals.

Four, giving the right response of gratitude. If my existence and all the things in my life that are the sources of true and deep happiness are gifts for which I want to be grateful, for which I realize I should be grateful then they are gifts of God; and I must give God my response of gratitude. Or, it is infinitely better to *believe this* when *it is not so*, than *not to believe this* and thus fail to respond adequately if *it is so*. How terrible if God was after all the Giver of these good gifts and I didn't respond! I cannot risk that: the non-parallelism of the two diagonals.

Five, preparing for the Final Judgment. What happens at death? If there is no God, we will probably just cease to exist; then it wouldn't matter all that much how we responded to the God-question. But if God does exist, and I come before God to be judged in some rightful manner by God, what will I say if I have ignored God in this life? Why did I not at least seek God? Whatever the details of a final judgment, and however serious its consequences, not seeking God, if God does exist, is perhaps a situation I should avoid. Better to seek God even if God doesn't exist than not to seek God if God does after all exist. The believer who dies in a universe without God is not really in a painful situation. He loses his existence as we all do. But the atheist who dies in a universe with God: doesn't he run the terrible risk of finding himself in a very sad and perhaps dreadful situation? Should we risk this non-parallelism of the two diagonals?

Six, preparing for immortality. Suppose God exists and is the giver of a life after death, an immortal life of happiness and fulfillment in union with God. If this is so, could it also be the case that not everyone will be in a position to receive such a gift? Could it be that I must be a certain kind of person to be able to truly receive such a gift? John Henry Newman says *yes*. He claims that I must be holy to be the kind of person who can truly receive the gift of eternal happiness with God. His reasoning is that God is holy, infinitely holy, Absolute Holiness. Doesn't it somehow seem to follow that only those who are holy in their own measure can stand to be with God, can bear to see God and receive God's love and God's gifts?

---

[8] Soren Kierkegaard, *Works of Love*, tr. Howard and Edna Hong (New York: Harper and Row, 1962) 23-24.

"We see, then, that holiness is necessary to our admission into heaven, because heaven is *not* heaven, is not a place of happiness *except* to the holy." Newman goes so far as to say "that if we wished to imagine a punishment for an unholy, reprobate soul, we perhaps could not fancy a greater than to *summon it to heaven*. Heaven would be hell to an irreligious man."[9] What we experience depends not only on what is given to us but also on what we are. If we must be holy to receive God's gift of happiness then surely the first step is to turn to God, to seek God and to believe in God; and thus to avoid the path of unbelief. Better to seek God when God is not than not to seek God if God is. In the first I lose very little. In the second I may lose infinitely. Perhaps I lose eternally, for I lose my chance to attain the holiness necessary for future blessedness: the non-parallelism of the two diagonals is a matter for consideration and wonder.

Seven, being on the side of ultimate meaningfulness, of good triumphing over evil. The world presents us with many high and sublime goods but also many terrible evils. Which will triumph in the end? If God is, God is the source of ultimate meaningfulness, of the triumph of good over evil. Better to believe this and commit to it even on the chance that it is not so, than not to commit to it if it is so. Committing to God means committing to the hope that the ultimate truth is the triumph of good over evil. That truth, if it is the truth, is infinitely more significant and important both in itself and for me, than the opposite truth, if that is the truth, namely that evil ultimately triumphs over good. If the hope in this ultimate truth that good will defeat evil carries the risk of being mistaken, the opposite stand also carries a risk. And Pascal's Wager is the thesis that these two risks, these two possible ways of going wrong are not parallel. Going wrong by not believing in God as the ultimate triumph of good over evil if God in fact exists is infinitely worse than the opposite way of going wrong: believing in God when in fact God does not exist. Once again we see the non-parallelism of the two diagonals.

Eight, recall Pascal.[10] Nothing is so important to a person as his own state. And thus, it is not natural that there should be persons who are indifferent to the

---

[9] John Henry Newman, "Holiness Necessary for Future Blessedness." *Parochial Sermons*, 1, Italics in original.

[10] Chapter 3, section 6.

loss of their existence. It is a monstrous thing to see in the same heart this sensibility to trifles and this strange insensibility to the greatest things. For it is not to be doubted that the duration of this life is but a moment and that the state of death is eternal, whatever may be its nature. The immortality of the soul is a matter which is of so great consequence to us, and which touches us so profoundly, that we must have lost all feeling to be indifferent as to knowing what it is. All our actions and thoughts must take such different courses, according to whether there are or are not eternal joys to hope for.

[4] PASCAL'S WAGER II: SEEKING GOD

The logic of Pascal's Wager is that it is better to believe in God even on the chance that God does not exist than not to believe in God if God does after all exist. But I cannot command belief; it is not in my direct control. I may wish to believe; I may see that believing is better than not believing, but these do not constitute belief. Very well: I can seek God. And so Pascal's Wager can be recast with *seeking God* and *not seeking God* in the lower left corner and the lower right corner, respectively. This is the second level of Pascal's Wager; belief is the first level. The second level of Pascal's Wager looks like this:

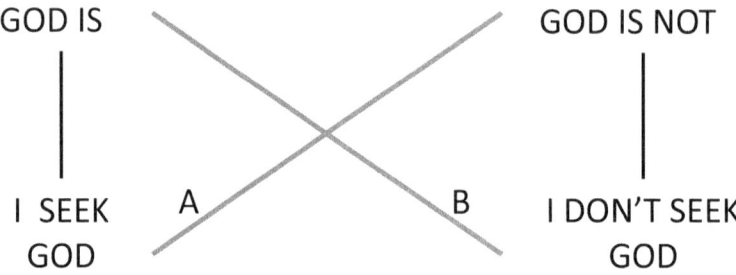

Again, the vertical lines are clear [bottom to top on each side]. If God exists I should seek God; if God does not exist there is no point in seeking God. It is the diagonal lines [A: LL to UR and B: LR to UL] that are crucial; both are ways of going wrong. Which is worse?

(A) I seek God when in reality God doesn't exist. Or:
(B) I don't seek God when in reality God does exist.

Again, Diagonal B is infinitely worse than Diagonal A, is it not?

I call this the second level because it follows the first, the original Pascal's Wager which is in terms of belief. For some people it is actually primary, and in this sense first, because they first seek to believe and then hopefully find what they are seeking and actually do believe. The second level is firmly based on Pascal for whom seeking God is of the greatest importance, as we will see in the next section.

Deep down, doesn't the God question haunt all of us? Isn't God a supreme cause for wonder? Are we alone in the universe? Or do we exist before a Supreme Person? When we die, is it the absolute end, utter annihilation? Or is there a God who will sustain us beyond the grave to a life after death? Just as questions are these not matters that should stir our hearts? Are these not questions that should move us and even trouble us in the most profound way? Is it natural to walk away from profound questions just because we think we have no answers? Imagine finding yourself in an utterly strange place. You don't know where you are, you don't know how you got there and you don't know what will happen to you. You feel lost and in fact you *are* lost. Wouldn't you be curious? Wouldn't you try to find the answers?

The classic example of a thinker who sees the human situation in this way is Pascal. He always saw the God question as central to human life especially when he was plagued by terrible doubts. These doubts led him to seek God, to seek answers to the great questions of life. Here is Pascal's vision of human existence and his response in his own words:

[5] SUMMARY THOUGHTS FROM PASCAL

1. *When I consider the short duration of my life, swallowed up in the eternity before and after, the little space which I fill and even can see, engulfed in the infinite immensity of spaces of which I am ignorant and which know me not, I am frightened and am astonished at being here rather than there;*

for there is no reason why here rather than there, why now rather than then. Who has put me here? By whose order and direction have this place and time been allotted to me? (Pensées, #205)

2. *This is what I see and what troubles me. I look on all sides, and I see only darkness everywhere. Nature presents to me nothing which is not matter of doubt and concern. If I saw nothing there which revealed a Divinity, I would come to a negative conclusion; if I saw everywhere the signs of a Creator, I would remain peacefully in faith. But, seeing too much to deny and too little to be sure, I am in a state to be pitied. (#229)*

3. *Wherefore I have a hundred times wished that if a God maintains Nature, she should testify to Him unequivocally, and that, if the signs she gives are deceptive, she should suppress them altogether; that she should say everything or nothing, that I might see which cause I ought to follow. Whereas in my present state, ignorant of what I am or of what I ought to do, I know neither my condition nor my duty. (#229)*

4. *It is incomprehensible that God should exist, and it is incomprehensible that He should not exist; that the soul should be joined to the body, and that we should have no soul. (#230)*

5. *Surely then it is a great evil thus to be in doubt, but it is at least an indispensable duty to seek when we are in such doubt; and thus the doubter who does not seek is altogether completely unhappy and completely wrong. (#194)*

6. *There are only two kinds of people one can call reasonable; those who serve God with all their heart because they know Him, and those who seek Him with all their heart because they do not know Him. (#194)*

7. *My heart inclines wholly to know where is the true good in order to follow it; nothing would be too dear to me for eternity. (#229)*

8. *I would have far more fear of being mistaken and then finding that the Christian religion is true, than of being mistaken in believing it true when it is not true. (#241) [The logic of the Wager: the error of the atheist would be far worse than the error of the theist.]*

9. *Atheists. What reason have they for saying that we cannot rise from the dead? What is more difficult, to be born or to rise again; that what has*

never been should be, or that what has been should be again? Is it more difficult to come into existence than to return to it? Habit makes the one appear easy to us; want of habit makes the other impossible. A popular way of thinking! (#222)

[6] WHAT IS THE LOGIC OF A MIDDLE POSITION?

IS FENCE-STRADDLING THE AVIODANCE OF A POSITION?

We have two options: *believe* that God exists and *not believe* that God exists. Is it only these two? Some people want to follow a third option, a middle road, not taking any position; neither *believing* God is nor *not believing* God is but "staying out of it" by remaining neutral and non-committal; "straddling the fence" (no position) on the question of God's existence.

The reason for wanting to straddle the fence seems pretty clear. If we commit to belief in God, we could go wrong: what if God doesn't exist? And if we commit to non-belief we could also go wrong: what if God does exist? Isn't it better to avoid risk of error and stay neutral?

But is staying neutral, straddling the fence on this great question really the avoidance of a position, taking a stand? Does staying neutral between belief and non-belief really avoid taking a stand? The person who wants to follow this path walks away from the God question. He turns his attention elsewhere. Is this not a stand? If my neighbor is in danger of death, and calls out to me for help, and I walk away from him, have I not taken a stand? Walking away in such a case is as much a stand as actively doing something.

Consider another example. Charlie and Sandy are deeply in love and plan to get married. A date is set. But two weeks before the date Charlie gets cold feet and asks Sandy if they can postpone the wedding. Fine, a second date is set. Charlie again gets cold feet. A third date. The series continues to date number five. Sandy is very patient but now she puts her foot down: this is it; if you pull out again it's all over. Charlie pleads one last time but to no avail; it's all over. Sandy is gone from his life and eventually marries someone else. Charlie never explicitly said *no*; he just hesitated, straddled the fence. But this straddling, this middle position was effectively a *no*. It was not logically distinct from a *no* in its practical meaning. He might as well have said *no*. So, it is with the fence straddler on the question of God; he might as well have said *no* like the one who simply asserts his denial of God. The alternative is believing-seeking God.

If God does not exist, the fence-straddling position will turn out to be justified. "You paid no attention to the God-question? Fine, you lost nothing because there is in fact no God!"

But suppose a God of love does exist. "You paid no attention to the God-question? This is not fine!" The fence straddler has not acknowledged the God of love. He has not given the right response to God. He has cut himself off from the all-important, ultimate, absolute reality. At death he will come face to face with God. How will he answer that he has ignored the God of love? Fence-straddling does not seem to be a prescription for ultimate happiness.

We see then that fence-straddling is in fact very much of a position. If God doesn't exist, you luck out. Isn't this exactly the same thing that applies to denial? If God doesn't exist, both the one who denies God and the one who straddles the fence win. But if God does exist both of these lose. They both fail to recognize the real God and give the right response.

In short, fence-straddling is a position that ultimately *comes to the same thing as denial.*

WILLIAM JAMES ON FENCE-STRADDLING

William James shows how fence-straddling is a position that comes to the same thing as denial; that it is not really a way of being neutral and avoiding the risk of error. He speaks of the fence-straddler as a skeptic: we don't know whether God exists or not so we should hold back and veto any claim to belief or faith. But that too is a position. Recall Charlie, who hesitated to make the commitment to Sandy. He lost! James offers the same comparison:

> It is as if a man should hesitate indefinitely to ask a certain woman to marry him because he was not perfectly sure that she would prove an angel after he brought her home. Would he not cut himself off from

Chapter 28: Is God Real?

that particular angel-possibility as decisively as if he went and married someone else? Skepticism, then, is not avoidance of option; it is option of a certain particular kind of risk. *Better risk loss of truth than chance of error*, -- that is your faith-vetoer's exact position. He is actively playing his stake as much as the believer is; he is backing the field against the religious hypothesis, just as the believer is backing the religious hypothesis against the field. To preach skepticism to us as a duty until 'sufficient evidence' for religion be found, is tantamount therefore to telling us, when in presence of the religious hypothesis, that to yield to our fear of its being error is wiser and better than to yield to our hope that it may be true. It is not intellect against all passions, then; it is only intellect with one passion laying down its law. And by what, forsooth, is the supreme wisdom of this passion warranted?

When James compares two ways of going wrong, two ways of being deceived, two ways of being duped, "dupery for dupery," he is actually invoking the logic of Pascal's Wager. Hope stands for believing-seeking God: hoping God exists; fear stands for not doing these: fearing God doesn't exist. Each could be a dupery. Dupery through hope would be diagonal A: hoping God is, believing-seeking God when in reality God is not. Dupery through fear would be diagonal B: fearing God is not, not believing-seeking God when in reality God is.

> Dupery for dupery, what proof is there that dupery through hope is so much worse than dupery through fear? I, for one, can see no proof; and I simply refuse obedience to the scientist's command to imitate his kind of option, in a case where my own stake is important enough to give me the right to choose my own form of risk. If religion be true and the evidence for it be still insufficient, I do not wish, by putting your extinguisher upon my nature (which feels to me as if it had after all some business in this matter), to forfeit my sole chance in life of getting upon the winning side, -- that chance depending, of course, on my willingness to

run the risk of acting as if my passional need of taking the world religiously might be prophetic and right.[11]

There are then two basic positions, two logical categories:

1. Not believing God is and/or not seeking God: by denial or by straddling the fence.
2. Believing God is and/or seeking God, ***perhaps in a spirit of wonder!***

---

[11] "The Will to Believe," in *The New World*, June 1896, 26-27. Italics in original.

EPILOGUE

This book is the compilation of over fifty years of teaching Ethics, Metaphysics, Epistemology, Philosophy of the Person, and Virtue Ethics in the classroom setting. We have tried to reproduce that classroom dynamic for you as much as possible on the written page. It is our hope that we have raised questions, provided many possible answers to those questions, guided you in discerning how to evaluate the answers, and encouraged in you further questions beyond the scope of this book. Philosophy that begins in wonder is open to proceeding further in a lifetime journey of wonder, avoiding the unnecessary pitfalls of cynicism, pessimism, and despair. This spirit of wonder offers to one a life of amazement, joy, gratitude and, therein, often the unexpected moments of knowledge, understanding, insights, and occasionally wisdom.

Blessings on the journey!

Stephen D. Schwarz
Kiki Latimer

www.ingramcontent.com/pod-product-compliance
Lightning Source LLC
Chambersburg PA
CBHW082102230426
43671CB00015B/2588